Copyright © Nick Campbell 2021
All rights reserved

Falls, Brawls and Town Halls

The History of Professional Wrestling in Northern Ireland

1932 to 2002

Nick Campbell

Author's Note

I first became interested in the Irish wrestlers of the past after meeting "Kung Fu" Eddie Hamill in March 2017. Eddie was then, as he still is now, an absolute gentleman with terrific stories to tell. This positive experience inspired me to learn more about the World of Sport era of pro wrestling. It was a brief encounter with the Finlay family and a great chat with Billy Joe Beck in the summer of 2019 that inspired me to seek out others and start working on a book. It was then after meeting the living legend that is Darkie Arnott in March 2020 the writing really began in earnest.

I hope this book serves as a reliable timeline of wrestling in Northern Ireland across 70 years, from 1932 to 2002. It was truly a test to track down all those interviewed and an even greater challenge piecing together a puzzle with many missing pieces. So unfortunately a small margin of error does exist. However, all detailed dates are exact and events presented with the utmost accuracy. I just wish I'd been born about 10 or 20 years earlier as there's so many great characters who have passed away relatively recently. Still, I'm forever thankful to everyone who took their time to share their stories. I can honestly say each one brought something unique, special and significant to the project.

It must be noted that, while the storytelling hasn't been compromised, this is a fairly positive piece of work. I genuinely like a lot of the characters I wrote about and so there isn't much in the way of scandal nor strong negative feelings.

2022 Updated Edition

I published this book in April 2021 on Amazon using its Kindle Direct Publishing (KDP) service. A year later I decided to update the book and in parts rework it. This was largely because since publishing the book I hadn't read it in one full year. Upon re-reading I realised there were further parts to expand upon or remove altogether, especially with new information I'd learn in the time between.

I believe this June 2022 update has left the book much tighter in production. I've added many more photos – which are always a bonus in a book. Plus I tracked down a few more wrestlers or their family members and have added or updated profiles as a result.

Chapters

Chapter 1   Ulster Goes All-in (1932 to 1936) .....*Page 1*

Chapter 2   The Great Scot & The English Innovator (1937 to 1939) .....*Page 11*

Chapter 3   Wrestling During World War II & The First Class (1940 to 1945) .....*Page 28*

Chapter 4   Worldwide Promotions & Direct Rule (1946 to 1949) .....*Page 53*

Chapter 5   Darkie & Glory Days at the Guildhall (1950 to 1955) .....*Page 71*

Chapter 6   Interval (1956 to 1961) .....*Page 98*

Chapter 7   The Milo Wrestling Club & Butcher (1962 to 1963) .....*Page 106*

Chapter 8   Class of '64 (1964) .....*Page 125*

Chapter 9   The Star-Studded Sixties & "The Ref's A Woman" (1965 to 1969) .....*Page 145*

Chapter 10   Finlay Family Business & The Mastery of Kung Fu (1970 to 1974) .....*Page 185*

Chapter 11   Shirlow & Monroe Shows & The Last Class (1975 to 1979) .....*Page 237*

Chapter 12   Fit & The TV Times (1980 to 1985) .....*Page 303*

Chapter 13   Ring the Bell (1986 to 1989) .....*Page 357*

Chapter 14   The Real Americans & Albion Street Alumni (1990 to 1993) .....*Page 374*

Chapter 15   Ulster Turns Tribute (1994 to 2002) .....*Page 391*

Introducing first...
Northern Ireland

The history of Northern Ireland has been covered in many other books, so in short; Ireland has thirty two counties across four provinces. In 1921 the island of Ireland was split, creating Northern Ireland and the Republic of Ireland.

The majority of the province of Ulster is situated in Northern Ireland and the counties there-in are Antrim, Armagh, Derry / Londonderry, Down, Fermanagh and Tyrone.

Colloquially, Northern Ireland is often referred to as "Ulster" or "The North", and the rest of Ireland is sometimes simply called "The South".

For simplicity sake the island of Britain (England, Scotland and Wales) is referred to as "the UK" here-in.

And its tag team partner...
Professional Wrestling

Wrestling was one of the nine sports at the first Olympic Games in 1896. The types of wrestling contested at the Olympics being *free-style wrestling* and *Greco-Roman wrestling*. These styles, as well as *catch wrestling, submission wrestling* and *jiu-jitsu wrestling* come under the umbrella term of *amateur wrestling* and are legitimate sports.

However, historically like any sport, wrestling could sometimes be tedious to watch as a spectator. As early as the mid-to-late 1800s there is evidence of "worked" wrestling in America, where in order to attract an audience wrestlers would work together / co-operate with one another and add theatrics to provide a more entertaining match. As people were willing to pay to see these entertaining matches, promoters / organisers of this worked wrestling could make money from it, and the wrestlers involved could get paid for their "performances". With enough events those willing to "work" matches could make a job out of wrestling and thus it became their profession. *Professional wrestling* was born. Professional wrestler became an occupation.

A controversy with pro wrestling is that despite its co-operative nature, for much of its existence (really until the 1990s / 2000s) its proponents and participants defended it publicly as being a totally legitimate sport. Today wrestling is largely defined as "entertainment", however throughout much of the timeline covered in this book pro wrestling was treated as a sport. Indeed, the training the wrestlers went through and the majority of moves used in matches were much closer to the sports styles of wrestling than they are nowadays. Regardless of the sport or entertainment status, pro wrestlers are comparable to athletes in being incredibly fit and both physically and mentally tough people.

As entertainment, pro wrestling has great appeal across all ages, genders, nationalities and religions.

Prologue

There is no record of professional wrestling on either side of the Irish border in the 1920s, for a man with the distinctive name of Atholl Oakeley hadn't yet reintroduced pro wrestling as entertainment in Europe.

Atholl Oakeley was born in Wales in 1900 to a wealthy English family. He lived a privileged life with money never being a matter of concern for him. "Sir" Oakeley grew up in the early 20th century when professional wrestling attracted huge crowds, though its performance style was much different than we know it today, being much slower and methodical like the sport styles.

One of the first icons of professional wrestling was a strongman from Estonia called George Hackenschmidt, who was skilled in Greco-Roman wrestling. "The Russian Lion" (Estonia was part of the Russian Empire at the time) Hackenschmidt wrestled around the world in the early 1900s, representing Europe as master of the ring. In 1911, George

Hackenschmidt retired from wrestling after being beaten by American wrestler Frank Gotch in front of a reported 30,000 spectators at a Chicago baseball stadium. Another early icon, Gotch was from a farming family in rural America and accomplished in catch wrestling. "The Iowa Ployboy" Frank Gotch would retire from pro wrestling right before the outbreak of the World War in 1914.

After the war ended in 1918 wrestling didn't recapture its old glory, with matches being bashed by newspapers on both sides of the Atlantic for being fixed. However, in America wrestling remained a form of entertainment. Largely as a side-show attraction at fairgrounds and carnivals where the wrestlers would work with one another and then challenge audience members to try their luck in the ring (where they would be promptly and painfully dispatched). America then led the way in the 1920s with a return to successful standalone pro wrestling shows. The UK and the rest of Europe stuck instead to the sports styles, producing many talented amateur wrestlers, including one Atholl Oakeley who claimed to have taken up wrestling as self-defence after a mugging.

In 1930, after meeting an American wrestling promoter, 30 year old Atholl Oakeley began talking about *"all-in wrestling"* which, like pro wrestling, would be an amalgamation of all the different sports styles of wrestling. It would mix free-style, Greco-Roman, catch, submission and jiu-jitsu wrestling all into one.

Oakeley stressed to the press that all-in wrestling was the real deal with one of the key changes being that all-in wrestling would be contested under rounds. Rounds meant that pro wrestling matches – like a boxing bout – would have a definitive ending time if a decision wasn't gained by either competitor. This eliminated one of the less entertaining elements of pro wrestling previously; matches could go on far too long, with wrestlers like Hackenschmidt or Gotch locked in a half-applied submission hold for an extended period of time to give the illusion that if one man made the wrong move the other could spring to action and take the advantage.

Unless timed out, matches were usually two falls to a finish (more modernly known as *"best 2 out of 3 falls"* only with a time limit).

On Friday the 13th of November 1930 Atholl Oakeley give an exhibition of all-in wrestling at a London sports club. Some reporters, particularly the sports pundits, were cynical about all-in, believing it to be the old antics of professional wrestling disguised under a new name. They were right of course, but it didn't matter; it was enjoyable entertainment.

Oakeley soon rose to prominence in the ring as a wrestler, and behind the scenes as a promoter of the UK's first standalone post-war pro shows. It was fairly modest in the beginning as the wrestlers (mostly heavyweights) all came from amateur backgrounds and could technically wow as they traded holds or tossed an opponent with a throw.

Then in mid 1931 Atholl Oakeley travelled to America, wrestled on some shows there and learned many more tricks of the trade, particularly of the theatrical, to incorporate into his all-in attractions once he was back home. Influenced by the no holds barred American bouts, all-in wrestling soon became its own wild west world of figurative cowboys and indians where there seemed to be no rules. Being proficient in a sports style of wrestling was still all-important, but all-in matches could descend into all-out brawls usually with one of the wrestlers or the referee sent flying out of the ring.

Unlike any amateur form of wrestling, striking an opponent with the hands or feet was allowed in all-in wrestling. Another American adoption was wrestlers with "gimmicks" – that is they'd sometimes play the character of a good guy or a bad guy, with a cultural stereotype usually being the simplest way to achieve this i.e. a patriotic English war hero or an evil German or a cocky American cowboy, etc.

Due to its exaggerated elements and at times violent and bloody performances, all-in wrestling began catching even more criticism than the pro wrestling before it. Still, this new entertainment form was extraordinarily popular with those paying to see it and all-in action played to packed out halls across England, Scotland and Wales before making its journey across the Irish sea…

Chapter 1

Ulster Goes All-in

1932

In the summer of 1932 Northern Ireland had its first taste of pro wrestling when *The Imperial Troupe of Lady Wrestlers* – who were touring the UK at the time – brought their travelling show to the *Empire Theatre* in Belfast. Matches were held each night for a week from Monday August 8th to Friday August 12th.

The Troupe consisted of ten women wrestlers. There was no ring used, only mats, and it was called "catch wrestling" but it is clear this roadshow was pro wrestling incognito. Some of the ladies, who were advertised from countries all over the globe including Australia, Canada, New Zealand and South Africa, would later take up careers as all-in wrestlers. One of the women even went on to wrestle as "Jean Hackenschmidt" (no real relation to George). Similar to the setup at American carnival shows, the lady wrestlers would compete against one another in exhibition matches then challenge women in the crowd to step up and see if they could survive on the mat. One evening a "local lady" did just that; she accepted the challenge and beat one of the Troupe to win the grand prize of £700 (nearly £50,000 in today's money). She did so wearing a black mask… Neither the identity of the masked lady nor her incredible winnings were picked up by any newspapers because she was no more a native than she was a novice; she was a planted audience member.

The man who organised the Imperial Troupe was a jiu-jitsu wrestler from Manchester called Adam King. During the all-in craze King was integral in introducing women's wrestling around the UK despite it often being banned from buildings by those more traditional in mindset. One of the men credited with training the Troupe was Jack Carroll from Wigan, an accomplished catch wrestler who turned to all-in wrestling when it started to pick up popularity. During the week as a special side attraction Jack Carroll wrestled to a draw with a Belfast boxer. On the final evening however the boxer defeated Carroll by disqualification, and it was a sure case of shenanigans that the Belfast boxer – the hero for the hometown to show their support for – would be able to match a master of the mat like Carroll in his own game.

The following summer the fierce females returned to the Empire Theatre for another week. They continued to tour the UK for several more years but this was the last time the act appeared in Ireland. However, by then both the North and South had already had their first official all-in wrestling events.

- - - - -

A few months after the first Troupe tour of Belfast, Jack Carroll was back on the bill when Ireland hosted its first ever all-in wrestling show. It was at *Portobello Barracks* in Dublin on November 19th 1932 and the show was the first in a series commissioned by controversial political figure General Eoin O'Duffy. Half of the money raised from wrestling events in the South throughout November and December went towards funding sports development nationally.
  The man who General O'Duffy passed organising the wrestling over to was William Willis. Born in Australia in 1899 to Irish parents, William Willis had moved to Ireland and with money left to him by his father opened his own restaurant, *The Green Rooster*, near St. Stephen's Green in Dublin. A keen entrepreneur Willis had experience with wrestling and boxing promotions in the land down under, and over the next few years would bring wrestling to many counties in the South for the first time.
  In the autumn and winter months of 1936 in Dublin, William Willis even ran the first weekly wrestling events in Irish history. As well as promoting he would occasionally referee matches too.

- - - - -

"The Belfast public will have an opportunity on Monday evening of seeing first hand what exactly all-in wrestling is when leading exponents of this form of entertainment will be unleashed in the Ulster Hall. It is claimed for all-in wrestling that it is more attractive

than dog racing, or dirt track riding, or any of these new-fangled sports. At any rate it has caught on tremendously in America and seems to be coming very popular in England and on the Continent"
- Northern Whig newspaper, December 3rd 1932

On December 5th 1932 Northern Ireland's first all-in wrestling show took place. The event was held near the city centre of Belfast at the *Ulster Hall* which reportedly had a capacity for around one thousand spectators. Days before the event the *"Rules of the Game"* were printed in local newspapers.

The main event was scheduled to be Fred "Half-Nelson" Keys of England vs. American heavyweight Billy Bartush, whom Atholl Oakeley had met on the other side of the Atlantic the year before. On the undercard were two bouts featuring Irish-born, English-trained wrestlers; *"middleweight champion of Ireland"* Jumping Jim Moloney vs. Englishman Richard Willis, and *"heavyweight champion of Ireland"* Barney O'Brien vs. Gino Marlow the *"champion of the gypsies"*

No doubt the ring used would have been a boxing ring, which has no give nor spring and minimum padding. It wouldn't be until wrestling picked up enough popularity that a ring designed to lessen the blow on the body crashing onto the canvas was created, so rings of this time were very painful to fall in.

Come the night Billy Bartush was a no show, replaced by fellow heavyweight "The Knockout King of Europe" Norman the Butcher. In the end Half-Nelson Keys would be disqualified, a brawl would break out, the referee be knocked out, and the curtain would close on Ulster's inaugural all-in wrestling event.

"There were three all-in wrestling contests at the Ulster Hall, Belfast, last night. The first pair entered the ring at about 8-15, and the last bout ended at 11-10. About 2½ hours of this time was devoted to wrestling, and it is probably not too much to say that in that period Belfast sportsmen saw enough of this new form of entertainment to last them a life-time"
- Belfast News-Letter newspaper, December 6th 1932

It would be four years before wrestling would be back on the big stage in Belfast...

1933

In the meantime, Armagh became the unlikely epicentre of wrestling in Ulster when from its tiny village of Killylea appeared Bob Wilson, who would be on the bill when wrestling was back in Belfast in a big way.

That June, Bob Wilson and his friend Jack Kirkwood of Keady (another tiny Armagh village) were invited to charity fundraisers in one another's local halls to give demonstrations in catch-as-catch-can wrestling and jiu-jitsu, respectively. In Killylea and Keady they ended their exhibitions by wrestling against one another on mats – both times to a draw. Wilson and Kirkwood were both reported as well-travelled, with Wilson claiming to be the *"heavyweight champion of New Zealand"* in the catch style.

In September, Bob Wilson competed in a special attraction wrestling bout on a boxing show held in *Armagh City Hall*. In a match vs. Dublin's Pete Connolly, Wilson would win and dethrone Connolly in the ring as *"Irish Champion"*. The rules were stated as under catch-as-catch-can regulations but it's suggested it was really under the pre-determined winner pro style. The referee even being Wilson's friend and sparring partner Jack Kirkwood.

In November at another boxing bill in Armagh, Keady man Kirkwood presented Killylea man Wilson with a physical belt for his victory, making Bob Wilson the first found crowned wrestling champion in Ulster's history.

The wrestling champion of Ireland would go on to compete in several more special attraction matches on boxing shows in Armagh over the years. Wilson also appeared in Belfast on events organised by one of the boxing's only female promoters, Clara "Ma" Copley.

However, while Bob Wilson's wrestling was billed under the catch brand some of his other associates most certainly practiced the pro style in their own public performances.

1934

"The wild-cat tumbles and sudden somersaults of the wrestlers now and again sent no end of thrills through the large crowd of eager onlookers. In the very late stages the order of the boot and fists were brought into the action by the participants, particularly Kennedy, and the forcing of the latter through and over the ropes by Cowan on several occasions, which caused those in the near vicinity of the ring to scramble for safety, for a period at least, were the notable features of the exciting contest"
- Lisburn Standard newspaper, October 26th 1934

On October 19th 1934 during a boxing bill at the *Conservative Flute Hall* in Lisburn, Bob/Bert Cowan wrestled local weight-lifting champion Sam Kennedy. As reported, during the duel Cowan and Kennedy attacked one another with their fists and feet and even hurled one another out of the ring; actions not permitted in any sports style of wrestling.

Born in Lisburn in 1910, 24 year old Robert "Bob/Bert" Cowan was a sailor in the navy who said he learned wrestling through travelling the seven seas, and credited *"Finns and Swedes"* as training him in the throws and holds.

Always bouncing between being billed as "Bob" or "Bert", Cowan was said to have only recently returned from New York. His match vs. Sam Kennedy is the first found match in a remarkably inconsistent run for Lisburn local Cowan who lived in Warren Park in the city.

In terms of notable local names from wrestling history in Ulster, Killylea's Irish champion Bob Wilson and Lisburn's salty sailor Bob/Bert Cowan are the very first.

That December, Bob Wilson would referee a Cowan vs. Kennedy rematch when they too appeared on a Ma Copley boxing event in Belfast as an added attraction wrestling match.

1935

On February 15th 1935 at the Conservative Flute Hall in Lisburn, Sam Kennedy promoted a *"boxing and wrestling tournament"* with Bob/Bert Cowan wrestling and Irish champ Bob Wilson again acting as the referee. Two wrestling matches were mixed in with three boxing bouts in the closest wrestling had come to being the attraction all by itself, albeit the style still credited as catch.

Despite going as far as to give himself the gimmick name of "Joe Steele", organiser Sam Kennedy's notion for being thrown around a boxing ring took a turn shortly after, as the bodybuilder quit wrestling and shot down talk of a sequel event.

- - - - -

Around that same time, on February 24th *"Sensational American All-in Wrestling"* was advertised at *The Ring* on Thomas Street in Belfast (reportedly The Ring was a temporary marquee on rented ground, inside was a boxing ring and seating / capacity is unknown). The event was again organised by Englishmen and to feature wrestlers from the UK, none of notoriety.

No further reporting on this event or any subsequent shows of the same sort speaks to its success, or lack there-of.

- - - - -

A time later Bob / Bert Cowan would place a public challenge in a newspaper demanding Bob Wilson defend his Irish wrestling championship against him, and though the Armagh man accepted the match (replying via newspaper advertisement) it doesn't appear to have taken place.

However there was another challenge Killylea's Bob Wilson did answer, an even greater one, one that would bring about the biggest wrestling bout of his lifetime and tie his curious catch-style contests into the proper pro style.

Bob Wilson
Irish wrestling champion, from Killylea, Co. Armagh

1936

"Bob Wilson, the Killylea (County Armagh) wrestler, who is champion of Ireland and New Zealand, has accepted the challenge of Danno O'Mahoney, wrestling champion of the world"
- Portadown News newspaper, June 13th 1936

Born in Cork in 1912, in his adulthood strongman Danno O'Mahoney was plucked from the Irish Army by an American pro wrestling promoter, trained up in the tricks of pro wrestling in London, and then sent to be the star of shows in Boston. As high emigration from Ireland to Boston meant its Celtic connection was strong, Danno was to be the idol of Irish eyes.
    All the giants of the grappling game of the time had a trademark move – today termed a "finisher" – and so Danno was made the master of his own manoeuvre called the "Irish whip", that is still in use to this day (though with a different technique to it).
    Debuting in the States in 1935 Danno would shoot to stardom with his Irish whip, and that July the 22 year old ex-soldier from Cork was pushed to the pinnacle of pro wrestling when he was crowned the undisputed *World Heavyweight Wrestling Champion*. Unfortunately the "undisputed" nature of wrestling titles of this era is one of its greatest misnomers as wrestling titles of the time were nearly always in dispute. Regardless, Danno O'Mahoney's big win had him hailed as one of Ireland's great sporting heroes.

A year later in the summer of 1936 Danno O'Mahoney returned to the Irish isle for the first time since he made headlines worldwide, and while his World Champion status was by then itself in dispute nonetheless he was considered to be coming home a champion. Heart-warming news footage of the time shows a massive crowd gathered to greet their hero as his ship docked on the Cork coast.

"Some years ago Belfast was given a sample of the 'all-in' game, but although the audience was entertained by the newest sporting novelty during the first couple of bouts, the rest of the programme, which was of a similar type, began to pall because of the repetition of

the same stunts over and over again. Those who said 'never again' to the stuff put on at that Ulster Hall bill can rest assured that the King's Hall show will show them real wrestling (not the 'all-in' variety)"
- Belfast Telegraph newspaper, August 31st 1936

The homecoming of "The Irish Panther" was of course marketed with a wrestling tour as Irish boxing tycoons Gerald Egan and Jim Edgar teamed together to promote shows spanning the island.

At huge sports grounds in Dublin and Kerry crowds of 10,000+ were reported that August, with the third stop to be on September 2nd 1936 at the *King's Hall* in Balmoral on the outskirts of Belfast. The King's Hall was the biggest indoor arena in Ulster and until the previous year was primarily used as a cattle mart. That is until – wanting a building with a bigger capacity than the Ulster Hall – Irish boxing bigwig Jim Rice renovated the agricultural centre so it could host huge fight nights. At the time the King's Hall was believed to accommodate an audience of between 6,000 to 8,000 (reports differ).

Due to the poor reception of the all-in attraction years before this wasn't a standalone wrestling show, instead it was co-promoted with boxing. On the grand stage wrestling and boxing would continue to share space, and a ring, for the best part of the next forty years as many promoters of wrestling would be first and foremost boxing bosses.

This time thankfully all went well, making pro wrestling a success on the big stage for the first time in the North.

"A top-notch wrestling and boxing tournament staged by Mr. Jim Edgar attracted a splendid crowd of over eight thousand sports fans to the King's Hall, Balmoral, on Wednesday evening, and thrills galore were the order of the night ... Dan O'Mahoney, the famous 17½st. Cork man, retained his world heavyweight wrestling championship after a herculean struggle with Carl Hansen, an 18st. Swede, who was vanquished in the seventh round, when O'Mahoney gave an effective demonstrations of his much-talked-off Irish Whip"
- Belfast Telegraph, September 3rd 1936

Despite "accepting" Danno's challenge, Bob Wilson was never actually scheduled to succumb to the Irish whip, though he was on the bill vs. American wrestler Charlie Strack in a poorly-reviewed loss.

Interestingly, the Killylea man's opponent should have been Steve Casey, an accomplished boat-rower from Kerry turned wrestler who too went on to great success in America. In fact if "Crusher" Casey hadn't pulled out of the match due to injury, Bob Wilson's *"Heavyweight Wrestling Championship of Ireland"* would have been on the line.

After completing the tour Danno O'Mahoney returned to America, but sadly his star was on the fall after losing his title. Tragically, on a visit home to Ireland in 1950 Danno would be killed in a car accident age 38. In 2000 his home village of Ballydehob unveiled a statue in recognition of its sporting hero.

Danno's statue is one of only two in Ireland recognising the achievements of professional wrestlers; the other belongs to Steve Crusher Casey, who represented his country six times as a champion in America in the '30s and '40s before passing away in 1987. His statue was unveiled in his little village of Sneem in County Kerry, also in 2000.

Similarly on the downward like Danno, after his defeat Bob Wilson and his Irish wrestling belt quietly disappeared. However, the last man to issue him a challenge for his championship Bob/Bert Cowan does make the move into full-on pro wrestling features, even getting his own outing in the King's Hall the following year.

Chapter 2

The Great Scot & The English Innovator

1937

"Belfast is to have wrestling as a new winter attraction, and if it is as successful here as it has proved in cross channel centres it will rival boxing in its appeal. Its sponsor in Belfast is Mr. W. Bankier"
- Northern Whig, September 17th 1937

Born in Scotland in 1870, William "Bill" Bankier was famous on the circus circuit in the late 1800s / early 1900s as strongman "Apollo, the Scottish Hercules". After his side-show days ended he began promoting catch wrestling contests in the early 20th century. Then caught up in the all-in wrestling craze 60 year old Bankier began promoting pro wrestling as everyone else did under the auspices of "all-in" in the 1930s.
However as all-in wrestling as a brand was being relentlessly bashed by critics for its bloody violence and outlandish offerings of mud wrestling and men vs. women matches, ever the opportunist Bill Bankier decided to join in on the criticism and instead starting promoting his own pro shows as *"free-style wrestling"* – which was already the name of a legitimate sports style of wrestling, however (like catch wrestling) free-style was misused as a masquerade for pro wrestling and its pre-determined winners. Confusing? It was meant to be!

"Mr. Bankier is enthusiastic for honest wrestling and is empathetic in his condemns of the abuses and hoaxing which have been foisted on the sport under the guise of all-in wrestling"
- Belfast News-Letter, October 14th 1937

Historically, Bill Bankier and Atholl Oakeley are considered rivals; a battle between elderly businessman Bankier and his free-style wrestling vs. rich kid Oakeley and his all-in wrestling.

Seeking to succeed where the English aristocrat's all-in failed, the Scottish strongman expanded his brand of wrestling entertainment onto the Irish isle. Bankier invested in building up business in Northern Ireland by booking three shows three weeks apart at the King's Hall starting on October 16th 1937.

The power of print was well-utilised by Bankier with advertising in all of Belfast's major newspapers. The superiority of free-style wrestling was of course stressed over all-in wrestling, however...

"Despite the statement that the wrestling at the King's Hall, Belfast, on Saturday evening, which attracted a fair attendance, would be of the free style at times it bordered closely on all-in methods. This was notably so in the bout between Anaconda, the 17 st. 7lbs Swede and Phil Siki, an Algerian scaling 16st. 10lbs. These magnificent giants thrilled the crowds with their 'rough-housing'"
- Belfast News-Letter, October 18th 1937

The Swede was really an Englishman while Phil Siki was the first of several hammerlockers of African heritage featured on Irish bills for the next 60+ years, as the two heavyweights helped Bill Bankier's event become the North's first successful standalone wrestling show.

The follow-up phoney free-style feature three weeks later then demonstrated how strongly scandal sells as the antics outside the ring of one of the wrestlers brought more to the box office than any of the advertised matches. Bob Gregory was the wrestler, and was a good-looking grappler who was dating the beautiful blonde Valerie Brook aka "Princess Baba of Sarawak". At the time Sarawak was a British-owned state in Malaysia governed by Princess Baba's father the "White Rajah of Sarawak" and his public disapproval of his royal daughter dating a common wrestler caused a stir with the paparazzi who began treating the lovebirds as a celebrity couple.

Bob Gregory and Princess Baba loved the media attention, often posing for photographers and making headlines around the world when they announced they were going to get married. The marriage story coincidentally came out around the same time Gregory was booked to appear on a wrestling bill in Belfast, so it was a huge story that his bride-to-be would be sitting ringside at the King's Hall to cheer on her future husband. Adding further fuel to the fire, the odd couple even attempted to tie the knot on the quick in Liverpool right before their scheduled flight to Northern Ireland for the wrestling. Possibly a publicity stunt? Definitely. Their witness to the failed wedding attempt was Bill Bankier, who understandably adored all the attention his wrestling event was getting. Whenever the trio landed in Newtownards airport via private plane on November 6th, the morning of the heavily-hyped wrestling show, Bankier posed for pictures alongside Gregory and Baba.

Princess Baba and Bob Gregory (at plane door) arrive into Newtownards airport on November 6th 1937. Bill Bankier is standing with his hands on his hips.

It was a promoter's dream to be gifted all the free publicity the young lovers garnered, and Bankier's second bill in Belfast was arguably the show that solidified wrestling in Ulster going forward.

"The free style wrestling programme at the King's Hall, Balmoral, Belfast, attracted a large crowd on Saturday night, and 6,000 roaring and at times vastly amused fans got first-class entertainment for their money"
- Northern Whig, November 8th 1937

The show was a great success, the eventual marriage of the wrestler and the royal wasn't; it soon ended in divorce with Bob Gregory retiring from the ring (a wealthy man from not signing a prenup) and Princess Baba going on to marry three more times (but thankfully for her father to no more bloody wrestlers at least).

A lesser-reported failure on that same free-style fixture was a lock-up between local wrestlers; when 27 year old "Sailor" Bob/Bert Cowan returned to the ring vs. a Lisburn school teacher called Dick McCullagh. It was yet another poorly-received match involving local representation (after Bob Wilson's bout the year before) and it even seemed to put off potential future participants as despite Bill Bankier's public proclamation that he would train up any interested men at a dedicated gym in Belfast free of charge, no-one answered the call.
   The teacher learned his lesson and stuck to the classroom, however Bob/Bert Cowan was a resilient sort of fellow and would be back in bouts in the future…

"Mr. Bankier, in introducing the 'pull and push' game to Ulster, has also enlarged the by no means considerable vocabulary of the rapidly increasing army of wrestling fans, several thousand of whom cheered, booed, laughed, groaned and were thrilled to the core in turn at the third international tournament at Balmoral on Saturday evening. 'Boston crabs', 'Japanese locks', 'submission holds' and 'body scissors' are but a few of the bewildering series of technical terms which are coming into everyday use among followers of the new sport"
- Belfast Telegraph, November 29th 1937

After the success of his third bill the great Scot announced that shows would continue to be staged in Belfast on a monthly basis going forward.

1938

In the new year the King's Hall was unavailable so wrestling returned to the Ulster Hall for the first time in over five years and in the very building Atholl Oakeley's all-in wrestling had failed to launch, Bill Bankier's free-style wrestling played to rave reviews.

These shows were overseen by boxing head honcho and bookmaker Jim Rice, whose job was keeping Belfast's biggest indoor sports buildings clear of any competition for the Scot. Yet neither Rice nor Bankier accounted for downright deception to try and sully the name of the suspicious sport when wrestling was back in the King's Hall that March.

- - - - -

On March 5th 1938 a fundraiser in support of the *Dr. Barnados* charity (today known as just *Barnados*) was hosted in the King's Hall. The organisers put together a star-studded variety show with film actor James Hayward as the host, heavyweight boxer "The Gorgeous Gael" Jack Doyle singing a few songs, and then in the wrestling portion English rugby-player-turned-wrestler Douglas Clark thrilling the 2,000 in attendance.

The show also featured the first found match for 35 year old shipyard worker and career criminal Alexander Robinson aka Buck Alec.

Born in Belfast on May 12th 1902, books have been written about the life, times and crimes of Alexander Robinson who was first in front of a judge in his early teens and continued to be trouble for the courts throughout much of his life. As a boxer in the early '20s the short, stocky and stern-faced Robinson developed the nickname "Buck Alec" (sometime spelled "Buck Alick"). In the late '20s he journeyed to America where he insisted he was an associate of infamous Chicago mobster Al Capone. By the mid '30s Buck was back in Belfast and working at the *Harland & Wolff* shipyard. The shipyard – where the Titanic was built – was the city's largest employer of the working-class, and here Buck Alec was seen by some as a loveable rogue whose crimes were a rebellion against the authority of the higher classes.

A controversial character, it's somehow apt that Buck Alec's first found wrestling appearance should be on a show shrouded in scrutiny of its own; Barnado's were never given the money raised from the charity event, the organisers were arrested and accused of pocketing the proceeds, and the mastermind behind the scheme even went on the run. Thankfully wrestling's name wasn't tarnished too much due to the event being a variety show, and to be clear Buck Alec didn't seem to be blame for any of it.

- - - - -

Going forward Bill Bankier wisely promoted his productions with his own name up front. *"A Marvellous Bill Bankier Promotion"* being a stamp of quality assurance for anyone suspect about future wrestling bills.

Bankier's return to the King's Hall on March 26th also featured Whipper Billy Watson, a Canadian wrestling legend, who was short and sturdy with a little black moustache and was touted as the real master of the Irish whip manoeuvre. Notable too was Watson's opponent that evening, "The Masked Marvel" who was the first masked wrestler to appear in action in Ulster (that wasn't a "local lady").

> *"Covered head to foot in an 'all-black' costume, with only his eyes and mouth visible, and who will not reveal his identity until he is beaten … The story is the 'Marvel' was so good in America he could get no one to meet him, and so he had to fade out and reappear in the masquerade costume … It is his custom to bet £20 on himself on each of his fights, and, on his behalf, a special challenge has been issued to anyone in Belfast who can produce a man whom he will fail to throw in six five-minute rounds. The 'Marvel', who, by the way, is said to be of Ulster birth, engages only in one-fall contests, and in his bout with Whipper Watson he kept his £20 safe by disposing of Watson in the fourth round"*
> *- Northern Whig, March 28th 1938*

Bill Bankier's events continued to be positively-received, so much so there was no more need for the stressing of his free style wrestling style over all-in wrestling. Or so it seemed.

- - - - -

Bankier's success in Northern Ireland didn't go unnoticed in the UK. After the Scot's "season" of shows finished in April and he took an early summer break, other wrestling organisers looked to get in on the action, and they went all-in.

That May an English wrestling promotion openly advertised all-in wrestling to be held in *Belfast Stadium* (a smaller boxing arena for those unable to promote in the premiere venues in the city). Buck Alec was also back and billed as *"Your own local All-in Champion"*. The shipyard worker was notably never given a bout in the King's Hall by Bill Bankier – mind you the notorious street fighter from Belfast wasn't the quite the company the Scottish strongman was used to keeping, especially not when he'd already spent time sitting on private jets with royalty!

On May 25th 1938 the all-in English crowd held the first live pro wrestling promotion in Derry City, the second biggest city in NI, in its historic *Guildhall* which could reportedly sit 600-700 spectators. Despite the Guildhall event (and Stadium event too) being stated as the first in a series of shows, after May there are no further reported live wrestling events until late that summer.

- - - - -

A battle began as the promoters of the all-in wrestling attractions sought to seize control of Belfast as their own territory. They announced they would be running the *Belfast Arena* (another venue booked by boxing rivals to Jim Rice) on a weekly basis beginning in late August – one week before Bill Bankier was set to start his second season at the King's Hall in early September.

A year earlier live wrestling in Belfast was virtually non-existent and then suddenly rival promoters were going head-to-head against one another, hoping to attract the bigger audience, make the most money and run the other out of the city. Though the promotional war pitting all-in wrestling at the Arena on a Friday night vs. free-style wrestling in the King's Hall (*"Ulster's Home of Wrestling"*) on a Saturday night wouldn't last long and proved to be the undoing of both parties interests on the Irish isle.

On September 2nd at the Belfast Arena and September 3rd at the King's Hall rival wrestling shows were held 24 hours apart, splitting the total audience in half, with the cheaper ticket at the all-in and better atmosphere and action at the free-style.

Right away the all-in advertisers played a dirty game. As the huge African heavyweight Phil Siki was one of the Scottish strongman's fan favourites, on the first all-in show they advertised Phil Siki as wrestling for them, only for it later to be revealed that it wasn't the actual Phil Siki but another black wrestler pretending to be him. In fact, whenever he was then billed on Bankier's events it was as *"The Real Phil Siki"*.

The battle went just seven more days. Bill Bankier announced he too would be running weekly and so again on September 9th and September 10th it was all-in vs. free-style. It was unfortunately the latter who actually ended up worse for it as the main event ending in disqualification angered the audience, with Bankier having to get on the microphone to try and explain it. There was even a fist-fight in the crowd, described as an all-in brawl by newspapers, ironically in the hall of a free-style event.

The battle for Belfast offered an option for crowds, but it also brought about more criticism from those who detested wrestling. One newspaper expressed disbelief that wrestlers were able to survive punishing throws and torturous submission holds for so long. Another paper referred to wrestlers as *"actors"*. Why exactly some of the newspaper writers were suddenly vilifying wrestling would soon be explained… Before that however, both Bill Bankier and the all-in wrestling louts cut their losses.

After the negativity during the second head-to-head showdown, Bill Bankier decided to pull his promotions out of Belfast and boarded his private plane for departure at the Newtownards airport for the final time that September. The great Scot was the man who established professional wrestling as an entertainment form to be expected in Northern Ireland. He always brought his A team to the King's Hall and Ulster Hall, and until the end his shows were tremendously well-received. While he wasn't interested in Ireland anymore, Bill Bankier would continue to promote pro wrestling in the UK right up to his passing, age 78, in 1949.

Meanwhile it was a pyrrhic victory for the all-in promoters who soon sailed back to their own shores after struggling on for a few more weeks with no-one but themselves to blame for poorly-reviewed shows and falling attendance figures. It's something that on their final show in late September they went out the same way they came in; falsely advertising Phil Siki.

After the battle for Belfast ended with no winners, there was little about wrestling reported until November. The media's openly antagonistic attitude to pro wrestling's legitimacy as a sport – all-in, free-style or otherwise – was then explained.

> *"a timekeeper and referee of wrestling bouts, said that all the so-called contests were fake. The only people kept in the dark were the public"*
> *- Northern Whig, November 10th 1938*

In a court case as chaotic as the promotional battle, Ireland's first wrestling promoter William Willis had taken legal action against the *Irish Press* newspaper in a court case in the South that got extensive coverage in the North too.

No longer a promoter, the year before Willis had outed the fixed nature of wrestling fights to the Irish Press in an interview by giving a specific example involving two wrestlers he'd booked in a match. In short, he'd told one to lose, they refused, so the other wrestler then had to intentionally injure the dissident wrestler to end the match and get the desired result. However, as the two wrestlers involved were still active at the time they disputed Willis' claims and demanded the Irish Press print a retraction. Not wanting (or caring enough) to challenge the wrestlers the paper did so, but then when William Willis read this he was furious, taking it as defamation against the honesty of his character and so sought damages from the nationally-syndicated newspaper.

> *"(the judge) addressing the jury today said that he could not help feeling that they were dealing with a world of unreality, small and circumscribed, that, according to the evidence, had a code and language of it's own, a language that smacked very considerably of American gangsters"*
> *- Belfast Telegraph, November 12th 1938*

So much ink was dedicated to this curious case by every national newspaper that Bob Gregory and Princess Baba would have been jealous! This was the first time in Irish news that the results of wrestling had being openly outed as pre-determined.

In the end the jury actually found in favour of the Irish Press and its retraction. As William Willis' case had been built around the question of his honesty this was turned against him when it was put forward that he'd previously played along in dishonesty when promoting his wrestling shows as legitimate sporting contests. So even though Willis was telling the truth, the newspaper's lawyers spun the story against him and his case was dismissed.

The Aussie-born restaurateur understandably harboured a hatred for the Irish Press for the rest of his life, until his passing aged 60 in 1960. Regardless of the details of the case William Willis should be remembered as the first man to organise pro wrestling in Ireland and for successfully promoting it in the South during years when the Northern scene was nearly non-existent. The period 1932 to 1936 when Willis was active was one of the only times in the 20th century when wrestling was more prominent in the Republic of Ireland than it was in Northern Ireland.

- - - - -

That December one of the most important men in the history of pro wrestling in Northern Ireland brought wrestling back to Belfast, his name was Harry Joyce.

Born in England in 1898, skinny with a sharp face Harry Joyce worked for a time as a grocery store owner. In the 1920s Joyce and his family moved to live in Canada where he owned his own gym and through getting to know wrestlers who regularly visited the gym in order to keep themselves in condition for the ring, Harry became involved in pro wrestling. Then whenever the Joyce family returned to live in England, Harry arranged to bring several Canadian grapplers, among them a not-yet-famous Whipper Billy Watson, over for a wrestling tour of the UK in 1936. Successful in doing so, in short order Joyce established himself as a promoter, matchmaker, referee and on rare occasion an all-in wrestler himself. He would organise several more short-term expeditions to Europe for his Canadian comrades as well.

Having heard good reports of the audience's appetite for wrestling there, 40 year old Harry Joyce then seized the opportunity and made the move to take control of the barren Belfast territory after finding himself a promotional partner in bookmaker Nat Joseph.

> *"The fun at the King's Hall, Belfast, last evening, when Mr. Nat Joseph presented a wrestling card was quite up to the standard enjoyed at this venue, and as the fans had not had a real outing for quite some time they were more than satisfied with what the 'killers' had to offer"*
> *- Belfast Telegraph, December 3rd 1938*

Beginning December 2nd 1938 the King's Hall was run on a bi-weekly basis by Nat Joseph, who was born in London but settled in Belfast and was one of Ireland's premiere boxing promoters with wrestling shows simply being an extra money-maker on the side for him. Every two weeks *"all-action wrestling"* – the newest rebranding of the form – would fall in the former cattle mart on a Friday night. The partnership between Nat Joseph & Harry Joyce was beneficial to both parties in that Joseph had the connections and knowledge in promoting locally, while Joyce had the connections and knowledge in wrestling and its unique workings.

"The Sport That Drives You Crazy" was the slogan for the Joseph & Joyce events, and the debut event featured English brawler Jack Atherton, heavyweight star of all-in wrestling in the UK.

The premiere also presented 38 year old Tommy Nelson, who was profiled as a Belfast man via way of the nearby village of Glenavy (which was/is closer to Lisburn).

Born in Glenavy in 1900, when he was very young Thomas "Tommy" Nelson's family moved to Canada and it was there he was raised. In his adult life Tommy worked as a bus driver before entering the wrestling business with his early career spent working as a wrestler on the fair ground / carnival circuit in Toronto. Introduced to Harry Joyce by their mutual friend Whipper Billy Watson, Tommy Nelson was among the first crew of Canadians brought over to do battle on the British wrestling scene in 1936. When wrestling in England he was always cited as a Canadian but once he landed on Irish shores the short, lean and technically-talented Tommy Nelson was as Ulster as the fry.

Heralded as Belfast's hometown hero "Hell-Cat" Nelson picked up the win vs. assumed American wrestler Frank Carr to delight of the audience in the first positively-received match for a wrestler with Irish eyes at the King's Hall.

A week later another Ulster-born brawler appeared for Joseph & Joyce, and in his 30s Pat Magee was one of the most delightful ring dynamos of his time.

Born in the seaside town of Ballycastle in Antrim in the early 1900s Patrick "Pat" Magee was raised locally before emigrating as an adult to England. In England is where Pat turned pro after missing out on the Olympics as an amateur wrestler. The very fit Magee, in the standard black trunks and black boots of the time, was one of several Irish wrestlers who appeared in action in the UK but he was the only Ulsterman of his time who was a staple of the British wrestling scene.

While a solid light-heavyweight wrestler the Ballycastle brawler with perfectly combed black hair was most memorable for sporting a real rarity in the ring at the time – a beard.

> *"Von Brockau conceiving a tremendous liking for the beard of Antrim's wrestler, took hold of it, and did things to it that weren't ordinary. Magee was hurled backward and forwards, from one side of the ring to the other, while one wondered could the beard hold out"*
> *- Belfast Telegraph, December 17th 1938*

An instant fan favourite, Irish audiences loved Pat Magee's beard. They would boo when it was used against him and cheer loudly whenever he'd use it as a weapon himself by rubbing it quite literally in an opponent's face when he had them trapped in a submission move. It was truly a sight to see in a simpler time.

At Joseph & Joyce's follow-up fixture on December 16th at the King's Hall, Pat Magee and his beard took a brutal beating courtesy of von Brockau, an evil German (likely English) who came complete with Nazi salutes – as the country's leader Adolf Hitler was already an unpopular figure. The match was Ulster's first ever tag team match pitting Pat Magee & England's Stan Garside vs. von Brockau & England's Ronnie Hurst. The two vs. two bouts were treated as something special on shows, often positioned as the main event of the evening, and in these matches Pat Magee was the man, and his brilliant beard the show-stealer.

Positively, both Tommy Nelson and Pat Magee became frequent features going forward, with one or the other – and occasionally both – usually in action for Joseph & Joyce.

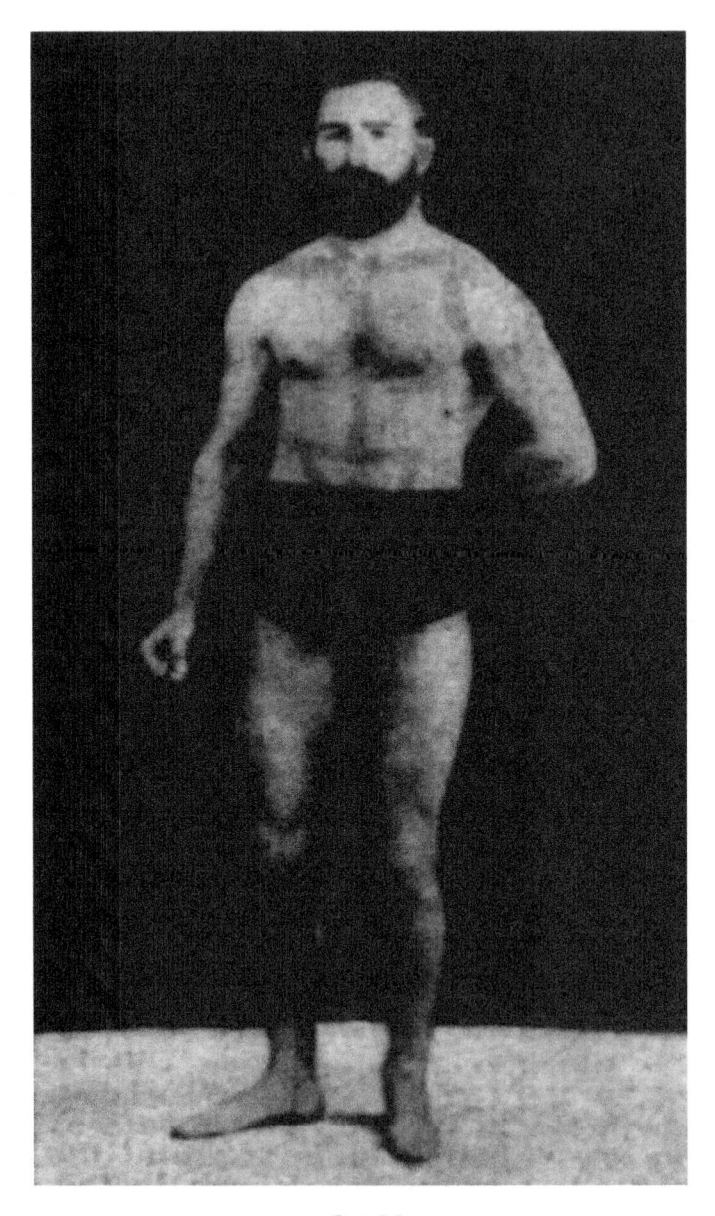

Pat Magee
Beloved bearded wrestler from Ballycastle

1938 could be considered Northern Ireland's first full year for pro wrestling (albeit confined near entirely to Belfast) with Bill Bankier's shows opening the year and Harry Joyce's closing it.

1939

On January 13th a curiousity was on in the card in the Ulster Hall in the form of the *"relay match"* which was a 4 vs. 4 team match with a scoring system; if you eliminated a member of your opponent's team you scored your own team three points. The match reportedly lasted an hour and a half (the show ended up being 3 ½ hours long as a result) and the scoring system was a little redundant as the match was for all intents and purposes an elimination team match. The relay element was the inability to tag out of the match once you opted in. One resilient wrestler spent 45 minutes in the ring, and really the only way to reach your distance was to be eliminated or survive and win the match. In the modern day multi-man elimination team matches are more common – though always with the option to tag in and out – however this relay match was unique for its time and appears to have been the only one to take place in Ireland in the 20th century.

"All action wrestling has a very definitive feminine following now. During the first odd dozen 'meetings' the fair sex were somewhat of a rarity, and members of the audience have even been known to look curiously round to see what type of girl had the audacity to break into the ranks of spectators of what was considered essentially a man's sport. The number of young women who patronise this latest sort of civilised fun has been on the upgrade, until Friday evening at Mr. Nat. Joseph's Ulster Hall promotion, there were so many that their shrill cries of excitement could be heard above the roars of their male escorts. Incidentally, if you want to see another side of a woman's nature watch her reaction to the gladiatorial contests in which wrestlers indulge"
- Belfast Telegraph, January 28th 1939

- - - - -

In the opening months of the new year the sports that drives you crazy was again housed in the Ulster Hall. However, less than six months after Bill Bankier was pushed out by all in-wrestling outfit there was then competitors to Nat Joseph & Harry Joyce as *London Promotions Ltd* looked to spark another battle for Belfast by somehow booking themselves back-to-back weeks on a Monday night in the Ulster Hall that February.

This time though there was no nonsense. Nat Joseph was one of a collective of powerful boxing promoters of the time who kept outsiders out of their halls and themselves and their associates in prime positions. The bookie showed his significance to Harry Joyce by having the Londoners booted right back out of Belfast by signing an exclusivity deal to be the only one able to promote wrestling in the King's Hall and Ulster Hall.

So after seeing out their two shows that February London Promotions sombrely sailed back home, defeated.

- - - - -

"Tommy Nelson (Belfast) became light-heavy-weight champion of Europe amid frenzied cheering when he defeated Mike de Mitre (Greece) who has held the title for two years, by a single fall in ten great rounds. De Mitre placed the championship belt round Nelson's waist"
- Northern Whig, March 11th *1939*

Nat Joseph, Tommy Nelson, Harry Joyce and Mike de Mitre pictured following Tommy's light-heavyweight title win on March 10th 1939 at the King's Hall

"Nelson Champion of Europe" read the headlines after Glenavy grappler Tommy Nelson made history by becoming the first Ulster-born wrestler to win a recognised title belt, defeating Mike de Mitre to win the *European Light-heavyweight Championship* at the King's Hall in an exciting bout on March 10th 1939. Mike de Mitre was a popular performer from Canada of Greek heritage, who in fact was credited as having discovered Nelson wrestling at fairgrounds and helped him get into the business full-time.

That April Tommy Nelson successfully defended his Light-heavyweight title at the final King's Hall spectacular for quite some time on Easter Monday 1939. The massive venue was being made into Ireland's first ever ice-rink (indoor anyway, some of the roads may otherwise have qualified during the winters months) and so was closed for an extended period.

After another successful defence for Nelson in May – during which a move called the "Castlecaulfield flip" was used (Castlecaulfield being a remote little village in the Tyrone countryside) – on June 16th Mike de Mitre reclaimed his championship at *Grosvenor Park* (the home ground of *Disterilly FC*) at Ulster's first outdoor wrestling event, and yes, it rained.

Unfortunately Tommy Nelson's title loss coincided with his final appearance in an Irish ring. He was pulled from promotions the following month due to injury, and was back in Canada by the end of the summer. In Canada the Hell-Cat continued to wrestle before retiring from the ring in the mid '40s. He kept involved by working in the office of promoter Frank Tunney in Toronto, and in the mid '50s was a matchmaker for wrestling cards in the territory. In the mid '60s, aged in his mid 60s, Tommy Nelson wrapped up his wrestling career for definite, and while his eventuality isn't known the former light-heavyweight champion of Europe did remain a physically fit man even in old age.

"Pat Magee, the conquering hero, his beard an example of what the well-dressed man is wearing this spring, walked to the ring with the cheers of the fans ringing in his ears"
- Belfast Telegraph, March 25th 1939

Meanwhile, on a winning streak in his speciality team matches, Pat Magee was one of the first Irishman to enter the ring to entrance music by being accompanied by the cheery folk tune *"The Ould Lammas Fair"*. The song is in reference to a family fun fair dating back to the 1600s that is still held to this day every summer in Ballycastle. The place would be jumping as the gramophone was pumping Pat and his beloved beard's theme song.

Joseph & Joyce continued to promote all-action wrestling in the Ulster Hall in the summertime. Though with the people of the province likely to soak up the sun when they sparingly had it, wrestling wisely became a once a month affair.

That summer are also the first found "sold shows". A sold show in wrestling is a show paid for and promoted by an independent party who'd make all the money on the door after paying the wrestling organisers, in this case Joseph & Joyce, a fee upfront. On July 13th the seaside resort town of Bangor hosted wrestling for the first time, and then on July 19th Ballycastle welcomed home its own wrestling sensation Pat Magee and his celebrity beard, complete with a live band to blare "The Ould Lammas Fair" on their entrance.

"A huge crowd, including many Scottish and English visitors, yesterday attended Ballycastle Amusements Development Committee's most attractive programme. The programme opened in the afternoon with a fancy dress parade. It was led by a novelty band with the topical title of 'Pat Magee's Band', and to provide the realistic touch all the members wore beards".
- Northern Whig, July 20th 1939

Credit here to Joseph & Joyce on their focus in promoting successful Ulster-born stars, as the big victories of Pat Magee in his fantastical team fights, as well as Tommy Nelson winning the European title billed as a hometown hero would help inspire the first wave of homegrown professional wrestlers…

Indeed all was going so strong when it all suddenly stopped after Nazi Germany invaded Poland on September 1st 1939 and forced Great Britain, including Northern Ireland, to officially declare war on Hitler, beginning World War II. In preparation the Ulster Hall cancelled all its entertainment contracts, in order to free up the building for government matters, specifically food control as rationing became a reality.

Wrestling, rightly, was not a priority.

Chapter 3

Wrestling During World War II & The First Class

1940

At the start of the year the food rationing office was relocated to its own premises, meaning the Ulster Hall could get back to business as usual. Busy with boxing Nat Joseph handed over wrestling promotion to his brother Dan Joseph who made up for lost time with weekly wrestling shows on a Friday night at the Ulster Hall. From one Joseph to another the appetite for all-action wrestling was appeased with live events from February onwards playing to packed houses.

Harry Joyce still organised the wrestlers, bringing back Pat Magee and his beard as well European light-heavyweight champion Mike de Mitre and a slew of UK/international stars. In a sign of the times many of the good guy Englishmen were billed as "Sergeants", "Corporals" and "Privates" while the bad guys had gimmicks based on current events too.

"When von Ribbentrop and Molotoff signed the Navi-Soviet Non-Aggression Pact – it created a world-wide sensation, but two of the nationals of the states involved apparently never heard of it, for at the Ulster Hall, Belfast, on Friday night they wrestled like enemies, not friends. Leaving it to conjecture as to who is Germany's No. 1 villain, Heinne Stack was billed as the No. 2 bad man of Hitlerland. Lord Haw Haw may have something to say about that, as Field-Marshall Goering was heretofore recognised as the successor in line. Herr Heinne's hammer and sickle opponent was Mil Slackovitch"
- Belfast Telegraph, February 17th 1940

The German would win here, but the Russians would get the last laugh.

- - - - -

Starting in April, for a short but significant stint, Ireland's #1 boxing boss Jim Rice – former promotional partner of Bill Bankier – would be the third promoter to team with Harry Joyce to present all-action wrestling.

"Harry Joyce is keen to get more local lads into the wrestling ring and has kindly offered to train free of charge any of them who wish to seek fame and fortune in the grunt-and-groan game"
- Northern Whig, April 19th 1940

On April 18th 1940 a local man stepped into the ring at the Ulster Hall to challenge Mike de Mitre, only to be defeated 2-0. However, the following week the local man was back and managed to score a fall in a 2-1 loss, this time to faux-Austrian Vic Hessle (whose sons Bert Royal & Vic Vaulkner would become well-respected wrestlers in their own right). The local man was 29 year old engineer Vic Fulton

Victor "Vic" Fulton was born in Belfast on February 4th 1911. Well-built with dark hair, Vic had the rough good-looks of Hollywood actor of the era Humphrey Bogart. Strong and determined Vic Fulton was one of the very first homegrown pro wrestlers in the history of Northern Ireland, having been trained in Belfast with Harry Joyce as his head coach.

The weekly events allowed Harry Joyce time to train interested novices in the hours before shows, showing them how to properly apply submission holds, how to counter them, how to throw an opponent using the right technique and how to land as safely as possible should they be the one being thrown.

Make no mistake "the secret" – that is, pro wrestling is co-operative – was not exposed to men like Vic Fulton until they had proven they could be trusted to keep it. Submissions were legitimately applied and bodies hurled full force, and most limped away battered and bruised, never to return, as only the strongest survived this weeding out process. While the matches were worked, pro wrestling training was treated as a genuine sport and so prospective pros had to be physically fit and mentally prepared and wouldn't be accepted unless they got genuinely good at grappling.

This was the way wrestling training existed throughout much of the 20th century, and is why many pros of the era felt they should defend its honour; they suffered to survive in it and so respected pro wrestling in a way the layperson couldn't understand. It's why so many wrestlers could justifiably call it a sport as considering the training methods it's hard to argue it was anything but legitimate when trying to break into the business.

Whilst Vic Fulton was the one getting the opportunity to wrestle in fronts of hundreds there were many more notable names of the first class waiting in the wings, among them Vic's 26 year old little "big" brother Bob.

Born in Belfast on September 16th 1913, Robert "Bob" Fulton was younger in age but physically bigger than his older brother in both height and weight. Bob stood 6 foot 2 and weighed 18 stone. Big Bob Fulton didn't have Vic's good looks nor technical talent, but he was the strongest local man on the mat and its only super-heavyweight. Though intimidating when it came to wrestling, in real-life Big Bob was regarded as a gentle giant and worked with horses in a yard on the Fall's Road.

27 year old Harry Browne was another action-man in training. Born in Belfast on November 4th 1912, Henry "Harry" Browne lived on the Shankill Road, worked in the shipyard and was a lighter weight than the heavyweight Fulton siblings. Harry's skills were that he was very fit and very fast on his feet, and in time he learned the holds and throws being taught by Joyce so well that he was arguably the most talented at them in his class.

Another gentleman (when he wasn't wrestling you) Harry like all others locally had no doubt attended previous wrestling promotions in the city, and it seems Harry was particularly mesmerised by the mysterious masked wrestlers…

Harry Browne and his wife Lena were also friendly with the family of 16 year old apprentice electrician Gerald "Gerry" McSorley, who was one of if not thee youngest of the trainees at the coaching sessions held before the Ulster Hall shows.

Born in Belfast on September 9th 1923 and living on the Falls Road with eleven in his household, Gerry McSorley was a quiet youngster. At training he impressed with his athleticism and agility but hid what he was doing from his family whom he believed would disapprove. That is until one day when his family discovered red marks on his back and angrily demanded an explanation. Reluctantly Gerry had to go and get Harry Joyce himself to come to his parents house to reveal that the red marks were due to running the ropes – that is, bouncing against the ring ropes. Thankfully the family found Joyce to be a good man, and trusted the former grocer enough to continue teaching the teenager.

The McSorley household from then on always welcomed Joyce and his wrestlers for a visit on show days, with Mike de Mitre one of many who enjoyed a cup of tea in its tiny kitchen.

"In this contest an invitation was given for any spectator to referee, and a Mr. McQuitty courageously accepted. The boys cut out very rough stuff and the referee did quite well"
- Belfast Telegraph, May 3rd 1940

The courageous Mr. McQuitty was 26 year old shoemaker David McQuitty, another very memorable member of the first class.

Born in Eden near Carrickfergus on July 29th 1913, David McQuitty was better known to all by his nickname "Dave Mack". Mack was a confident character and another lighter wrestler whose quickness made him lethal. Slim, trim with slick black hair and defined cheekbones Dave Mack's true speciality however wasn't in wrestling (or even shoemaking) but in sweeping woman off their feet with his charm. While wrestling was his past-time his passion was the opposite sex, and plenty of them! Amusingly his first appearance on May 2nd 1940 at the Ulster Hall was on a show with "*Ladies Specially Invited*" in the advertising.

Fitting too that Dave Mack's first foray should be in a non-wrestling role as it's in this capacity he would be best remembered. His "invitation" to referee of course being set-up for him to accept so he could experience what it was like being in the ring in front of a live crowd. In the role Mack excelled, he was a natural showman.

Every week Vic & Bob Fulton, Harry Browne, Gerry McSorley and Dave Mack, among many others, would arrive at the Ulster Hall early and be trained by Joyce, or at times by one of his Canadian contacts who were set to compete on that night's wrestling. Mike de Mitre, Carl von Wurden (a Mountie who always got his man in his native land) and the legendary Whipper Billy Watson all had a hand in helping grow the first crop of locally-sourced and locally-produced pro wrestlers in seminars of sorts before shows.

However while Vic Fulton got to grapple on live events in the first half of the year, the others would all have to wait until after the summer due to the war intensifying. On May 10th 1940, the same day that Harry Joyce brought wrestling to the town hall in Ballymena for the first time as part of fundraising effort for the families of those serving in the war, Germany invaded France. Soon after the Ulster Hall again went off-limits as it looked to be needed to house fleeing refugees from Belgium and Holland, whose countries had already been conquered by Hitler.

Heroically, after picking up his first victory in a bout at the Ballymena show Vic Fulton's toughness and tenacity can be further measured in that he missed much time in wrestling by serving as a gunner in the *Royal Air Force (R.A.F)*; Vic was too busy shooting Nazis out of the sky to bodyslam anyone.

- - - - -

Wrestling once again fell to the wayside. That is until later in the year when Dan Joseph resumed his role as promoter and advertised his pro show at the Ulster Hall on October 25th 1940 as the *"revival of the sport"*.

The event was a landmark. For the first time a wrestling show in Ulster was loaded with local wrestlers. All five matches showcased homegrown stars who made up 8 out of the 10 combatants on the card. Several of the first class made their debuts, and one polarising personality returned to the ring.

> *"A Belfast gentleman, Buck Alick by name, seemed to be on more than just nodding terms with the hundreds who packed the Ulster Hall on Friday night for the wrestling tournament, established a reputation by trouncing two referees. True, one of them, Harry Joyce, tiring of the tough end of the game (refereeing) appeared in the role of an opponent, but ex-referees and referees were all the same to Buck"*
> *- Belfast Telegraph, October 26th 1940*

Buck Alec
wrestler and controversial character

Not spotted on shows since the all-in attractions two years prior, 38 year old local legend Buck Alec was back on bills. With the bearded Pat Magee on sabbatical (he'd joined the army) Buck became the new show-stealing Ulsterman.

After this obvious trial run vs. Harry Joyce the convicted criminal would meet many of the English wrestlers (all the Canadians went home after the fall of France) in matches in Belfast, and in sporadic shows in Newtownards as well. Billed as *"Belfast's Public Enemy No. 1"*, to his credit Buck Alec was a draw at the box office. Buck's matches were unmissable due to the chaos caused during them. Any cheering from the crowd would eventually turn to booing the short-fused street fighter who was always the villain, breaking rules, battering refs, and bowling shoe ugly brawling his way to knockout wins or disqualification losses.

Among the three noteworthy wrestling debuts that evening was "Whipper" Dave Mack – the moniker explained as the likeable Lothario being taught the Irish whip by master exponent of the move Billy Watson – and in his match vs. Red Frew the light on his feet Mack wowed with a fast-pace.

Harry Browne meanwhile may have quite literally wooed as the first homegrown Ulsterman to wrestle under a mask as "The Black Owl" in his bout vs. Young Capollo. Harry's ring persona was inspired by a previous Grey version of the Owl name that wrestled in Belfast the year before. The Black Owl was a villain and a real rough-house, and wrestling tradition of the time dictated that if the Owl was ever decisively defeated he would have to unmask in the middle of the ring, revealing his identity (Harry from the shipyard!) to all. So to keep the mystery alive the Owl needed to prove he was able to put in a performance worthy of a win and so Harry Browne needed to be exceptionally skilled in both striking and grappling.

Finally for that revival feature, while brother Vic was flying high in the airforce Big Bob Fulton's feet were firmly on the ground and at his size really he was rarely knocked off them. Big Bob's first match coming on the card in a bout vs. popular English Sergeant Cab Cashford.

Unfortunately for Bob Fulton his appearances in action were rare as Joyce struggled to find opponents to suit his size as many of the UK's leading heavyweight mat-men were off fighting overseas.

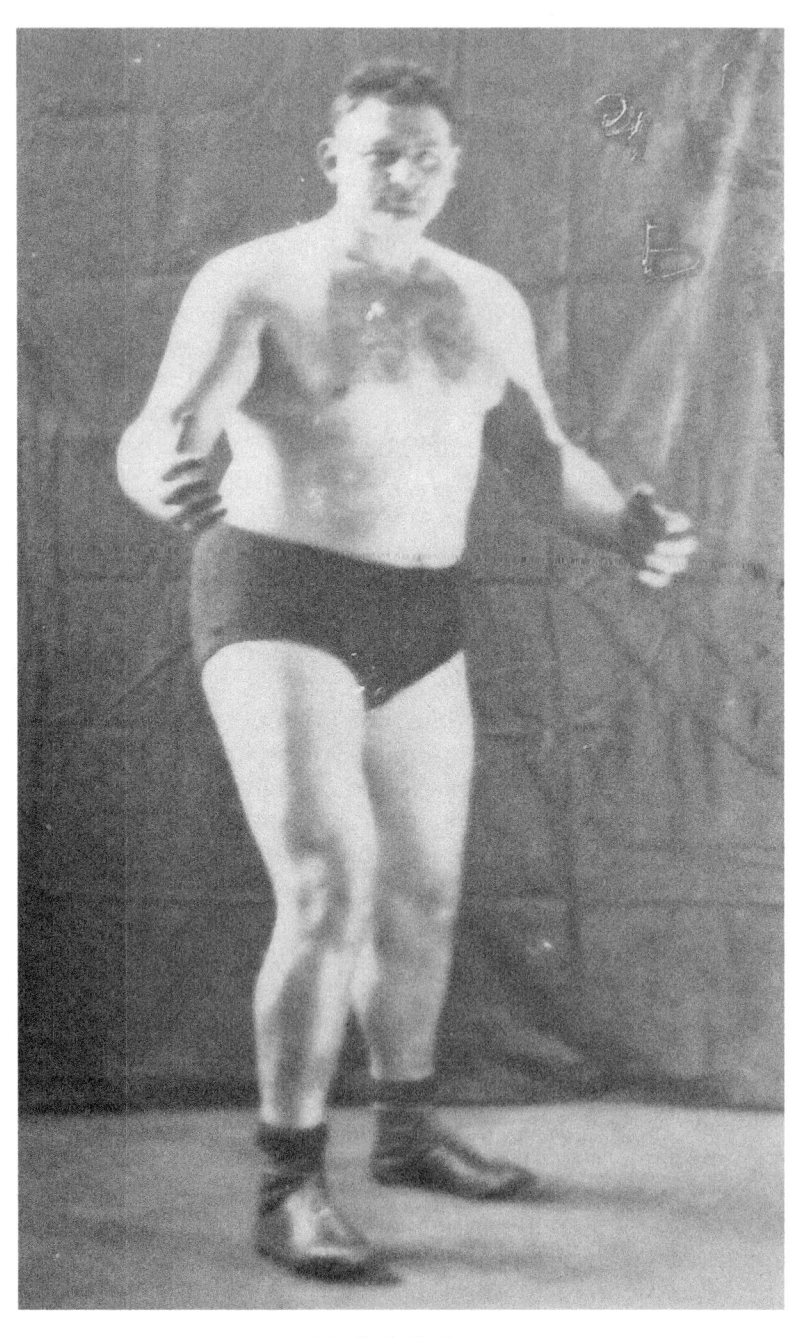

Big Bob Fulton
heavyweight wrestler, later billed as "Ulster Champion"

"that sinister figure, the Black Owl ... satanic in his black cowl and long skin-tight trousers, was not prepossessing, but his strange garb at any rate added a note of glamour"
- Belfast Telegraph, November 9th 1940

After the sold out revival show with thousands reported as turned away at the door, it was again standing room-only two weeks later on November 8th when Ulster's finest brawled again in the hallowed Hall. The Black Owl marvelled in a match vs. the debuting Bob Scott in the first well-reviewed match pitting two notable names of the first class against one another.

One of the oldest of the first class, 33 year old Robert "Bob" Scott was born in Belfast on September 9th 1906 and worked at the Harland & Wolff shipyard or *Short & Harland* aerospace factory (both were owned by the same people). Due to the sheer size of the work force the shipyard and factory had their own sports and recreation clubs. Bob Scott was a coach of the boxing club and it isn't too surprising that he and some of the other boxers took an interest in another ring sport. It's difficult to say for sure without experience but being thrown on your back does sound a little better than being punched in the face. As well as wrestling, should Harry Joyce be wrestling or unavailable due to injury, level-headed Bob Scott was also trusted enough to appear in the role of referee.

Cecil Creighton was another boxer of the time who dabbled in wrestling. In real life Cecil owned a popular pet shop in Belfast, and so whenever he acted the villain in the ring the crowd would apparently taunt him with animal noises.

A fortnight later on November 22nd 1940 it was Whipper Dave Mack (who also reffed on occasion) who was given the task of testing the intensity of the last remaining notable name of the first class to debut; young Gerry McSorley, whom Harry Joyce give the gimmick name of "Jumping Joe Peters". The Jumping Joe name was inspired by the lad's impressive agility with one of his best moves being a flying crossbody, and the teen more than held his own in a lively match vs. Dave Mack, closing out a card that got rave reviews in the newspapers.

Indeed the reviews were rarely anything but rave as Joseph & Joyce hit lucky with the local lock-up artists mixing well with the English body-scissor experts.

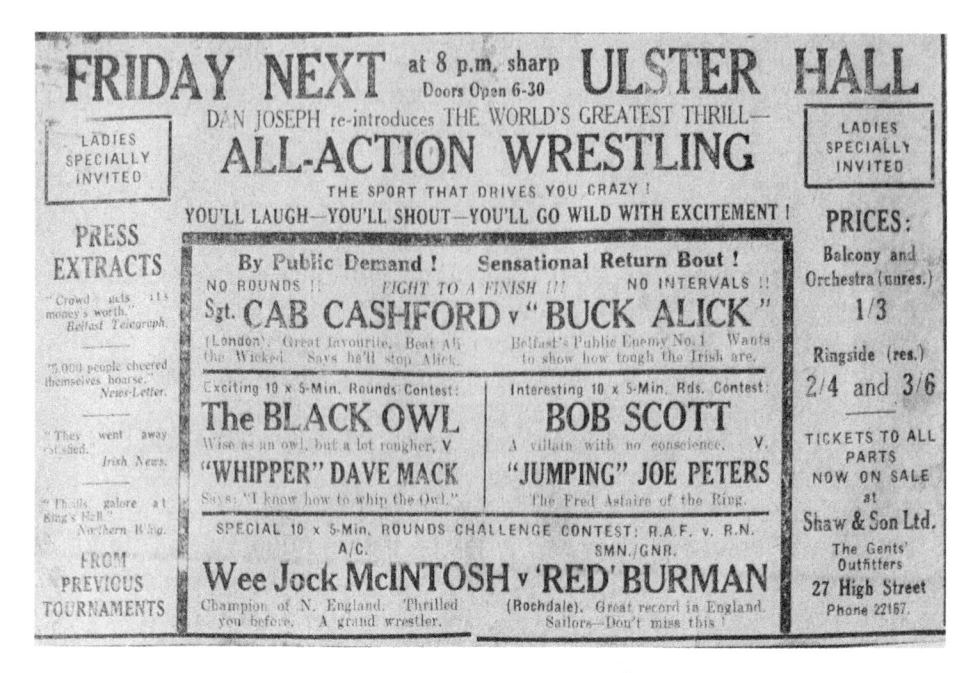

Wrestling bill at the Ulster Hall from 6th December 1940

"'Better than ever' seemed to be the popular verdict at the Ulster Hall, on Friday evening, when Mr. Dan Joseph promoted another of his all-action wrestling contests. Excitement, entertainment, showmanship, speed – all these went to make up a programme that gladdened the heart of the most exacting 'fan'"
- Belfast Telegraph, December 21st 1940

Harry Joyce's hard work had paid off; a league of homegrown wrestling heroes and villains had been established. Local men were finally active participants in pro wrestling instead of idle punters. It benefited Joyce's business too as English, Scottish and Welsh action-men were harder to come by because of conscription, whereas the politics of Northern Ireland prevented this from happening and so meant his roster wouldn't be wrecked by the wrestlers being constantly called away to war.

    Common on cards going forward were top act Buck Alec, heavyweight hitter Bob Fulton, lighter weight wonders Jumping Joe Peters and the Black Owl, utility men Whipper Dave Mack and Bob Scott, and when on rare reprieve from the R.A.F. Vic Fulton.

1941

All the local lads were part-time wrestlers who worked full-time jobs during the week, then wrestled at the weekend. They certainly didn't do it for the money – there was never a living wage for it in Ireland – they did it for the unexplainable love of the pro wrestling experience.

"anybody wanting free instruction in all action wrestling, please write or call – Harry Joyce's wrestling gymnasium, 124 Durham Street (Corner Grosvenor Road)
– Ireland's Saturday Night newspaper, February 22nd 1941

Harry Joyce's gym on 124 Durham Street in Belfast is the first found pro wrestling gym in Northern Ireland, and it would seem for a time that Joyce took up residency in Ulster. The gym, not far from the Ulster Hall, was the first hub for local level wrestling.

In early April, Whipper Dave Mack, Jumping Joe Peters and Bob Scott travelled to thrill when Joseph & Joyce staged a show in the Guildhall in Derry City. It was the first pro show documented in Derry since all-in wrestling walked in with little warning and left with even less fanfare three years before. Unfortunately, wrestling fans either side of the *River Foyle* would have to wait longer still for wrestling to feature again owing to actions by villains outside the ring far more vile than any in it.

On the night of April 15th 1941 Nazi planes bombed Belfast, with Hitler's terror of the air destroying the city with bombing raids twice more in May. Over 1,000 people were estimated to have died and more than 100,000 left homeless.

A young Belfast boy named Noel Arnott, 11 years old at the time, forever remembers the carnage.

"The war had a great effect upon everyone in Northern Ireland. It resulted in shortages. Food was rationed, and all aspects of industry was directed to the war effort. Belfast, like most major cities, had its share of German onslaught. A hundred yards from where we lived a whole block of houses was razed to the ground"
- The Life & Times of Noel 'Darkie' Arnott (2005)

"Pat Magee, the bearded wrestler from Ballycastle, is serving with H.M. Forces as a physical instructor in Northern Ireland. He is very eager to organise a wrestling performance, the proceeds of which would go to the purchase of sports equipment. Pat no longer wears a beard but a moustache"
- Belfast News-Letter, May 30th 1941

When wrestling resumed in the Ulster Hall in June, Pat Magee returned with it, joining Buck Alec in being the biggest billed local. However the diddley-dee tune of the Ould Llamas Fair was surely drowned out by gasps of shock and horror from wrestling fans when it was revealed Pat had shaven his big beloved beard down to a miniscule mediocre moustache! Long-time followers were devastated at the loss of the famed facial hair. They then quickly got over it.

That June 13th event was a fundraiser in aid of those effected by the bombing campaign. Importantly, in the interim wrestling had passed hands from one big-time boxing family the Joseph's to another in the Connell's. Harry Joyce's new partner was John Connell, yet another Belfast bookmaker and boxing promoter and who was better known as "J.C.". J.C. was quick to get wrestling back to bi-weekly as it became quintessential escapism entertainment for the public.

Nat Joseph had facilitated the first recurring Ulsterman in the ring (Pat Magee), Jim Rice the first homegrown feature (Vic Fulton), and Dan Joseph the first home-grown-heavy fixtures, and so that summer J.C. presented the first championship honours for local pro wrestlers.

"Will all Wrestlers send in their entries for the All-Ireland Championships"
- Belfast Telegraph, July 10th 1941

The weight-classes were in the divisions of middleweight and welterweight and the titles were represented by gold trophies not championship belts. The design of the trophy was a statue of a gold figure in a crouching ready-to-wrestle stance fixed to a black plinth. Runners-up received a gold medal.

That July two elimination tournaments were hosted on a bill so big it was promoted as *"2 shows in 1"* with ten matches promised but only seven delivered. Jumping Joe Peters and Bob Scott were among those knocked out of the tournament early while Whipper Dave Mack made it to the finals on August 7th 1941 in the Ulster Hall.

> *"The All-Ireland Championship finals also provided some keen wrestling. In the under 10st. class Whipper Dave Mack beat Lee Moore in the seventh round, and in the under 11st. section Jack McMullan accounted for Bill Peacock also in the seventh. Both these bouts were fought at a terrific pace"*
> *- Belfast Telegraph, August 8th 1941*

"Irish Welterweight Champion" Dave Mack and *"Irish Middleweight Champion"* Jack McMullen became the first ever homegrown wrestlers to be presented titles, with the proud Whipper keeping his trophy for at least 40+ years.

Jack McMullen was a technically-talented wrestler from Lisburn who didn't go for thrilling moves like some of his peers. Instead, McMullen grappled a good clean wrestling contest.

The first finding of McMullen was that March vs. fellow Lisburn leg-locker Bob/Bert Cowan. Cowan the 31 year old ex-sailor was by then working in the shipyard as an electrician and back in wrestling bouts for the first time seemingly since his match in the King's Hall for Bill Bankier three and a half years before. Cowan sharing the distinction along with Buck Alec of being the only local men to have had matches in the Bankier era and Joyce era.

The following month, September 1941, golden boys Dave Mack and Jack McMullen teamed together to represent Ireland/Ulster in a team contest against "England" competitors Dick Lacey and Red Jakes. The team of champions won the bout over the dubious duo who might have English heritage but were by then most certainly living and working locally.

Dick Lacey's real name was Donald Condren with an address in Bangor and a job in the shipyard as a repairman. Dick Lacey would quickly figure significantly into the NI wrestling scene.

Whipper Dave Mack, the Welterweight Champion of Ireland

Jack McMullen
Middleweight Champion of Ireland

The Lisburn lad McMullen's tenure in wrestling was prolific yet short, wrestling only during World War II, roughly from 1941 to 1943.

The middleweight championship however would have many more incarnations over the years.

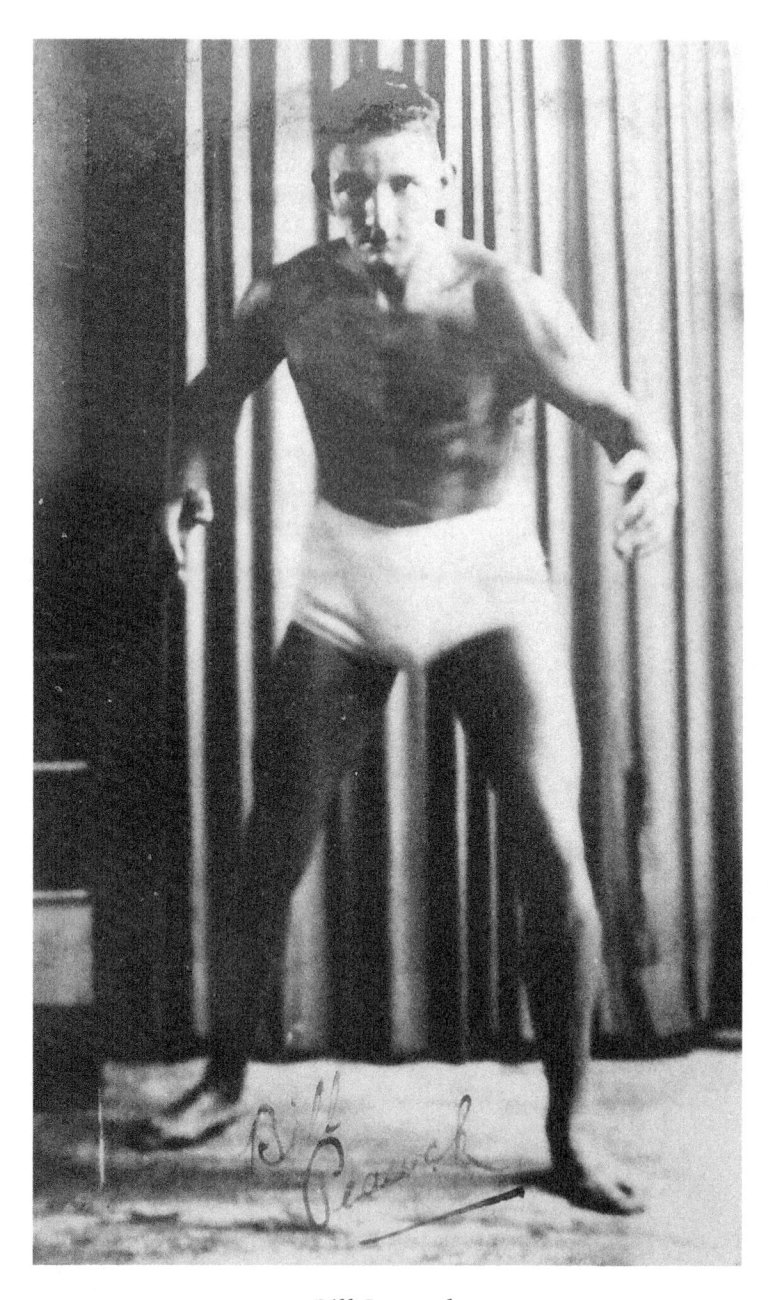

Bill Peacock
who Jack McMullen defeated to win the Middleweight title.
Little can be found for Bill Peacock but he can be found frequently on wrestling cards from 1941 to 1950

1942

On New Year's Day 1942 in the Ulster Hall it was Dick Lacey, Red Jakes and fellow Englishman Jock McIntosh vs. Pat Magee, Terry O'Brien and Ace Mooney in the North's first ever six-man tag team match. The three vs three contests meant more wrestlers meaning even more exciting and archaic matches. They were the newest hit attraction with audiences over the next few months.

- - - - -

"The N.I. Wrestling Promotions wish to let it be known that they are prepared to go to any camp of H.M. Services desiring free entertainment. All they expect is a means of transportation"
- Belfast Telegraph, February 14th 1942

On Friday the 13th of February wrestling moved temporarily to a sports hall called the *Rialto* on Peter's Hill in Belfast. Wrestling at the Rialto would only last a few months but provide three noteworthy tidbits.

Firstly, these monthly events were presented under the auspices of *Northern Ireland Wrestling Promotions* with Harry Joyce surprisingly partnered with Dick Lacey. Events were even marketed with *"Dick Lacey Presents Ireland's Greatest Show"*. Borrowing a boxing ring, the relationship between Lacey and Joyce was the same old song, though unlike the rich businessmen boxing promoters before him Dick Lacey was a working-class man from the shipyard and so was more hands-on with the promoting i.e. putting out posters, drumming up interest, etc.

Secondly, the March 20th wrestling at the Rialto showcased the first found *"free for all"*, that would today closely resemble a battle royal. Five men including Bob Scott and Dick Lacey himself all battled each other in the ring at the same time but only one man walked out the winner (and it was Lacey).

Thirdly, it was at the Rialto that the young Noel Arnott would witness live wrestling for the first time, particularly remembering Jumping Joe Peters among the all-action all-stars. Aged 12, it would still be a time before the lad, with an unusually darker skin complexion than many of his pale school peers, would himself join the wrestling ranks…

DICK. LACEY.
LONDON.

That April wrestling was back in *Ballymena Town Hall* for a fundraiser. Two years on it wasn't just for the families of the troops, morbidly it was for the war's widows and orphans. Notably, this feature was a first in being presented by the "*Short & Harlands sports & social club*" with Dick Lacey and Harry Joyce the organisers, and wrestlers like Welterweight Champion Dave Mack working for free.

By this time Harry Joyce no longer had at a gym at 124 Durham Street. Instead the wrestlers would have trained at a gym at Huss Street on the Shankill Road in Belfast. This gym was named after the Short & Harlands aerospace factory but seems to have facilitated workers from the Harland & Wolff shipyard as well. The club was meant to be exclusive for workers-only, but exceptions were of course made. The Huss Street gym would then serve as pro wrestling's hub for years to come.

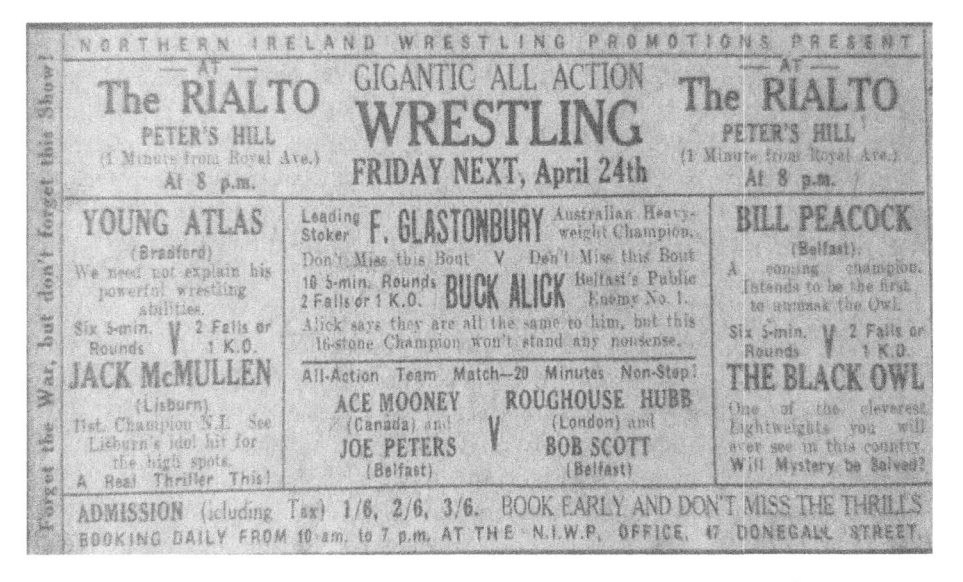

Northern Ireland Wrestling Promotions bill at the Rialto
for April 24th 1942

- - - - -

On June 11th 1942 Harry Joyce would reunite with J.C. and run the Ulster Hall for its final found time during World War II with Pat Magee and Buck Alec the stars of the show.

    The event may have marked an interval for wrestling in the big venues in Belfast, but it also marked a definitive end for two of the most notable names in the history of pro wrestling in Northern Ireland; one of its most notorious, the other one of its most important.

In early 1943 Alexander "Buck Alec" Robinson was heralded as a hero for saving three people from a burning building – he was out walking his dog, spotted the blaze, alerted the authorities, then rushed into the building and saved two women and a 4 year old child. Later that same year he was sentenced to six months in prison in connection with a robbery – during which he assaulted two of his co-accused believing they double-crossed him…

Buck Alec; a working-class hero in his community or a cold-blooded career criminal are the polar opposite public opinions of the man gimmicked as Belfast's Public Enemy No. 1.

Amongst his all-action peers however Buck was well-liked and didn't discriminate. The family of Jumping Joe Peters recalled that as the real-life Gerry McSorley's aunt was disabled and needed crutches to walk, it was arranged that she be given free entry to all events at the Ulster Hall so to see her nephew wrestle. However when a new manager for the venue wasn't made aware of the arrangement he refused entry to her, and even when the other wrestlers protested the manager stuck to being stubborn and still refused. Buck Alec then had a word and the manager not only let the lady in for free but offered her a pillow.

In later life Buck Alec would famously buy a fully grown lion from a visiting circus and keep the animal in the backyard of his Belfast home. Developing into something of folklore it has often been cited that Buck owned two lions but it was only ever one. This is something of a reflection of the man himself; over time Buck became a mythical figure to some, with it often being difficult to determine the fact to the fiction throughout his life. That said for the period of 1938 to 1942 he most certainly competed as a pro wrestler and a very popular one at that. After wrestling the real-life Alexander Robinson remained a peculiar personality for the rest of his life, until he passed away age 93 in 1995.

And Harry Joyce; due to all the stopping and restarting immediately after the June 11th event the English innovator would pull the plug on his promotions in Northern Ireland after three and a half years. At least four of Belfast's boxing elite had teamed with Joyce as did the province's first nationally-named promotion and the events he helped bring to the King's Hall and later to the Ulster Hall were hugely successful and influential in embedding the sport that drives you crazy in the city.

Harry Joyce's greatest achievement of course was being paramount to the development of pro wrestlers at a local level in Northern Ireland; all roads lead back to him in this way, and Vic

Fulton, Big Bob Fulton, 'The Black Owl' Harry Browne, Jumping Joe Peters, Bob Scott and Whipper Dave Mack among others all continued their passion for pro wrestling long after Joyce left the Irish isle for the last time.

Harry Joyce later operated his own wrestling gym in Northamptonshire in England, and stayed relevant in the grappling game right up to his passing in 1965 aged 67. The Joyce legacy was carried on thereafter by Harry's son Ken Joyce – who actually made his wrestling debut aged 17 in Belfast in April 1940 – and who became a well-regarded wrestler, referee, matchmaker and promoter in his own right on the British scene.

After that summer of '42 wrestling on a grand stage was few and far between as the war was getting more intense and the priority was supporting the effort to free Europe rather than provide entertainment at home.

1943

Army camps did take up the offer of free wrestling entertainment from NI Wrestling Promotions. Evidently, that February at a base in Co. Down a boxing ring was set-up by promoter Bob Gardiner who paid tribute to the troops with a free evening of boxing bouts, with Dick Lacey working in partnership to present a special exhibition wrestling match featuring Pat Magee vs. Dave Mack.

For further publicised wrestling promotion it was a quiet year. The sole show on record was from March 12th 1943 at the *Ulster Stadium* (the Rialto renamed) cited as the first in a series with a Mr. Bob Jardine the promoter and Dick Lacey the organiser.
    Though moustached master of the mat Pat Magee officially secured his sixth successive year in an Ulster ring, more noteworthy was the debut of 19 year old Jack Raymond in 2-1 losing effort vs. similarly aged Jumping Joe Peters.

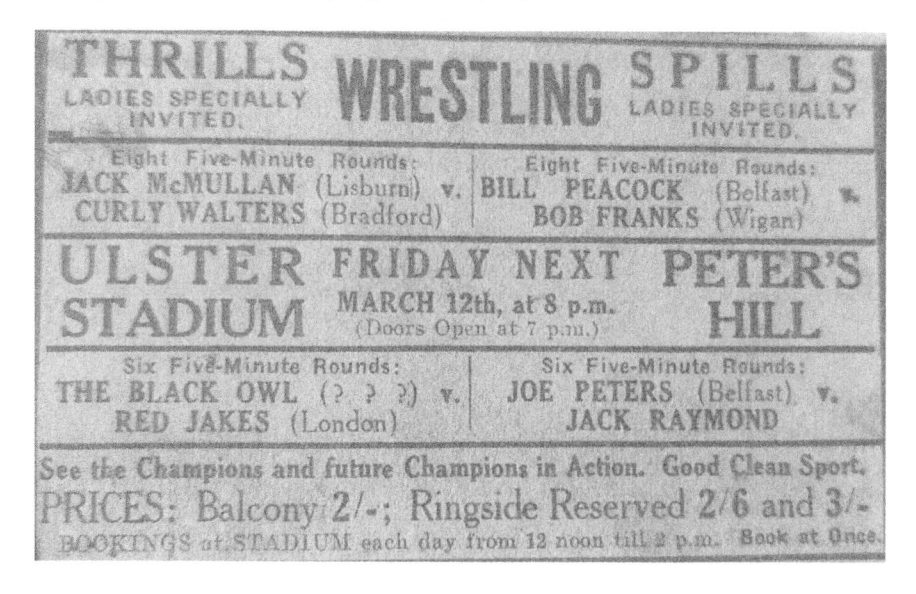

> **THRILLS WRESTLING SPILLS**
> LADIES SPECIALLY INVITED.   LADIES SPECIALLY INVITED.
>
> Eight Five-Minute Rounds: | Eight Five-Minute Rounds:
> JACK McMULLAN (Lisburn) v. | BILL PEACOCK (Belfast) v.
> CURLY WALTERS (Bradford) | BOB FRANKS (Wigan)
>
> **ULSTER STADIUM** FRIDAY NEXT MARCH 12th, at 8 p.m. (Doors Open at 7 p.m.) **PETER'S HILL**
>
> Six Five-Minute Rounds: | Six Five-Minute Rounds:
> THE BLACK OWL (? ? ?) v. | JOE PETERS (Belfast) v.
> RED JAKES (London) | JACK RAYMOND
>
> See the Champions and future Champions in Action. Good Clean Sport.
> PRICES: Balcony 2/-; Ringside Reserved 2/6 and 3/-
> BOOKINGS at STADIUM each day from 12 noon till 2 p.m. Book at Once.

Born in Belfast in late 1923, John "Jack" McClelland was a keen footballer in his youth and there was belief that if he'd stuck at the beautiful game he could have played it professionally. However as football wasn't the big money maker it is in the modern day Jack's father dissuaded him from accepting a trial with the *Arsenal FC* youth team and recommended a more routine career path.

McClelland's destiny was instead to become a very successful engineering draughtsman. Indeed, Jack was destined for success in many endeavours in life; forgetting the football he was an incredible swimmer too and working as a draughtsman at the shipyard is where he got into the wrestling and chose the stage name of "Jack Raymond".

Jack McClelland / Raymond's rise to prominence is swift.

Jack Raymond
(190 LBS.)

15 NEVIS AVENUE,
(Holywood Road)
BELFAST.
Telephone No. 55781.

1944

"Wrestlers desirous of engagements should write AT ONCE to: Jack McClelland, 15 Nevis Avenue, Belfast"
- Ireland's Saturday Night, April 1st 1944

Short in height but a heavyweight with a big 50 inch chest and an even bigger personality, while his contemporary Dave Mack could sweet talk the ladies, Jack McClelland used his gift of the gab in business meetings. Yet it is still surprising that at just 20 years old Jack became the first undisputed homegrown promoter and organiser of pro wrestling in Northern Ireland.

April 7th 1944 at the *Andrews Memorial Hall* in Comber is the first found Jack McClelland show. Promoted as all-in wrestling with the tagline *"See Some of Ireland's Best Matmen in Action"* it has claim to the honour of being the first ever wrestling event in Ulster to feature a full card of homegrown talent.

McClelland as Jack Raymond, The Black Owl, Jumping Joe Peters and Bob "Tiger" Scott all competed on the card. Though some of the names advertised that evening are billed from London, Canada and Algiers and it is difficult to determine if these wrestlers were actually born on the Irish isle or if they did come from another country (but were now living in Ulster).

A week later Jack's second found show was scheduled for April 14th at the Ulster Stadium in Belfast but was cancelled, maybe mercifully as the original main event was advertised as a team match featuring *"2 U.S.A. Blacks vs. 2 British Whites"*. Instead it was rearranged for April 28th and again featured the Owl, Jumping Joe, Tiger Bob and a reworked main event team match pitting Jack Raymond's team vs. Dick Lacey's team, in the final found appearance for the suspected Englishman.

It isn't unreasonable to suggest that Dick Lacey, with his experience as a wrestling promoter/organiser, likely acted as an aid to Jack McClelland or simply someone Jack sought advice from. It is then unfortunate the finality of Donald "Dick Lacey" Condren is unknown but his legacy remains in helping establish the first nationally named organisation in N.I. Wrestling Promotions. Indeed, Jack was to follow directly in Lacey's footsteps in this regard with his own branding in the future…

1945

While there was no publicised wrestling promotions this year, importantly World War II came to a close. Backed into a corner Nazi dictator Adolf Hitler took his own life that April, followed up by Germany officially surrendering on May 7th 1945 ending the war in Europe.

However, though the war in Europe was over, allowing the rebuilding to begin, its effects would be felt for a long time and for some a life time.

"Two brothers who found a detonator in a field previously used by the Army were injured when it exploded while they were playing with it in an air raid shelter. They were David Finlay, aged 9, and William Finlay, aged 11"
- Northern Whig, July 18th 1945

In Northern Ireland the army had been stationed on the east coast around the Carrickfergus area. Unfortunately a dangerous detonator had been misplaced in a field in nearby Whiteabbey, and when two local boys came across the unassuming item they were lucky to be left alive after it exploded.

Elder brother Billy would survive relatively unscathed but young Dave Finlay would lose his right eye as a result of the shrapnel.

In the years to come young Dave Finlay would be told he couldn't play certain sports due to his partial blindness. This however only served to motivate him more to prove himself in all the sports that were available to him. One in particular becoming Dave's passion in later life…

Chapter 4

Worldwide Promotions & Direct Rule

1946

"ALL-IN WRESTLING TABOO IN THE ULSTER HALL"
- Belfast Telegraph, January 29th 1946

During the war all-in wrestling's rough and reckless reputation had gotten so rotten that it was outright banned by councils. First in epicentre London and then throughout the UK, with Belfast soon following suit. Losing key venues dealt the brand of "all-in" its deathblow as promoters of pro wrestling stopped using it altogether when styling their shows. They reverted instead to the faux free-style terminology (used by Bill Bankier).

That January, John "J.C." Connell approached the Ulster Hall with intentions to organise boxing/wrestling again. However his request to have an exclusivity contract in place was turned down, and this opened up an opportunity for Jack McClelland.

"Belfast will shortly have it's first opportunity of seeing free-style wrestling bouts between the best British and Continental exponents of the art. Jack McClelland and Jack Crane, youthful local wrestlers and promoters, have leased the Ulster Hall for eleven dates, the first of which will be February 25, when it is hoped to have, among others, the leading British heavyweights on the bill"
- Mid-Ulster Mail newspaper, February 16th 1946

The headstrong McClelland partnered in promotion with John 'Jack' Crane who was born in 1924 and was from a family of eleven children. The Crane family where originally from

Cookstown in County Tyrone and were military-minded; Jack Crane was a member of the merchant navy, and one of his brothers was in the R.A.F. but was tragically gunned down during the war.

Jack Crane, wrestler and promotional partner of Jack McClelland

There was no bad blood between the Jack's and J.C. - with the boxing Don even giving them his blessing as he decided to focus on his fist fights instead. So bright-eyed 22 year old McClelland and 21 year old Crane would present wrestling on a weekly basis at the Ulster Hall for roughly three months.

To secure top talent smooth talker McClelland travelled to England and made a deal with Yorkshire-based wrestling promoter Ted Beresford who operated *Globe Promotions*. Like the Dick Lacey & Harry Joyce relationship before them, the agreement was that Beresford would act as the liaison on the wrestling end of things; choosing the wrestlers, arranging the travel, making the matches, etc while the two Jack's would be hands-on in promoting the events.

Thankfully any money McClelland & Crane gambled with by starting to promote their own pro shows they more than made back and then some as audiences, starved of entertainment, flocked to the features.

There was a catch though; the hey-days of homegrown wrestlers appearing in action at the Ulster Hall were over. When the war started Harry Joyce hadn't the option of bringing over the best of British wrestling as many were off fighting the Nazi regime, so local competitors were given more chances and filled the bills. Now with the world back to business as before Ted Beresford had his selection of stars to choose from and more importantly to keep. If Beresford wasn't providing his wrestlers with work – wrestling being a full-time career on the British isle for the top talented few – then they weren't getting paid and would go elsewhere for a wage. Belfast was just another day on the job for the grapplers of Globe Promotions.

  Local lads might have been the ones promoting the events, but local representation in the ring would be sorely lacking on the big bills in Belfast for decades to come.

- - - - -

It was with consideration for the men missing out that Jack McClelland helped organise what is the first found indisputable all-local wrestling show on April 12th 1946 at the *Short & Harland Gymnasium* on the Shankill Road in Belfast. It consisted of a card and crew comprised entirely of homegrown head-lockers.

  That evening 22 year old Jumping Joe Peters picked up a victory over Billy Steele (the new name for Bill Peacock), 35 year old Vic Fulton defeated Jack Raymond (in the main event of sorts), and 36 year old Bob/Bert Cowan overcame Bob Kane (in the match that closed the card).

Along with Jack Raymond the only local lads selected to wrestle on the grand stage of the Ulster Hall for J.C. / Globe Promotions that year were Jumping Joe, Vic and Bob/Bert; speaking to their standout skills (and good relationship with McClelland).

  Jumping Joe Peters was an asset to any feature that needed fast-pace action. Along with his signature flying crossbody Jumping Joe added being dynamite at dropkicks to his arsenal as well. The dropkick was one of the most devastating and delightful-looking moves of the time, and successfully hitting one on an opponent usually gathered a big response from an audience.

Gerry McSorley aka Jumping Joe Peters
Hailed as "The Fred Astaire of Wrestling" in reference to the famous
American actor and their shared quick feet
– Fred's for dancing, Joe's for dropkicking

Having survived the shootouts above the clouds with the R.A.F, Vic Fulton was back home a war hero. Not only highly respected as a wrestler by Jack McClelland, Vic also became a close friend of the young promoter. So it shouldn't be too surprising that Vic was always the first approached should a substitute be needed at the Ulster Hall for a JC/Globe bill.

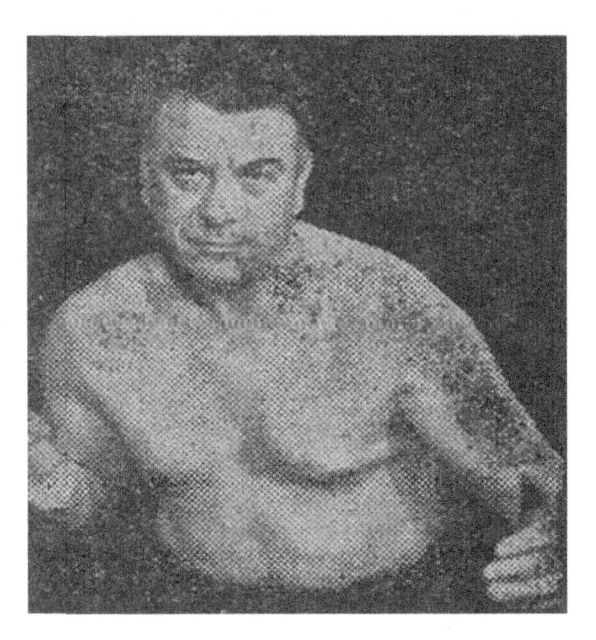

Vic Fulton
Wrestler and R.A.F. gunner

While always acting as a villain Bob/Bert Cowan – with a particularly bad habit for attacking the referee – was the only man who could say that over the last eight years he'd wrestled through every era of pro wrestling in Northern Ireland so far.

39 year old Bob Scott was another all-action man who was quite close with Jack McClelland. The boxer was also likely a father figure to the younger lads in the wrestling club and so was no doubt proud to be involved in the first found match for 21 year old engine repairman Joe Moore. At that April 12th all-Ulster show (albeit in a losing effort vs. lesser-spotted competitors called Jack Morgan and Tom Burns) Bob teamed with Joe in a tag match.

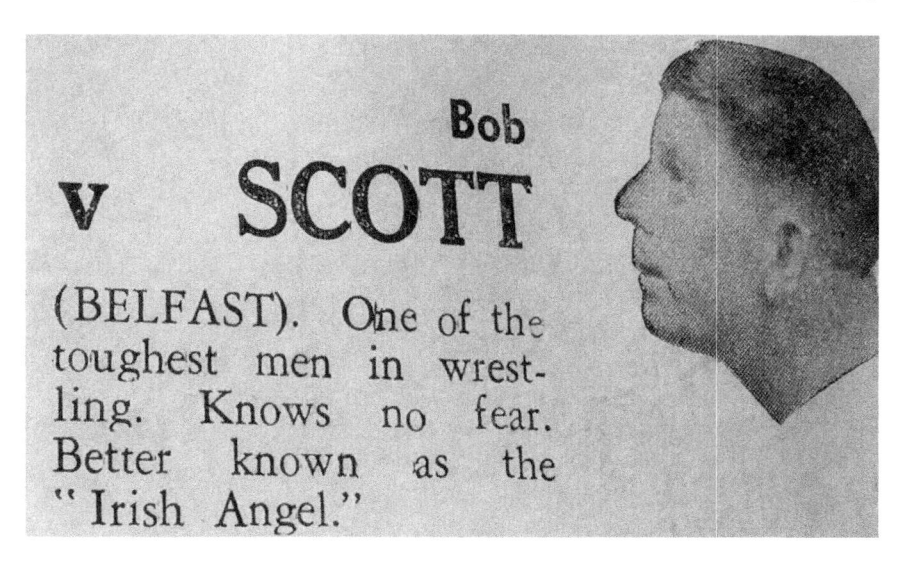

> **v** **Bob SCOTT**
> (BELFAST). One of the toughest men in wrestling. Knows no fear. Better known as the "Irish Angel."

A headshot of Bob Scott from a wrestling programme
Note: the "Irish Angel" is a lesser-found nickname,
"Tiger" is more common

Born in Belfast on March 14th 1925, Joe Moore is believed to be the skinny featherweight cousin of speedy lightweight Harry "The Black Owl" Browne. Joe also lived on the Shankill and was a very mild-mannered man who didn't go for any gimmicks like the Owl. Instead Joe sorted himself with sufficient skills to technically trouble anyone he got into a good grappling match with. Some wrestlers liked the "cowboys and indians" approach to presenting a pro bout, but Joe Moore was content to just be on the card in the straight wrestling match that often opened shows of the era. Joe would wrestle a clean, respectful bout, easing the audience into the experience so later when a villain began his dirty tactics the audience would be even more incensed as they could see all the rules abided in a match like Joe's being broken.

Later, from the same school of thought that made Jack McClelland into Jack Raymond, young Joe Moore adopted the surname "Reynolds" to become Joe Reynolds in the ring.

Meanwhile 33 year old Harry Browne was happy just to help out as referee on the gym show, while 32 year old Big Bob Fulton acted as the MC – because there was still no-one who came close to matching his weight and putting up a believable fair fight.

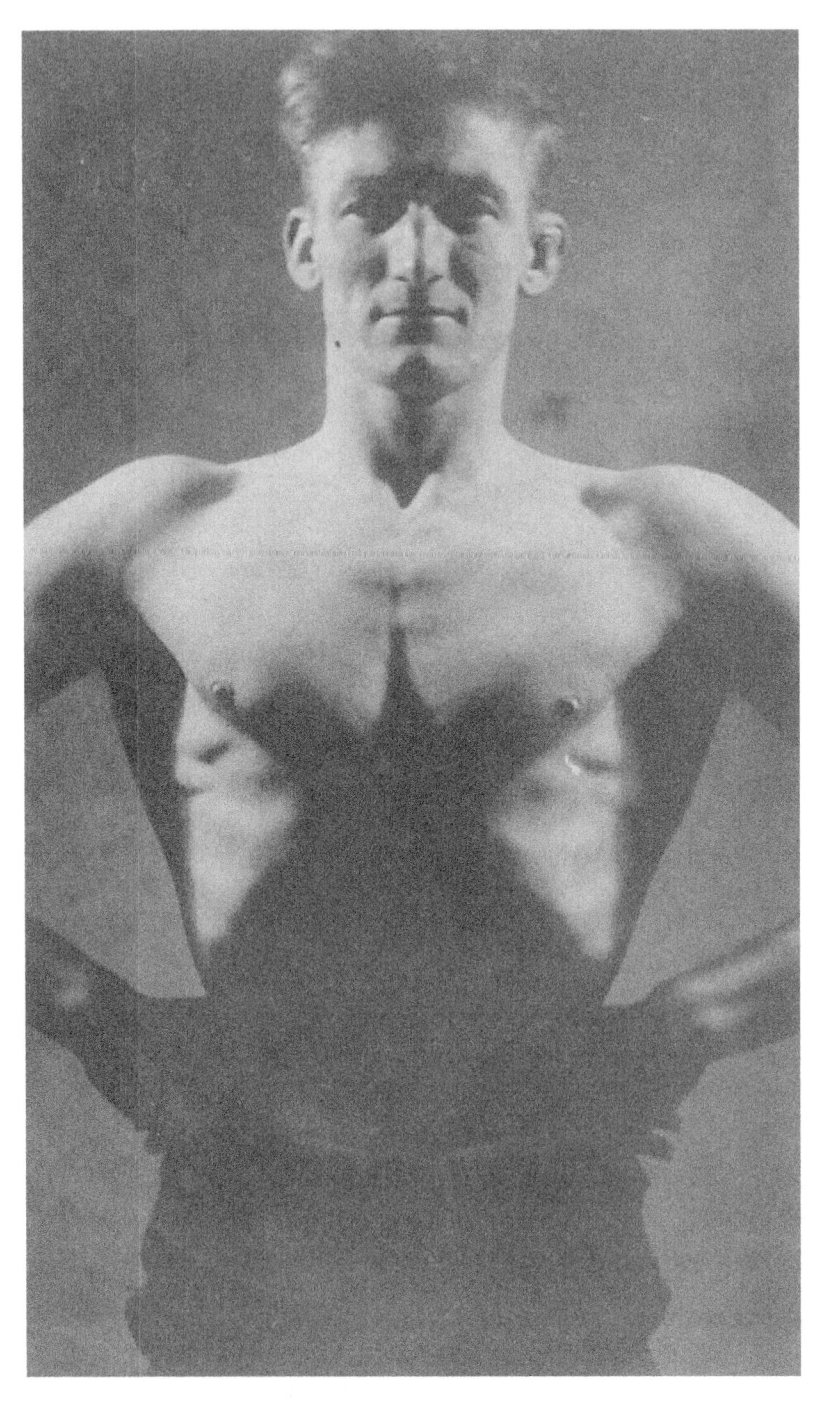

Joe Moore aka Joe Reynolds

- - - - -

After the two Jack's agreed-on dates concluded, J.C. resumed control of wrestling promotion that May. The Belfast bookie then presented the *"He-Man Sport"* with Globe Promotions matchmaker Ted Beresford. Beresford would go on to bring in some top quality UK talent like the Field brothers, *British Heavyweight Champion* Bert Assirati and one of the most notable names to make his first appearance in Ireland this year was infamously eccentric Englishman Les Kellett.

Meanwhile in the UK, something that would change the course of British and Irish wrestling happened this year.

> *"A British Wrestling Board of Control, intended to have the same function in professional wrestling as the British Boxing Board of Control has for boxing, was established last night at a House of Commons meeting... The Board's purpose is to control all professional wrestling in the United Kingdom, and a constitution and rules are being drawn up and stewards appointed"*
> *- Northern Whig, November 21st 1946*

Still feeling the fall-out from all-in, British wrestling's most powerful promoters realised a very pubic clean-up was needed to convince councils that wrestling wasn't what it used to be.

Boxing had closely resembled bare-knuckle fighting until the end of the 19th century when Hugh Lowther, a figure in British high society better known as *Lord Lonsdale,* acted as President of a club aiming to clean up its image. The influence of Lord Lonsdale helped legitimatise boxing and in turn the sport formed its own official governing body. Pro wrestling sought to do the same, and World War 1 hero – and more importantly a member of high society who was wrestling fan – Edward Evans, better known as *Admiral-Lord Mountevans*, was made President for the *British Wrestling Board of Control* on November 20th 1946.

However, Lord Mountevans was simply used to attract public attention and positive newspaper print. The de facto decision-makers were really the powerful promoters who that December wrote up the *"Mountevans Rules"*. The Mountevans Rules favoured cleaner technical wrestling over free-for-all brawling. This meant that lighter grapplers superb at realistic-looking submissions were able to rise up the ranks (and pay ladder) in the wrestling business much faster than when it was dominated by heavyweight brawlers who freely kicked, punched, bruised and abused their way through matches. This impacted the British wrestling scene in a big way as though heavyweights were still star attractions, smaller and snappier wrestlers became much more prevalent and popular.

The rules also included which holds were legal to use, and – as boxing had *Lonsdale belts* – "Official" Mountevans belts were created in the various weight-classes. Matches between two different weight classes, i.e. a welterweight vs. a middleweight were called *catchweight* contests. Often if two wrestlers weren't in a similar weight class they might never wrestle one another.

While the Lord's name would be used in association with wrestling for years to come, Mountevans himself had no more direct involvement and the Board of Control would actually cease to exist in any actual form a few months into 1947. The fix was already in though and the influence of Lord Mountevans got the brain trust promoters back into their coveted council-owned buildings. Indeed, soon several of these same figureheads would *join* together to use their power to attempt to monopolise wrestling in the UK…

- - - - -

At the same time as the Wrestling Board of Control were first meeting up, Jack McClelland and Jack Crane were putting the finishing touches on founding the first official locally-run pro wrestling promotion *Worldwide Wrestling Promotions* – that openly embraced the free-style branding, the British Board and later the Mountevans Rules.

The two young entrepreneurs pooled their money and resources together, and wanting to keep in the good graces of J.C. – and as importantly the English overlords of pro wrestling in Belfast – the two Jack's decided to book town halls in lesser spotted stops in Ulster. In doing so they brought wrestling to places in the province for the very first time, presenting the *"Roughest and Toughest and Most Thrilling Sport in the World"*.

Worldwide Promotions hosted its first show on December 2nd 1946 in Ballymena Town Hall with "Sailor" Jack Crane vs. "Sergeant" Vic Fulton as one of the marquee matches.

A blank booking card that the Jack's would post to wrestlers to inform them of upcoming shows

The debut event is also the first finding of Harry Browne wrestling without a mask and under the name of "Jim Brown" vs. Tiger Bob Scott. Though the Black Owl gimmick wasn't gone for good Harry appeared far more frequently as Jim Brown going forward and was billed as the *Lightweight Champion of Ireland.*

Worldwide's next event was at *Downpatrick Town Hall* two weeks later on December 16th with usual suspects like Jumping Joe Peters thrilling with his terrific offence, and the ladies favourite 33 year old Whipper Dave Mack still billed as the undefeated Welterweight Champion of Ireland (5 years on!).

After another fortnight gap, on December 27th 1946 a reported crowd of 1,000 packed out *Portadown Town Hall* for County Armagh's first ever full-on pro wrestling show that included the rematch of Jack Raymond vs. Vic Fulton plus Jim Brown defending his lightweight honours vs. Joe Reynolds. This event ended the first year were an alternative to the big bills in Belfast was finally offered.

Harry Browne aka The Black Owl
aka Jim Brown, Lightweight Champion of Ireland

1947

The trio of successful Worldwide Promotions shows were a fantastic feat pulled off by Jack McClelland & Jack Crane. They then revisited Ballymena and Portadown that February and added *Coleraine Town Hall* to their circuit that same month.

Newry Town Hall near the Irish border followed in March.

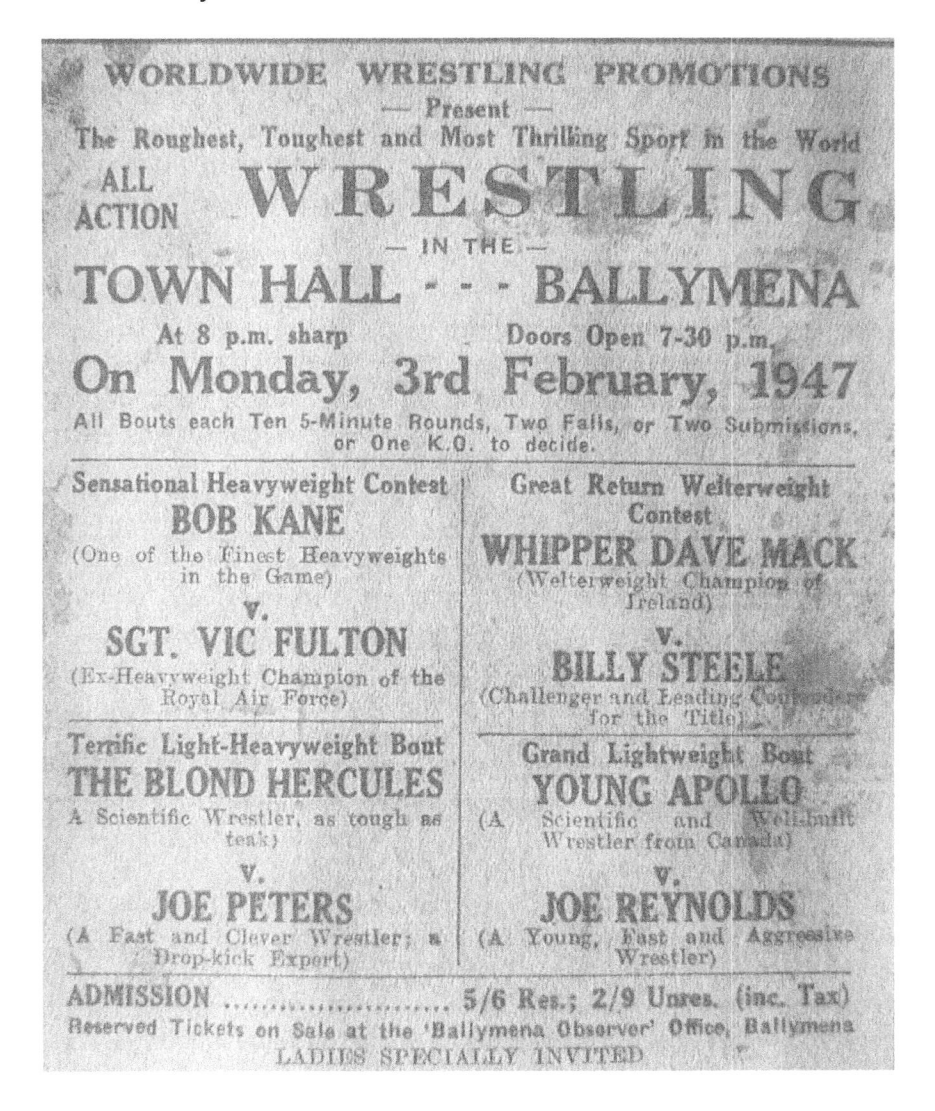

WORLDWIDE WRESTLING PROMOTIONS
— Present —
The Roughest, Toughest and Most Thrilling Sport in the World

ALL ACTION WRESTLING
— IN THE —
TOWN HALL - - - BALLYMENA

At 8 p.m. sharp　　Doors Open 7-30 p.m.

On Monday, 3rd February, 1947

All Bouts each Ten 5-Minute Rounds, Two Falls, or Two Submissions, or One K.O. to decide.

Sensational Heavyweight Contest	Great Return Welterweight Contest
BOB KANE (One of the Finest Heavyweights in the Game)	**WHIPPER DAVE MACK** (Welterweight Champion of Ireland)
v.	v.
SGT. VIC FULTON (Ex-Heavyweight Champion of the Royal Air Force)	**BILLY STEELE** (Challenger and Leading Contender for the Title)
Terrific Light-Heavyweight Bout	Grand Lightweight Bout
THE BLOND HERCULES (A Scientific Wrestler, as tough as teak)	**YOUNG APOLLO** (A Scientific and Well-built Wrestler from Canada)
v.	v.
JOE PETERS (A Fast and Clever Wrestler; a Drop-kick Expert)	**JOE REYNOLDS** (A Young, Fast and Aggressive Wrestler)

ADMISSION .... 5/6 Res.; 2/9 Unres. (inc. Tax)
Reserved Tickets on Sale at the 'Ballymena Observer' Office, Ballymena
LADIES SPECIALLY INVITED

The tour of town halls went on a hiatus soon after, but the Jack's were far from finished with shows. In fact, they'd barely even started.

Importantly, they wanted to work out the logistics of establishing their own base for frequent features, and they soon had somewhere in mind...

In the meantime, that year wrestlers in the North would travel down South to wrestle for the first time. Jumping Joe Peters, Whipper Dave Mack, "Bearded" Jack Raymond and Big Bob Fulton (they found someone his size vs. Irish wrestler Charles Geoghegan aka Young Atlas, who had a spell as a wrestler in America) starred on a wrestling show at the *Olympia Theatre* in Dublin. It was a showcase of lightning speed lighter competitors and hard-hitting heavier combatants, with Harry Browne taking charge as the referee that evening.

Shows in the South were few and far between by this point. The North, and Belfast specifically, was leading the way in producing wrestlers and promoting shows, with the South having only sporadic shows and a largely non-existent local level. Indeed for much of the rest of the 20th century, Northern Ireland was HQ for pro wrestling on the island of Ireland.

- - - - -

That year those trotted over by Globe included many old favourites like Mike de Mitre and Cab Cashford, and while the wrestling fanatics still wanted their fix J.C. recognised it would be wise to reduce weekly events to bi-weekly events. After a dispute with the city council over the increased entertainment tax (a way of recouping money spent on the war effort), J.C. stopped over the summer until the issue was resolved that autumn – by which point the Belfast faithful were begging for the he-men to come back.

In fact so popular was wrestling with enthusiasts that once they'd unwrapped their presents, ate their dinner and made all the small talk they could manage with their in-laws, they could throw on a warm coat and head on over to the Ulster Hall were there were *"Thrills Galore"* at the wrestling presented on Christmas night 1947.

1948

That summer J.C. retired from boxing and wrestling promotion and handed over the reins and his rings to a relative in George Connell. George Connell was born in Belfast in the mid 1900s, and followed the family business of being a bookmaker and boxing promoter.

Globe Promotions too were respectfully replaced, with the new name in bringing the best of British wrestling across the Irish sea being George de Relwyskow. Born in England in 1914, George de Relwyskow – a one-time tag team partner of Pat Magee during the Joseph & Joyce era – had been injured in a secret spy operation during World War II and forced to retire as a wrestler. However in 1942 Relwyskow's promoter father passed away and the younger Relwyskow took control of the family business. In the more prominent position of a promoter, like his father before him, Relwyskow became one of wrestling's bigwigs and had his hand in the Board of Control and the Mountevans Rules.

As well as upper England and Scotland, Relwyskow took on Belfast as his territory, and partnered with *George Connell Promotions* that September. The George's starting running the Ulster Hall on a regular basis; sometimes weekly, sometimes bi-weekly, sometimes monthly but always with some of British wrestling's best on the bill.

- - - - -

That same September, the Jack's at Worldwide Promotions expanded their enterprises by beginning to run regular pro wrestling in a place that had only ever presented it twice up to that point, the second highest populated city in the North; Derry City.

Travel at the time between Belfast and Derry was much longer as the roads weren't as developed as they are today, so the English never showed much interest in the west of NI. This left McClelland and Crane with their own exclusive territory.

On September 18th 1948 the Guildhall in Derry hosted its first of many Worldwide shows to come with Jim Brown vs. Joe Reynolds (a frequently found match) on the undercard and in the evening's main event it was Big Bob Fulton vs. English heavyweight Jack Atherton (who previously appeared on Harry Joyce's Irish debut show, ten years earlier, in December 1938).

> *"World-wide Wrestling Promotions staged the first of a series of tournaments, which they plan to hold in Londonderry, on Saturday night, when there was a good crowd in the Guildhall for the first taste of the free-style variety of the game. Top of the bill was a heavyweight match between Bob Fulton, the twenty-two stone Ulster Champion, and Jack Atherton, of Wigan, who conceded five and a half stone and was a decided loser".*
> *- Londonderry Sentinel, September 21st 1948*

Going forward the Derry Guildhall would host wrestling on a monthly basis. Events would feature only the odd UK/international star (coaxed over through Jack McClelland's contacts) on shows heavily supported by the local level's finest including Bob/Bert Cowan who added alliteration to his name to become *"Crusher"* Cowan, and Tiger Bob Scott who remained reliable in the role of referee or wrestler.

The Black Owl would woo again too in rare reappearances, but when not wrestling as the man in the mask or defending his Lightweight title as Jim Brown, the supremely skilled Harry Browne was along with Joe Moore one of the assistants at the Short & Harland's wrestling club. The club was apparently re-established around October of 1948 as an amateur club with a committee of names not involved in pro wrestling, but with Dave Mack credited as the head coach in a newspaper article.

The *Short Bros & Harland's Physical Culture and Wrestling Club* was still based in the gym on Huss Street in Belfast and in its desire to be recognised as an amateur club it even joined the *British Amateur Wrestling Association* – making the club Northern Ireland's first official amateur club, albeit with pro coaches in Harry, Joe and Dave Mack…

1949

Soon fans to the grappling at the Guildhall were being turned away. Wrestling proved a huge hit in Derry, and built off the back of top homegrown talent the second city became the second hot spot for pro wrestling in all of Ireland.

    The success inspired Worldwide to start a seasonal schedule. The Guildhall would be run once a month between September and May roughly, with other towns being visited whenever possible. Then in the summer Jack McClelland turned up his salesman tactics in order to sell shows to festivals or fundraisers.

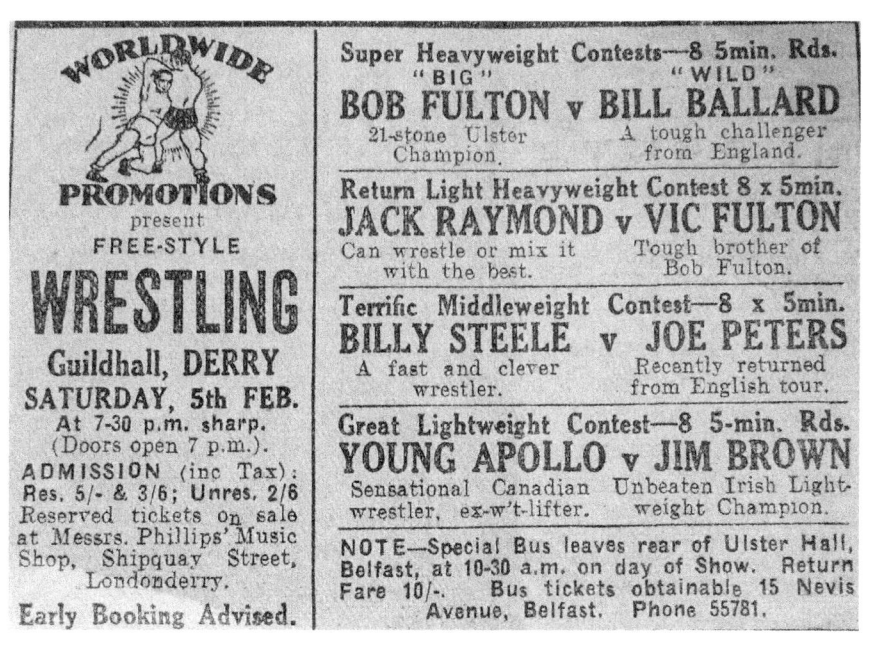

WORLDWIDE PROMOTIONS present FREE-STYLE **WRESTLING**
Guildhall, DERRY
SATURDAY, 5th FEB.
At 7-30 p.m. sharp.
(Doors open 7 p.m.).
ADMISSION (inc Tax):
Res. 5/- & 3/6; Unres. 2/6
Reserved tickets on sale at Messrs. Phillips' Music Shop, Shipquay Street, Londonderry.
Early Booking Advised.

Super Heavyweight Contest—8 5min. Rds.
"BIG" **BOB FULTON** v "WILD" **BILL BALLARD**
21-stone Ulster Champion.   A tough challenger from England.

Return Light Heavyweight Contest 8 x 5min.
JACK RAYMOND v **VIC FULTON**
Can wrestle or mix it with the best.   Tough brother of Bob Fulton.

Terrific Middleweight Contest—8 x 5min.
BILLY STEELE v **JOE PETERS**
A fast and clever wrestler.   Recently returned from English tour.

Great Lightweight Contest—8 5-min. Rds.
YOUNG APOLLO v **JIM BROWN**
Sensational Canadian wrestler, ex-w't-lifter.   Unbeaten Irish Lightweight Champion.

NOTE—Special Bus leaves rear of Ulster Hall, Belfast, at 10-30 a.m. on day of Show. Return Fare 10/-. Bus tickets obtainable 15 Nevis Avenue, Belfast. Phone 55781.

A Worldwide bill at the Guildhall from February 1949

Note; as previously mentioned Billy Steele used to appear in action as "Bill Peacock" during Word War II.
Uniquely, Peacock/Steele wrestled in white trunks (when black were the standard) and barefoot (again, not the norm).
As Billy Steele he was sometimes nicknamed "Tarzan", albeit billed from Ballymena.

At the conclusion of the first season at the Guildhall, Big Bob Fulton retained his *"Ulster Championship"* vs. Carl von Wurden; the Canadian Mountie who helped train the first class and respected his Irish success stories enough to take the loss.

That May event also featured the last match for Jack Crane who age only 24 retired from the ring and moved to Australia for work. On his final night after his final fight Crane was gifted a shillelagh – a traditional Irish weapon resembling a club – as a going away present. Crane's expedition to Australia left Jack McClelland as the sole trader of Worldwide Promotions, but it wasn't anything to worry the self-made man as he soon entered into business with one of the British wrestling's biggest players.

- - - - -

Jack McClelland's respectful relationship with J.C. extended to a friendly working relationship with his successor George Connell too and through the boxing boss Jack arranged an agreement with the other George – the English one – Relwyskow to get more of the UK's best grapplers onto Worldwide's shows.

Starting with the second season at the Guildhall, and depending on the availability of Relwyskow's UK/international regulars, a Worldwide show might feature several local wrestlers or very few, and at other times there would be a 50/50 split. Local lads might have built up business in Derry, but it didn't mean they were guaranteed to be featured as frequently anymore.

Of course it could too have been a sign of the times. Tiger Bob Scott was slowly transitioning from irregular wrestler to regular referee, and while some like Jim Browne and Joe Reynolds still filled bills as lightweight openers, others like Whipper Dave Mack and Jumping Joe Peters were already accepting less bookings, likely due to wear and tear on their bodies.

By coincidence or injury, as there was certainly enough heavyweights being brought over by then, Big Bob Fulton seemingly fell from grace. Bob would appear in action less and less until disappearing altogether from Worldwide cards.

Meanwhile, the newly monikered "Cyclone" Vic Fulton's stock only rose as he became the most consistent local man to get on cards for Worldwide. The Cyclone was even invited to appear at a charity event in Carrickfergus at the end of the year, being recognised as wrestling's local representative alongside other sporting celebrities of the day including iconic Belfast boxer Rinty Monaghan.

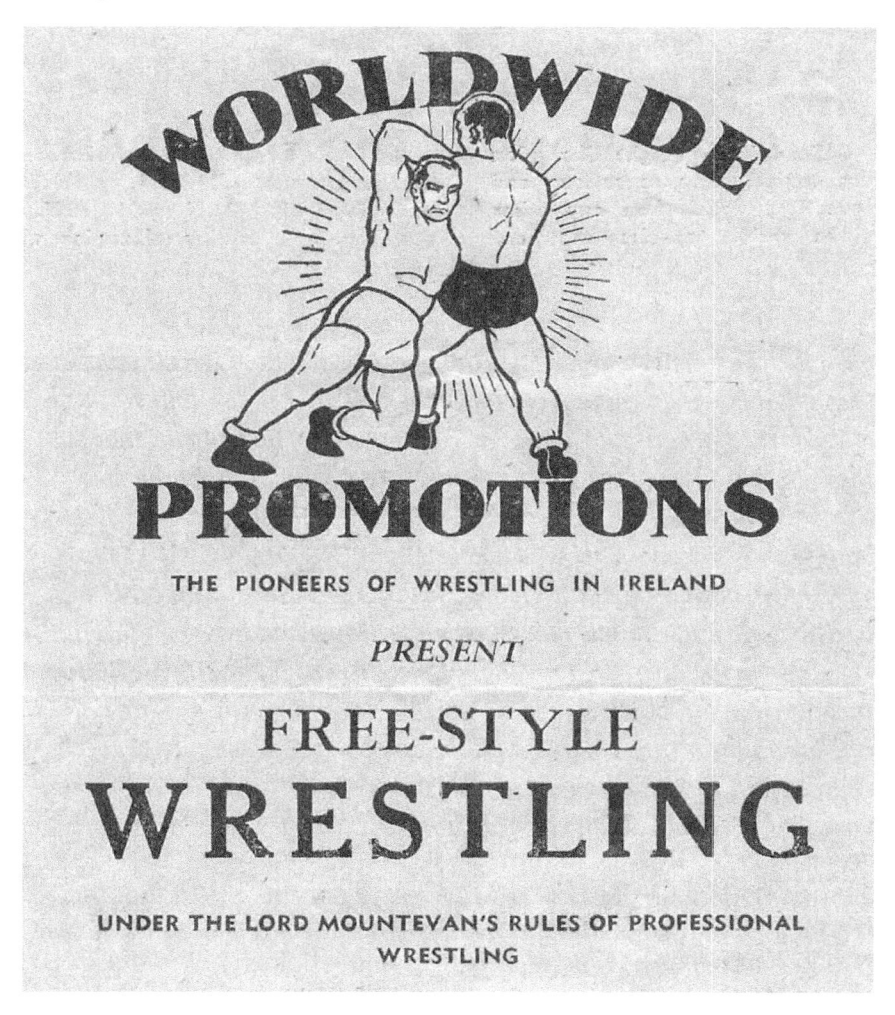

WORLDWIDE PROMOTIONS

THE PIONEERS OF WRESTLING IN IRELAND

PRESENT

FREE-STYLE WRESTLING

UNDER THE LORD MOUNTEVAN'S RULES OF PROFESSIONAL WRESTLING

- - - - -

That December – in a sign of wrestling's continued growth from strength to strength – George Connell & George de Relwyskow became the first men to promote pro wrestling in Northern Ireland in every month of a calendar year, January to December.

Chapter 5

Darkie
& Glory Days at the Guildhall

1950

Noel 'Darkie' Arnott: "I got into the Short & Harland wrestling club through a friend of mine. You had to be a worker to join but he put in a good word because he knew I was interested. The trainers there at the time were Harry Browne and Joe Moore, they brought me through. Joe was a featherweight, very light, very precise. Joe was very helpful to newcomers, he was a gentleman. The best wrestler who was there though when I joined was Harry. He was a wonderful wrestler. He knew numerous holds and throws and he was light in stature, maybe only 10 stone, a lightweight, but big in talent. He was an encyclopedia of wrestling. He'd work with me at the gym one-to-one for an hour three nights a week. And I'm not saying I was a great wrestler but that's how I got my experience. Anything I learned about wrestling it was through Harry Browne."

Born in Belfast on July 24th 1929 to blind parents (his father fully, his mother partially), in school Noel Arnott was nicknamed "Darkie" because of his swarthy-skin and jet black hair. As a young lad Darkie had a part-time job delivering newspapers for the *Belfast Telegraph*, and in his early teens he watched with wonder at the wrestling in the Rialto and dreamed of stepping through the ropes and into the ring himself. After leaving school Darkie took on the trade of an apprentice welder.

In late 1948, 19 year old Darkie Arnott got to join the grapplers at the Huss Street gymnasium, and over the next year the Belfast born-and-bred boy would learn the techniques and tricks of wrestling with Harry 'The Black Owl' / 'Jim Brown' Browne his mentor. Within a year Darkie was a seriously skilled wrestler, and his extensive knowledge of holds was matched by few others of his limited experience. However, when he represented the Short & Harland gym at an amateur tournament in Dublin in December 1949 it didn't work out exactly as planned.

Darkie Arnott: "The trouble was our coaches were professionals and I don't think they knew much about amateur wrestling, so they were teaching us professional holds. So when we went down to Dublin to wrestle a team there at Rathmines Hall, we had one winner, I was beat on points, and everyone else got pinned. And I was actually ahead on points at one stage, only I didn't know how it worked. I didn't actually know anything about amateur wrestling, so it was by luck. I just got in there and wrestled to the best of my ability. It was an interesting experience anyway."

Darkie's head and heart were in becoming a pro and thankfully good word of mouth spread to the right people. He was soon approached by an impressed Jack McClelland who offered Darkie the opportunity to properly turn professional and debut for Worldwide Promotions.

Darkie Arnott: "Jack McClelland was a bit of a book himself. He was a larger than life character. He was a great advocate for swimming and living a healthy lifestyle. He would go swimming in Victoria Park for miles a day. I liked Jack, he always looked after the local lads. Even though he was a wrestler, he was more for promoting it. He'd only wrestle to fill it out, if someone got injured or didn't turn up."

On Monday February 13th 1950 at Ballymena Town Hall, 20 year old "Bruno Arnella" from Italy debuted vs. Tarzan Billy Steele (who later this year wrapped up wrestling and joined Jack Crane in relocating to Australia). Bruno of course was Darkie, given the gimmick of first a full-blooded Italian, and soon after this show the slightly more feasible "Irish-Italian".
      That Saturday on February 18th "Bruno" had his second ever bout, vs. Whipper Dave Mack on the grand-stage of the Derry Guildhall for Worldwide.

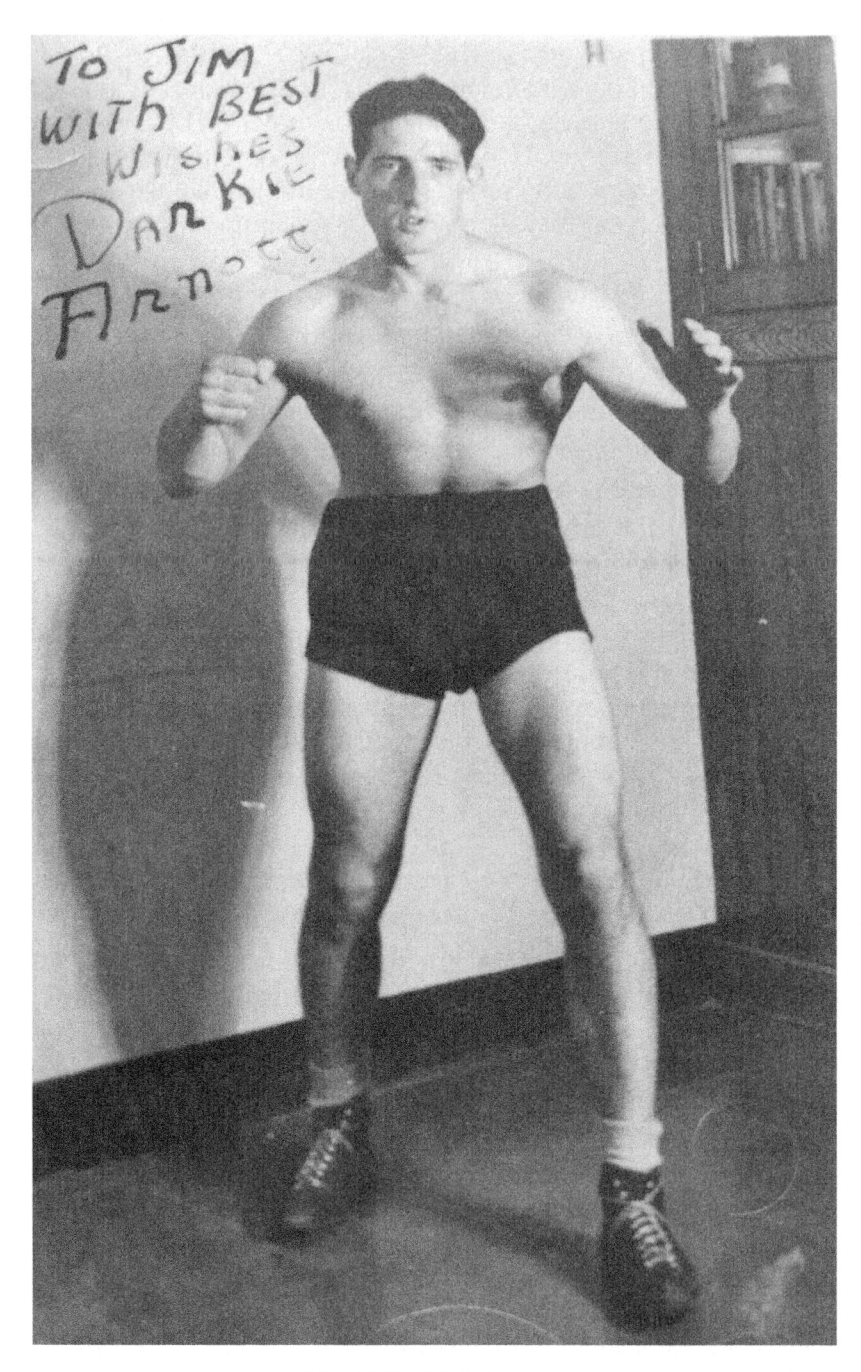

Noel "Darkie" Arnott
An autographed picture for Harry Browne's young son Jim

Darkie Arnott: "When I wrestled against the Welterweight Champion Dave Mack I hadn't a clue what I was doing. I would say Dave Mack carried me for half the rounds. He knew rightly I was a novice but he didn't take advantage. The night I wrestled Dave Mack, he wrestled for the two of us. Funny, I actually don't really remember Dave Mack wrestling much after that."

The match vs. Darkie is also the final found for 36 year old Dave Mack as an active pro wrestler. The undefeated Irish Welterweight Champion becoming the first of the first class to tap out after ten years. The always sociable Whipper would stick about the Short & Harland gym however, never getting involved physically but still dropping by to keep up with the craic and give advice and instruction to aspiring grapplers.

Darkie Arnott: "I used to get called 'Darkie' in school. So it just stuck when I got to the wrestling."

While the Irish-Italian billing stuck in advertising for shows, within the next couple months Bruno Arnella became "Bruno" Arnott and by that summer just Darkie Arnott, who gained confidence through showcasing his skills many more times for Worldwide as his coach Harry Browne's star pupil.

- - - - -

Darkie was also called upon as a sparring partner for more experienced wrestlers before their own big bouts. That July, Jack McClelland teamed with George de Relwyskow to promote two events at the grounds of *Crusaders Football Club* in Belfast. Jack even getting his good friend Vic Fulton a big bout on the first bill vs. longtime fan favourite the Canadian-Greek Mike de Mitre.

Darkie Arnott: "Vic Fulton and Jack McClelland would have been very close. I remember one time Vic was wrestling in the Crusaders, open air, and he asked me the day before to come down and have a pull-round with him. Vic was in the Air Force during the War, I think he was a gunner, he was about 15 stone".

- - - - -

That same year, Relwyskow & George Connell returned wrestling to the King's Hall for the first time post-World War II. In a huge two day happening, that February thousands packed the ice rink one day for the wrestling (headlined by de Mitre), and then the next day for a bill of boxing.

- - - - -

Meanwhile into his third successful season at the Guildhall, Jack McClelland relied on new names like Darkie Arnott as many of his old regulars of the ring weren't as active anymore.

Dave Mack was finished as a wrestler, Jumping Joe Peters got married that year and would soon start a family so had commitments elsewhere, and Big Bob Fulton remained missing in action. That said, Harry "Jim Brown" Browne and Joe "Reynolds" Moore along with Cyclone Vic Fulton were still frequently featured, and while Tiger Bob Scott wrested on occasion – including on one Guildhall bill in a battle of the "Tigers" vs. Scottish wrestler Tiger Robb – he soon settled solely as a referee on cards.

The old school was giving way to the new school but it took a little time for the transition to complete and local representation lacked as a result. From the first season at the Guildhall events had went from 90/10 for local representation to 50/50 in the second season to closer to 30/70 by the third as more UK/international stars, including notable names like Scottish lightweight legend George Kidd, made up most of the matches on a Worldwide show in Derry City.

Outside the city, wrestling cards in town halls were more homegrown heavy to their credit, though also more sporadic.

Harry Browne with a submission hold on Darkie Arnott
during training at the Short & Harland's gym.
Picture dated 1950

1951

Darkie Arnott: "*Jack McClelland worked with George Connell, when the opportunity arose anyway. I suppose Jack saw somewhere in the future he would get a turn or a deal out of it you know. So Jack worked with him when he was stuck, and George Connell would have helped Jack out at times. I used to have George Connell pestered you know? I'd always go to his office and ask when I'd be getting a bout at the Ulster Hall.*"

In exchange for Relwyskow being the official matchmaker for Worldwide's bills and adding importance by association, Jack McClelland would act as the local talent liaison if an extra body was needed on a Belfast show.

Darkie Arnott: "*The only time George Connell ever used me was when I was getting ready to go to the Ulster Hall one night with my girlfriend of the time. And big Jack McClelland and Connell turned up at my house, my mother's house, and said 'we need you to go on tonight, there's two wrestlers fog-bound in Manchester'. So they got me and then went and lifted Harry Browne, and we went on first.*"

Still in his rookie year, on January 5th 1951 Darkie was selected by McClelland to wrestle in the Ulster Hall for the first time, and vs. Harry Browne. It wasn't just eagerness that got Darkie selected for the show but how he had established himself in a relatively short space of time as one of the finest exponents of the locks and holds of wrestling on the island of Ireland.

Darkie Arnott: "*That's the only time really. I didn't get on there as much as I would have liked. It wasn't George Connell though, it was Relwyskow across the water who provided the wrestlers and he didn't want any locals on, because if he put a local wrestler on it would be taking away from one of his own. You can't blame him in a way.*"

- - - - -

Undeterred, Darkie continued to compete for Worldwide. He also kept up his training at the Huss Street gym where another new name would rapidly rise up the ranks in 21 year old shipyard driller Larry Casey.

Darkie Arnott: "Larry Casey was a bodybuilder. He was a driller in the shipyard and he came to the club one night and I was there and Harry Browne was there, there was a few of us. Larry came with his brother Dan and they wanted to try wrestling. So I was told by Harry to go in with him, and he was a bit bigger than me and heavier than me, but I had a bit of knowledge and he had no knowledge. So we went in, and I got the better of him, got two submissions off him. But he stuck at it and was spurred on to become a wrestler".

Born in Belfast in 1930, when the real-life Lawrence Ralston gained enough experience in grappling he too started wrestling for Worldwide. His first found match being on March 24th 1951 in a tag team contest in the Guildhall vs. a team captained by debuting Derry wrestler Andy McClea (more on him soon).

The "Larry Casey" name was perhaps picked by Jack McClelland to play to the perception that a member of Ireland's most famous wrestling family of the time, the Casey's, had been booked on the bill (Kerry wrestler Crusher Steve Casey was still active in American wrestling at the time, and several of his brothers were also known wrestlers).

Darkie Arnott: "Larry Casey was a pretty good wrestler after he was at it a while, he really was. However he always harboured the fact that I got the better off him that first night. And for years he was always trying to find a way to meet me in the ring and get his own back. He was obsessed, but I never give him the opportunity."

Casey and Darkie were to develop something of a real-life rivalry. As the two best young bucks to come out of the Short & Harland gym a rivalry between them was understandable, even inevitable.

Notable, the future of local level pro wrestling and its wrestlers was to be shaped by Darkie and Larry.

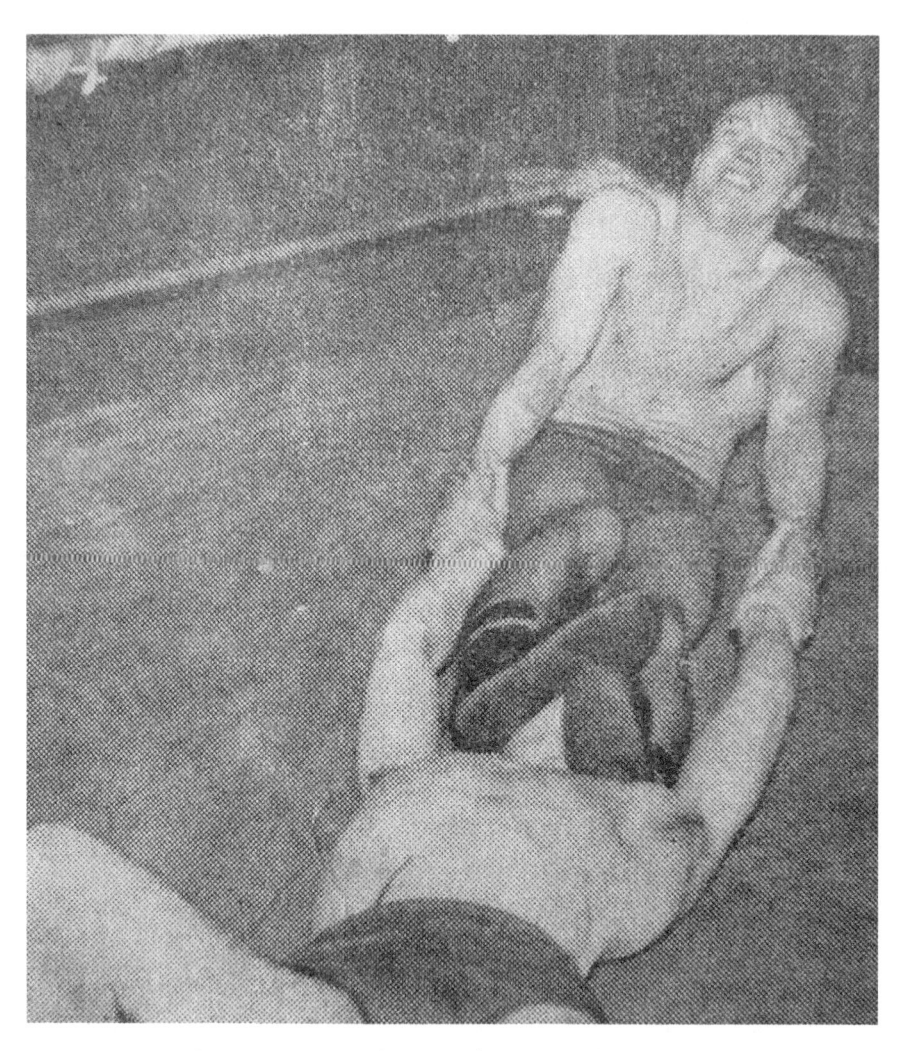

Larry Casey (top) applies a submission hold at training

Darkie Arnott: "Jack looked after the locals. When he ran the shows in Derry he always tried to have two or three Derrymen on the bill".

As early as the second season at the Guildhall, homegrown headlockers from Derry City started to appear on shows. Names like Roy/Rory Leonard, Jack "Buzz" Bradley and Jim Campbell were all frequent fixtures but the most significant of the Maiden City men was 22 year old football fanatic and gym owner Andy McClea.

Born in Derry on December 23rd 1929, sport was Andrew "Andy" McClea's life. By the time he was 21 Andy was already the president of a local football club in the city and operated his own weight-lifting gym at the team's training facility, the *St. Patrick's Athletic Club for Boys*. As many of the weight-lifters at the gym went on to become pro wrestlers it isn't a stretch to suggest the gym was not only a gateway into the grappling game but also the city's first dedicated space for pro wrestling practice.

Striving for excellence in sports and fitness wasn't just Andy McClea's life but his livelihood so unsurprisingly he was also the standout of the *Derry Wrestling Club.* In time the talented McClea got to mix it in matches with several UK/international wrestlers for Worldwide Promotions.

- - - - -

On the opposite end of the spectrum from the fresh faces of Darkie Arnott, Larry Casey and Andy McClea was the old one of Atholl Oakeley, then in his 50s, who the previous summer promoted in Northern Ireland for the first time.

After his all-in wrestling creation became Frankenstein's monster and was destroyed, Oakeley looked to reinvent. Refusing to recognise the Lord Mountevans rules instead Oakeley insisted on his own *"International Catch Wrestling Rules"* which aimed to bring wrestling back to its roots; when it was just two big men grappling in a ring with none of the thrills nor frills that his own all-in innovation had made synonymous with wrestling in the UK.

Darkie Arnott: "There was a man with plenty of money called Atholl Oakeley, and he tried to resurrect straight wrestling the way they done it in the 1900s, like George Hackenschmidt would have been wrestling. He would have two guys on doing every day wrestling, then the next bout would be old-fashioned style, no messing about, no gimmicks, no nothing. They could have a headlock on for five minutes. He interspersed them with two modern type bouts so the crowd wouldn't get disengaged. They were odd shows he done, but he was a very rich man so I suppose he had the money to burn."

When Atholl Oakeley came to Belfast in June 1950 he went big and booked the King's Hall. The star of his curious catch-styled card was Jack Doyle, an Irish boxer who had fallen from grace in his own sport and turned to wrestling as a substitute.

The back-to-bearded Pat Magee from Ballycastle also reappeared after a seven absence. Having went back to live in London during the war, an aging Pat bounced between refereeing and wrestling, and was surely paid a fine sum by Oakeley to show his skills one more time at the King's Hall. Following this event Pat Magee, then in his late 40s or early 50s, would slowly wind down his wrestling commitments before finally hanging up his black boots, putting away his black trunks and giving his greying beard a reassuring stroke that it wouldn't be used and abused as a weapon anymore.

Pat Magee with his brilliant beard was Ulster's first prominent player in British pro wrestling and a fun feature on the Irish circuit too. Unfortunately nothing could be found for his finality, though it is suggested his other sport was rugby and he taught it for a time at *St. Ignatius College* in London.

In June 1951, for only the third time in twelve months, Atholl Oakeley crossed the Irish sea and brought to the King's Hall American boxer "Two Ton" Tony Galento, whose claim to fame was knocking Joe Louis off his feet in 1939 in New York. Logistics for the show were sorted by Dublin boxing promoter Gerald Egan – who had helped organise Danno O'Mahoney's homecoming tour fifteen years prior – as Egan and Sir Atholl also worked on a wrestling event in Dublin the night before the bouts in Belfast. Lastly, Belfast boxer Rinty Monaghan completed a boxing hat-trick on the card, though little Rinty's appearance was only to sing a few songs in the ring during the interval with his signature being the traditional tune *"When Irish Eyes Are Smiling"*.

Darkie Arnott: "Your man Oakeley run a show in the King's Hall, and I was at it, and I don't know how but one of the Fulton brothers was on the bill, Bob. Bob Fulton worked at the bottom of the Falls Road, something to do with horses. Bob was about 18 stone, no particular great physique, just 18 stone of meat. Though Bob was a very genial man."

Having fallen from favour on Worldwide fixtures, Big Bob Fulton's stature meant he was the size of strongman Oakeley was after for these odes to a bygone era. However, Bob would again disappear after this match which ended in defeat and possible injury.

Darkie Arnott: "So anyway I made it my business to get down to ringside after the event had ended, and I had a minute's talk with Atholl Oakeley. I said I'd be willing to have a go you know, and he said, 'I have an Italian about your weight, I could match you with him'. But needless to say it came to nil. His efforts too would come to nil as the crowds didn't like it. It was too slow, people didn't want to watch that type of wrestling anymore."

Despite Oakeley's proclamation that his shows would bring back the grand old days of respectable wrestling, the Two Ton Tony match wound up with fists flying and a disqualification ending. His main event booed out of the building, it was to be Oakeley's final Irish show. The wealthy Englishman's events were unable able to match the mighty George Connell – who was well on his way to being lauded as one of Ireland's greatest ever sports and entertainment organisers – and so a defeated Oakeley decided to give up for good on promoting across the Irish sea.

A few years later, Atholl Oakeley would exit the grappling game and retire to spend his riches elsewhere. In 1971 he published his autobiography *Blue Blood on the Mat*. Sir Atholl Oakeley would pass away age 86 in 1987.

- - - - -

Tiny fist-thrower Rinty Monaghan singing on a wrestling show wasn't anything new; in 1938 he crooned on the phoney fundraiser in the King's Hall that featured Buck Alec's first match, and in the summer of 1950 Jack McClelland arranged for Rinty to sing a few songs during the interval of a wrestling show at a festival in the tiny seaside village of Burtonport in Donegal (which was also Donegal's first ever pro wrestling event).

In the summer of 1951 the wrestling was invited back to Burtonport with another extra add-on. This time it wasn't a singing boxer but a swimming wrestler as 28 year old Jack McClelland attempted to make history as the first man to swim the two and a half miles between Burtonport Pier and Arranmore Island, on the edge of the freezing Atlantic Ocean.

Darkie Arnott: "There's a story, it's not a very kind story, but Jack McClelland was a very talented swimmer. And we were doing a show on the Donegal coast and before the show Jack went for a swim, but there was basking sharks there you see. So a boat had to accompany Jack on his swim, with someone on board with a rifle ready to ward off any sharks on the chance they came across one. Well anyway as happened, a shark appeared, and a shot was fired and Jack got back on board the boat. Only for someone to quickly quip, 'you've shot the wrong shark'. It was a cruel remark, but we the wrestlers certainly found it funny when it was relayed back to us."

Despite the disparaging remarks (and sharks) Jack completed the swim and later that same day "Irish" Jack Raymond went on to wrestle vs. Cyclone Vic Fulton at the scheduled Worldwide show. It was a very impressive Wednesday for Jack!

That September the local league temporarily lost one of its best when Darkie Arnott headed to Canada with a friend to go work as welder.

Across the Atlantic, Darkie's passion for the pro style didn't subside. He continued in the craft by training in a Montreal gym owned by Olympian-turned-professional Paul Lortie, who was a Canadian wrestler/promoter who'd been on Bill Bankier's King's Hall bills in the late '30s. Impressing the former Olympian, Darkie even wrestled in the St. Henri area of Montreal, becoming the first known Northern Irish-born man to appear in action at a pro show in the Great North.

That same September, Larry Casey stepped in to fill a bill at the fourth season premiere of wrestling in Derry, subbing for an injured wrestler. Though relative rookie Larry more than just subbed in the spot; he stole the show vs. Tiger Robb. It was an encounter so well-received it was rewarded the rarity of rematch the following month at the Guildhall.

In October, Larry was called upon by George Connell to substitute for a missing UK/international star at the Ulster Hall. Twice in as many months Larry Casey excelled above those with more experience, and impressed enough to be kept in consideration for future cards for Connell & Relwyskow – who always stylised his name as "Laurie" Casey on their shows.

1952

In one of the many big happenings of a busy year, British wrestling legend Mick McManus made his first appearance in an Irish ring at the Ulster Hall. The demure McManus at 5'6 was dynamite between the ropes and would work his way up to being one of the best at being a bad guy. Crowds loved to hate the cocky cheat with jet black hair.

- - - - -

Mick McManus only ever worked for the elite promoters and it was this year that elite group would come together to try and take complete control of British pro wrestling as *Joint Promotions* was officially formed in England on March 13th 1952; George de Relwyskow being one of the founding fathers.

Joint Promotions was inspired by the American organisation the *National Wrestling Alliance (NWA)* who four years before in 1948 were created to maximise the profits of a few select promoters by crushing all other competitors. This is what Joint's objective was: to monopolise pro wrestling in the UK. Each promoter involved agreed to respect the others "turf" and not run opposing shows within so many miles of one another. They would also trade and rotate star talent to keep their shows fresh. Importantly, if you weren't with Joint you were against them. Those not associated with the new status quo would be referred to as "independent" or "opposition" promoters, for whom Joint wrestlers weren't allowed to work with or else they'd risk being blackballed by all in the collective.

Northern Ireland at the time didn't have any opposition promoters as Relwyskow controlled wrestling in Belfast and worked with Jack McClelland elsewhere in Ulster. Jack wasn't considered an actual member of Joint but was instead deemed an associate. However, his Worldwide shows did greatly gain from the merger when with help from Relwyskow he brought to his bills one of British wrestling's most mesmerising show-stealers; Masambula, a towering heavyweight gimmicked as an African witch-doctor who came to the ring wearing a cheetah headdress. The self-proclaimed voodoo man was a sight to behold for an Irish audience. Masambula was an instant fan favourite.

Mind you already in the Worldwide ranks was arguably the most popular wrestler of the glory days at the Guildhall. One with roots not too far from Derry City in Donegal's "Fighting Farmer" Frank O'Donnell.

Frank O'Donnell
(Ireland)

Born in Donegal in 1924 to a rural farming family, Frank O'Donnell left Ireland during the war to work as a farmhand in Dundee, Scotland. It was here Frank was introduced to wrestling and rose through the ranks with local lad George Kidd – who went on to be nicknamed "The Houdini of the Mat" for his superior wrestling skills. After debuting age 21 for George de Relwyskow in 1945, Frank O'Donnell moved to Yorkshire in England and there kept in shape at Ted Beresford's gym where he became a close friend of

Les Kellett. Quite simply, Frank was well-known and well-liked by many important figures in British wrestling.

Spotted as far back as the end of the first season of the roughest and toughest sport at the Guildhall, the short, balding but seriously skilled farmer would go from wrestling exclusively around the UK to crossing back over the Irish sea on a monthly basis from then on, only ever missing matches for Jack McClelland due to injury.

A great help in Frank's popularity was that the Gaelic-speaking grappler's home county of Donegal neighboured Derry, so his family, friends and proud supporters didn't have to travel far to see O'Donnell twist up his opponents in knots. In fact, such was the support for O'Donnell that advertisements for wrestling at the Guildhall noted a bus would be arranged to take spectators from Letterkenny (in Donegal) to Derry and back so they could enjoy an evening of wrestling from their home county hero. The newspapers loved Frank too with him receiving extensive coverage in interviews and positive write-ups of his performances.

That March of 1952, Frank O'Donnell defeated a Dubliner called Danny Flynn in Derry to become the "Middleweight Champion of Ireland" (another incarnation of a title by that name) and would be recognised with this honour for the rest of his days as a pro wrestler.

It was surely a big benefit to the box office for Worldwide Promotions to have Frank O'Donnell, Andy McClea and the local lads from the Derry City Wrestling Club to bring family and friends along to help pack out promotions at the Guildhall.

- - - - -

Along with Belfast and Derry, the town of Portadown, situated in the centre of Northern Ireland, became the unlikely third epicentre of pro wrestling for a short stretch in 1952.

Portadown had seen its share of shows (before the newly-renovated town hall banned wrestling and boxing from its building in the late '40s / early '50s) but the previous year two local bodybuilders Tony Stewart and Danny Livingstone unknowingly repeated history by wrestling in exhibition matches on boxing bills in their home county of Armagh (like Killylea's Bob Wilson before them)

Tony "Flash" Stewart and Danny "Nature Boy" Livingstone – their nicknames inspired by newspaper reports on the American wrestling scene – had trained in England and Belfast, respectively, when they decided to form the *Portadown Wrestling Club* at a weight-lifting gym, of which they were both members, called *Milo's*.

After training several bodybuilders in pro wrestling Flash and the Nature Boy rented a boxing ring and in March 1952 at the Armagh City Hall – Irish Wrestling Champion Bob Wilson's old stomping ground – they ran a very well-received show that was full of pro moves like dropkicks, aeroplane spins and Boston crabs. Though just like Wilson's style was considered "catch" wrestling, the club were credited as "amateur" (but this is likely owing to them not taking a payday for their performances).

The debut event also featured 15 year old Liam White who, born in 1937, was Ulster's youngest pro wrestler up to that point.

Liam White

A cousin of wrestling brothers called McQuaid on the bill, Liam would find work first as a butcher and then in later life as a travel agent with his own office in Portadown. After becoming especially friendly with many Canadians through travelling to the country with his job, Liam eventually opened his own pub called *The Maple Leaf* in nearby Gilford. Sadly in 1984 Liam White's life ended tragically at only 48 years old. The former bodybuilder always appreciated his time as a wrestler, and for nearly two decades was a record-holder in Ireland as the teenager of the ring.

That April of 1952 Tony Stewart and a member of Portadown's boxing club took up a united front to get their town hall to re-open its doors to their activities. It worked. By eight votes to four the town council voted in favour of the bodyslammers and uppercutters being allowed to use the premises. Unfortunately while the success here wouldn't go unnoticed, it would go unrewarded.

      Despite the availability of their town hall, owing to its rental charge the Portadown Wrestling Club instead hosted shows at the *Temperance Hall* in the town coming into the summer months. Tony Stewart and Danny Livingstone still engaged in exhibition bouts elsewhere too.

      Then it was announced that wrestling would be returning to Portadown Town Hall after all but it wasn't the local lads organising the event but Worldwide Promotions. Ever the opportunist Jack McClelland swooped in and vowed to bring his *"All Star Wrestling"* bills back to the town. They would be without any native representation other than a speedy, skilled wrestler named Dropkick Beattie (more on him in just a bit).

      Understandably disenchanted at being overlooked despite helping overturn the town hall's decision, Flash Stewart and Nature Boy Livingstone folded the Portadown Wrestling Club mere months after it started. In later life Tony Stewart moved to Canada and then moved back and opened a top-notch BBQ restaurant called *The Wagon Wheel* in his home town of Portadown. Danny Livingstone meanwhile became a milk man and was also a great hand at fixing radios and record players.

      Despite it being brief, the two men had laudably launched pro wrestling at a local level in their town from nearly scratch. The name of the Portadown Wrestling Club's base, the Milo club, would quite coincidentally be utilised in the future too for another DIY movement in homegrown pro wrestling…

As for Dropkick Beattie, his real name was William "Billy" Beattie, born on December 27th 1925 in Portadown, Co. Armagh. Billy too had learned how to lock-up at the Short & Harland's club and was obviously well-liked and respected by Jack McClelland as (after appearing in a few exhibitions in Armagh with Stewart and Livingstone) Billy was recruited onto the Worldwide roster, with his first found match, age 25, coming on November 11th 1951 at the Guildhall.

Given the gimmick name of "Dropkick" Beattie due to his expert delivery of the deadly dropkick move, Billy would appear in action throughout 1952. He would be greeted as the hero of the county whenever Worldwide was in Armagh for shows in *Lurgan Town Hall* that April and then later in the year when McClelland returned wrestling to Portadown Town Hall.

Dropkick Beattie would wrestle up until May 1953 when he decided to retire from the ring age 27 to focus on his family commitments. Though his stint was relatively short Billy Beattie wasn't finished altogether with wrestling, and in fact he would play a part in the second coming of pro training in Portadown in the future.

- - - - -

On July 21st 1952 Andy McClea and the Derry boys travelled to the town of Strabane for a sold festival show that made history by being the first ever pro wrestling event to take place in County Tyrone. This left Jack McClelland with just one remaining county to promote in Northern Ireland.

After that summer Worldwide Promotions hit a promotional peak when it operated a mini-tour of Ulster each month with stops in Derry, Ballymena and Portadown. From Saturday at the Guildhall to Tuesday the following week at a town hall, Worldwide would tour big names gained from its association with Joint Promotions.

That October, the 17½st big blonde muscle man Shirley Crabtree would be the star of the month's Worldwide shows. Crabtree who had only debuted in England that year was just 21 years old in these first appearances on the Irish isle, and of course would go on to become British wrestling legend "Big Daddy".

Fueled by the wrestling clubs in Belfast and Derry, Jack McClelland had no shortage of homegrown stars going forward, rarely struggling to fill a bill. It was just in time too as many old faces were disappearing from features.

This year are the final found matches for two more of the first class in 41 year old Cyclone Vic Fulton and 29 year old Jumping Joe Peters. Both of their last bouts – Vic vs. Jack Raymond that September in Ballymena, and Jumping Joe vs. Dan Casey (brother of Larry) that October in Portadown – were reported as ending prematurely due to injury.

Having brought two very different dynamics, Vic Fulton with his power and pose and Jumping Joe Peters with his speedy crowd-pleasing offence, they both bowed out after a decade plus as two of the local level's early standout stars.

Notably, Huss Street wasn't where wrestling training was based anymore. Those who'd taken up prominent leadership positions in the club over the years were more interested in amateur competitions than pro shows, but they'd become disillusioned that their best amateurs kept turning professional, and after cancelling entry into several tournaments due to lack of numbers they decided to close the club, and relinquish the gym.

Interest still high, the Belfast wrestlers established a new gym on the Shankill Road above a pub called the *Long Bar*, where they'd share the space with a boxing club. Positively, being independent from Short & Harland / Harland & Wolff also meant the club was no longer confined to just workers there (albeit its rules were relaxed anyway).

Harry Browne was by then the head coach and along with Joe Moore/Reynolds and Larry Casey (and visits by Whipper Dave Mack) other frequents faces in the Long Bar gym included ex-boxer Jim "Buddy" Dickson, Al "Smiler" Moore, Joe Maynard – billed from Limerick but actually from Antrim – and after he returned from Canada late in the year, Darkie Arnott.

1953

Darkie's first bout back that January was smack in the middle of the fifth season at the Guildhall and was a tremendous time-limit draw vs. Larry Casey. Though even with UK stars there, it was Jack Raymond's own match that proved the most memorable – as it had critics calling for a ban of pro wrestling in the city!

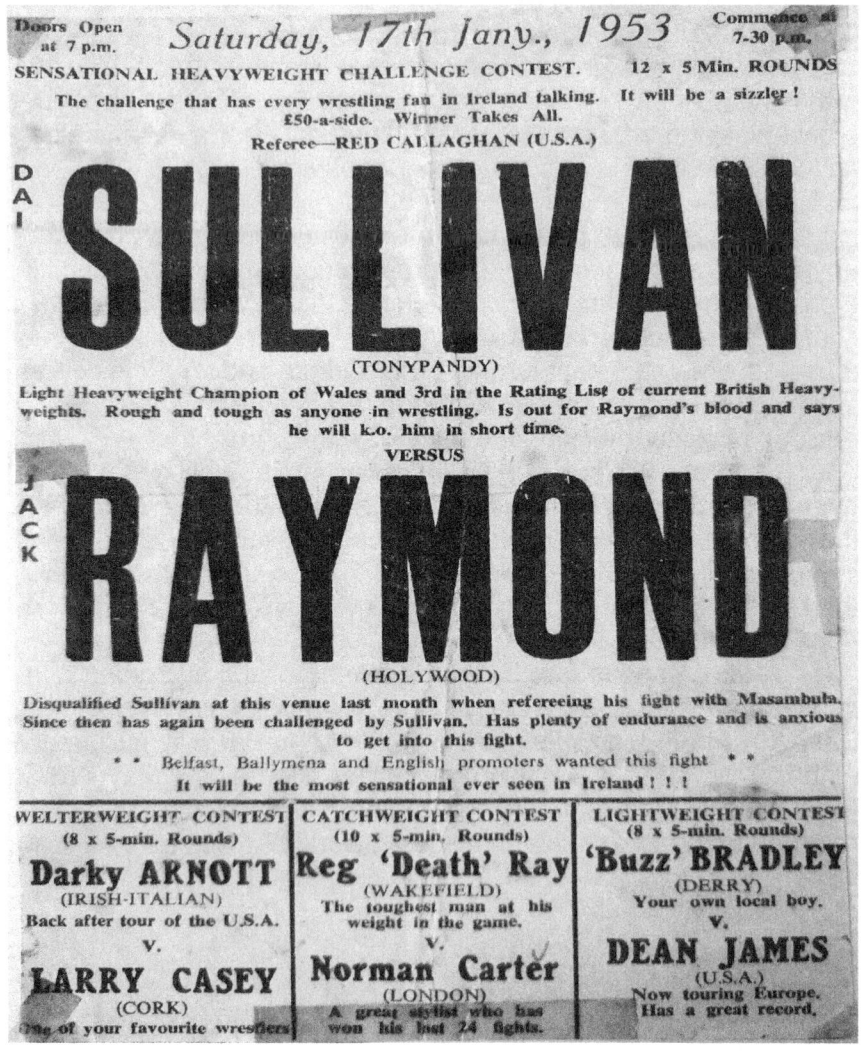

> **Doors Open at 7 p.m.** **Saturday, 17th Jany., 1953** **Commence at 7-30 p.m.**
>
> SENSATIONAL HEAVYWEIGHT CHALLENGE CONTEST. 12 x 5 Min. ROUNDS
>
> The challenge that has every wrestling fan in Ireland talking. It will be a sizzler! £50-a-side. Winner Takes All.
>
> Referee—RED CALLAGHAN (U.S.A.)
>
> **DAI SULLIVAN**
> (TONYPANDY)
>
> Light Heavyweight Champion of Wales and 3rd in the Rating List of current British Heavyweights. Rough and tough as anyone in wrestling. Is out for Raymond's blood and says he will k.o. him in short time.
>
> VERSUS
>
> **JACK RAYMOND**
> (HOLYWOOD)
>
> Disqualified Sullivan at this venue last month when refereeing his fight with Masambula. Since then has again been challenged by Sullivan. Has plenty of endurance and is anxious to get into this fight.
>
> * * Belfast, Ballymena and English promoters wanted this fight * *
> It will be the most sensational ever seen in Ireland ! ! !
>
> | WELTERWEIGHT CONTEST (8 x 5-min. Rounds) | CATCHWEIGHT CONTEST (10 x 5-min. Rounds) | LIGHTWEIGHT CONTEST (8 x 5-min. Rounds) |
> |---|---|---|
> | **Darky ARNOTT** (IRISH-ITALIAN) Back after tour of the U.S.A. v. **LARRY CASEY** (CORK) One of your favourite wrestlers | **Reg 'Death' Ray** (WAKEFIELD) The toughest man at his weight in the game. v. **Norman Carter** (LONDON) A great stylist who has won his last 24 fights. | **'Buzz' BRADLEY** (DERRY) Your own local boy. v. **DEAN JAMES** (U.S.A.) Now touring Europe. Has a great record. |

Bill for January 17th 1953 at the Guildhall in Derry City

What happened was a much-hyped and heated match between Jack Raymond vs. Dai Sullivan, the "*light-heavyweight champion of Wales*" was reported by a newspaper as having nearly incited a riot. Apparently there was an invasion of the ring by members of the crowd that ended with the police having to step in to regain law and order. After reading about this in said newspaper, the finance committee attached to the hall demanded an end to the entertainment for fears of the property being damaged if this was to happen again in the future.

    The matter was then picked up by all the national newspapers and was the sort of thing that brought about interesting insight into the minds of some people. One complaint from a columnist was that not only was it shocking that women attended wrestling – as by golly he'd seen them lined up to go into the Guildhall on a Saturday night – but that with some of the language he'd heard was used during the matches it was a sin a respectable woman's ears should be subject to such dirty words! As it is today it was then; those with the lowest interest in matters when they're at their best, seemed to have the loudest reaction to those same matters when there's any sort of scandal.

    To resolve the situation Jack McClelland would go to the press himself to reveal that the invasion only involved three rowdy individuals who didn't get far before being removed by staff. The staff themselves were plain-clothed which McClelland admitted probably contributed to the confusion that the ring had been invaded by a larger number of rogues. The police were never actually called, that part was pure fiction. Assurances were given to the Mayor of Derry that all was an exaggeration, and nothing of notoriety would happen when the wrestling was presented the following month.

    Indeed, like the Raymond vs. Sullivan rematch in Ballymena two days after the Derry debacle originally happened, the February event passed without incident and with the Guildhall's own caretaker content, much to the sure chagrin of the vocal anti-wrestling minority, wrestling would continue to marr the minds of the women folk in Derry for a while longer.

The conclusion of the fifth season would mark several ends with the monthly mini-tour being one of them. It is possible interest in wrestling wasn't as strong in Ballymena and Portadown as it continued to be in Derry, or simply the logistics of show-running in those towns were becoming more of a problem than profitable.

    41 year old Harry Browne's name is harder to come by after a match that April vs. his protege Darkie, while 46 year old Tiger Bob Scott took his final pay-off as a referee that May. Tiger Bob hadn't wrestled regularly in a while but refereeing could still be a physically demanding one on the body and so perhaps Scott was just getting too old for the job.

After thirteen years all members of the first class appeared finished as active wrestlers. However, there was still a match (or two) left for Harry Joyce's homegrown action-men, as the era of the originals would seemingly end as it started; with a Fulton brother wrestling.

    After a two year absence 40 year old Big Bob Fulton came back to compete for Worldwide in its sixth season. Big Bob was billed at 20 stone in weight and wrestled his and the first classes' seemingly final found match in a 2-1 loss vs. *"heavyweight champion of Wales"* Sandy Orford at the Derry Guildhall on December 12th 1953.

    At the sound of the bell to end the bout the first chapter of pro wrestling at the local level looked complete with the Whipper, the Owl, the Cyclone, Jumping Joe, Tiger Bob and Big Bob all retired as active all-in / all-action / free-style wrestlers.

- - - - -

That year in Belfast, George Connell went bigger and better than his predecessor J.C. when on Christmas Day 1953 Connell promoted wrestling in the King's Hall, followed by a huge boxing bill on Boxing Day. The endeavour may have proved too ambitious though, as this is the last time wrestling was held on Christmas Day in Northern Ireland.

1954

There wasn't much of a grace period in collective retirement for the first class. Tragically in early January 1954, less than eight months since he'd last stepped foot in a wrestling ring, Tiger Bob Scott would pass away suddenly age only 47.

Bob Scott's untimely death was mourned by his family and friends, as well as Jack McClelland and Jack Crane who expressed their deepest condolences for a loyal friend.

While Dave Mack and Harry Browne would stick around in coaching capacities at the Long Bar gym, the lives of the rest of the first class would play out as such:

After wrestling, Victor Fulton spent time as a steel erector in Alaska before resuming life in Belfast as a construction site foreman. Unfortunately in April 1959, in another premature passing, age just 48 Vic would succumb to an illness leaving behind a wife and four children. The Cyclone was Ulster's original homegrown headliner.

Gerry "Jumping Joe Peters" McSorley was a life-long electrician, and kept fit by being a keen cyclist. Despite wrestling across the island of Ireland in front of thousands, Gerry was remembered as a soft-spoken and humble man who when possible enjoyed an evening out ballroom dancing with his wife. Surrounded by a large loving family with many children and many more grandchildren, 67 year old Gerry would pass away from illness in November 1990. Having been born after the partition of the island Gerry may well be a history-maker in being the first ever pro wrestler actually born in Northern Ireland.

Finally, Big Bob Fulton would live a long life before passing away age 87 in November 2000. The gentle giant too surrounded by a large family circle. His legacy is being the inaugural heavyweight of Northern Irish wrestling, as well as being the only member of the first class to wrestle in the King's Hall.

- - - - -

Another who held Bob Scott in the highest regard was 29 year old Joe Moore. In tribute to the ex-boxer who teamed with him in his debut, after Bob's death Joe adopted the "Tiger" moniker in the ring. The newly christened Tiger Joe Reynolds would also become one of the only local wrestlers who competed on cards in the '40s left active after that summer of 1954.

Having just celebrated his 30th birthday, Jack McClelland would no longer feature "Jack Raymond" on his Worldwide fixtures after that summer. Jack's final found match coming on a sold show in Letterkenny in Donegal that August. In an interesting end to the eccentric's part-time career as a wrestler, Jack squared off vs. – for the first time in ages – a wrestling Nazi.
    By this time Jack was becoming prolific as a long distance swimmer and arguably was Ireland's most famous of the time by way of making and breaking records in the seas surrounding the island as well as competing in competitive swims in the UK too.

When wrestling was back in the Guildhall its seventh season served as the finale for the last long-time wrestler left when, sorely and strangely lacking any young guns from his Belfast and Derry reserves, Jack McClelland drove down to Lisburn to ask a favour from an old friend.
    On October 9th 1954 at the Guildhall, 44 year old Crusher Bob/Bert Cowan returned to the ring for a spectacular final found showing. Owing to the injury of another wrestler the sailor of the seven seas pulled double-duty. Cowan wrestled Tiger Robb and then Frank O'Donnell in separate singles matches on the same show, in losing efforts to both.
    Twenty years to the month he had an all-in bout masquerading as a catch contest as the special attraction wrestling match on a boxing bill, Bob/Bert Cowan had seen it all; from the tiny band hall in Lisburn to the 6,000 in the King's Hall there to stare at the exotic Princess Baba to wrestling during World War II to appearing in action at the first ever all-local promotion to battling for Worldwide in bouts throughout Ulster.
    Conflicting reports are that Bob/Bert Cowan lived out a long life in Lisburn or that he moved to Australia and seen out his days there. It's fitting that even in finality he's a bit of a mystery.

1955

At the end of the previous year it was reported that wrestling in Derry was starting to suffer a slight dip in attendance. After six and a half straight years of monthly matches (with only a summer break) it could be expected.

Not disheartened, Jack McClelland thankfully had his connections in Joint Promotions to send some notable names to help improve business. The biggest box office attractions brought across the Irish sea for both McClelland and George Connell this year were Masambula and Native-Canadian competitor Chief Thunderbird. Thunderbird in his huge headdress of multi-coloured feathers collected by his tribe wowed audiences, as Ulster wrestling fans always went wild for a man in head wear.

On January 15th 1955 it was "Whipper Watson" vs. Larry Casey at the Guildhall. Though this wasn't the Canadian wrestler famous for his Irish whip, but an actual Ulsterman called Billy Watson who was remarkable in his own way.

Darkie Arnott: "Whipper Watson was deaf and dumb. He was a very nice person. If he had have had his hearing, he would have been an excellent wrestler. You'd have to write the match down for him on pen and paper and do it that way. It wasn't ideal but I always got on well with him and wrestled him a few times over the years."

Born in Belfast on January 14th 1937, William "Billy" Watson was a young factory worker who was discovered by Jack McClelland working out at a gym and persuaded by the Irish swimming sensation to join the wrestling club at the Long Bar. Watson soon picked up proficiency in the pro wrestling trade. He was then given the Whipper Watson gimmick with his debut in Derry taking place just a day after his 18th birthday.

Someone who was particularly helpful to the new Whipper was the old Whipper, Dave Mack. Mack had grown up with deaf siblings so knew sign language and was able to communicate with Billy Watson this way during his coaching.

Whipper Watson would continue to wrestle on Worldwide cards going forward. In fact so impressive was the deaf dynamo of Irish wrestling, his family remembered he was even afforded the rare opportunity to appear in a match at the Ulster Hall for Connell/ Relwyskow that year.

Over the years Worldwide Promotions presented wrestling for the first time in Larne, Sion Mills, Limavady, Dungiven and all over Donegal, usually as all-Irish affairs with only the odd UK/international wrestler.

On July 23rd 1955 Jack McClelland became the first man to promote pro wrestling in every county in Northern Ireland when he brought a sold show to a festival in Enniskillen in Fermanagh. No mean feat as Fermanagh was (and remains) a very rural farming county.

Later that year efforts were made to establish Omagh in Tyrone as a new top town, however support for Larry Casey, Tiger Robb and the Derry Wrestling Club crew wasn't forthcoming after a trio of tri-weekly bills in *Omagh Town Hall* that September and October.

Regular wrestling just never really took off in the rest of the west of Ulster during this time like it did in Derry, likely owing to logistics like travel, a lack of local promoters, and a lack of local knowledge of or interest in pro wrestling.

The year ended on a high however as wrestling's popularity in Derry was reported as back to full strength with Jack McClelland praised for providing top quality entertainment and disproving the critics who didn't believe wrestling would be supported for one year in Maiden City never mind seven and a half.

That December at the Guildhall, Larry Casey challenged Frank O'Donnell in a heavily-hyped bout for the Irish Middleweight Championship, with O'Donnell retaining his title after a hard-fought battle.

All seemed on the up for Worldwide, but through no fault of Jack or his wrestlers, this was to be the final good year for wrestling at the Guildhall.

Chapter 6

Interval

1956

The biggest battle concerning the Ulster Hall in 1956 was within the Belfast city council chambers. It was over whether to ban wrestling and boxing from the hall over long-time complaints that its reputation for rowdy crowds was putting off potential concert organisers from hosting music events.

A Belfast city council meeting on the matter early in the year presented intriguing insight into the mindsets of the time. The defence stated that it was better to have sporting *"manly men than a lot of men interested in concerts"*. The opposition responded to requests for funding to refurbish the hall with, *"If you want it for boxing and wrestling, don't spend a half-penny on it"*.

The trouble was every time the opportunity to book events in the hall's diary came up, the boxing kingpins were the only ones to request multiple dates. Any repair work was delayed until the following year anyway when it was discovered that George Connell had smoothly slid in and extended his contract to run boxing and wrestling for another year in the historic hall… Come May the city council made up its mind to accept the motion to banish the offending parties from the Ulster Hall after Connell's contract concluded the following year.

Just a month later in June all was reconsidered and reversed as tax-payers were concerned that rates would go up in order to recoup the costs lost from the council not making money from its biggest entertainment income; the wrestling and the boxing. Later that month the council changed its course again and banned boxing and wrestling AGAIN from the hall.

Neither side was happy with this flip-flopping, so of course in July the council for the fourth time switched allegiances and agreed on the entertainment/sport continuing. Despite calls for the ban it was said the boxing and wrestling earned the hall around £5000 a year (over £100,000 today). This covered the cost of heating, cleaning and maintaining the premises, so losing that revenue would be detrimental to both the hall and local taxpayers.

Heated views were exchanged in the biggest national news story involving wrestling since William Willis turned state's witness two decades before. A female councillor believed it would *"make them the laughing stocks of the world if they went on record frowning at the manly sports of boxing and wrestling"*. When another councillor questioned if the people of Belfast were even musically-minded, a young woman in the public gallery shouted *"Yes!"*. In the local newspapers opposing opinions were shared, most amusingly with one pro-boxing/wrestling fan responding to the letter of a dissenter called "Felix" by signing off his own scathing letter in support with the signature "Anti-Felix".

The matter went as far as Westminster in England where MP Edith Summerskill (a feminist whose children took her surname instead of her husband's) showed her unsurprising support for the opponents of the manly men matters.

The date for the final clash of the city council was set for August. Tensions were high but when it was all over there was a decisive winner. By 25 votes to 17 boxing and wrestling give the KO/smackdown to its dissenters. Wrestling and boxing would go on in the Ulster Hall for the forseeable future. At their end of the year meeting the musically-minded, concert-crazies of the *Belfast Civic Society* expressed great sadness at the decision.

- - - - -

In a lesser-reported scandal, Jack McClelland similarly experienced venue problems that delayed the start of Worldwide's 1956/57 season. Jack went to the press, claiming the Derry council had increased the hire of the Guildhall by 60%. Showing some signs of this matter being a personal dispute between Jack and council members, they also increased the hire charge of the ring used at the venue – despite the ring being one Jack had sold the Guildhall some years before. They also refused the swimming sensation be allowed to use his own ring instead.

Around late November a compromise was reached on the rent, and the eighth season finally started. However the writing was on the wall. Wrestling in Derry was on the ropes.

1957

Come the conclusion of the eighth straight wrestling season the committee in charge of the Guildhall decided they'd no longer allow Jack McClelland to block book the venue anymore, meaning he'd have to secure the date for each show on a month-by-month basis. Jack decided enough was enough and made it publicly known that he wouldn't be promoting wrestling any longer in Derry. After nine years, the glory days at the Guildhall were over.

The knock-on effect was the demise of the Derry Wrestling Club as without opportunities to appear in action interest waned and ring regulars just moved on with their lives.

Age 28 Andy McClea already had enough on his hands. He was running his own health studio – the first of its kind in Derry – and the fitness guru spent the rest of life supporting others in sport. He even volunteered with disabled children to work out ways for them to enjoy and experience sports and exercise they'd otherwise be missing out on. Later in life McClea was on the board of directors for *Derry City Football Club*. On his passing in October 2013 at 83 years old, Andy McClea was celebrated as one of Derry's greatest sports ambassadors, with wrestling a footnote in his impressive life.

Without a base for its brawling Worldwide Promotions returned to a reduced schedule with only the odd show here and there, leaving Belfast wrestlers too lacking matches. So it was with the feeling he wasn't missing much that Darkie Arnott decided to voyage to Canada again that September.

At 28 years old Darkie was locked up in another ring, a wedding one with his wife Mary with whom he had a young son. The Arnott family travelled across the Atlantic where Darkie found work throughout Canada as a welder. He had terrific experiences and met some great characters, but as jobs moved him and his family around the vast country Darkie was unable to continue his passion of pro wrestling. Absence however not only made heart grow fonder but allowed the body of the motorcycle and boxing enthusiast to rest up after years of being thrown about stiff rings.

One day the Irish-Italian would be back but in the meantime local level wrestling in Northern Ireland, after 17 years, went into a decline.

1958

On June 14th 1958 Worldwide Promotions held a show at a festival in Bundoran in Donegal. Jack McClelland in a swimming challenge was also on the events programme. However, unlike last time the swimming wasn't a bonus but the big draw as 35 year old Jack was by then a sporting celebrity due to his successful feats in long distance swimming. Ever the sweet-talker, Jack dealed his way to £200 (nearly £4000 today) being wagered on the 15 mile swim between a lighthouse at St. John's Point to the Bundoran beach, and left heavier in the pocket as a result.

Top spot on the afterthought wrestling show was a match between Larry Casey vs. a localised Englishman called "Strangler" Stan Cooke. Stan Cooke was born in Liverpool but lived in Belfast and was a factory worker, a bouncer at pubs and clubs and claimed as the 3rd strongest man in Ireland.

Darkie Arnott: "Stan Cooke was a very strong person. He had held a couple of British weight-lifting titles and I think there was the claim he was one of the strongest men in Ireland. He preferred shooting to regular run of the mill wrestling. Stan was a very amicable person though, he didn't have a wicked streak in him. Very quiet."

Big, blonde and supremely strong Stan Cooke was also one of the last graduates from the Long Bar gym, as like the Huss Street gym before it, by happenstance of Darkie's departure, the wrestling club ceased to be. Though unlike previously there was no replacement space secured, leaving Strangler Stan and the rest of the Belfast wrestlers without a place to practice their moves.

There wasn't a platform for local wrestlers to ply their trade either when Worldwide Wrestling Promotions quietly folded soon after the Bundoran festival event.

After 15 years of wrestling all over Ireland, 14 of which he spent as a promoter, Jack McClelland focused his full attention on swimming. Over the next several years the half-man half-fish would become one of the best at the breaststroke in Europe and even wash up on African shores. In time the "Belfast wrestler" started to be better known as the "international long distance swimmer". After achieving numerous accolades in the swimming, in later life Jack became President of the *Irish Long Distance Swimming Association* and supported young swimmers along their own journeys in achieving sporting success.

Darkie Arnott: "Jack was very over the top but intelligent. He was the first man to introduce health food shops in Northern Ireland. He deserves a lot of credit for introducing wrestling on a wide scale in Northern Ireland too."

As well as opening his own health food shops Jack McClelland was a strict vegetarian. Jack was often in the newspapers extolling the virtues of leading a meat-free lifestyle, and even acted as secretary of the *Ulster Vegetarian Society*.

A wealthy man to the end, Jack McClelland and his wife shared time between their home in Blackhead on the Antrim coast, which he christened "Casablanca", and a holiday home in Alicante in sunny Spain. Upon his passing in February 1996 age 72, Jack's sister reported their shared belief that the poor health that led to his eventual death was a result of his swallowing the sting of a jellyfish during a swim in shark-infested waters between Spain and Africa in 1956 (some 40 years prior). In his obituary wrestling was noted as just one of the interests in the eclectic life experience of Jack "Raymond" McClelland, a true renaissance man.

1959

29 year old Larry Casey was the only local wrestler left active. Casey wrestled frequently at shows Connell & Relwyskow sold to festivals around the province and on occasion at the Ulster Hall.

As neither George Connell nor George de Relwyskow came to the Irish wrestling shows, instead overseeing things from their offices in Belfast and Leeds, respectively, the actual physical authority figure for the wrestling in Northern Ireland was usually Englishman Arthur Green. Green was a non-wrestler who had become George de Relwyskow's business partner soon after the formation of Joint Promotions. Together the two were *Relwyskow & Green Promotions*; with Relwyskow sorting the wrestling and Green everything else.

By this year Northern Ireland's most popular piece of technology, television, was starting to pick up steam, or rather signal. Beginning in 1953 TVs became more and more common in Ulster, however there were only two channels, the *British Broadcast Corporation (BBC)* and *Independent Television (ITV)*.

Launched soon after the station itself, on November 9th 1955 ITV began broadcasting wrestling as an annual series. It would run for a few months a year, initially showcasing pro and amateur wrestling on different weeks before settling for the former with a show titled simply *Professional Wrestling*.

On November 21st 1959 the fighting farmer and fan favourite during the Guildhall glory days, 35 year old Frank O'Donnell became the first Irishman to wrestle on ITV, coinciding with the launch of ITV's Northern Ireland affiliate *Ulster Television (UTV)* that came into transmission at the end of that October.

The soft-spoken commentator for the action was Egyptian-born Brit Kent Walton, and Mick McManus, Les Kellett and Masambula had all already appeared on the show before O'Donnell locked up on black & white screens around the UK and Northern Ireland – but only half of it. Irish eyes did get to see one of their own wrestling on the telly if they had the fortune of owning one, but it was also only if they were in the east of Ulster as Belfast and the surrounding areas got UTV transmissions originally while the west of Ulster, as always, would have to wait until a transmitter was installed in that part of the province.

1960

The monopoly men at Joint Promotions were the ones producing the wrestling for ITV with each promoter including Relwyskow & Green taking it in turns to tape matches on their shows.

Only the best were selected to scrap on television and so it was a testament to the talent of Irish Middleweight Champion Frank O'Donnell that he was filmed for another featured match. Indeed, over the next six years the Donegal man would make at least ten more televised appearances, including vs. his pal Les Kellett (who was a frequent visitor to the O'Donnell household).

The increasing popularity for the Professional Wrestling programme meant it began being broadcast more regularly, and this year – besides a summer break – it started being shown nearly every week.

In turn the British wrestling scene experienced a boom in business as attendance at wrestling events grew greater as people wanted to witness the stars of their tiny screens live in person. The demand for wrestling got so grand that Joint Promotions were able to run multiple events every day of the week. This meant 365 days a year there was wrestling show happening in a city hall, town hall, village hall or what have you hall in England, Scotland and (less frequently) Wales.

Northern Ireland quickly followed suit with weekly to bi-weekly wrestling at the Ulster Hall with Mick McManus and Masambula making appearances, and the local highlight coming that March when Larry Casey was selected alongside former foe Frank O'Donnell and the wrestling Dunleavy brothers, Seamus and Mike, from Mayo to represent Ireland in a points tournament vs. a team from Scotland.

1961

TV was key to Joint Promotion's empire. It was its greatest promotional tool and the bosses made sure to feature as many new wrestlers as possible so they could bill more of their exclusively-contracted performers as television stars.

As a result of the boom in business the King's Hall started seeing more wrestling shows too. Thousands turned up at Ireland's premiere ice rink to see stars like Sky High Lee, a Canadian wrestler who towered at 6'7, and Billy Two Rivers, a genuine Mohawk chief and a hugely popular performer on ITV, who were both in bouts in Belfast this year.

However the want for anything branded "Wrestling" inadvertently brought success to independent / opposition shows too. As Ireland slowly modernised these excluded British eyes started seeing green; thinking of all the money they'd make bringing wrestling to a land largely starved of the spectacle.

That March wrestling returned to the Derry Guildhall for the first time in four years as Englishman Max Crabtree, the brother of "Big Daddy" Shirley, toured the island of Ireland with a series of shows largely in the south, becoming the first opposition promoter to do so.

By the following year Max Crabtree had entered into a peace pact with Joint Promotions, and this allowed the family and friends of Frank O'Donnell to get back on the bus waiting for them in Letterkenny and see the Gaelic-speaking grappler at the Guildhall one final time in early 1962. Noteworthy too was this was Max and Shirley Crabtree's final tour of Ireland, with Derry City being one of the last to feature the future Big Daddy on the Irish isle. Something of a minor Mandela effect, Shirley never actually wrestled in Ireland in the 1970s or 1980s.

Meanwhile Frank O'Donnell would wrap up his days as a professional wrestler in the early 1970s. In later life the lovable Donegal drop-kicker rubbed shoulders with several celebrities, and was even the caddie for Irish golf legend Christy O'Connor. Living out his life in England and always one to reminisce fondly about his time as a wrestler, Frank O'Donnell would pass away in 2004 age 80.

Chapter 7

The Milo Wrestling Club & Butcher

1962

While Joint's big bills played to thousands at the old cattle mart, and independent promoters from the British wrestling scene tried their luck with the Irish, local level wrestling in Ulster had remained virtually non-existent since the late 50s.

However, after returning home from Canada in the summer of 1961, Darkie Arnott revived homegrown pro wrestling

Darkie Arnott: "When I came home I met Jackie Briers. Jackie was a fly-weight boxing champion. Jackie and I were always good friends. He said, 'are you thinking about getting back into wrestling?', and I said I wasn't sure how I'd go about it, because you see there wasn't any clubs about anymore. It had kind of died off a bit. So he says to me, 'if you want my gym you can have it for three nights a week?'. So I took him up on the offer and got to train there when it wasn't in use by his boxers. As more came along to it, I suppose then it became a club, so we called it Milo's Wrestling Club. The story of Milo the Greek was he was the strongest man in the world. He used to get a bull-calf over his shoulders and walk around with it all day, til he was able to carry a full-grown bull. Load of nonsense like. But nevertheless it made for a good story."

The gym owned by Jackie Briers – a retired boxer who was once red-hot in the ring for George Connell in the 1940s/50s – was on Foreman Street in Belfast and served as HQ for the *Milo Wrestling Club*.

OFFICIALS	
Promoter	GEORGE CONNELL
Matchmaker	G. de RELWYSKOW
Timekeeper	JAMES ALLEN
M.C.	MARK GREEN
Hall Managers	H. GREER
	S. WALLACE
Hall Steward	JIM NELSON
Referees	GEORGE WADE
	LAURIE CASEY

GEORGE CONNELL

presents

All-Star WRESTLING

★

SATURDAY, 17th FEBRUARY 1962

THE KING'S HALL BELFAST

Note: Larry Casey as the referee

Settled back into life in Belfast and still passionate about the pro style, the welding wonder (not just hyperbole; Darkie was considered exceptionally skilled at welding) breathed life back into the local league by sorting the new gym.

Though many ex-Worldwide Promotions wrestlers had moved on with their lives there was still several interested in locking up again. These included inspirational 25 year old Whipper Watson and fantastic featherweight 37 year old Tiger Joe Moore/Reynolds who both joined Darkie at the Milo club.

Another who reappeared was retired Welterweight Champion of Ireland Dave Mack. The always stylish-dressed ladies man was by then 48 years old and still without a single grey hair on his head – and not through dying it black as suggested by some of his peers, but through the secret of hair oil; a whole lot of it!

Dave Mack was no longer a shoemaker but was working as a storeman at the *PB Oil Refinery* in Belfast. He would regularly swing by Jackie Briers' gym to socialise, give advice to less experienced wrestlers, and eventually organise shows with Darkie.

Darkie Arnott: "Davey Mack was a very jovial character. A bit of a womaniser but everyone has their faults. He liked to dress up and look good for the ladies. Bit flamboyant but he was nice to work with. Usually Davey made the matches. He had a good knowledge of everyone and would reckon if one fella would work well with another and so forth. Sometimes it didn't work out but most times it did. Davey had a mind for it. He was usually the MC or the referee too."

On April 4th 1962 the boxing ring in Jackie Briers' gym hosted the first live event of the Milo Wrestling Club, and one of the advertised bouts was Darkie Arnott vs. Jim Brown, with Dave Mack as referee.

Yes, after a nine year absence from billed bouts 49 year old Harry Browne (who was on the show that launched local level wrestling in Northern Ireland in 1940) returned to the ring to grapple his protege on the second coming for Ulster wrestling. It's Harry's final found match and the last match of the first class after twenty-two years.

The following month at the *Shankill Road YMCA*, Jackie Briers came out of retirement to box his younger brother in an exhibition bout – and another yes, it only took 30 years for the tables to turn and boxing to be the special attraction on a wrestling bill.

For the love of wrestling, Darkie and Dave Mack would work together to keep their favourite past-time alive. The man with the year round tan managing the Milo club, and the former Whipper becoming the de facto promoter and matchmaker of the live events.

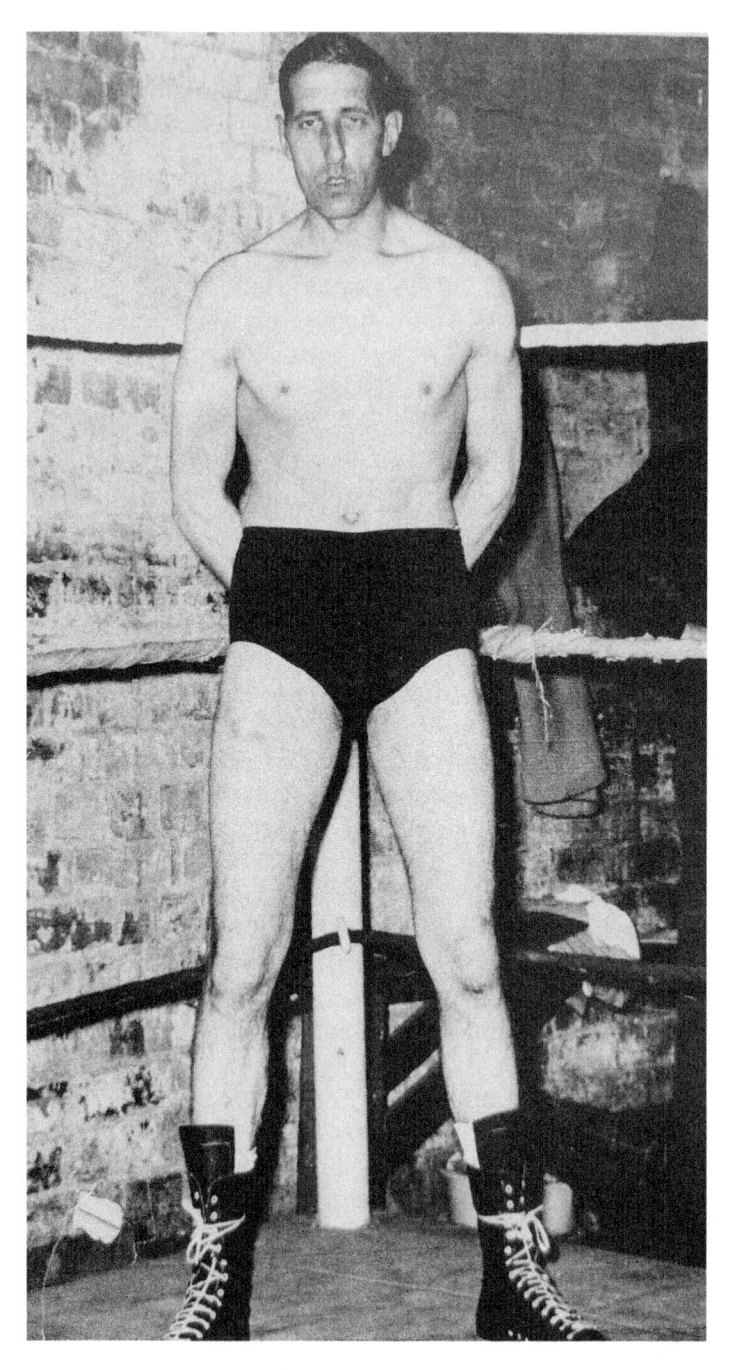

Darkie Arnott in the 1960s

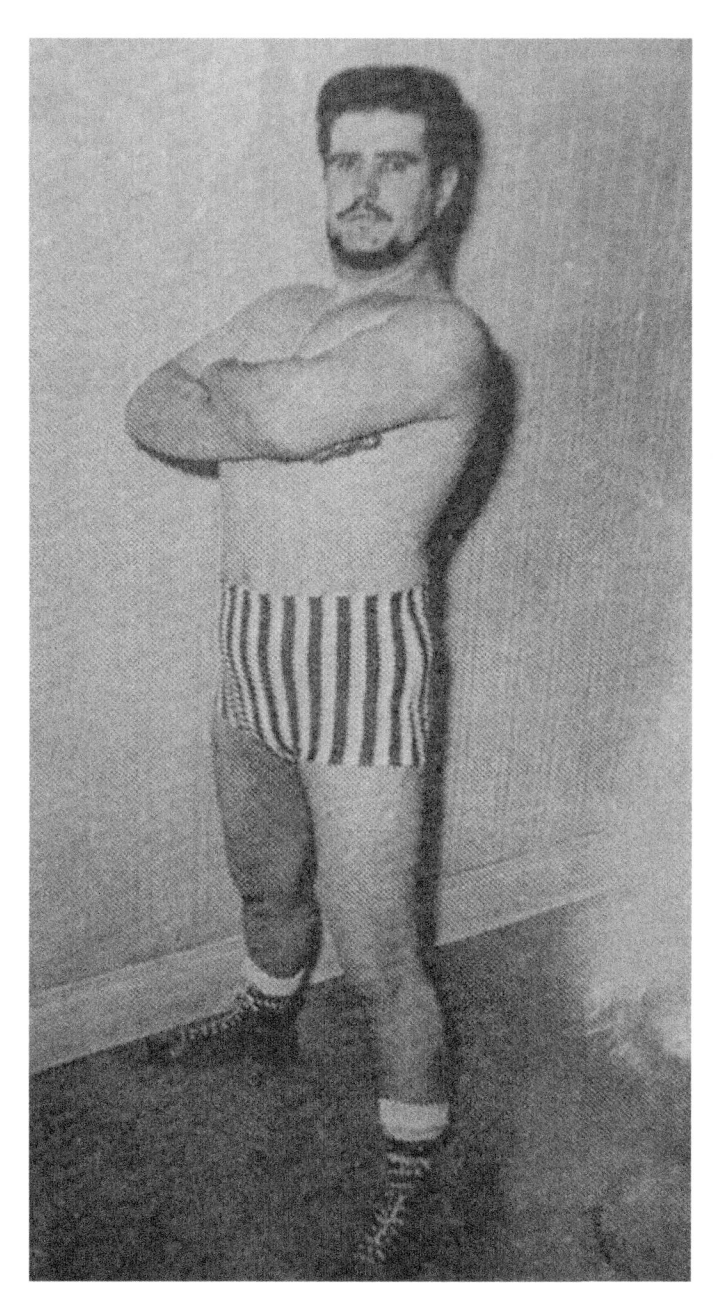

Whipper Watson
Deaf and mute wrestler

Tiger Joe Moore in the 1960s

Dave Mack in the 1960s

A wrestler from 1940 to 1950,
Later a promoter, matchmaker, MC, and referee
Always a sharp-dressed man

Shows were sporadic, and usually confined to Belfast city. Venues included community halls, as well as some sold shows for the workers at a huge linen factory based at *Ewart House* to enjoy.

Darkie Arnott: "If someone came to us and said 'would you put a show on?', we'd say, 'yes, it'll be this amount of money'. Then if it took off you'd be invited back and if it didn't, it would fizzle out."

The Milo Wrestling Club would pick up another past Worldwide player too when big, blonde Strangler Stan Cooke from Liverpool joined their ranks. In the interim Stan Cooke had been a constant at a weight-lifting gym run by Larry Casey.
    32 year old Larry Casey was then a regular referee at the Ulster Hall and an occasional wrestler on festival features for George Connell / Relwyskow & Green. Larry's gym was in Belfast too, and was first and foremost for bodybuilding. However though the shipyard driller was reluctant to break anybody into the pro wrestling business, Larry still enjoyed submission wrestling and so taught it to several local man, largely as a recreational sport.
    Stan Cooke too preferred shoot wrestling. Though without an outlet he didn't have the opportunity to really progress to amateur tournaments, etc. Stan was content to practice competitive wrestling at Larry's gym, and then experience the thrill of a live crowd when he wrestled for Dave Mack and Darkie.
    That isn't to imply the Milo club was an easy way into pro wrestling. Like anywhere else you'd be pushed to your limit before you'd be accepted into the brotherhood of break-falls and bodyslams. The only upside was that with gentleman Darkie at the helm, the wrestling club at Jackie Briers' gym was a little bit more fair and square for newcomers.

Darkie Arnott: "There was a lot of shooting at the gym, the real McCoy, going for submissions. You tested people like that. You got to know people, whether they'd take so much punishment, whether they'd fight back, whether they'd give up, whether they've got ability. Some people couldn't stick at it. We tried to keep the learners away from the more experienced though, we didn't want them being used as chopping blocks, as happens in gyms. We made it clear from the start no-one was going to get beat up there before they had the chance to defend themselves."

"Strangler" Stan Cooke

Irish wrestling's resident Englishman
A supremely strong wrestler who was later billed
as "Bulldog Bill Carter"

Someone who did stick it at the Foreman Street gym was 31 year old taxi driver Cliff Donaldson.

Born in Belfast on August 31st 1931, Clifford "Cliff" Donaldson didn't exactly match the immediate image of a pro wrestler conjured up in the mind; family man Cliff was short in stature, bald-headed (besides patches of hair on the side) and could easily pass for a much older man. However looks were definitely deceiving as Cliff was a very talented judo player, even teaching it at his local YMCA, where one of his students was a 19 year old lad called Eddie Hamill. With his background in the mixed martial art, Cliff the summer time ice-cream van man took to wrestling like a fish to water and was soon one of the Milo club's best on the mat.

Initially the taxi man wrestled under a mask as "Mr. X" or "The Black Bomber" or "Dr. Who" (in a curious case of copyright infringement), though the name he would later be best known by was "Butcher Donald". Butcher was an all-rounder who could mix it in any match. He impressed everyone with his exceptional skill and was quickly one of the most consistent in the gym for the Milo club and in the ring on live events for Dave Mack and Darkie.

Darkie Arnott: "I think Butcher Donald was one of the best I ever saw for a local man. He was a judo player so he was very good on the mat. And he was a very intelligent and nice man."

Eddie Hamill: "I was going to the Oldpark YMCA Judo Club, and the instructor there was a little fellow, and it was Butcher Donald. He was only an orange belt but he was teaching. Unbeknownst to me at the time, he was in the wrestling as well. He didn't look the part, but having said that you couldn't fault him for his wrestling. He was really good."

Darkie Arnott: "He was the sort you could put him anywhere on the card. If the promoter said, 'Butcher I want you to go a bit rough tonight, get the crowd going', Butcher could have done that. Or he could have wrestled dead-straight, or he could have wrestled funny. Butcher was a promoter's dream."

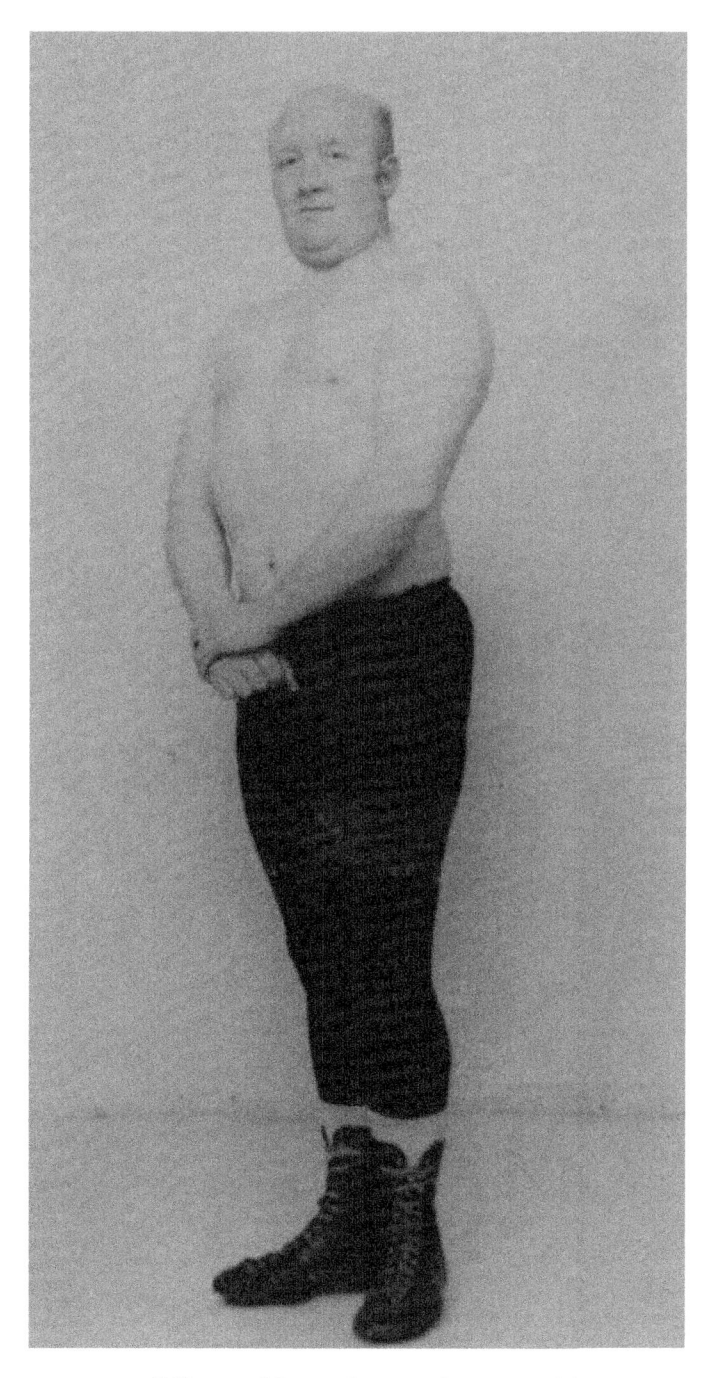

Cliff Donaldson aka Butcher Donald

1963

"George Gibb" was another new name held in high regard by Darkie Arnott but unfortunately Gibb would lose a leg in a car accident in early 1963, before his wrestling journey could really take off. Eventually the real-life Joe Burcombe would be awarded £9,000 (over £160,000 today) in damages, and a year after the accident be spotted successfully taking part in a swimming race, sans a leg. Wrestling truly attracted some of the most physically and mentally toughest people about.

Darkie Arnott: "I'd be billed as 'the referee's nightmare', always messing with the referee, acting the villain you know. I would take a walk round before the bout and find the old ladies in the front row and say to them, 'What are you doing at the wrestling? You should be at home washing your dirty dishes! I bet your house is boggin'! So once the match started they were ready to hit me with their handbags. You'd do things like that to rise the blood."

As Dave Mack sorted the logistics of the shows, Darkie was able to enjoy his experience as a wrestler and become one of Irish wrestling's best bad guys as "Dirty" Darkie Arnott – a very entertaining act that the crowd loved to hate.

Similarly self-fulfilling, and looking better in a tux than James Bond (the first film in the series was released the year before), 007 Dave Mack took on his preferred part of an MC on live events, leaving open the role of regular referee.

A blast from the past who refereed for Dave Mack and Darkie on at least one occasion was Jack Crane from Cookstown – the former co-promoter of Worldwide Promotions. Nearly 40 years old and back from Australia, Crane's diverse entrepreneurial efforts had seen him open Turkish bathhouses in the land down under. Bathhouses that were so popular with the Aussies their Prime Minister would apparently even drop in for some "me time" at the specialised spas. Jack Crane was interested in opening similar spa experiences in Belfast but their success, like his own eventuality, is unknown. This rare reappearance by the former merchant navy man was likely a favour to his friend Dave Mack.

Being one of the bosses was an advantage for Darkie too. He was able to ease entry into the secret society for his buddies Tommy "Ricky" Doak and "Roughhouse" Danny Beattie to be wrestlers, and the wise welder managed to land the local leagues a great referee in his 35 year old pal Syd Waddell too.

Syd Waddell
Referee, and occasional wrestler

Born in Belfast on March 23rd 1928, straight-laced Syd Waddell was welcomed as the first choice ref on cards going forward. Though Syd and Darkie met at the shipyard, Waddell was by then working as a bus driver for a depot in the Ardoyne area of the city.

Darkie Arnott: "Syd Waddell was the best man at my wedding. He was a welder, same as me, and the two of us worked in the yard together, that's how I met him. Then I brought him into the wrestling, and coached him into a referee. Syd was an excellent referee. He knew when to interfere and get tied up or when to let things go. We'd wrestled sometimes too. I remember one night we were on, Syd and I, and Davey Mack was the referee, and Syd KO'd me, well he didn't really, but I lay down for the count. It was good fun, wrestling your mate."

- - - - -

Since the start of the new decade, Manchester wrestler "Irish" Sean O'Shea was an independent promoter from the British scene who took to touring Ireland a few times a year for two weeks or so at a time.

Real name Jack Jefferson from England, ex-boxer O'Shea and his shows would span the South and up into the North. His final stop would be at a cinema in Belfast where he'd presented *"Late Night Wrestling"* (with a 10.30pm start time). The phony Irishman and his UK-only crew would then catch a ferry back to England.

That June the superstar of Sean O'Shea's shows was boxer-turned-wrestler Randolph Turpin, an Englishman who had fallen from grace and into debt after skyrocketing to fame by defeating one of the greatest boxers of all time in American 'Sugar' Ray Robinson for a World Championship in front of 18,000 in London in 1951. However over a decade later Turpin was a desperate man attempting to make money wrestling.

Darkie Arnott: "I was on a tour with Randolph Turpin for a promoter from Manchester. He'd ring me up and say, 'would you fancy doing a week or two's work down South, which would end up finishing in Belfast?'. So I brought my wee boy to meet Randolph Turpin, just so he could shake hands with him to say he had shook hands with a World Title holder. Turpin maybe wasn't the world's best wrestler, but he was a definitely a draw. People came to see him."

O'Shea would invite Darkie – whom he had made contact with through his cards at the Belfast cinemas – to join his crew, and so for a fortnight that June Darkie wrestled around Ireland supporting the shows with Randolph Turpin as the top act. At the end of this experience, the Manchester man was so impressed with Darkie he offered the Belfast bodyslammer the chance to go full-time and wrestle on cards throughout the UK. However, Darkie had realised living out of a suitcase wasn't the life for him, and so politely declined.

Darkie Arnott: "It was a kind offer but I wasn't interested. Wrestling at home was good enough for me."

As Dave Mack and Darkie started expanding their sold shows throughout Ulster, they assisted O'Shea with some very successful festival shows in Irvinestown, Fermanagh that summer.
     Then that September at a carnival in Enniskillen the two helped O'Shea stage a very memorable publicity stunt that saw native-American gimmicked wrestler Chief Sitting Bull ride a horse through the streets of the quiet farming town. Owing to it queuing up traffic for miles the police would step in and halt the horseplay, but the stunt worked as interest gained from the incident helped draw a huge crowd. Many of the local lads on card including Tiger Joe Reynolds competing in front of thousands who appeared to watch the wrestling that evening in a marquee set-up in a field.

- - - - -

The Milo grapplers would gain something else of significance from Sean O'Shea too; an actual wrestling ring. In the past the club had borrowed one of Jackie Briers' rings or rented from a boxing club local to the location they were scheduled for a show. This wasn't ideal, and being thrown about a rock-hard boxing ring wasn't either, so Darkie decided to ask the Englishman if he could buy one of his wrestling rings, which O'Shea agreed to.
     Wanting to split the cost and willing to share in the spoils of future success, Darkie and Dave Mack asked the Milo club

members if anyone else was interested in coming in as a third partner / investor and, his hulking chest leading the way, Stan Cooke stepped forward. Since his strongman days ended pro wrestling had filled the void and now big blonde Liverpudlian Stan was ready to return the favour.

Pooling together their own funds Darkie Arnott, Dave Mack and Stan Cooke committed themselves to growing the Northern Irish wrestling scene exponentially by buying their own wrestling ring from Sean O'Shea for the price of £50 (£760 in today's money)

The *Northern Ireland Wrestling Association (N.I.W.A.)* was founded, with its first mention in newspaper print coming from a review at a show held on October 2nd 1963 at *Woburn House* in tiny Millisle, Co. Down for a captive audience. Literally a captive audience as Woburn House was a huge mansion repurposed as a youth detention centre for wayward boys.

The first N.I.W.A. event is also the final found for Harry Browne in wrestling as he acted as the timekeeper at the show. Darkie did his best to keep the former Lightweight Champion of Ireland involved, giving him odd jobs and even debuting Northern Ireland's first ever second generation wrestler, Harry's son Jim.

Trained by his dad, Jim Browne carried on the "Jim Brown" name (this was all very confusing in research!) and wrestled as a lightweight from 1963 to 1964, further paralleling his father by often competing against Tiger Joe Reynolds.

Darkie Arnott: "Harry would have refereed the odd time but not as much as I would have liked. Then afterwards I think Harry took ill, and by that time I had moved from Belfast out to Newtownabbey, so I was removed from everything, any news. I didn't even know he was dead to tell you the truth until later. No-one kept me informed. He was a wonderful man. Anything I ever achieved in wrestling it was because of Harry Browne."

In his later years Harry Browne worked as a green-keeper at the *Belfast Castle* Gardens. Though sadly Harry was another of the first class to pass away too soon, from a sudden aliment age 59 in May 1972. While the true identity of the Black Owl was never publicly revealed and Jim Browne never dropped the Lightweight

Title, Harry Browne's greatest accomplishment was as a coach. Harry trained Darkie and Larry Casey, among others, into highly credible pro wrestlers. He also showed that you could be a larger-than-life character on shows while also being superb at the smaller details needed to make a match look as realistic as possible in the ring.

    In regards to pro wrestling coaches in Northern Ireland integral to its sustained history it was by then; Harry Joyce > Harry Browne > Darkie Arnott > …

Butcher Donald demonstrates a sleeper holder on Stan Cooke

- - - - -

That year the biggest name brought across the Irish sea by Relwyskow & Green was ITV wrestling's first bonafide breakout star; Jackie Pallo.

At only around 5'6, middleweight Jackie Pallo stood out aesthetically on television by simply wearing striped trunks, and he also fitted his hair into a little ponytail. Plus in the ring he talked the talk like no-one else, paying as much attention to giving the audience grief as he did grappling his opponent, Pallo was British wrestling's most theatrical wrestler. His cult of celebrity grew to were he was the guest star on non-wrestling TV programmes as well as appearing on stage in pantomimes. Nicknaming himself "Mr. TV", Jackie Pallo was the centrepiece of cards in the Ulster Hall and King's Hall whenever he appeared, with his name sure to sell-out the show.

Also notable this year was the west and rest of Ulster started receiving UTV broadcasts, so that all of Northern Ireland could join the UK in being proverbially pinned to their television screen on a Saturday afternoon.

On the British isle wrestling had in fact gotten so unbelievably popular that members of the royal family even attended matches at the *Royal Albert Hall* in London. The era often cited as the "Golden Age of British wrestling" was well under way.

The previous year George Connell too hit a high when he promoted the battle of the Belfast bantamweights, John Caldwell vs. Freddie Gilroy at the King's Hall. It was a match considered one of the greatest in the history of boxing in Ireland, and the sport's national peak at the time. However having reached the top of the mountain, Connell focused a little less on boxing, and the sport started to decline as a result. Less and less attention was given to staging big boxing bills anymore.

Beyond the words printed when the great Scot Bill Bankier first firmly established wrestling in Ulster in 1937, wrestling no longer just rivalled boxing in 1963 it arguably pulled past it to become the #1 ring entertainment in Northern Ireland.

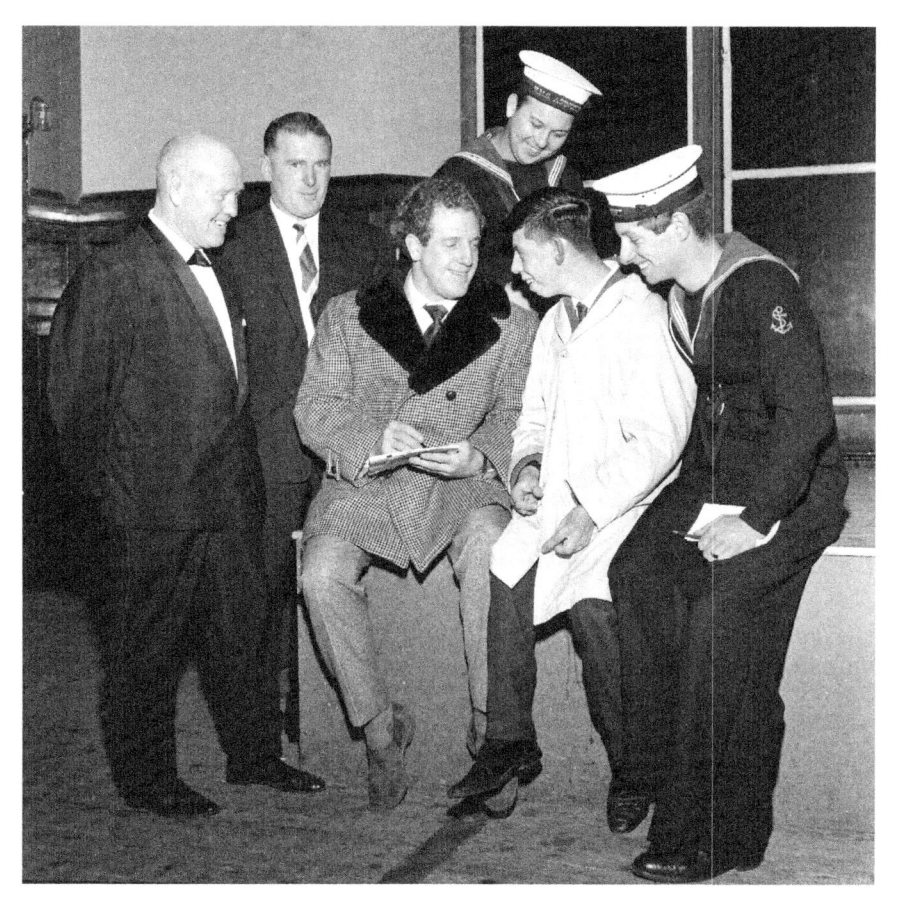

The Connell / Relwyskow & Green bills weren't confined to just Belfast during the boom period for wrestling in the 1960s, pictured here is Mr. TV Jackie Pallo signing an autograph before an event at the Guildhall in Derry.

Note: second from the left in this picture is then-retired Derry wrestler Andy McClea who helped promote bouts in the Maiden City during the '60s.

Picture credit and thanks to the Derry Journal

Chapter 8

Class of '64

1964

At the beginning of this year the membership of the Northern Ireland Wrestling Association / Milo Wrestling Club was noted as sixteen part-time pro wrestlers. This included head coaches Dirty Darkie Arnott and Strangler Stan Cooke, assistant coach Tiger Joe Moore as well as fan favourite Whipper Watson, ring general Butcher Donald and the astute Syd Waddell as referee. The roster was to nearly double within the next twelve months.

The first of many new names to make their debut in 1964 was 20 year old shipyard electrician Eric Wilson. Uniquely, Eric didn't come through the Milo Wrestling Club, he was taught the tricks of the trade by Larry Casey at his weight-lifting gym.

Eric 'Tug' Wilson: "I was a gymnast, a Junior Champion in Ireland, and I worked as an apprentice electrician in Harland & Wolfe shipyard and the driller there was Larry Casey. Larry was the referee at the Ulster Hall for Relwyskow & Green. He would have always reffed the last bout so the top Englishmen could catch their ferry in time. And I went to his weight-lifting gym to get stronger for the gymnastics and drifted into the wrestling, and I was trained by Larry. His gym was terrible. No ring, it was under-felt on a wooden floor, bit of canvas over it. If there was a hole in the floor they'd cover it with a weight. And when it snowed, the snow would come through the windows. I did shooting with Larry for about a year and a half. And the only reason he brought me in was because he couldn't handle me anymore. Tortured me for the longest time, a bit of white meat, but I started holding my own, getting better than him. So he clued me in."

Born in Belfast on October 31st 1943, Eric Wilson was one of the very few wrestlers to come out of Larry's gym. The reason being the fake Casey family member was very protective of exposing the truth of pro wrestling to just anyone, and so made breaking into the business an extremely tough experience. It was through sheer determination and true git that Eric survived these shoot wrestling sessions. Like many others of this era, it was toughing it in the beginning that made everything else after much easier by comparison.

As Larry wasn't interested in putting on wrestling promotions he instead asked Darkie about getting Eric his debut as a pro wrestler. So on January 24th 1964 it was Eric Wilson vs. Darkie Arnott in Holywood, on the outskirts of Belfast. The stocky-built shipyard shooter with curly hair faced off against the "The Referee's Nightmare" who lived up to his "Dirty" reputation and got himself disqualified in the match.

Tug Wilson: "My first bout was actually with Darkie Arnott, it was in the Civic Hall in Holywood, and Dave Mack was the MC. I was frightened to death, bundle of nerves, but Darkie was great with me. He even let me get the win, and he didn't have to do that."

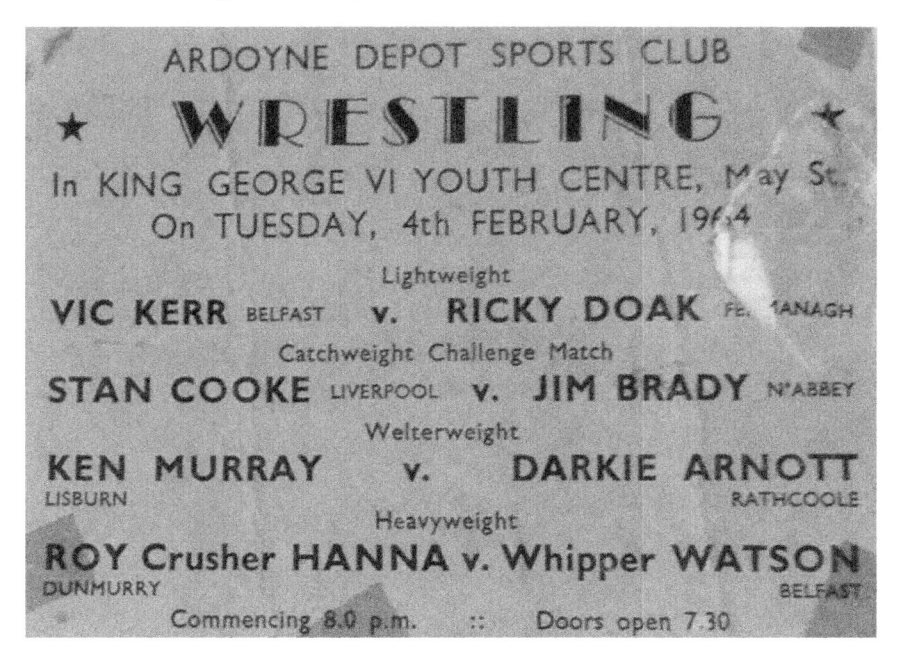

ARDOYNE DEPOT SPORTS CLUB

★ **WRESTLING** ★

In KING GEORGE VI YOUTH CENTRE, May St.
On TUESDAY, 4th FEBRUARY, 1964.

Lightweight
VIC KERR BELFAST v. **RICKY DOAK** FERMANAGH

Catchweight Challenge Match
STAN COOKE LIVERPOOL v. **JIM BRADY** N'ABBEY

Welterweight
KEN MURRAY v. **DARKIE ARNOTT**
LISBURN   RATHCOOLE

Heavyweight
ROY Crusher HANNA v. **Whipper WATSON**
DUNMURRY   BELFAST

Commencing 8.0 p.m.   ::   Doors open 7.30

That February the N.I. Wrestling Association started running shows at the *King George VI Youth Centre* on May Street in Belfast. The sports hall at the King George VI was a great spot for the wrestling, usually held on a Tuesday night and usually sponsored by Syd Waddell's bus driving bosses at the *Ardoyne Depot Sports Club*. The King George became the home ground in Belfast for local level wrestling as, besides a summer break, the venue would host monthly matches in seasons similar to the glory days at the Guildhall, from September to May (roughly).

Further regular hot-spots followed with the *Queen's Hall* in Newtownards in particular being a popular place for the wrestling.

Darkie Arnott: "We'd wrestle in Newtownards every fortnight. We had an arrangement with them that we'd split the proceedings. The wrestlers would wrestle for free and we'd put the money into the gym. Did that regularly."

That year the Milo Wrestling Club and its members moved from the shared space with the boxers on Foreman Street over to a home of their own on the Sandy Row in Belfast. The new gym was up some stairs and above a car mechanic's workshop at the address of *33 Albion Street*. The new gym had a makeshift ring and some weights in it.

Darkie Arnott: "We rented new premises on Albion Street and Davey Mack, Stan Cooke and I run the gym. It was our own place so we could train every night of the week if we wanted to. Then what I did was I put an ad in the paper for people who wanted to be a professional wrestler, saying to write to me if they were interested. I got hundreds of letters. They wrote from all over Northern Ireland. And I sifted through them and picked out the thirty best applicants. An awful lot didn't follow through with it, couldn't hack it, but some who did went on to greater things."

The new gym and new venues inspired the newly-named management to recruit new trainees. Darkie placed several advertisements in the Belfast Telegraph (the newspaper he ran errands for as a boy). The ads requested those interested write a letter to Darkie's home address in Rathcoole complete with their sporting credentials. It was the first time that the public were openly invited into the secret society since Harry Joyce called on more men to sign up for the first class during World War II, and that was nearly a quarter of a century before!

During an interview with the Telegraph printed on March 11th 1964 veteran ring villain Darkie acknowledged the closed door policy at the Ulster Hall and King's Hall to those in the local leagues. He also said that if anyone was lucky enough to go full-time they "*could*" earn up to £100 a week (£2000 in today's money).

So successful was the call-to-action campaign that the Belfast Telegraph used the huge response as an example of the advantages gained by advertising within their pages. At least 120 applicants at that count had put themselves forward for consideration into the Milo club. It was then the duty of N.I.W.A. management to pick the best, discard the rest, write back and hope some who submitted interest still felt the way they did when they put pen to paper.

Meanwhile another submission wrestling specialist adopted by the N.I. Wrestling Association from Larry Casey's gym was 24 year old factory worker Noel Ewart.

Larry Casey and Noel Ewart in the 1960s

Born in Belfast on Christmas Day 1939, Noel Ewart was brilliant at bodybuilding, sometimes even being billed as an "Adonis". Like Eric Wilson, Noel similarly stuck out the shoot wrestling sessions to gain not only the respect but genuine friendship of his coach Larry. So close were the two that when Noel's only son was born in 1964, he named him "Lawrence".

On the April 7th 1964 event at the King George VI, muscleman Noel Ewart completed the set for the Larry Casey crew by making his professional debut in front of an audience that evening at the youth centre hall that was reported as 600 fans. Times were good for local level wrestling and only going to get better.

By April Darkie, Stan and Dave Mack had settled on who would be selected from the newspaper write-ins to start at the Albion Street gym. Of those chosen several no-showed, several exited soon after they entered, and only a strong-willed few survived orientation. Among the top contenders to actually impress were 20 year old carpet-fitter Eddie Hamill and 22 year old factory worker Paddy Donaghue. Eddie and Paddy were good friends and gifted judo players.

Eddie Hamill: "I got into wrestling because there was an advert in the Belfast Telegraph that said it was looking for young men to train as wrestlers. Preferably judo-men, bodybuilders, boxers, that type, and I thought, well that would be something interesting to do. So I answered it, I heard back, and I went along with my mate Pat to start off in this little gym on Albion Street."

Paddy 'Pat Red Kelly' Donaghue: "I'll tell you why I got into it; the money! £100 a week?? We thought that was a fortune!! Then you got into it and you realised there was no £100, but by then you were already hooked."

Eddie Hamill: "Now I use 'gym' loosely, it was horrible. It was falling apart! No shower, no running water, no toilet. But that's where we trained, and that was how a whole lot of others came in. Darkie Arnott and Dave Mack trained us in that gym. Dave Mack was a good character, he was like the Strictly Come Dancing type, slim, well-presented. I never seen him wrestle and he never kitted out, just give advice, but he did a lot of MCing and refereeing. He was a nice fella. Darkie was the main man though, he showed us everything."

Pat Red Kelly: "I used to enjoy getting down to the gym. Especially on a Sunday. Sunday was thee day. You'd get to wrestle ten or twelve other wrestlers on one day. It be two of you in the ring, then the other lad would roll out and somebody else would get it in, then maybe they'd go out, somebody else in, then you'd jump out, but then eventually go back in again with somebody else, repeat the process. You could have wrestled three or four times in a row. It was hard work, a real test of endurance, but it was a laugh too. You could try to practice something new, come in and say 'aw this is a move I want to try out', 'what I want to do is this'. And you'd walk through it, explain it, then you'd do it at pace. It was great learning."

Eddie Hamill: "I knew how to fall from the judo, so whenever I went in and they threw me I would just go into a break-fall. So they'd say, 'oh so you've done something like this before?'. So they didn't have to teach me how to fall as I already knew how to. So I came along pretty quick."

Pat Red Kelly: "I think you needed a toughness in the body, or a thickness of the head to take the punishment and keep coming back."

Born in Belfast on November 2nd 1943, slim, trim, blonde-haired and with film star good lucks Edwin "Eddie" Hamill was a brown belt in judo who didn't realise until he started at the Milo that his judo instructor Cliff Donaldson was Butcher Donald the wrestler.
    While born in Belfast on March 13th 1942, red-headed and red-bearded Patrick "Paddy" Donaghue was a jolly light-heavyweight with a great sense of humour and full of witticisms. Paddy kept fit through cycling and hiking.
    It was through judo that Eddie Hamill and Paddy Donaghue became best of buddies and while they weren't fans beforehand the dynamic duo were intrigued by the uniqueness of pro wrestling. With their skills in mixed martial arts, the break-falls came easy to them and some judo moves transitioned well too, and so Eddie and Paddy soon stood out as star pupils.

131

Eddie Hamill
The future TV wrestling star Kung Fu

Eddie Hamill and Paddy Donaghue weren't the only ones who ascended quickly at the Albion Street gym. Another was 23 year old TV engineer Henry Shirlow.

Ian Shirlow: "It was my father, Henry's brother, who had seen the advert in the Belfast Telegraph for people who wanted to become pro wrestlers to go to some gym in Belfast, and he said to Henry as he had that sort of stocky build at the time. Henry was about 5'10 in height with a big barrel chest, you're talking a 50inch chest. Henry had done the amateur boxing, but my father thought the wrestling would be a better fit for him. All the family supported Henry. They really thought this was the ticket, that he would be big time in the wrestling."

Darkie Arnott: "Big Flash Shirlow was another Jack McClelland sort."

Ian Shirlow: "From what I gathered the training at the gym in Belfast was hard. They didn't pull any punches. If they hurt you and you came back, they'd hurt you again, and if you came back again, they'd still hurt you, until they weeded out the ones who wouldn't come back. The ones who stuck were the ones who were actually taught the game, the holds and the moves, and Henry was the persistent sort".

Born in Derriaghy near Lisburn on May 31st 1941, Henry Shirlow came from a boxing family, played cricket for his local team and raced sidecar on motorcycles, even competing on the *Dundrod Circuit*. So with his eclectic mix of recreational activities it wasn't surprising when his brother saw the advertisement in the Telegraph he thought of Henry.
     Henry had no problem writing up a resume of his accomplishments as, like Jack McClelland before him, Henry Shirlow had a big personality, the gift of the gab and a great look. Indeed, in wrestling Shirlow would go on to share a very similar path to McClelland.

Henry Shirlow
The future "Jack Flash Shirlow"

Knowing to give as good as he got from his boxing background, Henry Shirlow earned the respect of his coaches by easily embracing the new experience. Also impressive were 25 year old Hugh Beattie and 26 year old Frank Hughes, who were childhood friends, life-long thrill-seekers and paid ship-wreckers.

Frank 'The Blonde Duke' Hughes: "Hughie had seen the ad in the papers and come to me and said 'hey would you want to try this out?', and I said 'of course'. Hughie and I did everything together, we were best mates since school. And when we went to gym on the Sandy Row that was the other side of town for us, but I'd have to say, there was never any sectarianism in the wrestling club. Everyone was welcome. There was a lot of egos of course, but then we were all young. And if ever two guys took grievances against one another for whatever reason, Darkie would let them settle it in the ring. Best man left standing. It was seldom, but it certainly sorted things out."

Born in Newtownabbey on April 29th 1939, short in stature but huge in socialising skills, Elvis Presley-lookalike Hugh Beattie was a natural-born entertainer. Hugh was the craic of any party he attended and a big hit with the lads at the wrestling club long before he became a fan favourite on live events.
　　While also born in Newtownabbey in 1938, blonde-haired and well-built Frank Hughes had done amateur wrestling in the army during his time in the *Royal Ulster Rifles*. This amateur experience helped Frank in progressing at top pace in the pro style.
　　At the time Hugh Beattie and Frank Hughes were working as underwater demolition men; they'd dive into the ocean, plant dynamite on sunken ships, set off the explosives, and then reap the rewards of the scrap metal that could salvage with use of a crane. Yes, somehow wrestling was the second most interesting thing they were involved in.

Over the spring, summer and into the autumn months Eddie, Paddy, Henry, Hugh, Frank and the rest of the class of '64 were trained to a top level by Darkie and Stan Cooke. Butcher was by then acting as an assistant along with Tiger Joe, and of course the always dapper-dressed Dave Mack was usually at ringside too to provide some pointers.

Hugh Beattie
The future Whirlwind Monroe
pictured on a fishing trip with one of his best friends Eddie Hamill
whom he met through wrestling

Within just six months several of the new generation of homegrown grapplers were ready to showcase their skills in a ring in front of a paying audience.

Eddie Hamill: "What they done was, you didn't pay them but they said 'for the first six bouts you do them free. Then after the sixth bout we'll pay you the grand sum of £1.50'. That early on though we weren't bothered about making money, you did it as something to do, something different. Early on I wrestled as just "Judo" Ed Hamill or "Judo" Mike Hamill. Mike was because my father worked in the shipyard, and in them days everyone who worked in the shipyard had to be a Protestant. But my father was called Francis Hamill, which sounded very Catholic. So because his name sounded Catholic, they give him the name 'Mickey'. So he was called 'Mickey Hamill'. So I thought for a joke I'd name myself Mike after him. I told my father and he was delighted with it."

On September 1st 1964 at the King George IV, Eddie Hamill debuted as "Judo Mike Hamill" teaming with fellow judo expert Butcher Donald vs. bodybuilding brothers from Lisburn Ken and Earl Murray (Earl later wrestled solo as "Earl St. John").

That same show also featured the first match of the flamboyant Henry Shirlow as "Jack Flash Shirlow" – a name inspired by a well-known character from the *Beano* comic strip who moved so fast he could practically fly – vs. Whipper Watson, whom Henry worked everything out with in writing before the bout.

The final first-time feature on that evening of entertainment was Paddy Donaghue as "Pat Red Kelly" – his wrestling name coming from his red coloured gear, and as homage to the jovial judo man's favourite boxer, Spider Kelly from Derry. Pat's debut match being vs. The White Owl. The White Owl gimmick name itself was an obvious ode to Harry "The Black Owl" Browne and the wrestler under the mask alternatively appeared as *"Dropkick"* Jack Currie at times too. Pat would find out exactly how his hooded opponent earned the alternative moniker of "Dropkick".

Pat Red Kelly: "Our first fights, Eddie and I, where in the King George the 6th hall. I was fighting this guy called the White Owl. Wee small guy with a white mask and white trousers. I was all excited. People were chanting 'Red! Red!'. I was wearing red trunks and red socks and my towel was even red and the 'aul ones just loved me for some reason. Well the White Owl he was fast, he was good, and he had dropkicks like nobody else. Well he hit me one, I went down. I got up, he hit me another, I went down again. A boot right in the mouth again and again and again. I think I was either bouncing of the floor I was that excited or I hadn't the sense to stay down. Bell went, I went over to my corner and the advice I got from the fella in the corner; 'slow down and watch that dropkick'. 'No bother'. Bell goes, back in, dropkick. Finally, finally, it finished and I had a broken tooth and a missing tooth. Ended up I'd to go to an emergency dentist appointment the next day and I thought, flippin' hell. Then I was on again that night, and who was I on with... the bloody White Owl."

October at the youth centre hall then featured the debuts of Hugh Beattie and his best buddy Frank Hughes.

Hugh's colourful choice of ring-name was "Whirlwind Monroe", chosen to match his charisma and charm. 'Whirlwind' was in relation to his speedster style, and 'Monroe' (sometimes spelt as "Munroe" or missing the 'e' altogether) was a timely tribute to recently deceased American movie icon Marilyn Monroe.

Meanwhile Hughes was billed as an *"Ex-Commando"* due to his army days and became "The Blonde Duke" – the name in reference to his head of blonde hair, and a family nickname.

A month later, Whirlwind Monroe vs. Tiger Joe Reynolds opened the show at at the first pro wrestling promotion in *Carrickfergus Town Hall* on November 5th. A week and a half after that on November 16th the Blonde Duke was headlining vs. Strangler Stan Cooke when the wrestling returned for its regular evening of action on May Street at the King George VI.

Going forward Judo Mike Hamill, Pat Red Kelly, Jack Flash Shirlow, Whirlwind Monroe and the Blonde Duke would pop up on posters and programmes with more regularity each passing month. However, the class of '64 wasn't complete just yet. There was one very notable name left… 28 year old construction worker Dave Finlay. Finlay wasn't a big writer of letters, so he took a more proactive approach in introducing himself to head coach Darkie.

Dave Finlay
Patriarch of Ireland's most famous wrestling family

Darkie Arnott: "*Davey come in a middle of a show, came into the dressing room and spoke to me. And I said, 'well you were supposed to write a letter'...*"

Dave Finlay: "*I seen the ad for it and I wasn't one for writing so I went along to a show at King George the 6th there in Belfast. And I asked 'who's the man in charge here?', and that's how I met Darkie. And I thought he'd might take one look at me and say, 'away on' but...*"

Darkie Arnott: "*But I said come over on Wednesday night. Davey was always an athlete. He took to wrestling very easily.*"

Dave Finlay: "*As a young boy I lost my right eye, but I still took part in all sports. I ran for Northern Ireland in cross-country, and I was a decathlon champion when I was a teenager. But some sports like rugby, boxing, they turned me away because of my eye. In wrestling though it was no problem, it was never made an issue. I had got married to Evelyn in 1957 and we went on a long honeymoon to Canada for two years, and over there they had amateur wrestling. But when I got back from Canada, there was no amateur wrestling about over here. So when I seen this ad for wrestling I thought, that's for me.*"

Born in Whiteabbey on April 6th 1936, David "Dave" Finlay was the boy partially-blinded in the grenade blast in Whiteabbey in 1945. Since then excelling in several sports, as a youth cadet Finlay was taught gymnastics by a man called Sammy Cadelle, who was also an amateur wrestler associated with the *Belfast YMCA*. Cadelle had even turned professional to wrestle on a few Worldwide Promotions cards in late 1946 / early 1947. Cadelle taught the fundamentals of amateur wrestling to some of the young lads he took for gymnastics and the young impressionable Dave Finlay got hooked for life. Unfortunately Cadelle would quit amateur and pro wrestling when he got married, leaving teenage Dave without an avenue to advance.

So when he was told about the Belfast Telegraph ad, Dave Finlay decided the best thing to do was to sell his sporting successes directly to Darkie during a show at the King George VI at the start of the second season of wrestling in the hall that autumn. Finlay was by then living in Greenisland near Carrickfergus with his wife Evelyn, their 4 year old son David Finlay Junior and newborn daughter Wendy.

Though it was amateur wrestling that grabbed Dave's attention, pro wrestling was its own exciting experience and by the end of his first session on Albion Street a few days after his chat with Darkie, Finlay knew the ring in that grey and gritty gym on the Sandy Row was where he belonged.

- - - - -

However, it wasn't just the local leagues where noteworthy figures were appearing for the first time in Ireland. Early that year in March 1963 Darkie Arnott and Butcher Donald (billed as "Red the Fireball") were wrestling for Sean O'Shea at the *Troxy Cinema* in Belfast. On the same show was 29 year old heavyweight wrestler Wild Angus.

Born in Enniskillen on October 19th 1934, Frank Hoy was reared in a farming family in rural Fermanagh. Frank moved to Manchester, England age 20 to look for work, and towering at 6'3 and weighing around 18st, here Hoy was approached about becoming a pro wrestler and took up the offer. Hoy was coached in the late '50s by British wrestling veteran Billy Graham (not the American "Superstar"). Graham was particularly skilled at training heavyweight wrestlers. As well as Frank Hoy, Graham also trained a Manchester man called Martin Ruane; the future British wrestling legend Giant Haystacks.

After wrestling for a few years with little notoriety, Frank Hoy's part-time gig would become a full-time job when he was given the gimmick of "Wild Angus Campbell". Wild Angus with long hair and beard was a crazed kilt-wearing scrapper from the Scottish Highlands. The nationality-switching notwithstanding, it was probably a more eye-catching billing than fighting out of a farm in relatively-obscure Fermanagh.

Before he even stepped foot in a ring in Ireland, owing to his stunning size and lethal look Wild Angus was well on his way to becoming a full-time heavyweight feature of the British wrestling scene, with bigger moves for the big man to be made in the future.

Then, that October into November, the newest name to organise brawls in halls around Ireland was a very memorable one; Orig Williams.

Born in a tiny village in Wales in 1931, Orig was a prolific football player with spells at *Shrewbury Town* and *Oldham Athletic* in England, before taking on the dual role of player-manager for Welsh league team *Nantlle Vale*. It was noticing that attendance at football matches was much lower on a Saturday afternoon – when kick-off clashed with bell-time for the wrestling on ITV – that Orig got interested in promoting pro wrestling.

One of the men the Welshman approached for advice on making money in the surreal world mixing sports with showmanship was that Manchester man Sean O'Shea. O'Shea took a liking to the footballer and invited Orig to travel on a tour of Ireland with him. In doing so Orig Williams learned the lay of the land whilst falling in love with the Emerald isle. The proud Welshman eventually claimed Ireland as his second home.

Among the points for successful promoting that Orig learned from shadowing O'Shea was that if he was a wrestler himself it would save paying one more person. So the free-kicker learned "free-style" wrestling.

The proud Welshman picked up some of the faux-Irishman's stars, as well as another interesting promotional tactic; the curious concept of presenting some of his performers with names very similar in spelling to famous TV wrestling stars. So while you'd be hoping to see Mick McManus, Jackie Pallo and Billy Two Rivers on your television set, at your local town hall you could be tricked into taking in "Dick MacManus", "Mr. TV John Paul" and "Billy <u>Red</u> Rivers". Making money was the name of the game, and if fooling a few poor readers of the poster meant a few extra pound then so be it to the fluent Welsh-speaker.

In 1964 across the south, east and north of Ireland (wrestling still wasn't broadcast in the west making it something of a dead zone) Orig Williams respected Sean O'Shea's territories and ran towns of his own with Randolph Turpin as the headliner. These would turn out to be the boxers final Irish appearances as Turpin would pass away the following year under tragic circumstances.

Also on this tour Omagh became one of the first towns in the North to see the spectacle that was *"midget wrestling"* as Gorgeous Fuzzy Kay vs. Tiny Tim Gallagher became the first such match of this sort in Ireland. To his credit the Welshman's live events were always great variety acts with plenty to capture an audience's attention.

- - - - -

Meanwhile, as millions were glued to their small screens every Saturday afternoon, that year ITV decided to not only drop the summer break but to add a second wrestling show on a Wednesday night. The grapple game and its grapplers were given even more exposure, further strengthening Joint Promotions standing in British wrestling.

In 1964 George Connell Promotions staged four huge wrestling spectaculars at the King's Hall. Audiences of up to 8,000 were reported and that meant that four times this year Northern Ireland was the epicentre of pro wrestling in all of Europe. The bills reflected this as all of the biggest names in British wrestling appeared. Mr. TV Jackie Pallo never missed a night of it, sharing his spotlight vs. Scottish mat maestro George Kidd (in year 14 of a 26 year reign as *World Lightweight Champion*) and vs. boxer / ballet dancer / wrestler Ricki Starr from the USA. Entertainment for an evening's undercard was usually provided by hugely popular players like funnyman Les Kellett, African warrior Masambula and Native chief Billy Two Rivers.

That June Relwyskow & Green brought to Belfast the biggest tag team bout in British wrestling. It was the fabulous four of beloved babyface brothers Vic Faulkner & Bert Royal "The Royal Brothers" vs. bad boy Mick McManus & his tough-as-nails tag team partner "Ironman" Steve Logan.

Then, as pure trivia, that November in a career coup George Connell brought Belfast the biggest band in the world. The famous four of John, Paul, George and Ringo, *The Beatles*, who sold out two back-to-back shows in the King's Hall in front of 16,000 music maniacs combined. The Belfast Civic Society would have been delighted... only that blasted wrestling was tied in as the first few fans to buy tickets to the Beatles were given complimentary passes to see the he-men at the Ulster Hall as a bonus. Felix and the Belfast Civic Society just couldn't catch a break! (see 1956 for reference).

A star-studded King's Hall bill from October 3rd 1964

The monthly Ulster Hall matches were standing room-only as well. Besides referee / sold show wrestler Larry Casey, there was another Northern Irishman in the ring there too; 27 year old school teacher Sean Regan.

Born in Derry in 1936, Gerry Murphy moved with his family to England at the age of 10. A rugby player and amateur wrestler, by 1964 Gerry was London school teacher Mr. Murphy by day and secretly heavyweight wrestler "Sean Regan" by night. It wasn't until his first wrestling appearance on ITV on November 18th 1964 vs. Russian wrestler / actor Yuri Borienko (who appeared in the James Bond film *On Her Majesty's Secret Service*) that Gerry's double-life as Sean Regan was discovered. The Derry man of course embraced the media attention and took up being billed as "The Wrestling Schoolmaster"; paradoxically a teacher who broke up schoolyard fights at lunch time and then beat-up people on wrestling shows in the evening.

The 6'3 and 17st Sean Regan's television appearance also made him the first Northern Irish-born wrestler to feature on ITV. He'd make several more showings over the coming years vs. other heavyweights of the time like Bill Robinson and Albert "Rocky" Wall.

Similar to Wild Angus, Sean Regan was synonymous with wrestling elsewhere in the world. He never appeared on the local leagues in Ulster. Notably, whenever Regan would wrestle in Belfast for Relwyskow & Green to avoid the Derry / Londonderry problem he'd instead be billed from a village in Donegal called Muff.

Chapter 9

The Star-Studded Sixties & "The Ref's A Woman"

1965

Pat Red Kelly: "You'd be in the ring and if the other man was going over, you'd rise him up to make him a star. There were other boys couldn't see it that way; that sometimes you have to go down to rise somebody else up. I seen what the game was about. You had to be the showman, look the part, play the part, have the laugh, let the people laugh at you, so those people will come back to see you again and hopefully bring more with them, and that's the game."

On New Year's Day the N.I. Wrestling Association hosted an "American Battle Royal" at the King George VI; inspired by US wrestling magazines six men would be in the ring at once, if you went over the top rope to the floor you were eliminated, with the final two needing a pinfall or submission to win it. On that evening Whipper Watson was the victor vs. Honeyboy Walker (car dealer Jim Hoy in real-life) with Pat Red Kelly, Jack Shirlow, Darkie Arnott and Butcher Donald all left lying on the outside.

     In an interview with a newspaper reporter after the event MC Dave Mack noted that from the previous year the Milo Wrestling Club was up to thirty part-time pros. The well-presented promoter spoiled for choice in matchmaking.

Dave Finlay: "I think I was in awe of Darkie as he knew so much, he's a very clever man. Darkie was the top man when it came to technical wrestling. Butcher was another good one. Scientifically he was sound, knew all kinds of moves. Everyone liked the way he executed his holds. He was grand lad outside the ring too. He was a taxi driver, and he'd have brought me home from the gym at times."

No-nonsense when it came to training at the Albion Street gym, Dave Finlay excelled in all exercises. As the amateur and pro styles were much closer in comparison in this era Finlay's background in the former meant his grappling skills were already very strong, and so early in 1965 Dave Finlay made his debut as a pro wrestler vs. Jack Flash Shirlow in Newry Town Hall. When it came to the striking aspect of the pro style Finlay was very hard-hitting and this helped him mesh well with ex-amateur boxer Henry Shirlow. Their first match together was the beginning of a series of bloody Finlay vs. Shirlow brawls in town halls around the province. Though in the ring they were heated rivals in real-life Dave and Henry were really very friendly.

Dave Finlay: "Henry was a good friend of mine. He really looked the part but he loved himself. He'd come to the gym dressed to kill, like he was going to a party or something. I liked him though. We ended up socialising together, our wives too."

Someone else who Dave Finlay gelled well with inside and outside of the ring was his coach Darkie Arnott. Both men admired the other's wrestling ability and shared some life experiences like taking part in amateur wrestling tournaments, and spending time in Canada. They also loved to play the part of the villain in their matches, as unlike all other notable names from the class of '64 who were usually fan favourites, Finlay was another like Darkie who took pleasure in bending the rules whenever he could. Amusingly while "Dirty" Darkie was the "Referee's Nightmare", "Roughhouse" Dave Finlay took it in a different direction with his antics involving officials like Syd Waddell.

Dave Finlay: "In them days you got the referee included in the whole thing. Nowadays the referee is just there to referee. When I was a wrestling villain, I'd have shook the referee's hand and put my arms around him, and you know got him on my side. So the match would nearly become 2-on-1, with the referee having a favourite. That used to really annoy the punters, really get their blood boiling."

BANGOR F.C. DEVELOPMENT COMMITTEE
IN ASSOCIATION WITH N.I.W.A. presents

OUTSTANDING HEAVYWEIGHT CONTEST

10 x 5   8 o'clock   Doors open 7.30 p.m.

Co-op Hall, Bangor : Thursday, 29th April

BULLDOG BILL CARTER   v.   **BIG BILL MILLER**
(Liverpool)   (Belfast)
17 stone bully of the ring   One of Ireland's
No holds barred   Leading Heavyweights

GREAT MIDDLEWEIGHT CONTEST—8 x 5
FLASH SHIRLOW   v.   **DAVE FINLAY**
(Dunmurry)   (Greenisland)
All-action mat man   A boy with a good record

ALL ACTION TAG MATCH
DIRTY DARKIE ARNOTT   **BUDDY RODGERS** (Ex ...)
(Rathcoole.) Ireland's No. 1 Villian   Scientific Mat Man
              and   v.   and
WILD BUTCHER DONNELL   **JIM**
(Rathcoole). The referee's nightmare   who stands no nonsense

GRAND WELTERWEIGHT CONTEST—8 x 5
MIKE (Judo) HAMILL   v.   **BEARDED BOB REA**
(Belfast)   (Millisle)
Brown Belt Holder   Ex Unarmed Combat Instructor

Referee—Mr. DAVE MACK   M.C.—Mr. 8 A.M. JENKINS
ADMISSION 10/- Reserved and 6/-

A bill in Bangor from April 29th 1965

Billy "Buddy" Rodgers and Jimmy Rodgers were brothers who along with another brother Ronnie Rodgers were also part of the class of '64.

Sam Jenkins was pals with Dave Mack and did MC on some shows. "Mr. 8 A.M." must be an inside joke between friends

- - - - -

On January 2nd 1965 pro wrestling began being broadcast as one of a selection of sports on ITV's newest programme *World of Sport*. World of Sport featured the likes of ski-jumping and horse-jumping, and ran in direct opposition to the BBC's similar-styled *Grandstand* series which featured the likes of ice hockey and rugby, but when it came to viewing figures for the wrestling… every weekend without fail Jackie Pallo and the lads battered their competition. The year before the BBC had even added a third television channel called *BBC 2.* However it didn't matter because at 4pm on a Saturday afternoon the majority of households who owned a television set in England, Scotland, Wales and Northern Ireland were watching the wrestling on ITV.

In Belfast big businessman George Connell had become co-owner of the very popular ice rink at the King's Hall. This year acted as his settling in to his newest venture so all of the Relwyskow & Green shows were staged in the Ulster Hall instead. The Englishman sent their stars all the same and as well as the usual suspects was Japanese-American wrestler Harold Sakata; better known around the world as "Oddjob", the hat-throwing henchman who squared off against Sean Connery in an electrifying encounter in the James Bond classic *Goldfinger* which was released the previous year.
     The Irish isle also got to gawk at for the first time the unforgettable "Exotic" Adrian Street who – like Orig Williams – was a fiercely proud Welshman. Being born to a father who worked in the coal mines, Adrian Street's rebellion to his manly man upbringing was to play to the general public's unfortunate perception of homosexuality of the time by becoming a hated heel (bad guy) with his outlandish costumes, over-the-top camp antics, and being a man wearing lipstick and make-up in front of working-class crowds in the 1960s.

- - - - -

The wrestling boom was so big in the UK and Ireland that for the first time since the early 1950s a wrestling club was formed outside of Belfast or rather reformed in Portadown.

Elmer 'Bendix' Benson: "When I was young there were a few bullies about. And I was reared by my grandparents. My grandfather was a boxer and he had actually come through the Battle of the Somme. So he trained me up in boxing and after 6-7 months he said, 'right, now next time you get bother, you chin them', and that's just what I did, I hammered them, no more bullying. So I kept at the boxing and then I actually did a bit of street-fighting, but then I had to quit going to dances on a Friday night because I kept getting challenged. So I suppose the wrestling was just next in a succession of things."

Born on February 15th 1943 in Portadown, in his youth Elmer Benson played football and rugby and lifted weights. His brother-in-law was once a well known bodybuilder in the town called Tony Stewart – the original 'Flash' of Irish wrestling as well as the organiser of the Portadown Wrestling Club in 1952. Over a decade later in 1964 it was another former local wrestler who relaunched the wrestling club in the town, one whose specialty was dropkicks.

Elmer Bendix: "There was a club started here in Church Street, so I decided to go along, and there was maybe forty or so in it. And there was a man, and he'd come along and give a lot of pointers, Dropkick Beattie they called him. He was a great wee man. Very small, but very fit of himself, and he showed us a lot of stuff. All came fairly easy enough to me. I had boxing training before, and I was very fit."

39 year old Dropkick Billy Beattie had been Worldwide Promotion's action-man from Armagh from 1951 to 1953. With pro wrestling surging in popularity on television, Beattie decided to set up his own wrestling club in Portadown at the *Social Service Club Rooms* opposite *St. Mark's Church*.
  Elmer Benson was soon Beattie's star student, and would become acquainted with the N.I. Wrestling Association and its wrestlers whenever an event at Portadown Town Hall was organised with the help of Billy (working with old Worldwide associates Darkie and Dave Mack) in January 1965. Unfortunately on the night the ring van didn't turn up so the wrestlers had to cram into the dropkick dynamo's house until it was learned the event would have to be cancelled and rescheduled.

Elmer Bendix (right) throws a fellow trainee at the Portadown Wrestling Club

Sadly, for whatever reason and likely unrelated to the rescheduled show, the new Portadown Wrestling Club couldn't sustain either and soon shut down, this time for good. Everyone involved called it quits, except butcher Elmer Benson.

Elmer Bendix: "I was into dropkicks, and pushing and pulling and hitting but the first thing they taught you was your balance. If you haven't got balance, your opponent can just pull you and you'll go. But if you have balance, and they pull, it's them that ends up coming to you. It was a very good wee club, but then it broke up and out of it all, I was the only one who ended up wrestling. I was invited down to a club in Belfast on Albion Street, and I trained there, and that's where it really started."

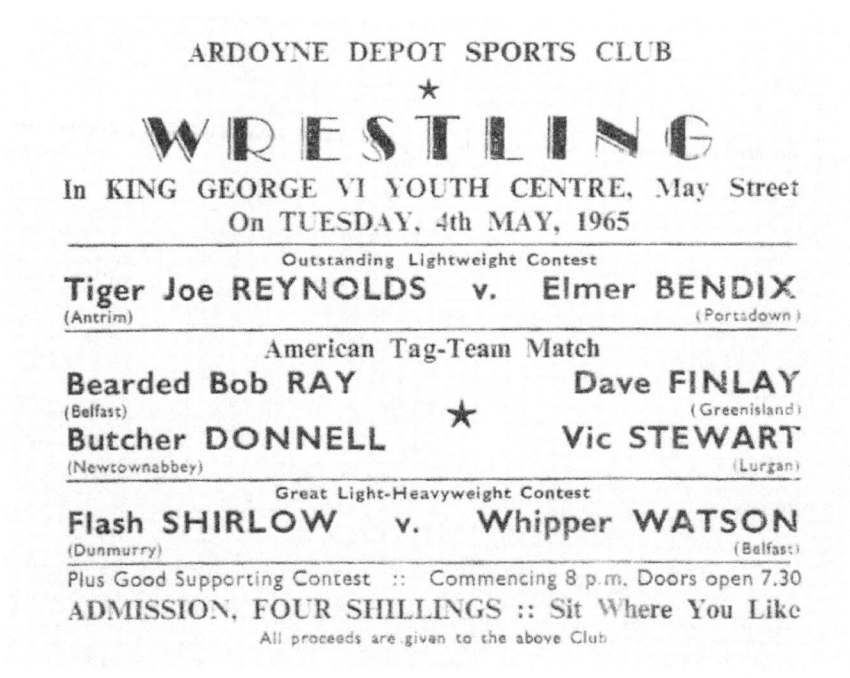

ARDOYNE DEPOT SPORTS CLUB

★

WRESTLING

In KING GEORGE VI YOUTH CENTRE, May Street
On TUESDAY, 4th MAY, 1965

Outstanding Lightweight Contest

Tiger Joe REYNOLDS   v.   **Elmer BENDIX**
(Antrim)   (Portadown)

American Tag-Team Match

Bearded Bob RAY   **Dave FINLAY**
(Belfast)   ★   (Greenisland)
Butcher DONNELL   **Vic STEWART**
(Newtownabbey)   (Lurgan)

Great Light-Heavyweight Contest

Flash SHIRLOW   v.   **Whipper WATSON**
(Dunmurry)   (Belfast)

Plus Good Supporting Contest :: Commencing 8 p.m. Doors open 7.30
ADMISSION, FOUR SHILLINGS :: Sit Where You Like
All proceeds are given to the above Club

On May 4th 1965 at the King George VI, 22 year old Elmer Benson as Elmer "Bendix" made his debut vs. Tiger Joe Reynolds, and in doing so – like his mentor Dropkick Beattie before him – became Armagh's only active pro wrestler.

Elmer Bendix: "The first one I don't remember much about it. You have to learn to forget about the crowd. You also have to show the crowd what you're doing, if you're doing it, that's OK, but you need to let the crowd see it. That's the way a good wrestler comes on. The name change from Benson to Bendix was decided the first night I wrestled. I think it was Darkie Arnott who decided Elmer Bendix. First thing that came into his head probably. That's how I ended up Bendix. I think it was to do with Bendix washing machines."

Meanwhile Elmer's original coach Dropkick Beattie stayed involved as a helping hand. Beattie would set up the town hall before shows whenever the wrestling revisited Portadown for years to come. A friendly familiar face to welcome the Belfast lads to the town hall until the end of the decade.

Dropkick Billy Beattie in later life

In work the real-life Billy Beattie was a maintenance manager at *Wade's* pottery factory in Portadown. Outside of wrestling the quiet family man put his skilled feet from his days of drop-kicking to good use whenever he took his wife ballroom dancing. In May 2001, age 75, Billy Beattie passed away but is still fondly remembered by Elmer, his most successful trainee.

Meanwhile the influence of Dave Finlay and Henry Shirlow ensured that Carrickfergus Town Hall and new monthly hot spot *Lisburn Orange Hall*, respectively, started seeing their fair share of pro wrestling promotions as both men were able to pull in the crowds as the hometown heroes.

The villains to these heroes were often masked wrestlers with a myriad of different personas. In the tag division there was "The Black Aces" and "The Stingrays" (based on a TV show of the same name) and in singles action you might be seeing "The Outlaw" or "The Executioner" or "The Skull" or "El Greco" (a reference to Greco-Roman wrestling) but above all the oddest attraction was the one conjured up by Darkie himself.

Darkie Arnott: "I resurrected the Mummy you know? I made this outfit, and Davey and I would wrestle under it as The Mummy."

Dave Finlay: "It was made out of long-johns, a white vest and crepe bandages. I think Darkie's sister-in-law stitched it together. You'd have talcum powder on your back, so when you where in the ring it would come off like dust, like you'd been in the tomb too long. You'd trail your leg too, it was a good gimmick."

Darkie Arnott: "We would switch it up. Most nights Davey would do it, but some nights I would do it and then I'd wrestle him, so people wouldn't guess who it was, or so was the intention."

Dave Finlay: "Of course they usually knew who you were once you started wrestling."

"The Mummy" was the surprising star of many Irish wrestling shows. As well as being alternatively played by Dave Finlay and Darkie Arnott, many others walked like Egyptian to the ring over the years with Eddie Hamill and Henry Shirlow suggested as having played the part of the zombie Pharaoh. The Mummy was a gimmick that shockingly lasted longer in Irish wrestling than most of its actual wrestlers.

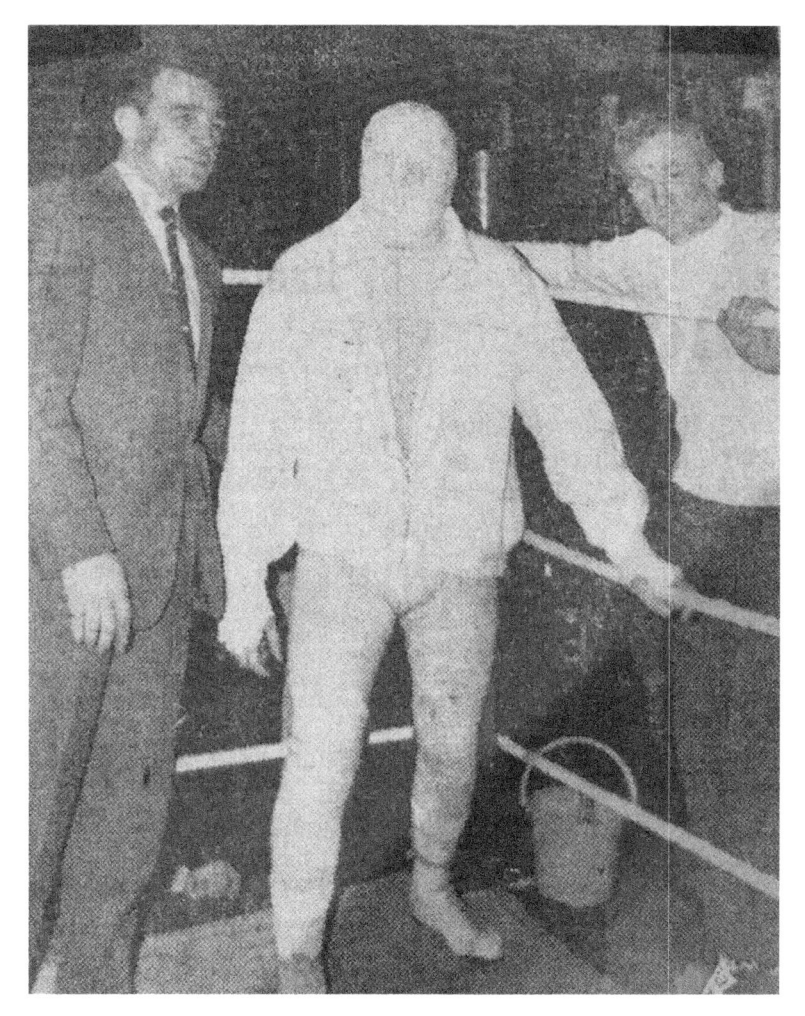

The Mummy, with Tiger Joe Moore (right) as a cornerman

- - - - -

Sometime in the mid '60s Orig Williams took over Irish operations completely from Sean O'Shea. Someone who was frequently on the ferry across the Irish sea for both was British wrestling icon Johnny Saint. Born in England in 1941, John "Johnny Saint" Miller turned pro as a teenager and worked his way to becoming the successor to the style of wrestling innovated by the British scene's most technically-talented wrestler of the time, George Kidd. The style was good clean wrestling full of cunning holds, clever reversals and little flares of slapstick comedy that's regarded today as the best example of the colloquially coined "World of Sport style wrestling". However, years before he made it onto television with Joint Promotions, Johnny Saint was a constant on independent wrestling cards around the UK, and thrilled audiences in Ireland too.

John 'Johnny Saint' Millar: "Sean O'Shea was a businessman. Quite shrewd at business. We had quite a few successful trips to Ireland with him. I remember Orig coming into the business. I remember Orig coming to the gym in Manchester and the next thing I knew he was into the promoting end. Orig then seemed to take over promoting in Ireland. I'm not sure what happened to Sean O'Shea. I think he went on to start some other business with photography."

34 year old Orig Williams became the leading opposition promoter on the island of Ireland, and while the N.I. Wrestling Association showcased its young blood and Relwyskow & Green matched up their made men, the Welsh-speaking ring warrior continued to present the most eclectic cards.
    That October Orig was the first man since the Imperial Troupe of Lady Wrestlers in the early '30s to bring women wrestlers to Ireland. One of the original bell-to-bell belles he brought over was English woman Mitzi Mueller. Mitzi was a blonde bombshell who wowed in the ring and even without television exposure was a huge hit on the independent wrestling circuit. Though while the venue in Belfast refused to allow her and her opponent to appear, Armagh welcomed the women and became the first in the North to see grappling girls actually in a ring.
    Orig the part-time promoter / footballer also continued with his brazen billing of names like "Johnny Kellett" (instead of Les), "Bill Royal" (instead of Bert) and "Zulu the African Witch Doctor" (instead of Masambula) throughout the following years because you can't teach a promoter new tricks until the old ones get him run out of town.

- - - - -

As 1965 came to a close homegrown wrestling in Northern Ireland arguably entered it's own "Golden Era". Over the next few years the old guard and the class of '64 would light up the cigarette smoke-filled halls of Ulster as the appeal of a night-out at the wrestling was rivalled only by live music, the cinema or taking your chances with what was on telly at the time.

A group picture at the Milo Wrestling Club on Albion Street in November 1965

Top row (L to R); Sam Jenkins, Darkie Arnott, Tiger Joe Moore, Jimmy Rodgers, Syd Waddell, Buster Shields, Billy Rodgers, Earl St. John, unknown, and Henry Shirlow

Bottom row (L to R); Stan Cooke, Dave Finlay, Ronnie Rodgers, Butcher Donald, Hugh Beattie, Eddie Hamill, Elmer Bendix and Dave Mack

- - - - -

Meanwhile that year Eric Wilson became the first Ulsterman not named O'Donnell, Casey or Regan to wrestle in the Ulster Hall in over 10 years. Through a good word from his coach Larry Casey, Eric had been billed on a sold show in Tandragee in Armagh for Relwyskow & Green in March 1965. He impressed enough to earn his slot on a sold out show in the historic venue that October.

Though Eric's mentor Larry got to see him follow in his footsteps, the shipyard driller sadly wouldn't get to see the shipyard sparky succeed at an even greater level in the future. That November the real-life Lawrence Ralston passed away under tragic circumstances aged only 35. Larry Casey was still an active referee and wrestler at the time, and his name was even advertised to appear in a match at the Ulster Hall that December. It was a death that shocked the local wrestling community. Despite never directly working together the N.I. Wrestling Association still expressed their sadness and sympathies for Larry's family following his untimely passing. Though his gym would close a short while later, Larry's legacy in wrestling lived on through his friends Eric Wilson and Noel Ewart.

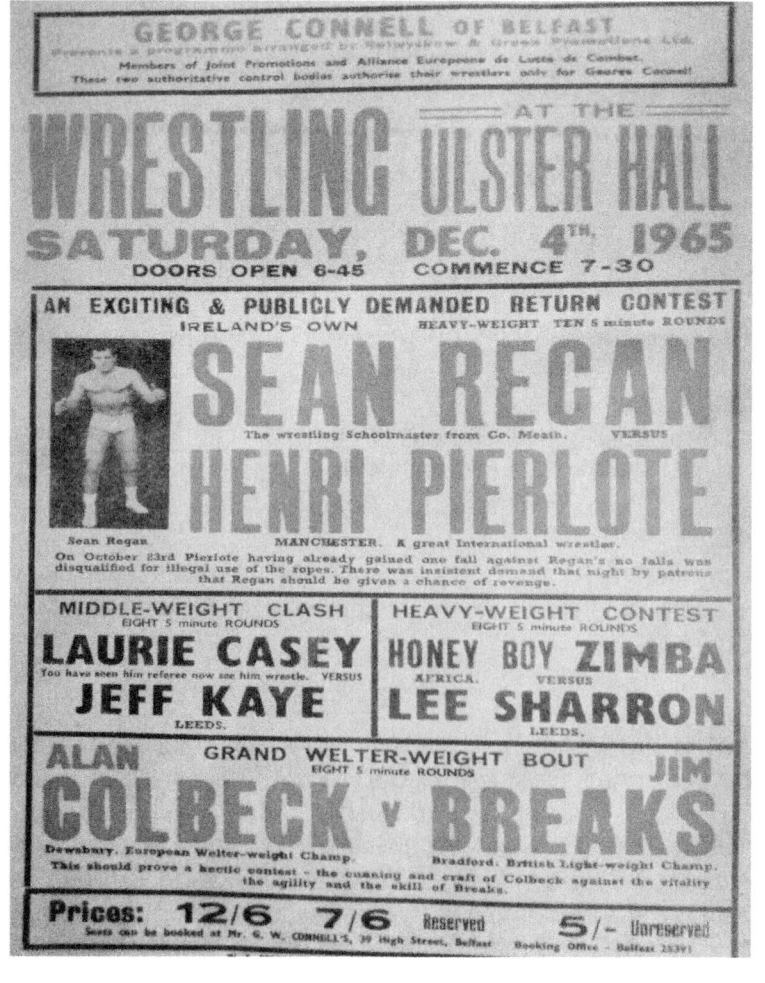

The match Larry Casey sadly never made

1966

The N.I.W.A. schedule continued to pick up pace with towns like Bangor, Ballymena, Comber and Cookstown all being semi-regular stops. At times there was 5-6 live events a month, a minuscule number by comparison of the British wrestling circuit but for part-time Irish performers it was invaluable time to shine in the squared circle in front of hundreds of fans.

By then the only former Worldwide Promotion wrestlers left were Darkie Arnott, Tiger Joe Moore, Whipper Watson, Strangler Stan Cooke and Dave Mack (as MC). Of those who came through on the boxing ring in Jackie Briers gym only Butcher Donald, Syd Waddell (as referee) and a few others were left remaining, and so it was the youth movement that was in full force with the likes of Judo Mike Hamill, Pat Red Kelly, Jack Flash Shirlow, Whirlwind Monroe, Dave Finlay and Elmer Bendix dominating local league bills.

New school vs. old school,
Dave Finlay and Darkie Arnott shake hands backstage before a bout in 1966

That summer is the final findings for "Ex-Commando" The Blonde Duke, age 28, in some tag team matches with Noel Ewart (who would sometimes wrestle as "Ace Mooney", a wrestling name also used on the Irish circuit in the '40s). At times the Duke and Ewart worked with one another in real-life too.

After self-admittedly missing some matches due to being busy with his job, the real-life Frank Hughes decided wrestling wasn't for him any longer as he had his eyes on enterprises that would actually make him money! To aid him in his dynamite discoveries Frank built his own specialised crane to lift exploded ship debris out of the waters around Ireland. Later he would travel around the world including America, Brazil, Puerto Rico and Oman, wheeling and dealing in different cutting edge machinery.

The Blonde Duke: "I liked wrestling but my greatest interests lay in making money, and unfortunately there wasn't much of it in wrestling. So I decided to focus my attention on other endeavours. I would still come to the shows from time to time, and of course stayed in touch with Hughie, but I moved on."

Dave Finlay: "The Blonde Duke, he lived in Whitehouse Park, very big houses in there. He was always ambitious in life. Though he seemed to sometimes be a millionaire, other times down and out. Didn't seem to bother him either way."

The Blonde Duke: "I enjoyed it for the time I was in it, and Darkie Arnott there's a man who deserves a statue for all he done for it. Mind you back then they called me The Blonde Duke because I had this great head of hair, and nowadays I'm more like the bald Duke!"

Even today in his early 80s and back living in Newtownabbey, Frank Hughes remains a colourful character still thinking up ways to make a few dollars more. In his retirement from the ring The Blonde Duke was the first noteworthy name of the class of '64 to concede the proverbially final fall.

However while losing one prominent player, Irish wrestling quickly gained another in 20 year old factory worker Rosemary Liddell.

Rosemary Gault (nee Liddell) aka Kim Starr
The world's first female pro wrestling referee

Dave Finlay: "Darkie just said to me, 'why don't you get Rosemary involved?'. She did really well with it, she appeared in magazines and on TV, only woman's referee in Britain, probably even the world."

Rosemary 'Kim Starr' Gault: "I had went to the shows, and Dave suggested I start reffing and was I more than happy to. So I used to go up three times a week to the gym in Albion Street to train, maybe for about a year or so. I really enjoyed it, and it was Butcher Donald who looked after me. He was like the daddy of the place. I remember once we where in the gym and some of the boys were swearing, and Butcher said, 'lads will you stop f'ing swearing, there's a lady here!'."

Born in Whitehouse on February 22nd 1946, throughout her teens Rosemary Liddell was successful in sports such as hockey, badminton, show-jumping, judo and gymnastics all before she became a history-maker in professional wrestling.

Rosemary's sister Evelyn was married to Dave Finlay, whose passion for wrestling was matched by few others on the Irish circuit. He lived and breathed it, and was rarely left off a bill, maybe in small part because of his friendship with gaffer Darkie but in larger part due to his skill and passion for the sport. The thrills and highs of wrestling were something Dave was only happy to share with his family and so Rosemary was to become the second member of the Finlay family (albeit an in-law) to get involved in pro wrestling. She was far from the last…

The only woman to ever train at the Milo Wrestling Club, Rosemary would learn the ins and outs of the form first hand from her brother-in-law Dave as well as Butcher Donald and the others. When she was ready Rosemary was given the ring name "Kim Starr" without any questions asked.

The petite, brown-haired Kim Starr was treated with the utmost respect by the rest of the roster and billed as *"Britain's only woman referee"* attracted national news attention. She was a little lady amongst the fighting "he-men" with one eye-catching headline reading *"The Ref's a Woman"*.

Kim Starr's debut and a place in the history books took place on Thursday September 29th 1966 at the Queen's Hall in Newtownards when she refereed the opening bout between Dave Finlay vs. Whirlwind Monroe. A few days later on Monday October 3rd at the King George VI in Belfast part of Kim's officiating a match pitting Darkie Arnott vs. The Mummy (her brother-in-law Dave in disguise) was filmed for a news piece for the BBC.

Darkie Arnott: "The only time I got on TV was once and it was for two minutes. I was wrestling Davey as The Mummy, and his sister-in-law she was doing the referee, and because of that there was great interest and the Telegraph they put a photograph of her in the paper, and did an interview with her. So that night a camera crew turned up and filmed the bout, and at the end of the match the two of us got knocked out as we ran head on into each over, boom, that was it over. I never seen the clip of it anywhere since."

Dave Finlay: "My sister-in-law when she was Kim Starr, I'd have pointed my finger at her, and she'd bite it. Crowd would love it."

Kim Starr: "I used to break up the wrestlers by twisting their ears. Once I was breaking up the wrestlers, and Darkie went to pull me back, and I swung my arm back. He said it was a karate chop, but I think it was an elbow, and I knocked his tooth out."

Kim Starr would share officiating duties with bus driver Syd Waddell going forward. She showed a woman's touch could be deadly when she got physical, her trademark to make sure she got a wrestler's attention being to grab the unruly sod by each ear and twist.

When she wasn't beating up the baddies like she was an all-in wrestling referee, Kim Starr was being treated with the best view in the house to top quality bouts. On the Irish wrestling scene there weren't many matches that brought the action and excitement like Judo Mike Hamill vs. Whirlwind Monroe, who inspired awe from the audience and their fellow wrestlers alike with their furious pace and thrilling sequences of moves and reversals. Why they worked so well was that the real-life Eddie Hamill and Hugh Beattie were constantly at the Milo club practicing new sequences and figuring out routines in the ring that they could then incorporate into their matches.

Dave Finlay: "Eddie Hamill and Whirlwind Monroe, they were really really good. Eddie was a great good-looking babyface, you could put him with anyone. Whirlwind was a great personality, very jovial. He was a good showman, always had the nice gear, very well-liked and the girls loved him."

Eddie Hamill: "We were great mates, me and Whirlwind. We liked the same things. We used to go shooting together, scuba-diving together, we lived in each others pockets. I met him through the wrestling, the gym. I don't know why but we just clicked together, we had the same sense of humour, and we just hit it off. With families, my wife became friendly with his wife, and we used to go to the others houses, and go out together and on holiday together. He was a great fella, great sense of humour, nothing upset him."

Becoming best of friends helped too, and both Eddie and Hugh pushed each other to be better. In time it was toss-up between a select few for the #1 talent on the local league but Judo Mike and the Whirlwind were top contenders for the honour. A guaranteed show-stealer they were a go-to for matchmaker Dave Mack whenever he was deciding who'd wrestle who in matches each month.

Though making the matches wasn't as hard as deciding who'd be in them as so many wrestlers were still coming through the Milo club at the time. The first found matches for two new names in 33 year old car dealer Harry Corr and 25 year old factory worker Roy Lynn were November 23rd 1966 on a bill in Lisburn Orange Hall.

Dave Finlay: "We had a lot of good lads at the club at the time. Harry Corr, he was a very nice man, would have took a wee sip of drink before a match to settle the nerves. He'd have been in with the body-building crowd. Roy Lynn, he was a Western Australia amateur champion. When he came back we give him the Australian gimmick, Roy Digger Lynch, had him do the accent and all."

TO-NIGHT'S PROGRAMME

INTERNATIONAL HEAVYWEIGHT CONTEST
10 x 5 Minute Rounds

BULLDOG BILL CARTER v **DIGGER LYNCH**
(LIVERPOOL) — Former Australian Cruiserweight Champion.
As Rough and Tough as they come.

Handwritten annotations: 1ST FALL. 3RD RD / EQUAL 4TH RD

LIGHTWEIGHT CONTEST
8 x 5 Minute Rounds

TIGER JOE REYNOLDS v **ACE MOONEY**
(ANTRIM) (NEWTOWNABBEY)
Both these Boys are Ex-Lightweight Title Holders.

Handwritten annotations: 2 Fall / 1 Fall

WELTERWEIGHT CONTEST
8 x 5 Minute Rounds

MIKE JUDO HAMILL v **WHIRLWIND MUNRO**
(BELFAST) (WHITEABBEY)
Irish Welterweight Champion. One of the Most Popular Mat Men of To-day.

Handwritten annotations: 1ST FALL. 2ND RD / EQUAL 4TH / WIN 5TH RD

AMERICAN TAG MATCH
No Rounds — 30-Minute Time Limit

DARKIE ARNOTT — **HARRY CORR**
(RATHCOOLE) (BELFAST)
The Referee's Nightmare.

v

BUSTER SHIELDS — **PAT MURPHY**
(BELFAST) (GREENISLAND)
Everybody's Nightmare. Two Minds with but a Single Thought— To Beat Darkie Arnott.

Handwritten annotations: WIN / 2 Subs

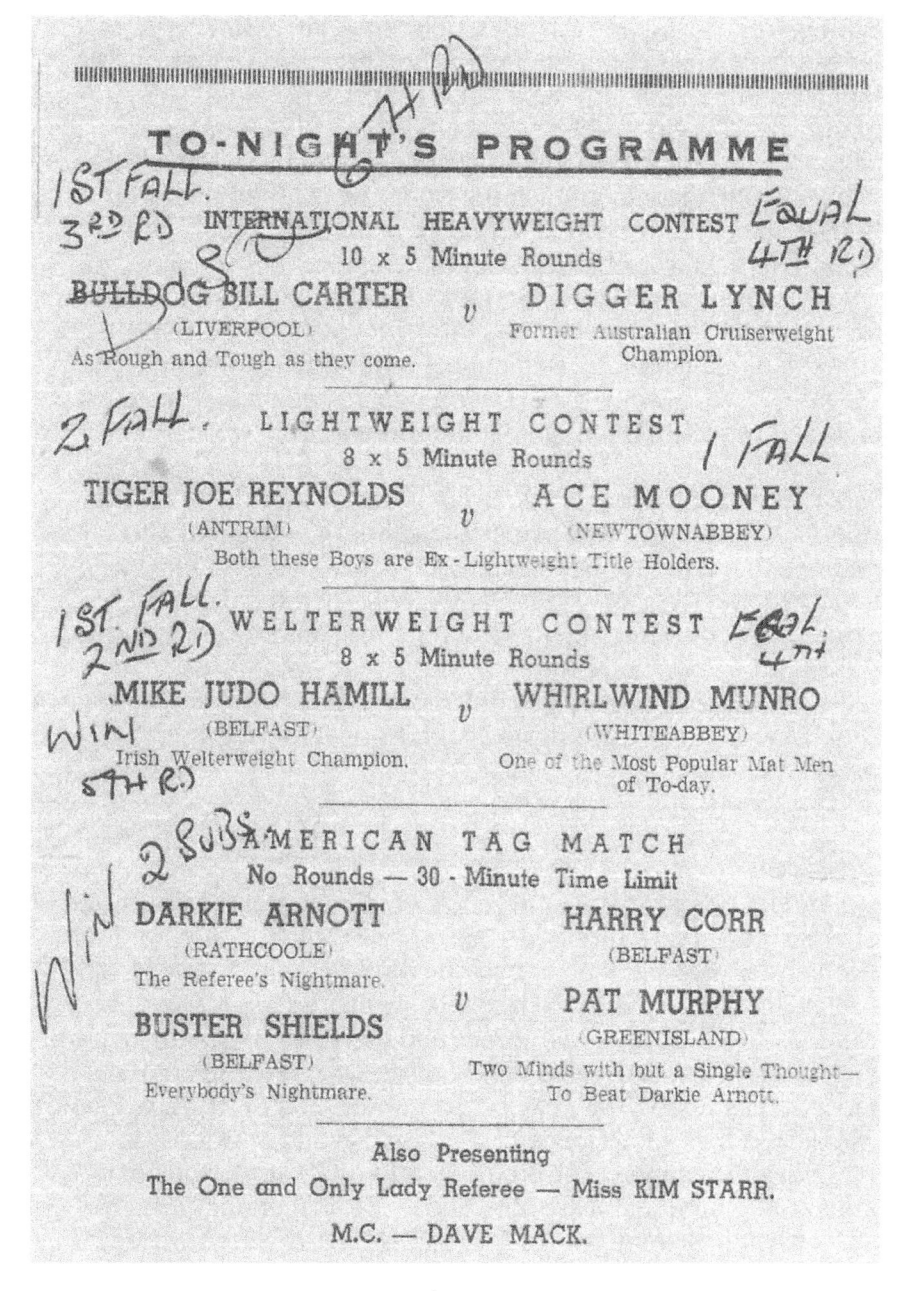

Also Presenting
The One and Only Lady Referee — Miss KIM STARR.

M.C. — DAVE MACK.

A bill from November 23rd 1966 at Lisburn Orange Hall
"Bulldog Bill Carter" is Stan Cooke
"Ace Mooney" is Noel Ewart

Born in Belfast on May 24th 1933, Harold "Harry" Corr was a fitness fanatic who opened several health studios with his wife Maureen in the '50s. In these health studios Maureen took some of the very first fitness classes in Northern Ireland that were women-only. It was through his gyms Corr found out about the wrestling and, like so many before him, he crossed over from bodybuilding into pro wrestling and instantly became a buddy of fellow weight-lifting enthusiast Stan Cooke.

"Strongman" Harry Corr was recalled by his family as a fairly straight-laced wrestler in black trunks and black boots who sometimes tagged in an odd couple team with the lively Whirlwind Monroe – who always stood out on shows because of his multi-coloured wrestling attire and vibrant personality.

Then born in 1941 in Carrickfergus, Robert "Roy" Lynn lived in Australia for several years in the '60s where he trained and competed in amateur wrestling, and so it was Dave Finlay who Lynn became friendly with as he was one of the only at the Albion Street gym able to match Finlay on the mat in amateur wrestling prowess.

A big, bald heavyweight Lynn was given the gimmick name Roy "Digger Lynch" and played his part as if he was from the land of dingo and didgeridoos.

- - - - -

On the big bills in Belfast the King's Hall was again the epicentre of pro wrestling in Europe in 1966 when it boasted another four evenings of star-studded wrestling entertainment that year. Mr. TV Jackie Pallo only managed a solo showing, so Les Kellett, Ricki Starr, George Kidd, Adrian Street and the Royal brothers instead supported the main events of box office smash Mick McManus, the jet-black haired villain who was either ITV's #1 or #2 biggest wrestling superstar (rivalled by Pallo) on World of Sport.

Some of the other Saturday afternoon sensations who appeared on the Irish isle that year also transcended from their TV show to others programmes and into films. Wrestler Leon Arras aka Charlie Glover later co-starred in the '70s television series *Porridge*, and the 6'4 "Bomber" Pat Roach went on to feature in supporting roles opposite both James Bond and Indiana Jones in the '80s.

However that June the wrestling at the King's Hall hosted its most unfortunate case of celebrity in Jimmy Savile. Savile was a much-loved television personality and radio DJ in the UK for 40+ years, but after his death in 2011 he was exposed for heinous crimes with his name since becoming a buzzword for 'evil'. For a short time in the '60s though, Jimmy Savile took the time to train and step into the ring as a pro wrestler on the British scene. He proudly claimed to have wrestled 107 matches and lost most of them, and one of those was in the ring in the old cattle mart.

- - - - -

While Relwyskow & Green maintained Belfast as one of their top tier territories, George Connell – having achieved his two greatest promoting successes in the last few years, first with Gilroy vs. Caldwell and then with the Beatles – wasn't the cut-throat tycoon he once was and allowed his lease on the Ulster Hall to lapse, meaning outside parties could finally promote in the city centre venue.

That December Orig Williams became the first outsider to organise pro wrestling in the Ulster Hall in 27 years, with his partner in promotion being a former school teacher from Belfast called Jim Aiken. The event was one of the earliest for *Aiken Promotions* who continue to this day as one of Ireland's most successful event management services. The show featured Orig's usual variety of grapplers including lightweight legend Johnny Saint, super-heavyweight star Klondyke Bill (who was said to weigh somewhere in the region of 40st / 560lbs) and the dwarf wrestlers Tiny Tim Gallagher and Gorgeous Fuzzy Kay – the latter of whom was advertised as having starred in the Disney films *Snow White and the Seven Dwarfs* and *Pinocchio*… despite both being cartoon movies??

The Welshman returned to the Ulster Hall the following year with another one-off with the main event match being Cowboy Jack Cassidy vs. Chief Thunderbird (not the original who'd appeared for George Connell in the '50s as he was dead by then) making Orig only the second man in Irish wrestling to promote a visual cowboy vs. indian match. The other of course being Sean O'Shea from years before.

1967

Bruce 'McDonald' Stevenson: "I was born closer to Scotland than I was Belfast, that's my claim anyway. No, it was actually Davey Mack who give me the name 'McDonald'. I had seen wrestling here at the Queen's Hall and I thought, that doesn't look too bad. So my uncle worked in the shipyard and he'd asked around on who was doing it and heard about the Albion Street in Belfast. So off I went and I started when I was 16 years old. The man who sort of brought me on was a guy called Joe Moore, wrestled as 'Tiger' Joe Reynolds. My first match was then in the town hall with Joe, and he was a lovely worker, smooth as silk. He kept my head calm and talked away to me. He was a really nice man, and didn't want to work too hard. Joe had respiratory problems and bear in mind this was when you could smoke in the halls during the shows. So there wasn't a lot of running about and cowboys and indians, it was all clean and clever. Which became how I worked really".

Born in Newtownards on April 20th 1949, Bruce Stevenson joined the gym as a teenager and a month before his 18th birthday debuted at the Queen's Hall in his hometown in March 1967 as "Bruce McDonald" vs. Tiger Joe Reynolds.
　　　　The smart short-haired college student was a lightweight wrestler well-suited to more straight-forward competitors, reflecting the mindset of his mentor Tiger Joe. Joe was by then in his 40s and as the longest active pro wrestler in Northern Ireland looked to take it a little easier during his rare in-ring experiences. Easy-going without any ego nor eccentricities, Bruce McDonald became a regular on the Irish circuit and just like Tiger Joe worked best in the opening match.

Bruce McDonald: "Joe and I worked a lot as the opening bout after that, and I think I was the only one Joe worked with towards the end of his time in the ring. I was able to look after him, and he was able to look after me."

Another who came up through the Albion Street gym at the same time as Bruce was 19 year old car mechanic Dave Stalford.

LISBURN SILVER BAND

PRESENTS

PROFESSIONAL WRESTLING

LISBURN ORANGE HALL

WEDNESDAY, 1st NOVEMBER, at 8 p.m.

TERRIFIC MIDDLEWEIGHT CONTEST

8 x 3 min. Rounds

"THE SKULL"　　V　　DAVE STALFORD
(Human or Animal)　　　　(Donegal)
　　　　　　　　　　The right man for the job.

Grand Lightweight Contest	Great Cruiserweight Contest
6 x 3 min. Rounds	8 x 3 min. Rounds
BRUCE McDONALD	JACK (Flash) SHIRLOW
(Newtownards)	(Lisburn)
	Former Irish Middleweight Champion
v	v
CHRIS REDFERN	ROY (Digger) LYNCH
(Belfast)	(Carrickfergus)
Two Fast and Clever Matmen.	Former Australian Cruiser Champion

---

FANTASTIC TAG MATCH

No Rounds — Thirty Minute Time Limit

By Special Request　　　　MIKE (Judo) HAMILL
THE FABULOUS　　V　　(Ex-Irish Welter Champion)
　　　　　　　　　　ACE MOONEY
"STINGRAYS"　　　　(The Pocket-sized Adonis)

A bill from November 1967

Born in Belfast in 1948, Dave Stalford was big, burly, bearded and infamously a hard man with a reputation comparable to Irish wrestling's past rogue Buck Alec. Similarly to the lion-tamer, Stalford's bouts often ended in chaotic KO wins or dirty disqualification losses, though he too was actually very well-liked in the locker room, particularly for his sense of humour. He had no problem playing The Mummy from time to time as well.

- - - - -

That February Derry-born Sean Regan vs. Dublin-born Pat Barrett in the King's Hall was this decade's North vs. South war to settle the score on who was the new "Irish Heavyweight Champion". It was also the first time in the nearly twenty year reign of Relwyskow & Green / Connell that there was a celebrated clash of two Irishmen on a big bill in Belfast.

- - - - -

Germany and by extension Austria were the only other European countries outside of the UK where pro wrestling was popular enough to be profitable. The Germans/Austrians would stage wrestling tournaments that could go on anywhere between a few weeks to over a month. These tournaments hosted matches in the same city and building every night until conclusion. Though British wrestling thrived on larger-than-life characters like Jackie Pallo and Mick McManus who were both under 5ft7 in height, in Germany/Austria size mattered. So Sean Regan and Wild Angus had been regular visitors since '64 and '65, respectively.

      Interestingly, at the tournaments Angus was given a new gimmick name. The Irish "Scot" became a mad monk called "Rasputin" – named after a real-life Russian holy-man who was mythically hard to kill. That summer of '67 the monstrous monk terrorised in a tournament in Vienna to stand tall above all, and the runner-up? Sean Regan. It was a good year for the Irish.

- - - - -

On October 21st 1967 the King's Hall was host to one of the biggest bouts in the history of British wrestling; Pallo vs. McManus. The villain vs. villain feud of sneaky Jackie vs. snarling Mick made the masterminds behind Joint Promotions even richer men, brought ITV wrestling some its highest ever ratings and for one night only Ulster got to stage the spectacular in front of thousands of wrestling fanatics. It was the grandest match ever before brought to Belfast and for many in the jam-packed arena that evening it would be their one and only time seeing the two television icons against one another live and in colour. Literally; Northern Ireland didn't get colour TV until 1970.

Frank Hoy aka Wild Angus
The original "Rasputin the Mad Monk" of wrestling when competing
on the German/Austrian tournaments
In 1967, Angus/Rasputin won a tournament in Vienna
Cheers to Gernot Johannes Freiberger for the picture

1968

The previous year Wild Angus signed on to Joint Promotions, and made his first appearance in action on the 21st November 1967 broadcast of World of Sport.

The giant Enniskillen grappler then made his debut in the King's Hall this February in a "Tag Team Eliminator". A staple of the Relwyskow & Green showcases in Belfast, the eliminator would see four top tag teams square off in two semi-final matches, with the winners advancing to a final held on the same show. The most successful tandems over the years being, among others, the Royal brothers (Bert Royal & Vic Faulkner), Mick McManus & Steve Logan, and "The Saints" (brothers Roy & Tony St. Clair).

Frank Hoy's family would get to herald the return of their famous son many more times as Wild Angus figured onto George Connell Promotions in the Ulster Hall for several more months in headline bouts.

Besides the huge faux-highlander, the newest sensation for Belfast fans to see perform in person was Kendo Nagasaki; a sword-carrying masked man of suspected Japanese heritage, with the mystique surrounding his true identity making him an almost mythical figure on ITV. In real-life Kendo Nagasaki was Peter Thornley, an English millionaire turned pro wrestler who was actually as elusive as his in-ring character

Then later that year fearsome Fermanagh man Hoy went off to conquer the Continent of Asia. Angus ran Wild in Japan as an invading "Gaijan"; a Japanese term of endearment for foreigners. Like Germany, Japan was also a profitable place to make a living as a journeyman wrestler, and another country that held heavyweight wrestlers in the highest regard. Angus' size made him a sensation and he was invited back many more times to the land of the rising sun and sushi. As a result Wild Angus was rarely on World of Sport as he loved to travel and accepted any chance to compete in Germany or Japan. His globe-trotting wouldn't end there either.

- - - - -

Eddie Hamill: "I liked Orig but he was the biggest rogue ever. He would put wrestling bills out with "MCMANUS" in big print, and "Mark" in small print. Another one he done was 'These wrestlers have been invited to appear, Jackie Pallo, Les Kellett', you name them. And then when it came to the show he'd say, 'well we invited a few people but they haven't showed up, but Judo Mike Hamill is here!'. So you'd feel a right prat going out to the ring."

In 1968 Orig Williams worked with the wrestlers from the Milo Wrestling Club when, in need of some top quality talent to fill some bills in the South, Sean O'Shea passed the retired soccer star the phone number of Darkie Arnott. The highly-recommended trio of Judo Mike Hamill, Whirlwind Monroe and Dave Finlay going on to tour across the island of Ireland that March with Orig.

Then in June the Welshman brought Mitzi Mueller to a cinema in Rathcoole (on the outskirts of Belfast) advertised as *"the bout that was banned in Belfast".* On the card too was a top class tag match in Hamill & Finlay vs. Dirty Darkie Arnott & Butcher Donald; the wrestling generation game.

Darkie Arnott: "Butcher and I used to form a tag team as two villains. What we used to do was I'd be in the corner and he'd be in the ring. And he'd get a headlock on one of our opponents and come running to me in the corner and I'd have my foot out through the ropes ready for Butcher to drive the other man's head into my boot. You'd tell the referee to way off of course. Then if you did it once or twice, and then did it again the man would then break free and push Butcher's head into my boot instead. The crowd would love it as the villains had got their comeuppance. It kept things going."

Going forward Orig William would feature Hamill, Monroe and Finlay frequently when he visited the Irish isle. Eventually he started offering them opportunities to wrestle in the UK too.

- - - - -

Kim Starr: "My future husband put his foot down. I think he was worried about all the men round me, he probably had right to be! It was a brilliant experience, travelling all over, I certainly enjoyed it."

After reffing around Ulster for nearly two years, that August of 1968 the real-life Rosemary Liddell got married and closed the Kim Starr chapter of her life. In later life Rosemary Gault worked as a secretary, and today in her 70s remains happily married. Though it's unknown how many times she's since resorted to the ear-twisting or back elbow smashes as a means of resolving a domestic dispute!

In Kim Starr's absence Syd Waddell resumed the role of the most reliable and trusted referee.

Kim Starr: "I'd still go to support the odd time though, sneak off when it was on nearby. Really all of us just wanted to support Davey. The whole family was behind him."

Around this time too, family matters played a part in a changing of the guard as 39 year old Darkie Arnott decided he needed to spend more time at home with his young family than at the Albion Street gym and so he handed over his half of the club to a man he knew had the same passion for pro wrestling as he did, 32 year old Dave Finlay.

Dave Finlay: "Darkie was giving up his third of the club so I decided I'd buy into it, then it was me, Dave Mack and Stan Cooke who run the gym. I then made sure the guys who came into it were well-trained. I wanted them to show up early, and if they didn't show up to train, they didn't get onto shows. It was disciplined that way. Guys used to come in their suits to the club and not do anything, showed up just for shows. I put a stop to all that."

Bruce McDonald: "Dave Finlay was a really good motivator. He instilled confidence in you, you believed what he said, and he had your back. He wasn't a bully, he would take it as good as he got without complaints."

Dave Finlay: "I taught shoot wrestling because you never know when a guy was going to take advantage of you, so you needed to be able to defend yourself. You wanted guys who knew how to present themselves in front of a crowd, how to hold themselves in the ring. You wanted a high standard, a good product. It was a brotherhood."

Dave Finlay took over as the head coach at the Milo Wrestling Club and with his amateur acumen acclimated incredibly well. Finlay wasn't someone who listened to excuses nor suffered fools gladly, and his stricter stance on who should he eligible to appear on live wrestling shows meant those who didn't attend training regularly missed out on getting matches. Many who fell victim to the new modus operandi were those busy elsewhere with body-building. Being physically fit was all important of course but more time weight-lifting might mean less time learning the finer techniques to wrestling holds and throws, and so slowly but surely fewer bodybuilders became pro wrestlers.

However, there were still those in the Milo club who balanced both well, Strangler Stan Cooke and his friend Strongman Harry Corr for example. Cooke remained a constant at the gym and on cards, with Harry Corr his sparring partner in shoot wrestling. Both muscle men being very skilled at shooting.

Even with the changes a large collective within the club respected Dave Finlay and his decision to weed out the weaker links while showcasing the cream of the crop. The thrilling two of Mike Judo Hamill and Whirlwind Monroe as well submission specialist Noel Ewart, accomplished amateur Roy Digger Lynch, solid shooter Bruce McDonald and hard-hitter Dave Stalford all accepted Finlay as the leader of their grappling gang and earned the reward of regular matches.

Also, while his sister-in-law Rosemary was finished with wrestling, that year Dave convinced his older brother Billy Finlay (the brother he'd survive the blast with during World War II) to join the Albion Street gym, making him the third of the Finlay family involved in wrestling.

35 year old Billy Finlay's stint as a wrestler was short, and not altogether sweet, but it did include tag team matches with his brother as "The Finlay Bros" and even a possible appearance as The Mummy!

Billy Finlay: "Davey had been doing it a few years, and he really enjoyed the wrestling, it took up all his spare time. So he wanted me to give it a go, and I did, but I couldn't make it as a wrestler. It just wasn't for me, so I packed it in. Just dreaded wrestling."

Someone who did adapt well to the wrestling was 18 year old apprentice carpenter Sean Montgomery, who even in his young age was already a judo prodigy and indeed was inspired into the ring by two former judo practitioners in Pat Red Kelly and Eddie Hamill.

Seany Rivers: "Well I was 18, and I liked watching wrestling on the TV, and Pat Red was a judo guy, and so was Eddie Hamill, and they'd left the judo totally to take up wrestling. So I went to Pat and asked him where I could train and Red directed me to Albion Street. So I was 18 years old, showed up to Albion Street – it took two buses to get to it, I had no car in them days – and the gym was really just a typical gym of its day. No frills about it, nothing fancy. So I introduced myself and three weeks later I had my first pro fight. It was because of the judo. I was a 2nd Dan in judo, an Irish international, fought for Northern Ireland, fought for Ireland. I found it easy to adapt. The break-falling system is almost identical. So the falling was straight forward. Really with the amount of judo I was doing and the level I was at with the judo, there wasn't much for me to pick-up other the showmanship side of it, which was probably the most enjoyable part of wrestling, playing to the crowd and winding them up or winding them down. Wrestling was fun that way".

Born March 6th 1950 in Belfast, Sean Montgomery was the youngest member of the Milo Wrestling Club, which at the time was largely a member-led experience.

Seany Rivers: "I think everybody coached each other. It was a thing of going in and trying stuff out, and working out moves. We all learned to know each other reasonable well. My first match was in the Buff's in Belfast and it was against Butcher Donald. I was young and he was old and the crowd hated him, they wanted to kill him. I was sort of a last minute stand-in that evening, so of course I had no wrestling boots, so I wrestled in my bare-feet. And that went down so well I think I became the only barefooted wrestler in the UK. It was a bit of a gimmick of mine, and with the judo it was only natural for me".

Sean was soon suited with a gimmick name too, given to him by Dave Mack, who remained the promoter and match-maker of local pro shows.

Seany Rivers: "Well some people already called me Seany, but it was Dave Mack who said to me, 'You look a bit like an Indian'. I'd very long hair then, down to my waist. This was the time of the Beatles and the Rolling Stones, it was the swinging '60s, and it was a very good image for the time. So Dave Mack says, 'You look a bit like an Indian, so we'll call you Seany Rivers".

No doubt inspired by popular TV wrestler Billy Two Rivers, Seany Rivers balanced between wrestling and judo over the coming years. Seany competed on cards held in regular venues like the King George IV and the Queen's Hall in Newtownards, as well as summer festivals where sometimes the weather wasn't the only thing that got the crowds hot!

Seany Rivers: "Bruce McDonald and I were teaming in the Orange Hall in Carryduff against Butcher and Stan Cooke. And we were younger and they were older and bad-looking devils. We got a right duffin' up, and the crowd went bonkers, so much so the police came into the hall. The police were outside because of the traffic with the fete, but they had to come into the hall because they started throwing chairs around!"

- - - - -

Unfortunately, while Ulster's wrestling scene both in the local leagues and on the big bills was stronger than it had ever been before, by this point Northern Ireland was on the verge of civil war. There's been many books written about the period known as *The Troubles* in Northern Ireland and 1968 is generally considered the year when the conflict began in earnest as decades of tension between the two communities finally boiled over.

Owing to the turmoil, on October 5th George Connell Promotions and Relwyskow & Green presented their final ever feature at the huge King's Hall. It was headlined by Mick McManus vs. George Kidd, in what is the final found Irish appearance for McManus.

The Ulster Hall continued to be run semi-regularly on a monthly or bi-monthly basis as the World of Sport stars helped keep people's minds off the increasingly desperate situation.

- - - - -

Billy Joe Beck: "I had a friend, Henry Shirlow, 'Jack Flash Shirlow'. And Henry used to do racing, sidecar racing, and he was in a crash, and he hurt his neck. And he asked me if I could help him out as I was doing the physical training. Back then I was very very fit guy. So I started trying to help him and we went to a gym, and because I was a brown belt in judo at the time, I says 'come on, we'll do a few forward rolls and a few break falls' to try and get his neck strengthened up again. And eventually Henry says to me, because I was able to do the break falls and rolling so well, 'would you not be interested in the wrestling?'. And I sorta hemmed and hawwed, but then I went down the Sandy Row, and the training was good. As I said I was able to do the break falls and stuff like that, but then I had to learn wrestling moves and holds, and as time went on I got to like it."

While membership of the Milo Wrestling Club had peaked, there was still a steady stream of noteworthy new names coming through the ranks. One of them was 23 year old physical training instructor Billy Joe Beck.

Born in County Leitrim on March 22nd 1945, William Joseph "Billy Joe" Beck joined the army in England in the early 1960s before being re-stationed in Lisburn in the mid '60s, settling there and starting a family, before eventually meeting Henry Shirlow.

Billy Joe Beck: "Sandy Row and the training, it was a dirty wee place. Up stairs, rickety stairs. And when you finished training there was no showers. They had a set of weights in there, and they had the ring. And at the back of the ring was just a wall, a stone wall, and if you hit your head... The floor too, the canvas, was reasonably hard, but otherwise it was alright. In there you took the rough with the smooth. If you went in there you had to take a slap, as well as give one. If you went in there, some guys would try you out to see what you were like, and see if you could take it and give it. They trained you hard, and I went down faithfully. I used to get a bus, I had no car then, so I got a bus down to Sandy Row on a Tuesday, Thursday and Sunday. And if you show that sort of dedication, they knew you were interested to learn."

Billy Joe Beck wasn't the only one whose interest in wrestling started with Henry Shirlow. Henry's teenage nephew Ian Shirlow was another who fell in love with it from going to see his uncle wrestle. Indeed, whenever the cricket-playing wrestler recovered from his sidecar racing injury Jack Flash Shirlow made his much-anticipated in-ring return that November at the Lisburn Orange Hall vs. long-time rival Dave Finlay, with Ian in the audience.

Ian Shirlow: "I got the bug for it going to see my uncle wrestle. I remember one bout in particular very vividly. It was in Lisburn. Henry raced sidecar at Dundrod, on the motorbike circuit, and had had an accident. Henry got a serious neck injury, that put him out for a while from wrestling. But eventually he came back, and he was facing Dave Finlay and they knocked ten bells out of each other. The two of them, their bouts together were unbelievable. It was an art form. And Finlay knew about the injury, and Henry's brother, my other uncle was there too, and he was about to get in the ring to have a go at Finlay, because Finlay kept working on Henry's neck. The crowd was hanging off the rafters that night. Once I seen that, the crowd going absolutely bananas, I thought, that's for me."

After the bout Henry Shirlow promptly took another extended leave of absence to fully recover! However, the action-packed shows that Shirlow helped organise in Lisburn where still highly attended, and the town was such a top spot that on December 26th 1968, an annual tradition was born; wrestling on Boxing Day.

Billy Joe Beck: "Wrestling was always very popular on Boxing Day, there was great support for it. Especially when it was in Lisburn. It would have always been on early in the afternoon, so people could get back home to spend time with the family or what have you in the evening. They went on for years and years."

The very next day on December 27th 1968, the wrestling was in Portadown Town Hall with the main event match being local lad Elmer Bendix vs. Butcher Donald for the new new new "Middleweight Championship of Ireland". This version of the middleweight title (like the one from World War II) was also represented by a trophy, with Butcher being the champion after defeating Dave Finlay for the honour over the summer – after Finlay traded the title back and forth with Jack Flash Shirlow the previous year.

Elmer Bendix: "I was actually a butcher during the time I was wrestling. It's a hard game, you had to have strength to be at it. I was a butcher and Butcher Donald wasn't! I think actually I quit after that match with Butcher. It was a good bout and he beat me in end up. Butcher was a good wrestler too, a crafty bugger. I had wrestled him quite a few times. It was the travelling that had me quit, it was travelling through the troubled places and never knowing what might happen. That was part of it, and I decided I'd have enough injuries. I got my teeth loosened. I bit through my tongue. One night in Ballymena I was in a tag team, and I ended up getting threw over the ropes and hit my shoulder hard, and I got back in and wrestled on, but see after a couple hours, I thought my shoulder had exploded. I did bouncing afterwards, in place of it I think. We didn't do the wrestling for the money, there was none. We did it for the love of it. Though it was tough and hard and you got injured, you enjoyed it."

25 year old Elmer was by then a master butcher at the *Denny's* meat factory in Portadown. The sectarian violence spreading throughout the North playing a part in his decision to lock-up for one of his last times.
     Elmer Benson was the last in Portadown's legacy in pro wrestling in the 20th century as the town would still host shows but wouldn't produce anymore pros. As a youth leader at the YMCA in Portadown in the mid 1970s, Elmer did attempt to get a wrestling club off the ground but without success.

        Interestingly, Elmer Bendix actually made a mini-comeback with some final found matches in 1980 (12 years between found matches) before finishing with pro wrestling forever.
        Today aged in his late 70s Elmer Benson lives a happily retired life in Portadown. He enjoys gardening and fishing. Notably, Elmer now has something he didn't when he was wrestling; American citizenship, owing to when he tracked down his father, an American soldier during World War II, whom he'd never met.

Elmer Bendix: "My Dad came over here at the end of '41. He was a military policeman and he was here to show the soldiers some things. My mother and him were going to get married but then the army moved him to Africa. Then in Africa he got wounded, he got seven bullets in his shoulder, and one of them they could never get out, he carried that the rest of his life, always trouble at airports. Anyway, in '92 I finally met him over in America. My wife had written to the army and they said they would deliver the letter to him, but they give us nothing in terms of a number or address. I think when he got it, it probably scared the life out of him. But eventually there was contact made and I went over to Lexington in Kentucky and met him, and recognised right him away because he looked just like me!"

1969

Billy Joe Beck "My first show was in a marquee in Drumquin. That was my first show, I'll always remember that. Was with a guy called Whipper Watson, who was deaf and dumb. Whipper used to carry a little notebook with him, and a pen. And he'd write you a note, and you'd have to answer him back, and he'd write you another note. That was just the way he talked to you by writing notes. He was a barber's model I believe, because he had this lovely head of hair, always styled, you'd swear it was a wig but it wasn't. I think he modelled for barbers, because I think there was photos up here, there and everywhere of the Whippers head and his hairstyles. Anyway, I didn't win."

On May 8th 1969 at a festival in the tiny Tyrone village of Drumquin it was the blonde-haired, sturdy and straight wrestling Billy Joe Beck vs. the wily Whipper Watson. This event as well as another festival in Newtownstewart a month later were promoted by P.G. McQuaid, a Dungannon businessman who also worked with Sean O'Shea and Orig Williams from time to time around the Tyrone area.

Billy Joe Beck would go on to wrestle regularly, his endless energy from being a fitness fanatic being a big positive. He was capable of some spectacular moves too like the "sunset flip" that involved leap-frogging over an opponent's head, and rolling them into a pinfall in the same movement.

- - - - -

That same summer the British Army were deployed in Northern Ireland and in a buy-out George Connell give over the King's Hall to the government so the army could take up base there; closing the ice rink for good.

To the credit of Relwyskow & Green they would continue to send top talent like Jackie Pallo, the Royal Brothers and the villainous Jim Breaks to the Ulster Hall on a monthly or bi-monthly basis, depending on the severity of the situation in the North.

- - - - -

Humorously, however dark, wrestling has a long history of playing up to turbulent times – what with its wrestling "Nazis" during World War II – and so for a short time a tag team called "The Rebels" were a feature on shows. The name being in reference to the Irish rebellion against the British, the team sometimes consisted of Seany Rivers and Dave Stalford and was actually a cross-community tag team featuring a Catholic and a Protestant.

Seany Rivers: "Davey Stalford and I became The Rebels, but we both far from that – Davey especially! We wore masks, really it was to help hide our identity. But because of the situation here we had to stop that very quickly because people took it seriously. We played it up so much it nearly became a dangerous situation. I remember we were out in Ballyclare, maybe at the town hall there, and they seemed ready to wreck the place."

That summer, particularly that August, acted as an intersection for several veterans of the Irish scene as Butcher Donald went into a semi-retirement and Tiger Joe Moore finished for good as a pro wrestler.

After eight years of wear and tear on his body, 38 year old Butcher decided to rest himself as a wrestler and started to referee whenever possible. The role of ref wasn't as physically demanding as it once was, but it still required a talented and trustworthy individual and Butcher was just that.

While 44 year old Joe wrestled his final found match as Tiger Joe Reynolds vs. Bruce McDonald in Carrickfergus Town Hall as part of its *Back Carrick Week* festival that August of 1969. Joe bowing out owing to age, injury and health concerns. A fan of western movies and classical music in his spare time, Joe was the last local level wrestler left who'd competed as a pro in the 1940s.

Butcher's time away from in-ring action on live events was temporary, Tiger Joe's permanent, but both men stuck about the Albion Street gym and became the coaches of the beginner classes for the Milo Wrestling Club. Sunday was the advanced class, reserved for N.I. Wrestling Association roster members, and sometimes taken by Dave Finlay. Tuesday and Thursday acted as the nights for novices to come along and learn the craft, and so over the next few years nearly every new local level wrestler got their start by being taught by short taxi man Butcher Donald and skinny shipyard worker Tiger Joe Moore.

Butcher and Tiger Joe continued in their passion for pro wrestling in different capacities but the same sadly couldn't be said for Whipper Watson whose time in wrestling ended unceremoniously.
 That unfortunately eventful August of 1969 the real-life Billy Watson was injured in a machine accident at the factory where he worked and lost sight in one of his eyes. Being deaf, mute and partially blind was a disability too many to overcome, and so after 15 years the Whipper was forced to quit pro wresting age 32. In 1974 the lifelong native of Dhu Varren in Belfast was awarded $15,000 (£157,000 today) in compensation for the accident.
 Though he wasn't around wrestling anymore, one of the men Billy did remain friendly with was Noel Ewart. The considerate Ewart learned sign language so he could communicate with his old wrestling buddy whenever they would watch football matches together at their local bar (the Whipper was a *Liverpool FC* supporter). A keen traveller Billy Watson would see sights around the world before passing away in October 2017 age 80.

That September the N.I.W.A. tried bringing both sides of the community together with a peace-building event at the King George VI but unfortunately the venue's position in the centre of Belfast was to its detriment. The event was cancelled as travelling became more difficult, with the army setting up road blocks to stop riots and checkpoints to search cars for weapons and explosives.
 After a final found show in 1970, the home of local level wrestling for seven years wouldn't promote wrestling anymore. Eventually the King George VI was abandoned, and today the site of the youth centre on May Street is a car park.
 This failed event was also the final finding of the Northern Ireland Wrestling Association who quietly disbanded with Dave Mack and Strangler Stan Cooke both no longer interested in promoting or organising wrestling shows during the turbulent times as riots, shootouts and bombings became more and more common.

- - - - -

Dave Finlay was left as the sole promoter of the local leagues and, in order to successful organise shows going forward, he turned to those he trusted the most for help. His family.

Planning for the future, Finlay was even beginning to bring his 9 year old son Dave Junior by the Albion Street gym. The elder Finlay slowly breaking his boy into pro wrestling – a passionate past-time that was soon to become a full-on family business for the Finlays.

Dave 'Fit' Finlay Junior: "I thought my Dad was Superman. All I was interested in was wrestling, I was fascinated by it. I'd been up at the gym on Albion Street as a kid in the '60s, and I think the first person I ever got in the ring with was Butcher Donald. That was my first introduction to it, and it got better and bigger from then on."

Dave Finlay launches himself like a rocket into Darkie Arnott during a live wrestling event in the late 1960s
The referee is wrestler "Johnny Glenn"

Chapter 10

Finlay Family Business & The Mastery of Kung Fu

1970

Dave Finlay: "During the Troubles this was the only entertainment about. My approach was to always try and sell the shows, so we'd have guaranteed money. There was a lot of festivals on then, and what I would do is get in contact with all the festivals, as well as the priest of every parish and come the summertime we would be going full at it. I would have to have two rings going sometimes. My wife Evelyn ran the accounts. She was my secretary. She would have handled the money, kept books, filled out any forms, made sure everything was running like clockwork. She was key to it all. Then my kids were experts at putting rings up. On show days we'd hire a van, get them off school for the day, and the three of us would build the ring."

Dave Finlay might have been the head honcho of Irish wrestling but as the saying goes behind every great man was a great woman and that great woman was Dave's wife Evelyn. Evelyn Finlay sorted out all the logistics of the shows for her working class promoter husband.

One of the first solo shows organised by the Finlay family was for the social club at the *ICI Fibres* factory in Kilroot, near Carrickfergus, which employed a huge workforce. Shows were also hosted on the floor of *Rothman's Cigarette Factory*, another of Carrickfergus biggest businesses. Dave Finlay quickly became known as the man about town for wrestling, and developed a good relationship with the local council in the process.

Dave Finlay with his dog Bruno and Darkie's dog Rex
Even the Finlay family pet was involved in the wrestling!

Undeterred by the dire situation in Northern Ireland, Finlay sought to promote shows anywhere and everywhere in the province. Though army and police checkpoints meant travelling from town to towns could be a hassle, Dave brought pro wrestling for the first time to many villages, where live local entertainment was greatly appreciated. Busy especially in the summer season with festivals, for the next few years Finlay and his stable of strong shooters thrilled in marquees in tiny townlands like The Loup, Ardboe and Glenravel, as well as around hotels, town halls, village halls, GAA halls, Orange halls, working men's clubs, pubs and wherever else they could fit a ring into.

Dave Finlay Snr with two of his best and most reliable roster members Jimmy Rodgers and Noel "Ace Mooney" Ewart

Dave Finlay: "The lads we had we didn't need to fly big names over all the time because our own guys were that good."

Pat Red Kelly: "If somebody said 'aw it's a fix', you'd say 'OK, you come try it. If I put you down, you buy this. If you beat me, I'll buy that'. You made it a challenge, a stake so it was something to prove and a price to pay physically and money-wise too. You'd have big

farmer boys up and down the country saying, 'ah I could beat you', but they hadn't a chance. We knew what we were doing, how to get them in a hold and have them squealing like a pig."

Bruce McDonald: "It wasn't as tight with us. You went out there and you had fun. You had the finish, you knew who was winning, but you worked the rest of it out there. Though I do remember one person in particular was very annoyed I won a coin toss to go over. Davey Finlay had flipped a coin and said, 'call it', I called it heads, 'right heads you're going over', and the person was not very happy about that. Some people could be like that. Though the rationale was nobody was going to hurt each other because if that's their living, you got to let them keep their living. And even if it wasn't their living, it wasn't mine, I had a day job, most of us had day jobs, you shouldn't effect somebodies ability to work."

The country might have been divided by politics determined by religion but the wrestling wasn't. The lads came from both sides of the community and worked together without identity ever being an issue.

Pat Red Kelly: "At the height of the Troubles we were a mixed bunch but we never talked about it, what was there to say? 'I was born a Catholic, this other fella was born a Protestant', so what? Who cares? It had nothing to do with wrestling. You could be up the Shankill Road wrestling one week, then down the Falls Road wrestling the next. Nothing ever said, you just got on with it."

When he wasn't a fan favourite, 28 year old Pat Red Kelly was one of "The Undertakers". The Undertakers were a villainous tag team in black masks who wore bowler hats on their way to the ring. Another ghoulish gimmick in similar vain to "The Mummy".

Pat's tag team partner in The Undertakers was usually a Belfast wrestler called Roy "Crusher" Hanna, who specialised in villainry. The Crusher, real name Bill Stockman, had actually been about from when the Milo Wrestling Club was founded at Jackie Briers gym in the early '60s, but wrestled only sporadically before reappearing in the early '70s.

Pat Red and Crusher Hanna as The Undertakers were a top tag team on the Irish wrestling scene, and took advantage of the turbulent times by playing up to the conflict during performances (or at least Hanna did!)

Pat Red Kelly: "Crusher Hanna and I were the Undertakers. We got on well. I used to go round to his house on the Shankill Road, we were friends like. Anyway, one night we were up at Broughshane and he'd said before to me, 'here Red, do you have a cross?', meaning a crucifix. I said, 'aye', he said, 'can I have a lend of it?'. So we're on the show, and we're the bad boys in the hoods. But then he takes out the crucifix and gets down on one knee, and crosses himself like he's at a Catholic mass! Oh boy, the crowd they did not like that. I had to follow suit, and get down on one knee beside him and I was like 'Jesus Christ, Roy you're gonna get us killed'. He said, 'you not listening Red? This'll get us more work'. A wrestler's mind like!"

- - - - -

Meanwhile Orig Williams was so taken by the talent of Judo Mike Hamill and Whirlwind Monroe (who'd both since been over to wrestle in England and Wales with him) as well as Dave Finlay that the Welshman would purposely leave some spots open on his bills for the terrific trio to fill whenever he'd cross the Irish sea.

At a show for Orig on May 19th 1970 at the *Starlight Ballroom* in County Louth, Hamill had just finished his match when a big fellow from the crowd – who'd been giving the wrestlers grief all night – jumped into the ring and demanded one of them fight him. The tale of this incident has since become folklore in Irish wrestling history. The big fellow was 27 year old Johnny Howard.

Eddie Hamill: "I think we were in Dundalk, and Johnny came along with his mates, sat in the front row and as the show went on started shouting, 'Load of rubbish! I could do better than that'. You know just shouting abuse with all his mates. And it was at the end of the show, and it was for Orig Williams, and Johnny's shouting 'Come on I'll wrestle any of ya! I'll wrestle any of ya!'. And all the punters were staying, they weren't moving out of the hall, they wanted to see what was going to happen.

Born in County Kildare in 1943, Johnny Howard lived in England for a while before making Carrickmacross in County Monaghan his home. Shockingly at this time he was actually employed at a different hotel as security?? However, had Howard been the bouncer at this event no-one would dare have tried to hijack it as at around 6'4 and 17st with a big beard, long hair and a mean mug Johnny looked more frightening than some of the wrestlers on the show!

Eddie Hamill: "So in the back Orig says, 'what are we going to do, the punters won't leave, he wants to fight somebody?'. So I said, 'here I'll fight him Orig'. Orig says, 'bloody hell Eddie, he's huge, you're going to fight him?' I said, 'yeah I've nothing to lose', I was only like 11½ or 12 stone, but I thought if he beats me, means nothing, because he's a bigger fella. Nut if I win, different story. So anyway I went out to the ring and Johnny's mates had all put money up, I think it was about a tenner, which was a few quid then. So we're in the ring, and I knew he wasn't fit, so I worked him round, worked him round. And he was starting getting out of breath, so I knew I had him. And so I put a choke on him, and he flaked out, tapped out, and that was it over, and I got the tenner! After it he actually shook hands with me, and we eventually became best of friends."

Dave Finlay: "After that I thought the only thing to do with this guy is just bring him into it. Better having a guy like that on our side."

When Eddie Hamill had walked back out to the ring, Dave Finlay had stood watching on from the wings, confident that the judo brown belt could handle himself but ready to rumble just in case some of the big bouncer's friends interfered. It was then when Finlay saw the sheer size of Johnny Howard he knew there was a star to be made. So despite the decisive defeat (and after the audience finally left) Dave caught up with Johnny in the car park and offered to train him to become a pro wrestler – so that next time he got in a ring in front of a crowd he'd be a properly trained paid participant instead of an unruly out-of-pocket punter. Johnny accepted the offer

- - - - -

Rather than risk a southern-sounding accent on the Sandy Row (where the Milo Wrestling Club was based) Johnny Howard and his truck driver friend Brian Tumelty soon started taking the long trip up from Carrickmacross in the South to Greenisland in the North for training sessions with Dave Finlay at his house. The humbled Johnny Howard learned the craft by locking up with Finlay in his living room and being thrown about the back garden either side of a peaceful Sunday dinner with the Finlay family.

Outside of lessons from Finlay, Howard got into shape by cycling, running and weight-lifting, by his own admission at times he sometimes training up to three hours a day.

Dave Finlay: "Johnny and another fellow would then come up to my house on a Sunday, we'd move everything back in the living room and try out some moves. Or we'd try it in the garden. And Johnny got really really good."

That June wrestling – at a local level – returned to the Guildhall in Derry for the first time in over 13 years. Dave Finlay broke away from breaking in Johnny Howard to do battle with another long-distance grappler with whom he'd become great friends with; 33 year old security guard Mickey Gallagher.

Dave Finlay: "Mickey Gallagher from Derry was a good friend, wrestled as Mick Shannon. He trained with a guy called John Doherty from Draperstown I think. Mickey would have come down to our gym an odd time, and I think him and Doherty trained together in Castledawson. Mick was a great guy."

Born in Derry on January 6th 1937, a teenage Michael "Mickey" Gallagher had seen the stars of Worldwide Promotions in the Guildhall in the '50s. Mickey even trained with the Derry Wrestling Club at Andy McClea's gym, but never got the chance to compete on a show. After spending several years serving in the Irish Army, Gallagher's interest in pro wrestling was reignited when he discovered the Albion Street gym and began travelling there along with his factory worker friend John Doherty.

Choosing "Shannon" in reference to Ireland's biggest river, Mick Shannon had debuted with N.I.W.A. in 1969. Instilled with confidence from cards he'd been on, in 1970 helped organise an event at the Guildhall. Leaving the wrestling logistics to the boys in Belfast, Mick's greatest concern on the card was making sure no damage was done to the treasured hall during the show – in particularly no-one was to throw anything for fear of chipping or breaking the hugely expensive windows around the building.

That June evening at the Guildhall the main event was fan favourite Mick Shannon vs. the hated Dave Finlay. Dave thankfully didn't have to rough up any ring invaders (less the finance committee lose its mind again) but he did take a bit of a battering from the disgruntled grannies defending "our Mickey" with loaded handbags and sharpened umbrellas their weapons of choice.

Having Mick Shannon in Derry meant the city would host many more wrestling cards going forward, with Finlay periodically bringing a car or two of wrestlers across the country to compete in the Guildhall, or the *Marian Hall* in the Shantallow area.

Mick Shannon (right) throws John Doherty during a training session with the Milo Wrestling Club at 33 Albion Street in Belfast

- - - - -

As the local scene strengthened itself in spite of the tense times, across the Atlantic one tough Tyrone man survived a very different hostile environment to become the first Northern Irish wrestler to compete for the legendary Hart family and their *Stampede Wrestling* promotion.

Peter McElhatton was born in Pomeroy on May 28th 1927 and as a teenager moved to England. It was there in the '50s that Peter – by then in his 20s and working as a tradesman – took an interest in amateur wrestling. Small in stature but powerful in winning prime position on the mat Peter became a decorated amateur competitor. As a member of the *Irish Amateur Wrestling Association* Peter proudly represented his home nation by taking home trophy after trophy from battles with some of the UK's best.

However it really wasn't until he and his wife Mary took the long trip to Canada to start a new life for themselves in late 1967 that Peter took an intrigue in turning pro. By then into his 40s and retired from amateur wrestling, it was through striking up a friendship with highly respected pro wrestler Stu Hart that Peter would finally be convinced to step in between the ropes.

In the summer of 1970 McElhatton, regarded as a highly skilled stone mason, was hired by Stu to extend the deck and porch of the Hart family mansion. When the work outside the house was done for the day, Peter would then be welcomed inside and down to the basement, to the infamous "Hart dungeon" – where Stu would train (though reports have always likened it closer to torture, hence the 'dungeon' name) prospective wrestlers. Stu pushed men to the breaking point to see if they had what it takes to be deemed worthy of appearing on the shows he promoted under the banner of Stampede Wrestling. And while many never returned after just one of Stu's shoot style sessions, some of those who braved the dungeon went on to become world renowned wrestlers. Though this fame wasn't in Peter McElhatton fortunes the Pomeroy man still held his own and earned Stu's respect enough to be taught the tricks of the pro style, and soon was booked onto Stampede bills.

That October of 1970 43 year old Peter McElhatton competed on cards in the Alberta area of Canada that also featured infamous bloody brawler Abdullah the Butcher.

Peter soon realised the pro ring wasn't for him and hung up his wrestling boots for good shortly thereafter, but he is the only known Ulsterman to train in the Hart dungeon and the first to compete on cards for Canada's most famous wrestling family.

A man of many talents who along with his wife was heralded as a great helper of fellow Irish immigrants to Canada, Peter would regularly return to Ireland to stay at a holiday house in Cookstown in his native Tyrone, doing so up until his passing in August 2017 at 90 years old. To the end Peter McElhatton, survivor of the Hart dungeon, remained rightfully proud of his time in the world of wrestling, both in his amateur accomplishments and short but noteworthy stint as a pro.

Peter McElhatton with his amateur wrestling trophies

- - - - -

As well as working with wrestlers down South and across the province, Dave Finlay always maintained a great working relationship with Orig Williams.

Orig was especially an asset when it came to sourcing women's wrestlers for shows as the Welshman was the #1 promoter of girl fights in British wrestling. So if one of Finlay's festivals requested it, William would send over two of his fiercest females. Similarly the door swung both ways and whenever Orig was in need of top Irish talent for his tours he'd ring up Dave Finlay and take his pick of the recommendations.

That November, for the first time since World War II, homegrown headlockers were featured prominently in a fixture at the Ulster Hall as the Welshman promoted a special "Ulster vs. Great Britain" themed show. Finlay, Judo Mike Hamill, Whirlwind Monroe and Dave Stalford were all in action on the bill as "Team Ulster" would walk out the winners with the score 2-1 (with an indecisive draw the other contest). Dave Mack was also the MC on this event (his first appearance in a wrestling ring in the Ulster Hall in 28 years) and Butcher Donald was the referee.

- - - - -

Notably, while Darkie Arnott and Strangler Stan Cooke did stay on as wrestlers after the N.I. Wrestling Association ceased to exist, Dave Mack assumed complete ownership of the Milo Wrestling Club and the Albion Street gym.

The 57 year old former Irish welterweight champion was by then a married man, and even after 30 years experience in pro wrestling was still in love with it. Dave Mack tried his best to draw in more trainees including advertisements in the newspapers offering coaching to men and, for the first time explicitly, to women. Sadly though these ads didn't pull in the same interest that brought together the class of '64. However with Butcher Donald as the de facto head coach (Dave Finlay often busy with promoting, though still showing up to take sessions from time to time), the Milo club would see several significant new names emerge in 1971…

ULSTER HALL, BELFAST

WRESTLING

TO-MORROW (SAT.), NOV. 14, at 7.30 p.m.
Doors open 6.30 p.m.

SENSATIONAL HEAVYWEIGHT CONTEST

THE WILDMAN FROM BORNEO v. **AL MARTINELLI**
The Incredible Half-Man, Half-Animal — Dynamic Anglo-Italian Star

SPECIAL TEAM CHALLENGE CONTEST

ULSTER v. GT. BRITAIN

WHIRLWIND MUNRO v. **JACK DEMPSEY**
(Belfast) Irish Welterweight Champ — (England) British Welterweight Champ

JUDO MIKE HAMILL v. **ORIG WILLIAMS**
Ulster's Top Wrestling Judo Star — Dynamic All-Action Welshman

DAVE FINLAY v. **GORDON CORBETT**
Ulster's Most Aggressive Middleweight — Midland Area Mid-Heavyweight Champ

DAVE STALFORD v. **WILD JOCK CAMPBELL**
The Toughest Heavyweight in Ireland — Ferocious Bearded Highlander

SEATS: 20/-; 15/-; 10/-; 6/-. Advance Bookings —
THE ATHLETIC STORES, WELLINGTON PLACE, BELFAST
Telephone 20491

Ulster Hall, November 14th 1970
"Wild Jock Campbell" was another phoney Scottish wrestler who from time to time teamed with Ireland's own faux Scot Wild Angus

One of the most unique settings for Irish wrestling started at the very end of this year when a Belfast nightclub called *The Piccadilly Line* began presenting *"Wrestling-Cum-Cabaret"* every Tuesday night from late December 1970 to mid May 1971. At these events live wrestling matches would be held prior to a full cabaret act. The big, burly men would batter each other from post to post, and then the audience turned to a stage and enjoyed the rest of the evening's entertainment that might include stand-up comedy, singers or more risque performances like burlesque.

It was definitely a very interesting backdrop for top bouts like Finlay vs. Shirlow, and Hamill vs. Monroe, but unfortunately these wrestling-cum-cabaret collaborations were short-lived. In late '71 The Piccadilly Line was destroyed in a paramilitary attack that thankfully no-one was injured in.

Dave Finlay: "There was quite a bit of publicity for them. First time it was ever happening in Ireland. But before we got another season out of it, they blew the place up. Guess that's how bad we were!"

Tug Wilson: "Dave was a good promoter. I worked a few of his shows. He had a good teacher in wrestling in Darkie."

Since Larry Casey's death, performing on live wrestling events hadn't been a priority for Eric Wilson. However in 1969 he'd got back into bouts on some festival shows at the local level and put on some particular great bouts vs. fellow gymnastics gem Dave Finlay.

Dave Finlay: "Tug Wilson and I had some good matches together. We both had a background in gymnastics. He was an all-round guy."

Seany Rivers: "I trained with Tug in Breen's Health Studio, a few of the wrestlers trained there, Harry Corr would've trained there too. Breen's Health Studio would have been the in-place to train at the time. It was run by 'Mr. Ireland' Winston Stewart. Tug and I used to do security around dance halls and that too. It was fairly well paid, and it wasn't that difficult then, people were fairly well behaved."

Working the door as a bouncer would in fact play a pivotal part in the future wrestling fortunes of Eric Wilson...

Meanwhile 20 year old wrestling and judo star Seany Rivers was getting more and more interested in weight-lifting, adding it as another recreation in his busy sporting life. Although an injury this year halted his wrestling for a time, the resilient multi-sport star recovered well and less than a year later in the spring of 1971 travelled to Cork and took home the title of Irish Junior Olympic Weight-lifting Champion.

Seany Rivers: "I did have a bad fall once at the Guildhall in Derry, I went for a dropkick and came down very badly on my shoulder. That required two operations. But ten months later I won the Irish Junior Olympic Weightlifting Championship. I was always a weight-lifter more than a bodybuilder, and when I say Olympic it's nothing to do with the Olympics, it's just that what they called the style of the lifting. I was very proud of that, especially when coming back from a shoulder injury".

- - - - -

Also this year, Eric Wilson was back too working on the undercard for George Connell Promotions at the Ulster Hall supporting the likes of Les Kellett (in his fourth decade in Irish rings), Johnny Saint (then signed to Joint Promotions) and Mr. TV Jackie Pallo in the final full year for Relwyskow & Green in Northern Ireland.

1971

Billy Joe Beck: "We were down at Sandy Row training, and who was over when we went down to train? Arthur Green from Joint Promotions. He lived in Leeds, but he had come over as they done the shows at the Ulster Hall. We were in the ring, and of course then when we found out they were over looking to see what the talent was like over here for wrestling we were in there trying to impress."

Bruce McDonald: "We all did an audition in Albion Street and Arthur Green just picked who he wanted from it."

It was the two worlds of wrestling in Belfast colliding as the big bills turned to the local leagues (for the first time since the War) for assistance. Relwyskow & Green had been finding it harder to convince the stars of World of Sport to travel to Belfast – that had developed a reputation as one of the world's four "B" destinations for tourists to avoid, the other B's being Bosnia, Beirut and Baghdad – and so co-promoter Arthur Green visited the Milo Wrestling Club to scout the talent.

That April it was unsurprisingly Judo Mike Hamill vs. Whirlwind Monroe in the Ulster Hall on a George Connell Promotion. Unusual was their typical show-stealing routine wasn't well-received by Arthur Green who let it be known to the two afterwards. It was criticism that Eddie would take to heart and make Green and his associates quite literally pay for in the future…

As the Troubles took their toll, Relwyskow & Green decided Northern Ireland wasn't worth risking anymore and so May 29th was their final show at the Ulster Hall, with the technically-talented 23 year old Bruce McDonald and Eric Wilson both on the bill. After a festival event in Belfast on June 28th 1971 – also featuring Bruce McDonald in a bout vs. Jimmy Rodgers – the Englishmen pulled their promotions completely. It was the end of an era. After 23 years George de Relwyskow stopped running wrestling events in Ireland.

These wrestling shows too were to be the last live entertainment promoted by George Connell, who quietly retired thereafter. By then all of the other boxing bigwigs of the 1930s/40s like Jim Rice, the Joseph brothers and J.C. had all passed away, and upon his own passing in 1977, aged in his 70s, George Connell was remembered as one of Ireland's greatest fight night organisers.

George Connell
Working alongside Relwyskow & Green, Connell was the promoter of pro wrestling in Ireland for 23 years from 1948 to 1971

That March ex-Army man Mick Shannon as well as Judo Mike Hamill and Whirlwind Monroe worked a few shows in the South for promoter Brian Dixon. Dixon was an Englishman who founded his own wrestling company in 1970 that would become best known by the name *All Star Wrestling*. Similar to his set-up with Sean O'Shea, initially Orig Williams and Brian Dixon worked together. However, they stopped collaborating after a messy split when Dixon got romantically involved with one of the retired footballer's biggest box office attractions, Mitzi Mueller.

Respectively, All Star Wrestling left the North to the local lads, and only ran sporadic shows in the South as Orig was for all purposes untouchable in terms of running live events in the Republic of Ireland. In time, Orig and Dixon became the top two independent / opposition promoters in British wrestling.

Meanwhile since his maverick start in the wrestling business Johnny Howard had developed into a formidable heavyweight, and debuted in a tag team with Brian Tumelty as "The Irish Rebels"; a gimmick somehow even more questionable than his original decision to jump the ring.

Dave Finlay: "The Irish Rebels were Johnny Howard and that other fella, and you'd have them wear green, white & gold. Then you'd have them on with guys dressed in red, white & blue. Places would be heaving. Do it in Carrickfergus one night, then Crossmaglen on another, play it both ways. Risky business."

Seeking to save travelling hours up the country each week, Howard and Tumelty actually founded the *Carrickmacross Wrestling Club* in November 1970 based out of the *Hotel Nuremore* where the former worked as a bouncer.

Howard and Tumelty in separate singles action or the Rebels as a tag team were the main event matches whenever they started promoting their own sporadic shows around Monaghan and Louth. Though while their wrestling club served as the South's first discernible pro wrestling school, it unfortunately didn't debut that many tenured mat-men and as a result wrestlers from the North often completed the cards in supporting roles. The popular pair of Judo Mike Hamill and Whirlwind Monroe were of course among the first called to action on Howard's promotions, and soon several others of Dave Finlay's wrestling stable were bringing their best in bouts around the South too.

- - - - -

Eddie Hamill and Hugh Beattie were in high demand across Ireland having worked for every wrestling promotion going, but that year the Troubles forced the terrific two apart when Eddie decided to get out of Belfast and start a new life.

Eddie Hamill: "When the Troubles started, there was a bit of trouble up where I lived in Belfast, and I just thought I'm not getting involved in this. So I phoned Orig Williams and I asked, 'is there any work over there Orig, over in Wales?'. And he said, 'Hamill, get on the next boat I have plenty of work for you', and that's what I done. I got a lorry in, packed all up, all the furniture and things, came over to Rhyl and that was the start of it."

The seaside town of Rhyl was the base of operations for Orig Williams. Rhyl was where (like the majority of big-time promoters in the UK) Orig ran an office to conduct business from, and the building also acted as accommodation for travelling wrestlers like Eddie and Whirlwind Monroe whenever they'd come over to wrestle previously as guest part-timers.
    That summer of '71, 27 year old Eddie Hamill decided to give up his carpet-fitting job in Belfast and make the permanent move to Wales to become a full-time pro wrestler, becoming the first homegrown hero of the ring to do so. It was far from your regular 9 to 5 job and as the Welshman knew no boundaries in promoting "Judo Ed" Hamill would be out on the road, driving to and from towns, wrestling, and repeating that week to week all over England, Scotland and Wales and bringing home more than £100 (nearly £1500 today) a week as a wrestler – just as his trainer Darkie Arnott predicted years before in the influential Belfast Telegraph advertisement.

Eddie Hamill: "The wives first impression was, 'why don't you grow up and get yourself a proper job?'. She always said that, she didn't like it. I can understand it because I was away six days a week, travelling all over. Back on a Sunday, day off then back on the road again on the Monday. So my kids never seen much of me, and the wife didn't, and that's why she didn't like it. Some of the other guys were good enough they could have went the whole way with it too. But Whirlwind had a business, so he only did the wrestling part-time. There was a lot of people like that, old Dave Finlay was the same. They had families, they didn't want to move, they preferred to have a job and wrestle as a hobby, you could understand it."

It wasn't the ideal lifestyle for some but by that point Eddie Hamill was arguably the best wrestler on the Irish scene and seeing the sights and entertaining thousands each week was more exciting to him than earning a living as a labourer.

As a firm fan favourite Judo Ed Hamill's travels as a journeyman wrestler weren't even limited to the British circuit, for Orig brought his wrestling bills into Europe and even as far as Africa.

Of course even though he wasn't wrestling in Ireland regularly anymore Eddie kept in touch with his mates. 32 year old Whirlwind Monroe sailed over to visit, stayed at the new Hamill family home in Rhyl and wrestled for a week or two with Orig every so often and Pat Red Kelly too would use his holiday time at work for some wrestling adventures with his old judo pal Eddie.

Paddy was a talented musician too with a great voice and so he'd even provide the after-party entertainment, playing guitar and singing while pints were being raised to a show well-done – traditional after every event for Orig Williams whose fondness for Ireland and the Irish extended naturally to Guinness.

Pat Red Kelly: "The few times I went over to Wales or England or the Isle of Man to wrestle I'd bring the guitar and have a session after the show. Few pints, Eddie would be there too, us being the Irish we had the craic. Working with the English was good. Eddie and I would even drive the ring van to make a few extra quid."

- - - - -

Though the Irish wrestling scene had lost one of its top talents, that same summer also offers the first findings for the newest action-men to be produced by the Albion Street wrestle factory. Among them 25 year old shipyard crane operator Cecil Brown.

Cecil 'Ricky Valentine' Brown: "My first name was Mickey Breen. Butcher Donald just said, 'you're Mickey Breen'. But I didn't like the name. So then they asked me to pick a name, and there was a guy over in America called Johnny Valentine who was wrestling at the time. I liked that name, but I didn't want to go as Johnny, so I just picked Ricky, Ricky Valentine. Definitely better name than Mickey Breen."

Born in Belfast on April 27th 1946, the tall, athletic, dark-haired and dashing Cecil Brown played football in his youth, was a talented swimmer, and a weight-lifter (who even worked out at Larry Casey's gym for a time) before joining the Milo Wrestling Club.

Ricky Valentine: "I started putting on a bit of weight, so I went down to this club that I knew about on Sandy Row to do some weight-training. What I didn't realise was they had a wrestling ring up, and a wrestling club going in the same building. So I was doing weights, and Butcher Donald, I didn't know him then but I certainly got to know him, come over and asked me if I wanted to get involved. I told him, 'nah I have no interest'. So he left me, but then came back ten minutes later, and said 'here, why don't you try it, and if you don't like it you can go back and do weights'. So I'll never forget, there was this big guy with a big beard on him like Desperate Dan, who I had to put in a headlock, and I swear I had this big beard rash down my right hand side afterwards. But actually as I done it, I got interested in it. And I got to eventually love wrestling. I'm not being bombastic but I was good at it, and when you're good at something you stick at it."

Naturally gifted at sports Cecil was soon show-ready and debuted as "Ricky Valentine" on bills for Butcher Donald.
	For a short time in the early '70s Butcher promoted his own shows with himself as the referee, Dave Mack as the MC and

some in-ring regulars including bus driver Billy "Buster" Shields (a lesser-known member of the Class of '64) and Butcher's own nephew Billy "Pastrano" Patterson, a forklift driver at the shipyard and considered something of a 'wild man'. The programmes for the Butcher bills advertised classes at the Milo club, largely took place in and around Belfast or surrounding areas, and relied on making money at the door rather than being sold shows.

Ricky Valentine and Dave Mack, in the 1970s

Ricky Valentine: "At first you had to do six shows without getting paid, it was like paying back the guys who trained you. After six shows you got paid, but let me tell you, you didn't really get paid, it was barely expenses. If you were trying to make a living at wrestling in Ireland, you were in the wrong trade."

"Ladies Favourite" Ricky Valentine shone right out of the gate as a grappler, but someone who took a little longer to find their feet was 21 year old blacksmith helper Dennis Millar.

Dennis 'Diamond Shondell' Millar: "I always watched wrestling when it was on TV, glued to it. Watched it on a Saturday afternoon like. I was fascinated by it. I liked Kellet. Mick McManus was big in them days. Steve Logan. Jackie Pallo. Soon after I left school, I started in the shipyard. And then somebody mentioned one day that there's a wrestler who worked round in the engine works, which was not too far from where I was working. And he was actually training wrestlers. And I went round to see him, and it was Joe Moore. And he says 'if you're interested, the place to go is up the Sandy Row, on Albion Street, above a place that fixes cars', so I went up there, and started training."

Born in Carrickfergus on September 6th 1950, the skinny, dark-haired and moustached Dennis Millar was among the first generation to grow up watching professional wrestling on TV, rarely missing World of Sport on a Saturday afternoon and occasionally watching the Wednesday night show too. Becoming aware of the Albion Street gym through Tiger Joe Moore, Dennis learned how to lock-up and everything thereafter from Butcher Donald. He then debuted on the taxi man's bills with the memorable ring name of "Diamond Shondell".

Diamond Shondell: "Diamond came from that whenever I'd go out, I always dressed up. I liked a nice suit, any trousers I wore I had to have the right buckle for them, always have nice shoes too. I loved jewellery, I wore like five rings. I liked the chains, a nice watch. And Shondell was the name of my favourite band the Shondells, they're from the '60s. I loved '60s music. Still do. So I put that that together."

Diamond Shondell settled well into the culture of the Milo Wrestling Club. Best known for bringing with him a good sense of humour, Diamond's in-ring persona wasn't defined yet and so he played it fairly straight on shows at the start.

When Butcher Donald's stint as a promoter ended Ricky Valentine and Diamond Shondell joined Dave Finlay's crew, with the latter always remembering or perhaps just never being able to forget the Sunday sessions taken by Ireland's then #1 promoter.

Diamond Shondell "There was one thing, dropkicks. You were taught whenever you hit someone a dropkick, the harder you hit them, the better a break fall you got. But if you go up and hit nothing, then your feet just go out and you drop down like a bucket of coal. That was painful. Used to be Dave Finlay would hold up a brush and you'd have to dropkick the brush. And if you got cocky, he'd move the brush and you'd go BAM to the ground. Well of course one day, I got cocky, and went up, he moved it, and I came crashing down, and I wasn't cocky after that like."

Training at the same time as Valentine and Shondell was 29 year old factory worker Ralph Hunter. While Ricky came into the club through Butcher, and Diamond was pointed in the right direction by Tiger Joe, it was another veteran of the Irish circuit who introduced the good-natured Ralph to the wrestling game.

Ralph 'Rocky' Hunter: "Years ago I worked as a machinist in Mackies, and I worked beside this big fella, and aw he was like the size of the Hulk, called Stan Cooke, and I didn't know at the time he was a wrestler. Working with him I got to know him pretty well, and he was a lovely guy, big gentleman. Anyway, Stan said to me one day, 'Ralph would you not think of coming down and giving the amateur a go?'. So he took me down to the club he was training at. And over time, I started getting good at it. Harry Corr was there too, doing the amateur. They'd have been good mates. And one day this guy called Dave Mack come along to a session and took me to the side, and asked if I'd ever thought about getting into professional wrestling. I really enjoyed the amateur but he talked me into it, so I joined the pro club."

Born in Belfast on March 2nd 1942, with a great big head of hair and a little black moustache Ralph Hunter was a fitness fanatic who came from a sporting family; his cousins Victor and Allan Hunter played football professionally, even being capped for Northern Ireland at international level. Initially interested in the shoot wrestling style that Stan Cooke and Harry Corr trained in at the Albion Street gym, Ralph was soon a very solid wrestler but did have to learn one lesson a particular harsh way whenever he apologised for his actions one night in the ring.

Rocky Hunter: "There was a guy there called Butcher Donald, and he trained us, and he was very very good. Though I mind one day we were training, and I was in with this big guy, and we were going back and forth, and I ended up hitting him a dropkick in the face, and he went right down. So me not being too long in the game, I give him a hand up and says, 'I'm sorry mate, are you OK?'. And yer man Butcher came over to me and says, 'did you do a dropkick there?', and I said, 'well I did my best', and he says, 'did you apologise to him there?', and I says 'aye', and he stuck one right on my jaw, decked me. Didn't like that I apologised for doing something well. They trained you hard in there."

Whenever he was set to debut on live events Ralph was given the gimmick name of "Rocky" Hunter. Though he was considered by his contemporaries as one of Irish wrestling's good guys in the locker-room, in the ring it was as a wrestling villain Rocky really excelled.

Maybe the most unique setting in which Rocky Hunter would play the part of a bad guy wrestler was at a Medieval-themed festival at *Carrickfergus Castle*. First ran from August 2nd to August 4th 1971 the local council provided a party like it was 1599. All those attending dressed like they'd come straight off the set of a William Shakespeare play and there would be food, drink and a variety of entertainment a plenty harkening back to ye olde days. Mixed in with the jesters, sword-fighting and archery was – no doubt inspired by the bard's play *As You Like It* – wrestling.

The set-up was simple; there was no ring, just a canvas with Dave Finlay usually acting in the role of the referee / MC while two wrestlers entertained for 10-20 minutes up to 2-3 times a night, and (long before people learned the power of the word "lawsuit") audience members could try their luck too before quickly paying the price of a bright red face – a little because of embarrassment and a lot because they'd just nearly had their head squeezed off by someone like Rocky.

Rocky Hunter: "I wrestled first for Dave Finlay. I really liked him, he looked after his wrestlers. He used to do these charity events in Carrickfergus Castle, like a medieval theme, everyone would be all dressed up. And they'd have us as entertainment, and you'd take turns being the champion for the night. The announcer would be all, 'Lords and Ladies, who will step up and challenge our champion tonight?', and you'd get these ones from the audience giving it a go, trying to beat you in a wrestling match. So you know, you'd let them go a bit then put them down. Well there was one night were I'd already wrestled three or four times, and this big lad could see I was tired and he wanted in, easy win he thinks. So Finlay could see the screw was in, so he stepped up, took my place and he annihilated that guy. Dave Finlay was a great wrestler, hardest man I ever wrestled. I know there was ones who wouldn't wrestle him because they were scared."

- - - - -

The dissolution of N.I. Wrestling Association led to some short-lived promotions by other wrestlers besides Butcher Donald, though fittingly it was to be one of Dave Finlay's long-time in-ring rivals who'd position himself as the next prominent local promoter.

Billy Joe Beck: "Shirlow, he was a bit of a Del Boy you know. He was the loveliest fella going, but he could sell snow to the Eskimos."

Retired sidecar racer Henry Shirlow was full of charisma, a smoothest salesman, and – as a coincidental parallel to Jack McClelland – helped bring in old boxer Rinty Monaghan (who had guest appeared for Worldwide Promotions in the '50s) as the special "presenter" of a short-term promoter's shows that summer. Rinty's propensity for singing as strong as ever.

Billy Joe Beck: "Rinty Monaghan used to be a world champion boxer so they'd used his name in promotions. There was a few shows we did with him, and there was one in Ballymena and Rinty loved to get in the ring and get on the microphone and sing. But when he went in, you couldn't get him out! So he'd be singing away, singing 'When

Irish Eyes Are Smiling' or 'Popeye'. You know, 'I'm Popeye the sailor man'. He'd just go on and on. So I had the idea, I went over to him in the dressing room and said, 'here's something we could do, you sing Irish Eyes, and then whenever you go into Popeye I'll come out with a few of the wrestlers and we'll carry you out of the ring, and you just keep singing away, the crowd will love it'. So it was a funny way to get him out of there and not offend him really."

That year 30 year old Henry Shirlow borrowed a boxing ring and started promoting his own shows, usually around the Lisburn area where he was well-known.

Billy Joe Beck: "He pulled them in when he was top of the bill, Lisburn especially. Henry was very popular in Lisburn as you'd expect he'd be."

Jack Flash Shirlow and Billy Joe Beck also won championships in 1971 that were noteworthy for being among the first ever titles on the Irish wrestling scene to be represented by physical belts. On October 11th 1971 Billy Joe Beck defeated Whirlwind Monroe at the Lisburn Orange Hall to win the new "Welterweight Championship of Ireland", and a fortnight later on October 27th 1971 at the *Top Hat Ballroom* in Lisburn Jack Flash Shirlow defeated Mick Shannon to become the first recognised *"Light-heavyweight Champion of Ireland"* – with Butcher Donald being the man in the middle for both bouts as the referee.
    The Top Hat was actually owned by George Connell and in the early 1960S the venue hosted some wrestling events. Unfortunately, like the Piccadilly Line, a year later in late '72 the Top Hat would be destroyed in a paramilitary bombing, ending Henry Shirlow's endeavours there and returning him to the local Orange Hall for live events.

Through Welterweight champ Billy Joe Beck's contacts at the local army barracks in Lisburn (though he'd since moved on to other work) he and Light-heavyweight title-holder Henry Shirlow were able to train at the gym there free-of-charge in their spare time.
    Someone who started joining Beck and Shirlow at their work-out sessions was 19 year old mechanic Dennis McMillan.

LISBURN ORANGE HALL
MONDAY, OCTOBER 11 1971

Light heavyweight Contest 10 x 5 min. round **Ricki Valentine** Recently unmasked the Red Devil V **Jackie Trent** Recently returned from a successful tour of France	The fight you have been waiting for? WELTERWEIGHT CHAMPIONSHIP OF IRELAND 8 x 5 mins. rounds **Whirlwind Monroe** (Newtownabbey), Irish Welterweight Champion V **Billy Joe Beck** (Lisburn). Has fought Monroe on several occasions to a draw. Now he's ready to take his title!

AMERICAN TAG MATCH
NO ROUNDS — 30 MINUTE TIME LIMIT

Roy Davies (Drumbo). Fast making a name in the pro. grappling game. "FABULOUS" **Le Hippie** (Lisburn). Fast and clever	**Rocky Hunter** (Belfast) V **'Buster' Shields** (Belfast) Ireland's No. 1 Villain

PLUS SUPPORTING CONTEST
Advance bookings obtainable from —
THE FACTORY SHOP, 33 Bridge Street, Lisburn
or phone Lisburn 5989
Also CORKINS BAR, Market Square

Bill for October 11th 1971 in Lisburn Orange Hall

Born in Lisburn on April 12th 1952, Dennis McMillan came from a boxing background. Dennis' father "Rocky" McMillan was a respected referee in the sport, even appearing on TV reffing fights featuring the likes of Barry McGuigan. Under his dad's guidance, a teenage McMillan even won honours as Ulster Junior Boxing Champion and once boxed vs. iconic English fighter John Conteh.

Ian Shirlow: "Dennis McMillan and I boxed together in the very early '70s. We were at the same weight at that stage. Then he came into the wrestling. Dennis was a fantastic athlete. He had the build, the looks with the jet black hair, and moustache, and the personality to be a villain."

Ricky Valentine: "Dennis was tough, he was a good boxer as well, very good amateur boxer. I mind going to see him box one time, and they stopped it in his favour within four minutes, it wasn't a match at all. He was very fit too. He and I were very fit. Some guys weren't that fit, thankfully it came naturally to us."

Ian Shirlow: "He did the doors at bars and pubs around Lisburn and Belfast. We were friends, he was a character, bit of a wild card. Dennis and I were actually married a day a part. I always remember it because it was in the headlines in the Ulster Star in Lisburn; 'McMillan beats Shirlow to the punch'."

Despite being brought up a boxer, Dennis was passionate about becoming a pro wrestler and so with his families full support his dad "Rocky" got him in touch with Billy Joe Beck.

Billy Joe Beck: "Dennis McMillian. It was actually me who trained him. He was from Lisburn. Dennis could be cocky, and sometimes people didn't like him because of that cockiness, but he was dead-on, and I knew how to handle him, and there was no harm in him. He was a good boxer too. And he was a quick learner in the wrestling."

Training him in the basics of wrestling first in the Lisburn army barracks Billy Joe then brought Dennis to the gym on Albion Street to be coached along with the likes of Ricky Valentine, Diamond Shondell and Rocky Hunter.
      During this year Dennis McMillan debuted on Shirlow's shows. His boxing background served him well as his style was aggressive and skill-set solid, and he'd often team with Billy Joe in

tag action. What wasn't so great was his first gimmick… "Lee Hippie" that seen the scowling hard-hitting man's man car mechanic styled as a 1960s liberal icon complete with tie dye, beads and a flower power headband?? Regardless of his curious costume, in the ring Lee Hippie could go and as a Lisburn local he was usually front of the line when it came to being picked to wrestle on shows for Henry Shirlow.

Dennis McMillan as Lee Hippie

- - - - -

Though many on the Irish wrestling scene worked part-time as bouncers at pubs and clubs, the only one who got a great wrestling gig out of their time on the doors was Eric Wilson.

Tug Wilson: "I was working the doors at Tito's in Belfast. And I had friends in the Strand Showband, and they hit it big in England. And they came to Tito's as an act, and Ray Millar, who was the bass player, he said 'if you ever need out, phone me', and he lived in Manchester. And shortly after that I phoned him, and he knew Roy St. Clair and Tony St. Clair and he introduced me to them. So they arranged for me to go to Bolton, and Wryton Promotions they had a permanent ring at Bolton Stadium, which was an old cinema. And Tony St. Clair give me a trial run, and after it he told the promoter Ian Burns, 'I'll work this man anytime'."

After a few final matches for Dave Finlay, that autumn 27 year old Eric Wilson was tired of the Troubles and escaped to England. After impressing popular wrestler Tony St. Clair, Eric was introduced to *Wryton Promotions* office man Ian Burns who he'd soon strike up a lasting friendship with. As Wryton were a partner within Joint Promotions, some strings were then pulled and Eric Wilson became the first homegrown pro wrestler from Northern Ireland to be officially signed by British wrestling's biggest players.

Playing the part of villain Eric was given the name "Tug Wilson" – similar to Whipper Watson, the name was actually in use by a British wrestler in the '30s – and Tug Wilson would bout with the best across the UK going forward, as well as work on wrestling shows at *Butlin's* summer camps.

Tug Wilson: "I wrestled full-time after I moved to England. You'd be on the road 4-5 times a week. It was tough. Wryton had all the Butlins camps. They were awful to work on, the money was awful."

1972

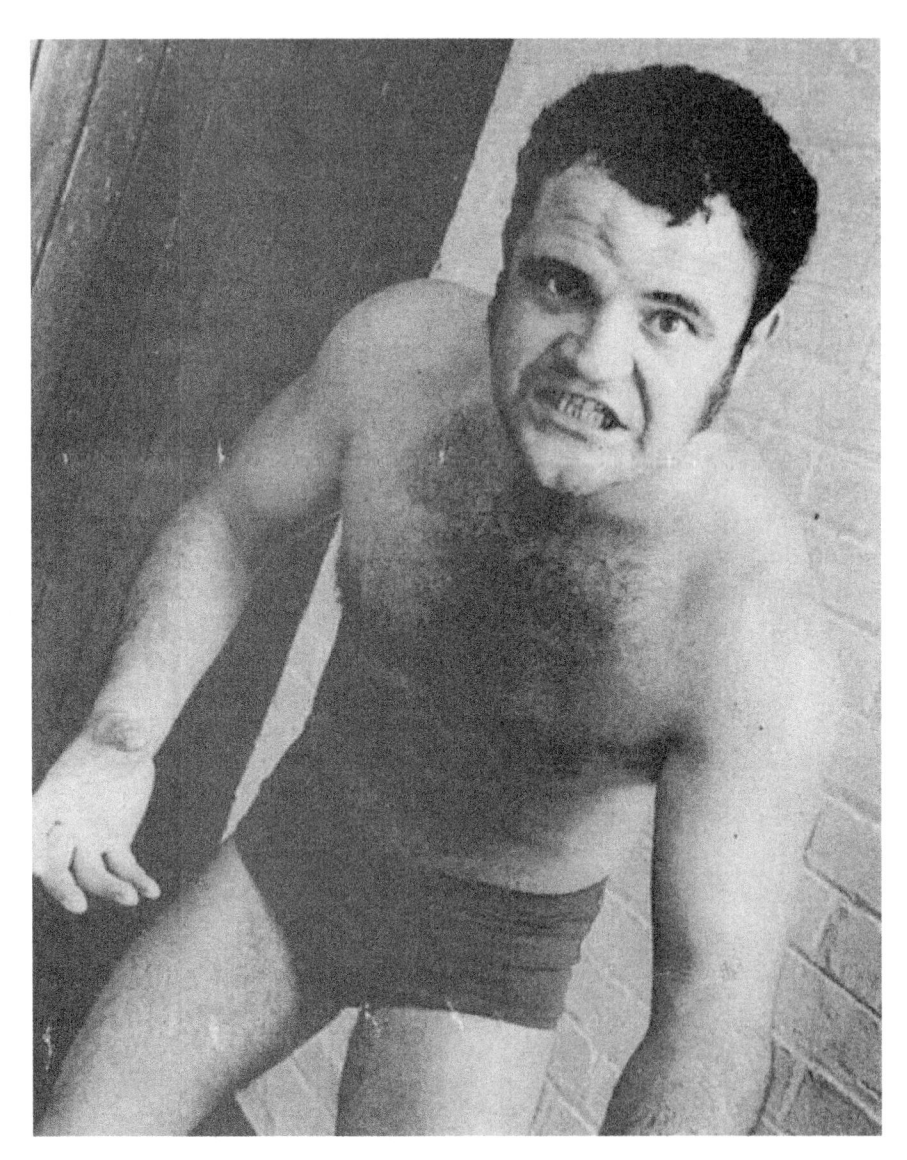

Eric "Tug" Wilson

Tug Wilson: "The money on TV was crap too. It was the equivalent of the going Equity rate for a non-speaking part on television, maybe 40 quid."

So successful was the former sparky's jump from part-time to full-time that on the April 22nd 1972 broadcast of World of Sport Eric Wilson made history by becoming the first homegrown wrestler to appear on ITV, vs. English wrestler John Casanova.

The poor pay aside, Tug Wilson would wrestle many more times on television; in singles action vs. Johnny Saint and in tag action vs. the Royal brothers. Always as the villain owing to his mean mug and aggressive shooter style. Tug would also tag team with Mark Rocco – whose father Jim Hussey had wrestled in Belfast for Relwyskow & Green from the '40s to the '60s. Mark would later became better known as "Rollerball Rocco", one of the pioneers of a newer, faster, more intense style of pro wrestling than ever seen before by audiences this side of the Atlantic.

Tug Wilson: "I was in a tag team with Rollerball Rocco, we were the Rockets. He was very dynamic, he could fly about, well we both could at that time anyway."

- - - - -

Tug's (and Eddie Hamill's) departure came as Northern Ireland was arguably experiencing the worst time in its relatively short but strained history. 1972 is considered the worst year of The Troubles in regards to casualties of the civil war. Some areas of the province were worse effected by the violence than others, but overall the mood across the counties was low.

Seany Rivers: "Wrestling had sorta dropped off, this was during the dark days, things in Belfast were pretty dire then. So I moved to New Zealand to start a new life, and I got on the New Zealand judo squad which was a massive achievement, and I lived in New Zealand for about three years."

Wrestling continued but on a much smaller scale, akin to World War II when bills were sporadic and many names vanished from the scene. Some temporarily, others entirely.

Seany Rivers himself would eventually return to Ulster and its wrestling scene, however in sporadic appearances. Wrestling being Sean's firm third passion after judo and weight-lifting.

Seany Rivers in New Zealand in the 1970s

Seany Rivers: "There was never great money to be earned in the wrestling, especially considering the effort put into it."

Following spells in the mid-to-late '70s and the early-to-mid '80s Albion Street alumni Seany isn't spotted on anymore pro shows, and come 1990 the championship-winning judoka decided to curb judo too, judging his body to have had enough of physical combat. By then Sean was no longer in carpentry but a successful salesman of heavy industrial woodwork machinery. For a time too he operated a popular nightclub in Belfast called the *Jamaica Inn*.

Today, happily retired in his mid 70s and living in Belfast, Sean Montgomery isn't long returned from living abroad for an extended time.

Seany Rivers: "Thankfully, life for me hasn't been too bad. I lived in Thailand for about seven years, in a rural village there in North Thailand. It was peace and quiet. The villagers, they took me into their heart. I'd cycle round the village. There was plenty of temples to visit. It was very enjoyable. From Thailand I used it as a base to visit China, Vietnam and India, and Goa. Goa is inside of India but it's like a different country altogether. I'd love to get back there. Asia is such a peaceful place."

- - - - -

This year 38 year old Wild Angus and 36 year old Sean Regan were off competing on other continents.

In 1971 "Angus Campbell" arrived to Canada to compete for the Hart family's Stampede Wrestling. In 1972 as "Black Angus", Frank Hoy was working for the NWA in the US, becoming the first Ulsterman to crack the American wrestling circuit. The huge Fermanagh heavyweight was surprisingly a face (slang for 'good guy') in America, and as well as picking up recognised championship belts in both singles and tag honours, Angus feuded with "Cowboy" Bob Orton (the father of modern day wrestler Randy Orton) and the legendary Harley Race (a 7x time *NWA Worlds Champion*).

Meanwhile Sean Regan wrestled his last televised World of Sport match in the UK on an October 1972 broadcast. The match was taped in September however, as in October the Derry-born stud was among the first gaijan to grapple for Japan's newest company, *New Japan Pro Wrestling (NJPW)*. In NJPW Sean Regan challenged in singles and tags vs. Japanese wrestling legend Antonio Inoki, who was also the promoter and would make worldwide headlines a few years later when he challenged Muhammad Ali in an infamous wrestler vs. boxer match. The strong-jawed school teacher also competed on the Canadian and America wrestling scenes in 1973 but didn't really leave a lasting impact.

Sean Regan was arguably more successful in Japan than Wild Angus, while Angus was more successful than Regan in North America.

- - - - -

Canada's long wrestling relationship with the Irish isle also includes the short story of Shillelagh O'Sullivan.

Born in Newtownbutler in Fermanagh on May 3rd 1937, Patrick "Pat" McMahon's life was an interesting one even before he considered a career in wrestling. In his childhood the police saved him and his family from a murder-suicide attempt by his father. In his adult years he joined the Irish army but when his service ended he refused to be recruited by the IRA, and fearing for his life fled the country for Canada in the mid '60s.

In Canada the sturdy, strong McMahon made a new life for himself as a truck driver, got married, had kids, and it wasn't until an attempted boxing career fell through that Pat wandered into the world of pro wrestling when in 1971, age 34, he started wrestling part-time at the weekends around Toronto. An affable sort, Pat was well-liked within the Canadian wrestling circuit. It was with good connections that Pat was introduced to American wrestling promoter Vincent James McMahon, a big boss based out of New York who the Newtownbutler brawler started doing odd-jobs for during a spell in the US (Pat was used to being away from home with the truck driving).

Finding favour through favours, on July 6th 1972 the ex-Irish army cadet was rewarded with a match vs. Japanese-American wrestler Mr. Fuji on a live event at a high school gymnasium in New Hampshire, for Vincent J. McMahon's *World Wide Wrestling Federation (WWWF)*. Pat McMahon, the Fermanagh man, became the first ever Ulsterman to wrestle for the WWWF. It would be his only appearance with them as by the end of the year he wasn't one of the powerful New York promoter's running men anymore.

1973

When he went back to Canada Pat McMahon was repackaged as "Shillelagh O'Sullivan", wearing a shamrock on his trunks and having a little person in a leprechaun outfit escort him to the ring.

The *Maple Leafs Gardens* was Toronto's ice hockey rink and a wrestling venue promoted by Frank Tunney, Vincent J. McMahon's associate in Canada – and the same promoter Tommy Nelson worked under when he retired as a wrestler to take an office job – and Shillelagh O'Sullivan was to be the star of Tunney's shows, or so it was hoped. Despite visions of a Danno O'Mahoney style smash-hit with the Irish contingent in Canada, it wasn't to be for Shillelagh O'Sullivan and after only a few appearances at the Gardens – which could hold a capacity of 16,000+ wrestling fans – Pat was back on the local leagues.

After several years wrestling around Toronto, Shillelagh O'Sullivan hung up his green boots age 43 in 1980. Always a colourful character, later in life Pat wrote poetry, a stage play and even attempted stand-up comedy. After bouts of poor health, in April 2012 Pat McMahon would pass away age 74. In the annals of Irish wrestling history he is easily forgotten about as he never actually wrestled in Ireland, the UK nor Europe for that matter.

- - - - -

As Judo Ed Hamill and Tug Wilson tore it up in the British independents and Joint Promotions, respectively, at home 40 year salesman Billy Finlay was brought (back) into the family business.

Born in Whiteabbey on December 1st 1933, William "Billy" Finlay, like his brother, was good at gymnastics and even played football for local league side *Carrick Rangers.* Mind you neither Dave nor Billy could touch the footballing accomplishments of their youngest brother Albert, who played goalkeeper for *Glentoran FC* and is regarded as one of the best in the club's history.

Dave Finlay: "My father-in-law John Liddell, he would have done MC for me, and my own father he used to be a sea captain, so he was able to sort the ring ropes, make sure they wouldn't snap and went on properly. And I brought my brother Billy into wrestle, but he was no good. So I said, 'Billy you're no good at this game but I want you to referee'. Billy became the best referee in the business."

Billy Finlay: "A few years after I tried the wrestling, Davey came to me and said he was stuck for a referee, I think your man Syd Waddell couldn't make it or something, and Davey asked would I help him out, so I did. I think my first one was in Ballyclare, and I really enjoyed it. The reffing came very easy, and I liked winding the crowd up. So I enjoyed the refereeing and stuck at it."

After a tough time as a wrestler in the late '60s, Billy Finlay put all behind him until he was brought back into the family business as a referee. Becoming his brother's main official, Billy would referee all over Ulster and eventually start travelling to shows in the south of Ireland through Orig Williams.

Cool-headed Billy Finlay was once again the third (or fifth including Dave's father and father-in-law's involvement) member of the family active in pro wrestling, with more relatives to follow…

That year is also the first finding of Johnny Howard in the gimmick he would become best known by; Rasputin the Mad Monk.

Dave Finlay: "I give Johnny the Mad Monk gimmick, as if you read into the real Mad Monk, the real Rasputin, they poisoned him, they shot him, they stabbed him, drown him just to keep him down. So here's this big fellow with long hair in the ring who you'd have to do everything to keep down as well. Johnny was great with his expressions, and shouting at the audience, and jumping outside and looking like he wanted to kill all round him. In them days the old women would have went after you with the handbags, so Johnny would have picked the handbags up and threw them to the other end of the hall. He played the villain really well. He was a real nice lad outside the ring, but once he went into the ring he was Rasputin."

Johnny Howard's significant size was one of his biggest strengths but it was the gimmick of "Rasputin the Mad Monk" that made the big bouncer a big ticket-seller.

Despite Wild Angus originally being billed as "Rasputin" in Germany/Austria it's Johnny Howard who is best remembered by the name in Irish and British wrestling history. As the Mad Monk, a wild-eyed Johnny would slowly walk to the ring wearing a long robe with a hood as orchestral music played. Though it would surely seem a strange sight to have a supposed "Monk" in the ring, once the bell went Johnny would get "Mad", with his energetic performances being a huge hit with crowds who loved to hate the holy terror.

The North's resident Southern wrestler on bills for Dave Finlay, Rasputin was a favourite for his fellow wrestlers to work. Even though cheery, chatty Johnny was often told to hide his heavy "Free State" accent in certain parts of the Trouble-torn country, he was always backed up by his wrestling brotherhood (including when a man pulled a gun on him during a bill at a loyalist bar in Belfast). Humour was even found in the bleak times.

Rocky Hunter: "We were wrestling up in the Shankill, and Rasputin was on and he was top of the bill, and I was wrestling him because I was local, I'm from the Shankill originally. So I goes to him in the dressing room, 'here you know tonight you're going down?', and he says, 'what do you mean I go down?', and I says, 'here let me tell ya you better or I'll tell the crowd you're a Catholic!'. So two years later, I was wrestling him down in Dublin, he says 'Rocky you know you're going down tonight?', I says 'oh?', he says, 'aye, or I'll tell everyone you're a Protestant'. We were both having each other on of course. That was kind of the humour you had at the time."

- - - - -

The timing coincidental, it was an inspired image overhaul that would also take Eddie Hamill from an independent scene standout to a bonafide box office star. Retiring the ring persona of Judo Mike / Ed Hamill, it was as a mysterious martial arts master called "The Amazing Kung Fu" that would take Eddie to the next level in his wrestling career.

Eddie Hamill: "We went on a tour of Turkey, and I had never heard of kung fu. And this high up in the army came to one of the shows, and we got talking. He was talking to me about the judo and those kind of things, and then he mentioned this kung fu to me. And he started telling me all about it, and how he was teaching the army this specialised self defence type thing. I thought, huh that sounds interesting. Then I was back home and there was an advert in the paper, and it was of a fella stood there with the judo outfit on and a mask on, and it was for a book to buy. And it was about this new martial arts called… kung fu. And it said it was a very secret organisation, and that the fella was wearing the mask because if they found out he was selling the secrets they might take reprisals. And I thought, what a great gimmick! Of course, it was just their con to sell the book, but I thought what a smashing gimmick, so straight away I was like I have the outfit, now I just need the mask. And that's how it got going."

Wearing colourful judo suits and performing in his bare feet, the transformation to Kung Fu included wrestling in a mask to hide his identity and add to the allure of the Amazing one being of assumed Asian origin – though never stated by Eddie himself the blurred nationality was along the lines of "Italian" and "Scottish" in regards to spicing up a show line-up.

Eddie Hamill: "I made the masks myself. Nowadays you can buy them or get them made no problem, but in them days you had to find someone who could make them. But I was fortunate because I had done the carpets and sewing, so I was able to throw a mask together. When the other lads first seen the mask, they said to ditch it because the thinking was if you wear a mask, you're the villain. I said, 'not necessarily because the Lone Ranger wore a mask, and he was the goodie, and Batman too'. They didn't agree. And when I first got into the ring with the mask, the crowd did boo. But being that I was on against the villains, and playing it clean, they quickly realised I was the good guy. So it was worth the risk because it worked."

Kung Fu

1974

Eddie Hamill was a game changer in British wrestling. Traditionally a masked wrestler was the villain but Kung Fu was a fan favourite. He was innovative too with an arsenal of audience-pleasing kung fu kicks and throws, and footwork that was second to none in a very unique way; being barefooted meant Kung Fu was able to use his toes to snatch and twist an opponent's ear or nose or hook them by the mouth. All this made the mystery man a joy to watch and positive word of mouth soon spread.

Eddie Hamill: "It was the hey-day of Bruce Lee films too. I think that's why I was so popular."

Eddie's creation of the Kung Fu character was perfectly-timed as it coincided with the UK release of Bruce Lee's film *Enter the Dragon*. The film launched the genre of the "kung fu film" to the Western world, and soon the Amazing Kung Fu was one of opposition wrestling's top attractions as the act picked up popularity from positive word of mouth.

The first appearance of Kung Fu on the Irish isle was on a tour for Orig Williams that February, vs. flamboyant heel the Exotic Adrian Street in places like Armoy, Kilroot, Portrush, Bangor and at the *Europa Hotel* in Belfast – which despite having only been opened a few years before, the Europa infamously was known as the "most bombed hotel in the world" during the Troubles.

Adrian Street had recently quit Joint Promotions to make more money with the opposition, becoming one of the first top television talents to leave the upper echelon of British pro wrestling to entertain instead on the independent scene. Street even came on with Orig as his co-promoter, and in his autobiography *Imagine What I Could Do To You*, Street wrote that he considered Eddie Hamill the most talented wrestler on the Welshman's roster and hand-picked him to be the hero to his villain in matches around the UK and Ireland.

Kung Fu was Orig William's golden goose, but time was ticking as the monopoly men would soon come calling…

Another Ulsterman who greatly benefited from working with the Exotic one was 26 year old Dave Stalford. The rough, tough

Belfast bruiser was curiously cast as a snotty butler character called "Charles" who would accompany Adrian Street in his matches, serving to heighten the hatred for Street who not only was presenting himself as a gay performer in front of the working class but then was rubbing his supposed wealth in their faces too.

As Charles, moustached Dave Stalford wore a suit and bowed to his master's every command. In reality when the shows were done and everyone went to the nearest bar to drink away their wages, Stalford acted as an actual back-up to Street if anyone picked a fight with him. According to Adrian Street himself, on at least one occasion Dave Stalford – with help from Whirlwind Monroe – actually saved Street's life from a man who pulled a gun on the flamboyant wrestler in a Belfast bar (Rasputin vs. Street in a bar in Belfast would've been madness!).

Seedy Belfast bars weren't the only place that Adrian Street had people baying for his blood; whenever he returned for another tour later that year, during a match vs. Dave Finlay in Omagh Town Hall, the audience started hurling objects into the ring, forcing the bout to be abandoned with the wrestlers chased out of the building by an enraged mob. Adding to the experience was that the journey home of Street and the Finlay brothers Dave and Billy was delayed as a prison was on fire due to a riot... Maybe Relwyskow & Green made the right decision!

The success of Dave Stalford's dual-role with Street led to him becoming one of Orig's most loyal lieutenants, and Stalford would start travelling over to Rhyl during the summer months to work full-time at wrestling and ring-building for the Welshman. More than just a business associate, Dave Stalford became one of Orig William's best friends.

Bruce McDonald: "Davey Stalford was like the son Orig never had. They just clicked together. Orig trusted Dave with his life, and his bank accounts."

- - - - -

Bruce McDonald, a close friend of the Finlay family, was another who started getting the call to action more often for Orig. The Newtownards native was usually driving the car with Dave Finlay his passenger whenever they would take the trip down South to wrestle for the Welshman or with the Carrickmacross crew or indeed for Brian Dixon, who that July journeyed Luke McMasters to wrestle in Ireland for the first time. McMasters being the then gimmick name of the future Giant Haystacks, who was vs. Johnny Howard that evening.

Bruce McDonald: "I was on the bill when Haystacks started. It was in the Green Isle Hotel in Dublin for Brian Dixon. Big Johnny wrestled him and looked after him."

- - - - -

That same summer Bruce McDonald wouldn't just be on the bill but in the bout vs. another future wrestling legend, when Bruce was trusted with taking on Dave Finlay's 14½ year old son in Dave Junior's first ever pro wrestling match.

Fit Finlay: "I had done amateur wrestling in Olympic style, I also did judo. I was first taught judo by Eddie Hamill. Eddie was a really good judo player. I think judo held me up quite well too. Judo, karate, I did a little boxing, all these molded me into who I was."

Born in Greenisland on January 31st 1960, Dave Finlay Junior was his father's son; a success at any sport he put his passion into. Ever since he could walk Dave Jnr was taught the art of amateur wrestling and given pointers in the pro style too by his dad.
	As the Finlay father and son shared the same first name, the wrestlers would refer to them as "Old Dave" and "Young Dave" to distinguish between them. If Old Dave wasn't able to get out of the house to gain Young Dave experience grappling at Dave Mack's Albion Street gym, he would home school him instead…

Dave Finlay: "I had a ring in the garden, and I trained up Fit in it from when he was just a kid. I trained him up in the style I had, that no-one took advantage of you."

Fit Finlay: "In those days, you had to prove yourself in wrestling, nothing was given to you, you had to earn it. Nowadays it would come across as bullying, but they had to make sure the guys they were training weren't wasting their time, that they'd stay a week and leave and give away all the trade secrets. Even as a teenager I had to prove myself, and they made me prove myself. My Dad too. In the ring he'd put me in holds I thought I would die in. And you weren't really taught the inside aspects of wrestling until most trainers, in this case my Dad, thought you were ready to get in the ring and carry the responsibility of being a professional wrestler."

The Finlays of Greenisland were the only family in all of Ireland to have a full-size pro wrestling ring in their back-garden – pending the weather of course! Kids in the neighbourhood would watch with wonder from the fence as Old Dave taught Young Dave the best techniques, throws and tricks to the trade, and so before he was even in secondary school Dave Finlay Jnr was a wrestling prodigy.

Besides training at the Albion Street gym and in the ring in his back garden, Young Dave also travelled with his father around Ulster as a crew member, putting up rings and acting as an assistant in the corner during matches. That summer of '74 he was only supposed to be serving as ring crew when wrestler Jimmy Rodgers didn't show up and a replacement was required.

Fit Finlay: "It was accidentally my debut. It was against Bruce McDonald. I think it was July 4th, and it was in Glynn, this little fishing village just outside Larne. It was for a rugby club, now they have a building, but then it was just a field, and they'd put a tent up. And we put the ring up in the afternoon and gone home, and came back in the evening time. And come the evening time one of the guys didn't show up, so my Dad said, 'well we're going to have to put you in'. I'm 14 years old. He says, 'you need to wrestle tonight', I'm like '...OK'. I didn't even have any wrestling gear, so I had to put my Dad's boots on that were too big for me. It was all his wrestling gear, so it was hanging off me."

Bruce McDonald: "Young David had done amateur, so he was a good worker to start with. So it was an easy bout."

Fit Finlay: "My second match was against Darkie, it was my first official match. I think we wrestled in Armoy at a little nightclub or bar, and the backstory to that was I had watched my Dad and Darkie wrestle as a kid in Carrickfergus in the town hall. And Darkie had these great horrible expressions, he looked like a murderer, with this awe of nastiness about him."

Darkie Arnott: "Davey said to me would you take young David on, help break him in. So needless to say, I acted the villain, got the crowd on young David's side."

Fit Finlay: "I'd watched Darkie wrestling my Dad growing up, my emotions going wild, sitting watching with my friends as my Dad got beat up at times, and I hated Darkie as he did it. So now I'm a teenager and I'm wrestling him, and now all these memories are coming back to me, and I'm like, ah this guy's a monster! But Darkie was so good with me, totally professional."

Teenage Dave Finlay Jnr was then Ireland's youngest ever professional wrestler, and the newest member of his father's stable. In his early days Young Dave always played the part of a good guy despite finding it wasn't a role he was comfortable with, preferring to be the villain like Dirty Darkie or his dad. What he was even less impressed with was his first gimmick (that give Lee Hippie a run for its money) when he was styled as a Roman soldier with the name "Young Apollo" – complete with a homemade costume that included beer tins as pieces of armour and a toilet brush as a helmet.

Fit Finlay: "As a young wrestler I didn't like being a babyface, and having to smile and wave at people but my Dad would say 'you gotta', but it just wasn't in me to do that. So I said, 'Dad what about if I wear a mask?', he says, 'it doesn't matter if you wear a mask or not, you're built like a stick'. So I got my Mom to make this mask, with a skull and flames coming out of it, and the first time I was wrestling with it, I realised it didn't have a mouthpiece so I couldn't breath. So it was like wrestling with a shopping bag over my head. So I had to go out of the ring, under the ring and use a stanley knife to cut a mouthpiece and breath, and then go back in the ring."

Dave Finlay Jnr as Young Apollo

Over the next few years Young Apollo battled with the best of Irish wrestling while being shown no favourtism by his father.

Fit Finlay: "So early on I wrestled Whirlwind Monroe quite a bit, and I never scored a fall against him. For the first few years my dad would never let me get a fall. It was best out of three at the time, rounds and all that, and I'd just be beat two straight. So I was getting so sick of being beaten by Whirlwind Monroe, like he was a great guy, but as a young kid I was like, 'please dad, let me win just once'. But my dad was like, 'no, you haven't learned the lesson yet'. And you know I don't think I ever got to beat Whirlwind Monroe!"

That summer is also one of the few findings for another wrestler whom Dave Finlay had a close connection with, 25 year old aircraft factory worker Marty Robinson.

Billy Joe Beck: "Davey treated Marty Robinson like another son. Good wrestler."

Dave Finlay: "Marty Robinson, he was dynamite".

Marty Robinson: "I'd seen Davey Finlay wrestling in Carrickfergus, and I thought I might have a go at it. Though I really can't mind how I found out about the club in Belfast. The training was tight enough, you had plenty of rope burns and cuts and bruises. Diamond Shondell, I was around exactly the same time as him, Rocky Hunter too. They were my training partners. I done the wrestling for Davey, and I done a few on the Isle of Man, and a few in the Ulster Hall for Joint Promotions, but mostly Davey".

Born June 25th 1949 in Greenisland, Marty Robinson was training at the Albion Street gym as early as 1970 coached first by Butcher Donald and Tiger Joe Moore and then fine tuned by Dave Finlay.
Dedicated and a quick learner, Robinson's style was straight, clean wrestling. Early on he stood out as skilful enough to be selected by Arthur Green to wrestle on the final few Joint bills in 1971, before finding a spot in Finlay's stable. Whether it be in bouts against local lads like Bruce McDonald or television stars like Adrian Street, Robinson was impressive.
However the wrestling was strictly a hobby for Marty Robinson who winded it down in the mid-to-late 70s for a variety of real-life reasons, among them the attention.

Marty Robinson: "You had to keep yourself reasonably fit and you just don't have time for it when you get married and have a family. I wasn't so keen on the limelight either. Never really felt comfortable with people coming asking for autographs and the like. I think that's what put me off a little too. Just my nature. I just wanted to do it for the sport of it".

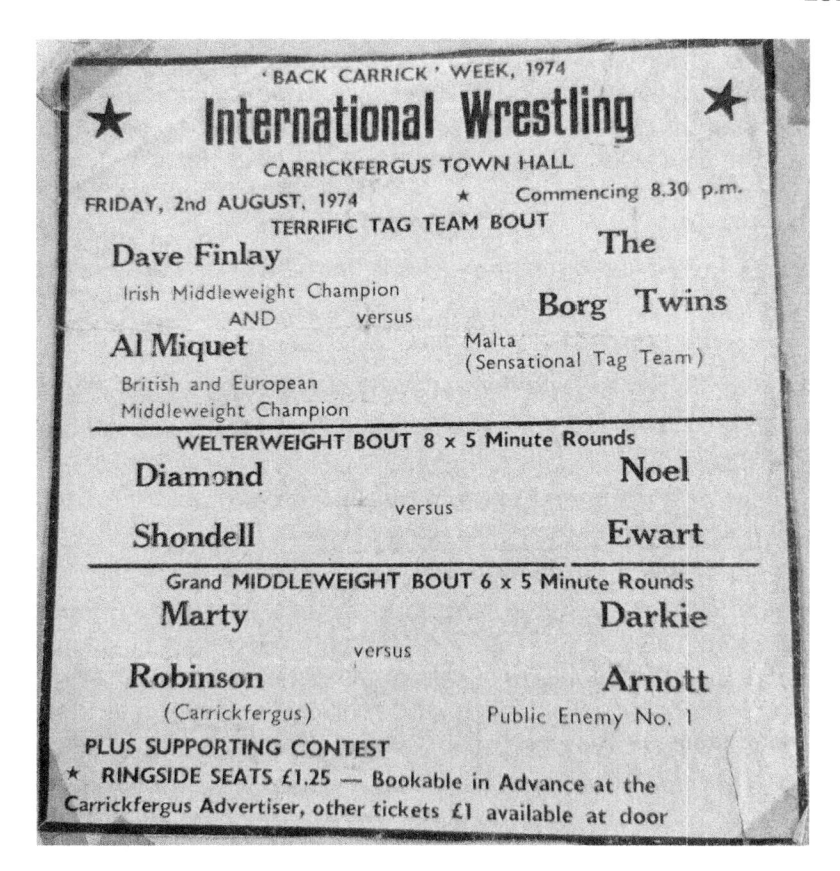

> **'BACK CARRICK' WEEK, 1974**
>
> ★ **International Wrestling** ★
>
> CARRICKFERGUS TOWN HALL
>
> FRIDAY, 2nd AUGUST, 1974 ★ Commencing 8.30 p.m.
>
> **TERRIFIC TAG TEAM BOUT**
>
> **Dave Finlay** **The**
> Irish Middleweight Champion
> AND   versus   **Borg Twins**
> **Al Miquet** Malta
> British and European (Sensational Tag Team)
> Middleweight Champion
>
> **WELTERWEIGHT BOUT 8 x 5 Minute Rounds**
>
> **Diamond** **Noel**
> versus
> **Shondell** **Ewart**
>
> **Grand MIDDLEWEIGHT BOUT 6 x 5 Minute Rounds**
>
> **Marty** **Darkie**
> versus
> **Robinson** **Arnott**
> (Carrickfergus) Public Enemy No. 1
>
> **PLUS SUPPORTING CONTEST**
>
> ★ RINGSIDE SEATS £1.25 — Bookable in Advance at the Carrickfergus Advertiser, other tickets £1 available at door

Bill for August 2nd 1974 at Carrickfergus Town Hall

- - - - -

In England history was made that year when Eric Wilson became the first and only ever Ulsterman to hold a position of power in an office for Joint Promotions.

Tug Wilson: "I worked for Wryton Promotions as a matchmaker. I had become friends with Ian Burns, he did all the paperwork and the accounts and booked the halls and all that. And he didn't get on with the previous matchmaker, so he got me in. I was still wrestling as I did the matchmaker for Wryton. I had no airs about the job."

As matchmaker, Eric booked bouts for shows around Liverpool, Manchester and Bolton and at times the matches he made were broadcast on World of Sport. Eric's office job also afforded him the opportunity to hire those he believed would benefit Joint to have in their ranks. Though his offer was respectfully declined by Dave Finlay Snr, Eric's influence helped bring in Eddie Hamill.

Tug Wilson: "Eddie Hamill was great. He had the touch, a smashing worker. Kung Fu was a top gimmick too, and it was actually me that put in the word for him to Joint."

Eddie Hamill: "When Joint got in touch with me Orig wasn't pleased about it, understandably. He said, 'I brought you over here Hamill to work for me'. I said, 'I know Orig but it's a chance for me to get on TV. If I get on TV, after a few years I'll come back to you'. It was all about the money, I had to make a living."

That summer – 10 years into his journey as a wrestler – Eddie Hamill would sign on to make the Amazing Kung Fu an exclusive star of Joint Promotion shows. He'd make the move worthwhile by playing hard-ball on Joint's initial offer owing to the run-in at the Ulster Hall with one of the organisations head honchos Arthur Green years before.

Eddie Hamill: "Story is: the Ulster Hall in Belfast, George Relwyskow and Arthur Green, they were promoters at the time for Joint Promotions, and they wanted some Northern Irish wrestlers so me and Whirlwind were picked. So we done our bout, and to be honest with you it wasn't a great bout, things were just off that night. Anyway we came off, and after it Arthur Green said to me, 'What do you do for a living son?'. Then I was doing carpet-fitting, so I said 'Oh I do carpet-fitting Mr. Green'. He said, 'Take my advice son, stick to it!'. So years later when I started to make a name in the business, they phoned me up and asked if they could bring me on. And I thought I'll get my own back, so I said I'd only come on if they paid me double my wages. And they did!"

On November 2nd 1974 edition of World of Sport, broadcast to the millions on Eddie's 31st birthday, the well-paid Kung Fu would win his ITV debut vs. Englishman Clive Myers.

Instantly amazing viewers, Kung Fu would make many more prolific appearances, with matches vs. "Cyanide" Sid Cooper, vs. Bert Royal and vs. Rollerball Rocco among his best ITV bouts. On a winning streak the simple but still effective story was that if Kung Fu was ever decisively beaten by pinfall or submission he would have to remove his mask in the middle of the ring, revealing his true identity…

- - - - -

Since Relwyskow & Green's exit no-one had attempted to bring active TV wrestlers to Ireland in the interim, and that's were Henry Shirlow saw an opportunity. By then Shirlow owned his own heath studio in Lisburn and one of the instructors there was long-time wrestling fan George Crothers. George served as a confidante to the charismatic Jack Flash and supported him when he made his move to become Ireland's new #1 promoter of ITV wrestlers.

George 'Lone Wolf' Crothers: "Henry used to do wee shows like the Orange Hall in Lisburn every Boxing Day. Seemed to be all small shows then, only a few times a year. Then Shirlow went over to England, to the big promoters. And they agreed on allowing some big names to come over here to wrestle. Henry met up with George de Relwyskow, met him in a bar in Leeds. I was over with him."

Ian Shirlow: "My uncle Henry had a very big personality, and was very persuasive, and had went over to Relwyskow & Green of Joint Promotions, and he said to them he'd bring their wrestlers over to Northern Ireland, look after them, and fill the halls. He assured them everything would be kosher, because this was during the Troubles, dangerous times. Henry would fly the wrestlers in, put them up in hotels, pay all their expenses, and promote them on the bills. He'd have sold all this to them with his personality."

Lone Wolf: "I remember going to see Billy Two Rivers when he was on at the King's Hall when I was 15, and then whenever he was on for Shirlow I went to the airport to lift him. He was fantastic. Every time he got paid he said, 'that'll buy a few more acres for the reservation'."

That March of 1974 Shirlow brought over the incredibly popular Billy Two Rivers to be the World of Sport star of shows supported by, among others, Whirlwind Monroe, Billy Joe Beck, Lee Hippie, Butcher Donald (who'd since returned to wrestling regularly) and 60 year old dapper Dave Mack as the MC.

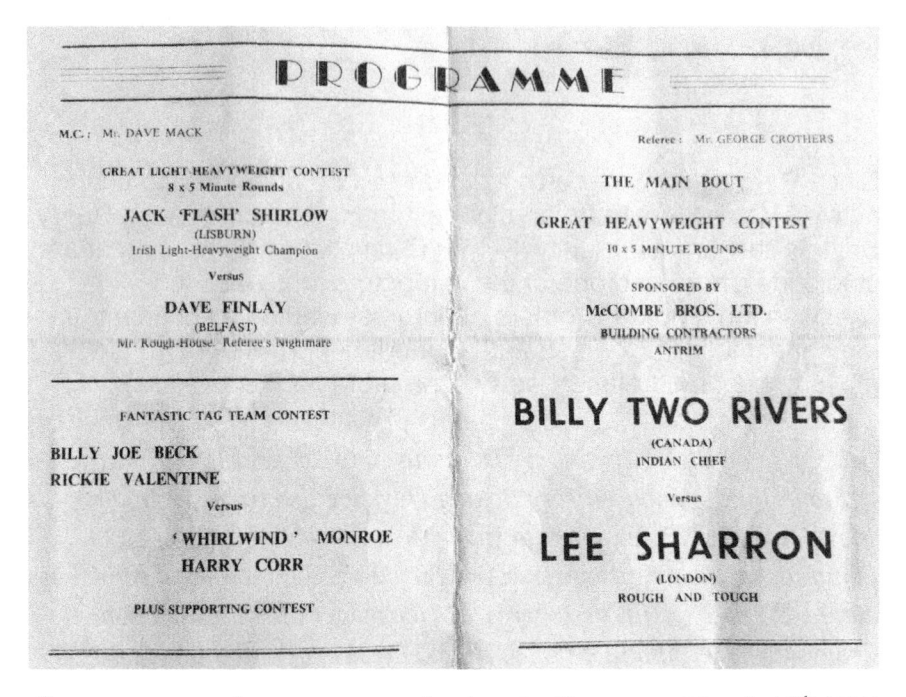

PROGRAMME

M.C.: Mr. DAVE MACK
Referee: Mr. GEORGE CROTHERS

GREAT LIGHT-HEAVYWEIGHT CONTEST
8 x 5 Minute Rounds

JACK 'FLASH' SHIRLOW
(LISBURN)
Irish Light-Heavyweight Champion

Versus

DAVE FINLAY
(BELFAST)
Mr. Rough-House, Referee's Nightmare

FANTASTIC TAG TEAM CONTEST

BILLY JOE BECK
RICKIE VALENTINE

Versus

'WHIRLWIND' MONROE
HARRY CORR

PLUS SUPPORTING CONTEST

THE MAIN BOUT

GREAT HEAVYWEIGHT CONTEST
10 x 5 MINUTE ROUNDS

SPONSORED BY
McCOMBE BROS. LTD.
BUILDING CONTRACTORS
ANTRIM

BILLY TWO RIVERS
(CANADA)
INDIAN CHIEF

Versus

LEE SHARRON
(LONDON)
ROUGH AND TOUGH

The programme for an event at the Antrim Forum on March 15th 1974
Note: George Crothers as the referee

- - - - -

Then – that same November that Eddie Hamill was showcasing his skills for the first time on Saturday afternoon television – Whirlwind Monroe and the terrific Lisburn trio of Jack Flash Shirlow, Billy Joe Beck and Lee Hippie travelled throughout Scotland and England on a mini-tour for Relwyskow & Green. The Lisburn crew +1 competed on a series of "Ireland vs. Scotland" shows as well as at Manchester's own King's Hall (better known as *Belle Vue*) one of British wrestling's premiere venues.

Billy Joe Beck: "It was through Henry Shirlow that we got the call from Relwyskow & Green, Joint Promotions, to go over and wrestle over there. And one of the biggest ones I did for Joint was in Manchester. We were driving through Manchester to go to the show and I couldn't believe our names were up on this big screen in lights. I thought it was brilliant."

It was the start of a beautiful business relationship between Henry Shirlow and Joint Promotions as – just like Jack McClelland before him – the silver tongue ex-boxer became an associate of the monopoly men. Though it would be a little time until all the pieces of the puzzle fell into place to make the venture financially-viable for both parties…

- - - - -

It was a peak time for the class of '64 in particular; Kung Fu and Tug Wilson were ITV wrestling stars; Dave Finlay Snr was Irish wrestling's #1 promoter and Jack Flash Shirlow was on his way to bringing premiere television wrestlers back to Ireland. Unfortunately, around the same time, after 12 years the Milo Wrestling Club ceased to exist.

Billy Joe Beck: "There was times you could hear the shooting outside on the streets, and I think it just sort of put off people going to the place."

The gym's address on the Sandy Row, a hotspot for social unrest, was to its detriment during statistical the worse years of the Troubles. Whenever the car mechanic in the building below closed shop the landlord of the premises on 33 Albion Street soon sold the site to be demolished.

Dave Finlay: "The place on the Sandy Row, Albion Street, it was pulled down. Once it was gone, you might have went to a leisure centre and done some training, I had the ring in the backyard, but once the premises went at Albion Street everyone just did their own thing."

Chapter 11

Shirlow & Monroe Shows & The Last Class

1975

Fit Finlay: "During the school holidays I would go over to Rhyl for Orig Williams, and I would spend those two months just wrestling everyday. He'd have a circuit in Scotland, a circuit in Wales, so my summers were spent wrestling. It was a great time."

Working with the Welshman in his first matches outside of Ireland, the Greenisland gladiator Young Apollo got to battle with some of the UK's best, and even tag with his old boy.

Fit Finlay: "My Dad and I, we wrestled in the Isle of Man where they would have these weeks were they'd cater to the Scots, the Welsh, the Irish, the Northern Irish. So we went over there and we'd tag, and on one of my first ones, when I was like 15, we actually flew in a four-seater plane from Newtownards to the Isle of Man, and I thought I was a superstar. Just me, my Dad and the pilot, and we flew in, wrestled and flew out the next day. Unbelievable I thought, 15 and flying on a private plane."

On the Irish isle the Finlay family dynasty of Old Dave, Young Dave and referee Billy Finlay were sure to be on the Welshman's variety wrestling shows along with the ladies, the midgets and the giants. They were joined too by lethal lightweight Bruce McDonald and Orig's best buddy from Belfast Dave Stalford.

- - - - -

While the British independent scene was buzzing, Joint Promotions was in something of a slump; the extra time-slot on a Wednesday night had since been dropped and viewership for World of Sport on Saturday had taken a dip. Many believed the TV product had grown stale from not creating enough new stars as well as losing old ones like Jackie Pallo that it built its brand around in the '60s.

That summer Joint went in a new direction as Max Crabtree (formerly one of the first independent promoters to tour Ireland in the early '60s) became top dog of the organisation. Crabtree had successfully acted as an associate of the monopoly men for years, and built up a reputation for being creative in his match-making and coming up with gimmicks for wrestlers. One of Max Crabtree's first moves was to bring in his own people, and that July his brother Shirley – who'd wrestled for Worldwide Promotions in the '50s – debuted on ITV, and was soon rechristened "Big Daddy" and interestingly was initially a villain.

Tug Wilson: "When Max Crabtree took over Joint Promotions totally, I got the sack."

For Eric Wilson his days with Britain's biggest wrestling organisation were numbered, as he and Wryton Promotions associate Ian Burns weren't a part of Crabtree's future plans.

Relieved of his office duties Tug Wilson would move over to the independent wrestling circuit and later that year tour Ireland for Orig Williams with Dave Finlay Snr, Rasputin, Malta tag team the Borg Twins and ex-World of Sport star Ricki Starr on the bills. A career villain Tug would actually find wrestling as the 'bad guy' much easier when he wasn't restrained by the confines of Joint's TV contract (which didn't allow for over the top violence – somewhat understandably as it was shown at 4pm in the day!)

Tug Wilson: "I worked for Orig Williams and Brian Dixon, and you could do stuff with them that you weren't allowed to do with Joint Promotions. You could be more villainous. There was stuff you weren't allowed to do on TV, blade and that".

Meanwhile the only original owners to keep themselves active in new look Joint Promotions were Relwyskow & Green, with George de Relwyskow working peacefully with Max Crabtree right up until his passing in 1980 aged 66, after which his daughter Anne carried on the family tradition as a third generation promoter.

George de Relwyskow
Promoter of pro wrestling in Ireland for 23 years

- - - - -

Lone Wolf: "I trained with big Henry. We trained all over the place. Any leisure centres that take us. At the Wallace Park in Lisburn, we'd run up and down there, in the winter the frost be coming out of our noses. It was important, keeping fit. You didn't want to get in and run out of puff."

That summer of 1975 features the first found matches of 28 year old handyman George Crothers. George was trained by Henry Shirlow on mats in leisure centres around Lisburn. A life-long fan who used to watch the wrestling on ITV, George had already proven to be integral to Shirlow's shows even before he stepped into the ring as a wrestler.

Lone Wolf: "First, whatever town we where in I'd go down beforehand and put all the posters up. Then on the day of a show I'd go and build the ring up too. We'd actually use Whirlwind Monroe's lorry. He had an engineering firm, so we used his lorry to transport the ring about, and one of Monroe's workers would have drove it and helped me set up the ring. Then we'd set the chairs all out, and have the place looking pristine for that night. I was a second for a long time too, maybe a year or so, and then even when I was wrestling, I still did all those jobs, I just loved it."

Born in Lisburn on July 20th 1947, George Crothers was a handyman by trade who through working on Henry Shirlow's home had become friendly with the reigning Light-heavyweight Champion of Ireland.

Incidentally, as a young man in the '60s George met Jack McMullan in a similar way through doing work at his house. McMullan being the Lisburn man who became Irish Middleweight Champion on the same evening at the Ulster Hall in the summer of 1941 that Dave Mack won his welterweight honours.

After a year of helping with the ring, acting as a cornerman and taking on ref duties when required, George Crothers debuted as "The Lone Wolf" on one of Shirlow shows. The Lone Wolf was the newest member of the colloquially coined "Lisburn crew" along with Henry Shirlow, Billy Joe Beck and Dennis McMillan.

Lone Wolf: "I always wrestled as the Lone Wolf. I have a big tattoo on my chest of a wolf. Henry suggested it to me. I used to come out with a cloak, used to belong to Henry, had a big flash on it, I just took the flash off, came out with it. I have a funny feeling my first bout was in Portrush and was against Billy Joe. And on the night of my first show, right before it, Dennis McMillan, he was Lee Hippie at the time, he called me into the toilets, and I was thinking... right, what's going on here, this boys calling me into the toilets? But he says, 'you know, it's like this', and he squeezed my hand gently. 'Not like this' and he twisted my hand. They thought I didn't know, but I knew."

George Crothers aka The Lone Wolf

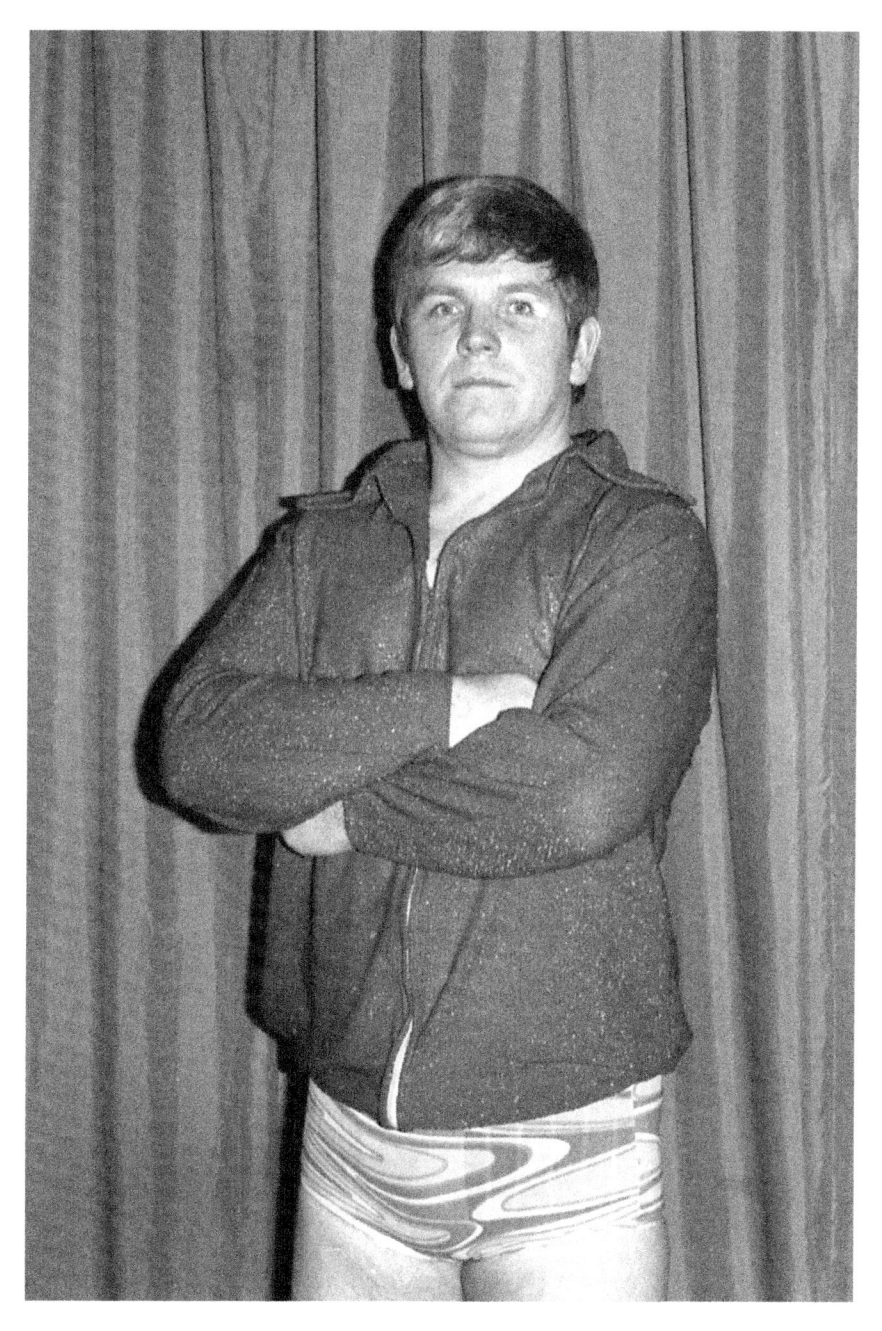

Billy Joe Beck
a Welterweight + Middleweight Champion of Ireland
Picture credit to Peter Nulty

Jack Flash Shirlow
Light-heavyweight Champion of Ireland
and one of the co-promoters of the TV talent tours

1976

Professional wrestler was just another notch in the workman's belt as George Crothers went from important to invaluable to the Shirlow shows when he built Henry his own ring, saving him from having to borrow one from boxing clubs.

Lone Wolf: "At that time I was a jack of all trades, so I said to Henry 'if you get the stuff I'll weld it, I'll build a ring for you'. I think it was actually Pat Red Kelly that got us the four corner posts, and they were actually the big pipes that go underground for heating, and boy they were ideal for the wrestling ring with the size and shape of them. And we built a bit of it then in Whirlwind Monroe's back garden, real DIY job you know, everyone chipping in. Monroe was a good lad. He had a pony tail and then he cut it off and hung it in a picture frame in the living room for a laugh. He was very good in the ring too. So anyway, I built the ring for Shirlow and he just had the one ring, it was the one used for all the promotions. The very first time we used it after it was built, Gerry Hassett from Belfast was promoting boxing for Barney Eastwood. And the very first fight they promoted in it was Charlie Nash against Bingo Crooks in the Ulster Hall. First time it was used it was for boxing, not even wrestling."

That boxing event was March 3rd 1976 and by then 34 year old Henry Shirlow was preparing for a week-long tour of wrestling around Ulster. Joint Promotions agreed to allow the Amazing Kung Fu and Les Kellett to be the stars of these shows.

Importantly, Henry was no longer promoting by himself. Happy-go-lucky 36 year old Hugh "Whirlwind Monroe" Beattie was by then Henry's part-time business partner. In real-life Henry and Hugh were very good friends, holidaying together with their families. It didn't even take much sweet-talking from Shirlow to convince Beattie to join him as Hugh was always up for an exciting experience. Hugh was financially in a good way too; since his days dynamiting sunken ships he'd become a master carpenter with his own business. Pro wrestling promotion was to be just another money-making enterprise for the highly-rated ring rogue from Newtownabbey.

Shirlow and Monroe had a third partner in English gentleman Brian Page, a 41 year old plumbing instructor who lived in Finaghy (between Belfast and Lisburn), and who – like George Connell, Arthur Green and Evelyn Finlay – sorted the non-wrestling logistics like booking venues, arranging travel, etc. Meanwhile Hugh transported the Lone Wolf ring from town to town using a van he owned, and stored it from time to time in space offered by his friend Frank "The Blonde Duke" Hughes. Shirlow's role was sorting the wrestling side of the shows, using his connection with Joint Promotions to secure top World of Sport wrestlers, as well as booking the Irish wrestlers and the subsequent bouts to be on each bill, etc.

Notably, unlike Worldwide Promotions who always advertised with their brand name, the trio of Shirlow, Beattie and Page never seemed to concern themselves with a dedicated promoting name. So while a multitude of versions appeared over the years including *Island Wrestling Promotions* the events they collectively organised were usually just referred to as "Shirlow & Monroe shows" by the other wrestlers – not discounting Brian Page's role but just as short-hand for the two more prominent players within the local scene.

The first found Shirlow & Monroe show is from April 5th 1976 at the *Arcadia Ballroom* in Portrush followed on April 6th at the *La Mon House Hotel* in Comber (a popular spot going forward) and running through to April 10th at the Antrim Forum.

It was off to the races as Shirlow, Beattie and Page became the first homegrown pro wrestling promoters to semi-regularly tour Ireland with top talent fresh off of World of Sport, beginning with Kung Fu and Kellett and continuing with many more famous fighters for years thereafter.

Ian Shirlow: "When it was big time Henry seemed to go every eight weeks or so. Maybe three months a part. It just depended on the availability and getting the guys released from Joint Promotions, and getting them over here at the same time. He'd have got a lot of big names over. He'd then do a full week of shows, Monday to Saturday, six nights. Sometimes he'd fly in a guy for three nights, then fly him home, and fly in another guy in for the other three nights."

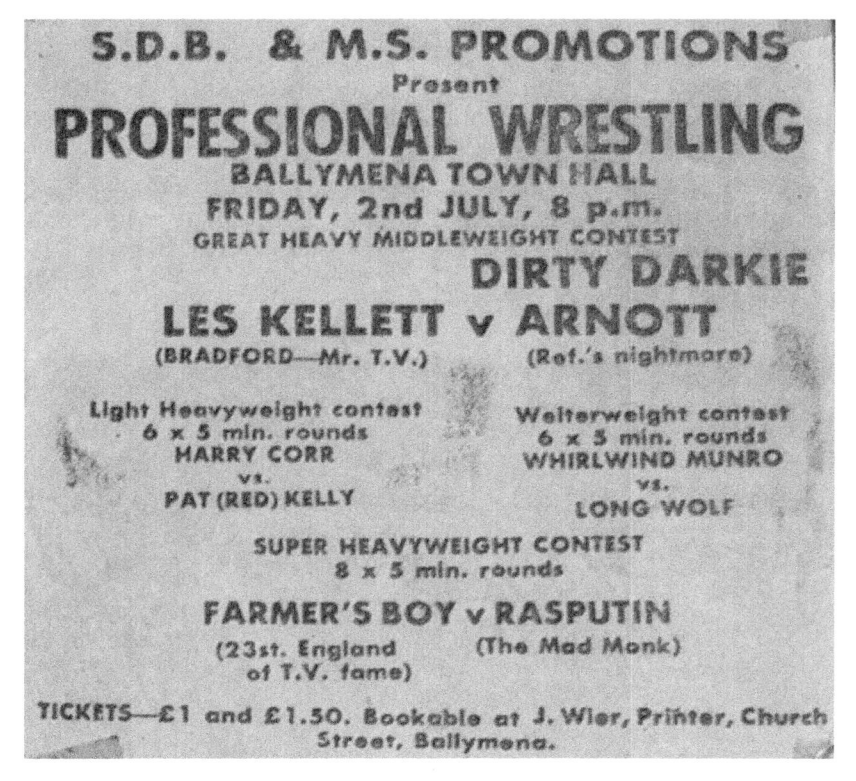

> **S.D.B. & M.S. PROMOTIONS**
> Present
> # PROFESSIONAL WRESTLING
> BALLYMENA TOWN HALL
> FRIDAY, 2nd JULY, 8 p.m.
> GREAT HEAVY MIDDLEWEIGHT CONTEST
>
> **LES KELLETT v DIRTY DARKIE ARNOTT**
> (BRADFORD—Mr. T.V.)   (Ref.'s nightmare)
>
> Light Heavyweight contest   Welterweight contest
> 6 x 5 min. rounds   6 x 5 min. rounds
> **HARRY CORR**   **WHIRLWIND MUNRO**
> vs.   vs.
> **PAT (RED) KELLY**   **LONG WOLF**
>
> SUPER HEAVYWEIGHT CONTEST
> 8 x 5 min. rounds
>
> **FARMER'S BOY v RASPUTIN**
> (23st. England   (The Mad Monk)
> of T.V. fame)
>
> TICKETS—£1 and £1.50. Bookable at J. Wier, Printer, Church Street, Ballymena.

A Shirlow & Monroe show in Ballymena Town Hall on July 2nd 1976

For some these shows came as they were closing their accounts. That year 43 year old Strongman Harry Corr retired from the ring after a final found match that summer vs. Pat Red Kelly. In his decade as a pro wrestler Corr was common across cards for the N.I. Wrestling Association, then Dave Finlay and finally Shirlow & Monroe. His ability as a shoot wrestler and decency as a person were appreciated by all.

Billy Joe Beck: "Harry Corr was a lovely man, he was a gentleman too. Good wrestler. Harry enjoyed wrestling, but his job was more important to him."

Bodybuilder Harry wasn't just brawn but brains too. Harry worked in finance for a local company and later became the Northern Ireland manager for a much larger organisation.

In January 2008 Harry Corr would pass away at the age of 72, though he has been immortalised forever by his artist son Terry, who commemorated the ten year anniversary of his father's passing by producing a series of pieces entitled *"The Wrestlers"*. As well as artwork depicting his Strongman dad, Terry Corr created caricatures of the wrestlers he remembered seeing in the ring in childhood including his dad's sometime tag team partner Whirlwind Monroe and fan favourite Judo Mike Hamill.

Strongman Harry Corr artwork
by Terry Corr

Whirlwind Monroe
artwork
by Terry Corr

Judo Mike Hamill
artwork
by Terry Corr

Ian Shirlow: "With Henry on his shows, no-one was ever wrestling the same guy every night. If say there was four or five lads around the same weight, you'd have wrestled a different guy on a different day of the week. It was mixed and matched, it was never two bouts the same. Every venue that he had it would be different. That's what helped promote it. Because there was some people that followed it and would say, 'sure I already seen this match last night', 'I seen that fella wrestle that fella the other day'. Henry would never put on the same match twice in a week. So a lot of the bouts would have been catchweight, as sometimes there'd be a big weight difference between the lads on the card."

Being top talent themselves Jack Flash Shirlow and Whirlwind Monroe were of course frequently featured on their own shows. Irish Light-heavyweight Champion Shirlow was usually in the heavier weight contests, and the talented Monroe suited for all shapes, sizes, and styles of wrestlers.

Billy Joe Beck was another often in action. Retiring undefeated as the Welterweight belt-holder he then moved up a weight and won the Middleweight Championship of Ireland, which was by then represented by a physical belt too (which Billy Joe is still in possession of today). The other Lisburn crew regulars in Lee Hippie and the Lone Wolf competed on many Shirlow & Monroe shows. As the event regularly showcased the World of Sport stars vs. the local lads, the Hippie and the Wolf gained much experience grappling with the best of the British wrestling circuit. Meanwhile Ian Shirlow learned on the sidelines when sometimes acting as a cornerman.

Others to get opportunities across Ulster included "Ladies Favourite" Ricky Valentine, Derry's Mick Shannon, the always affable Pat Red Kelly and Rasputin the Mad Monk – whose manic performances were so memorable he'd soon become one of the biggest billed names on the posters.

Billy Joe Beck: "Johnny Howard was a gift to wrestling, and a gift to wrestle as well. Great villain. As the Mad Monk he'd enter wearing a cloak, and carrying a bible, and they'd put the lights down and play this funeral music. If you were in the ring with Johnny, he made you look good."

Brian Page would initially act as the timekeeper for the supershows with the referee usually being Billy Finlay or the returning Syd Waddell. MC was once again Irish wrestling icon Dave Mack. By then well into his fourth decade in wrestling and still dressed to impress at any show, being aged into his 60s wasn't without its disadvantages for the former speedy Whipper, especially when travelling long distances to shows.

Pat Red Kelly: "Thing about Dave Mack, he couldn't drive in the dark. He'd be driving and duh duh duh duh duh he'd hit every cats-eye, just so he knew he was still on the road. I remember there was a show out in the country. And because we ended up on this wee road with no cats-eyes, Dave ended up in this ditch. So some sight for the farmers then passing by and seeing us big wrestlers lift this little car out of it."

Dave Mack and Kung Fu backstage at a Shirlow & Monroe show

Shirlow & Monroe also showed appreciation for the men who acted as their coaches way back in '64 by booking Dirty Darkie Arnott, Strangler Stan Cooke and Butcher Donald in bouts with the best of British wrestling, with all three getting the opportunity to match-up vs. the infamous hard man Les Kellett.

Darkie Arnott: "Les Kellett was a hard man. There used to be a gym where he lived and a lot of heavyweights would have come to it, and one of them was in wrestling with him one night and they got his finger tight and said, 'submit Les, or I'll break it'. Les wouldn't submit, says, 'go ahead, break it'."

Ricky Valentine: "He wasn't liked in wrestling fraternities. I had a few friends who were English wrestlers and they didn't like him at all. Les was a good showman, good wrestler for his age, he was a lot older than me, but Les was very eccentric. Whenever I wrestled him, and we'd finished up, because they didn't have a cup of tea ready for him he went on the huff. He loved his cup of tea after wrestling."

Ian Shirlow: "Les Kellet, I remember being on tour with him. He was a total tea-drinker, loved tea. No matter where he went, he wanted a cup of tea. He was a farmer, had hands on him like shovels. I remember we were coming back from somewhere, and we stopped off at a pub. And Kellett was having his tea, and this big farmer came up to him and said, 'you're Kellett? Sure you're only a wee small man, I could beat you'. And Kellett just got up, rubbed his two hands together, said 'right', and decked him, laid him out, and then sat back down again. He wasn't to be messed with. He was a hard man".

- - - - -

The same month that Eddie Hamill made his return to an Irish ring (since signing with Joint) he suffered his first televised loss as Kung Fu, vs. Mick McManus on the April 24th 1976 edition of World of Sport. Per stipulation the marital arts master then unmasked in the middle of the ring, revealing he wasn't of Asian persuasion at all but a fair-haired Irishman.

The decision to reveal the true identity of the mystery man was actually a strategic business move. The character of Kung Fu had proven so popular with the millions watching on a Saturday afternoon that copycat acts emerged on the independent scene, and any poor performance by a phony "Kung Fu" hurt the appeal of the real Amazing one.

Eddie Hamill: "When I wore the mask there was a lot people imitating me, there was at least five people going around the country saying they were Kung Fu. So Mick McManus was the booker in London and he said, 'look we have to get rid of all these people, and the only way to do it is to unmask you, so people can see your face and know it's you'. So that's what we done. We had the match on TV, and Mick unmasked me. So what I then done on shows afterwards was go into the ring with the mask on, and then MC would say, 'well as everyone knows, as you seen on TV, Kung Fu was unmasked so now unfortunately he must take off the mask', so I would take it off in the ring and go from there. And eventually it got to were I didn't wear the mask at all, it was common knowledge."

Kung Fu made even more World of Sport appearances after his public unmasking, with some of his best bouts being in rematches vs. Mick McManus, as well as action-packed encounters vs. the energetic Rollerball Rocco.

Eddie Hamill: "Mick McManus was great, we had the craic together. He was a great worker, he'd do anything for you. He'd say, 'you make me look good and I'll make you look good'. I don't know how many bouts I had with Mick but they were all over the country and packed the halls out. I used to have good bouts with Rocco too. It was all go with him, which I enjoyed. I hated slow bouts, and Rocco was the same. As soon as the bell went he'd rush across at you, the excitement was there, then you'd slow it down, then you build it up again. We always had a good bout."

- - - - -

Tug Wilson: "Ended up I wrestled in Germany, Zambia, Belgium and Mexico. Mexico was tough, I couldn't get into their style there, lucha libre."

Tug Wilson's time working on the independents was arguably as interesting as his tenure in the office for Joint. The ex-bouncer grappled on the German tournaments as well as becoming the first documented Northern Irish wrestler to compete in the wrestling-crazy country of Mexico when he toured for a few months with its premiere wrestling promotion, *Empresa Mexicana de la Lucha Libre (EMLL)*, starting in August 1976.

In order to stand out in a territory of high-flying masked men, Eric made the bold move of bleaching his curly black hair blonde. Wilson would wrestle in *Arena Coliseo* and *Arena México* – two of the country's most famous wrestling venues – and it was in the latter that October that Tug would take part in one of Lucha Libre's most famous match types, a "Lucha de Apuestas" match. The stipulation of the match was that both wrestlers had to wager something, and so while his opponent El Cobarde ("The Coward" in English) bet his mask, Tug would put up his newly bleached blonde hair, only to lose and then have his head shaved bald in the middle of the ring immediately following the match. Between Kung Fu's unmasking and Tug's head shaving there was no luck of the Irish in high stakes matches in 1976.

Tug Wilson wrestling in Mexico

OTRO PELON. El rufián inglés, Tug Wilson, acabó siendo rapado, después de perder su encuentro de apuestas ante el Cobarde.

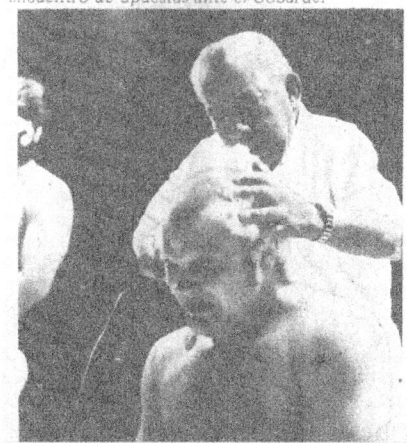

LA PLATINADA cabellera quedó esparcida por el ring de la arena México. Tug Wilson sufre la humillación de la derrota, al perder su greñero.

Tug having his head shaved after losing a match in Mexico pictures from Mexican wrestling magazines, provided by @LuchaBlog on Twitter

Tug Wilson: "My hair was a mess when it was sheared off, the black roots showing through then orange then yellow and a white frizz on top. I couldn't get peroxide strong enough in Mexico to bleach it!"

After returning from Mexico, Tug Wilson would continue to wrestle up to 1978 were aged 34 are his final found matches in England. Soon thereafter the real-life Eric Wilson would call it quits to become a bar owner in Manchester. His pub *The Clarence* being a popular lounge, particularly for *Manchester City* fans, for many years. Today in his late 70s Eric is retired from pulling pints too and lives a content life in England. As an indirect result of being involved with this book, Eric and his friend from Wryton Promotions Ian Burns attended their first *British Wrestler Reunion* (hosted in Leeds) in the summer of 2021.

- - - - -

That November of 1976 Kung Fu was back in a week of bouts for Shirlow & Monroe, and wrestling was back in the Ulster Hall for the first time in five years, sold on the fact that it would feature the first appearance of Giant Haystacks in Northern Ireland.

Towering at nearly 7 foot tall and billed as weighing a walloping 45st (530lbs) in real-life "Giant Haystacks" was Martin Ruane from Manchester whose family where from County Mayo in Ireland. The mountain of a man even claimed that only his heavily pregnant mother travelled to England two days before his birth, he'd have been born an Irishman. On TV at the time Haystacks was actually in a tag team with Big Daddy as two big, bad brutes. In Ireland the Giant was a bonafide box office attraction for the Shirlow & Monroe shows. As a result of his drawing power 'Stacks would be brought over time and time again with Irish audiences just captivated by his sheer size alone.

Through mixing massive names in British wrestling with some of Irish wrestling's finest, the first year of the Shirlow & Monroe shows were a huge success. Ballymena, Ballynahinch, Comber, Craigavon and Portrush joining Lisburn in becoming top spots for live pro wrestling shows for years to follow.

- - - - -

Meanwhile Dave Finlay Snr and his crew continued on the festival circuit. Though Dave's focus was turning from pro to amateur...

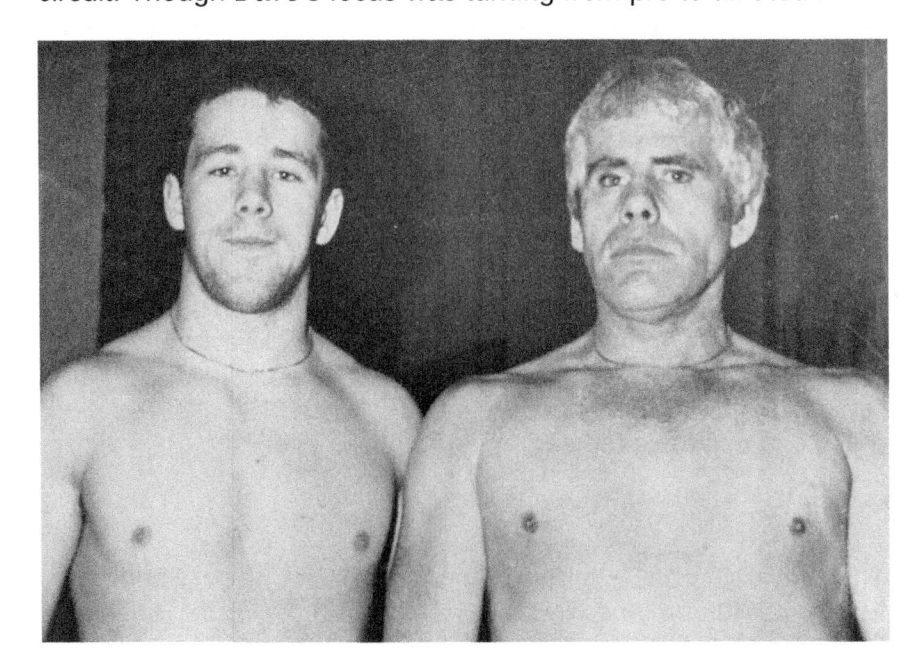

Young Dave and Old Dave

1977

Following up on his first wrestling passion, Dave Finlay Snr founded the *Carrickfergus Amateur Wrestling Club* with his goal being to re-establish the Olympic sport styles of wrestling in Northern Ireland (which had largely lay dormant since the Short & Harland's club closed over two decades before). Member #1 was of course Dave Finlay Jnr, leaving both father and son to balance between amateur and pro commitments.

The club also allowed Tiger Joe Moore a way back into wrestling in much the same way he started; through the amateur ranks. Then in his 50s, Joe was brought in as a senior coach and bridged the gap between the grappling at the members-only Huss Street gym in the 1940s and this new club in the 1970s that was initially based in a room on the top floor of a factory in Carrickfergus. In the beginning practice took place in a pro ring.

Dave Finlay: "Joe Moore was very good at shoot wrestling, so I said to Joe I was going to do the Olympic wrestling so he started helping me out. He was a decent guy, and him and I teamed up until he took very ill."

Sadly poor health would eventually force Joe Moore to finish in the amateur wrestling too. Still, Joe would visit the pro shows near to his home, and kept in touch with the scene through working with Rocky Hunter – who by chance went from working beside Strangler Stan Cooke in a factory to working beside Tiger Joe Moore in the shipyard.

Rocky Hunter: "Joe and I worked in the shipyard together, and he'd always bring to work two sausage rolls. And the way it was in the shipyard you couldn't bring food in on the job, so he'd always have to hide them somewhere to get later. Used to hide them inside the pipes hanging up on the wall. Anyway one day Joe had a heart attack at work and he collapsed, and the ambulance arrived, and as the ambulance men were carrying him out, he asked them to stop a wee minute by me, just so he could say real quietly, 'Ralph, those sausage rolls, you can have them if you want'. Cheers Joe!"

Married but without children, Joe Moore would succumb to his illness just over a week after his 63rd birthday in March 1988. Joe's greatest legacy was coaching across four decades, from the Short & Harland's gym to the space shared with boxers above the Long Bar to Jackie Briers gym to 33 Albion Street and finally with the Carrickfergus club (in strictly the amateur sport).

Rocky Hunter: "Joe was about as skinny as your finger, but he was brilliant."

Tiger Joe wasn't the only pro to follow Finlay into amateur wrestling, as several of those displaced by the ceasing of the Milo club kept themselves in shape by joining the classes.

Diamond Shondell: "Dave Finlay put me through the amateur, put me through Olympic style wrestling, while still doing the professional. That got me totally lost, because I was then doing things that give the other fella points!"

Someone who came into their own on cards around this time was 27 year old Dennis "Diamond Shondell" Millar. The partially-deaf grappler (affectionately nicknamed 'Deaf Dennis') was gifted with great comic timing, and it was after receiving some positive feedback that Shondell started playing up the part of a villain while incorporating slapstick comedy into his matches.

Diamond Shondell: "The turning point for me was I was wrestling one night, and Darkie Arnott was the referee, and after the match was over he said to me, 'where did you learn that funny walk?'. I said, 'what?', he said, 'you did a very funny walk when you where in the ring there'. I didn't know, I didn't think when I was doing it, but after I did it a few more times, they told me, 'keep doing that'. So after that, I just did what I wanted, did something funny or said something funny, or give off to the audience, and it seemed to work well."

Billy Joe Beck: "Diamond Shondell, Dennis was a natural. He acted like a dirty wrestler, but he was a funny wrestler. And the way he got on with things and doing things, people used to love him and hate him. He was so good to work with."

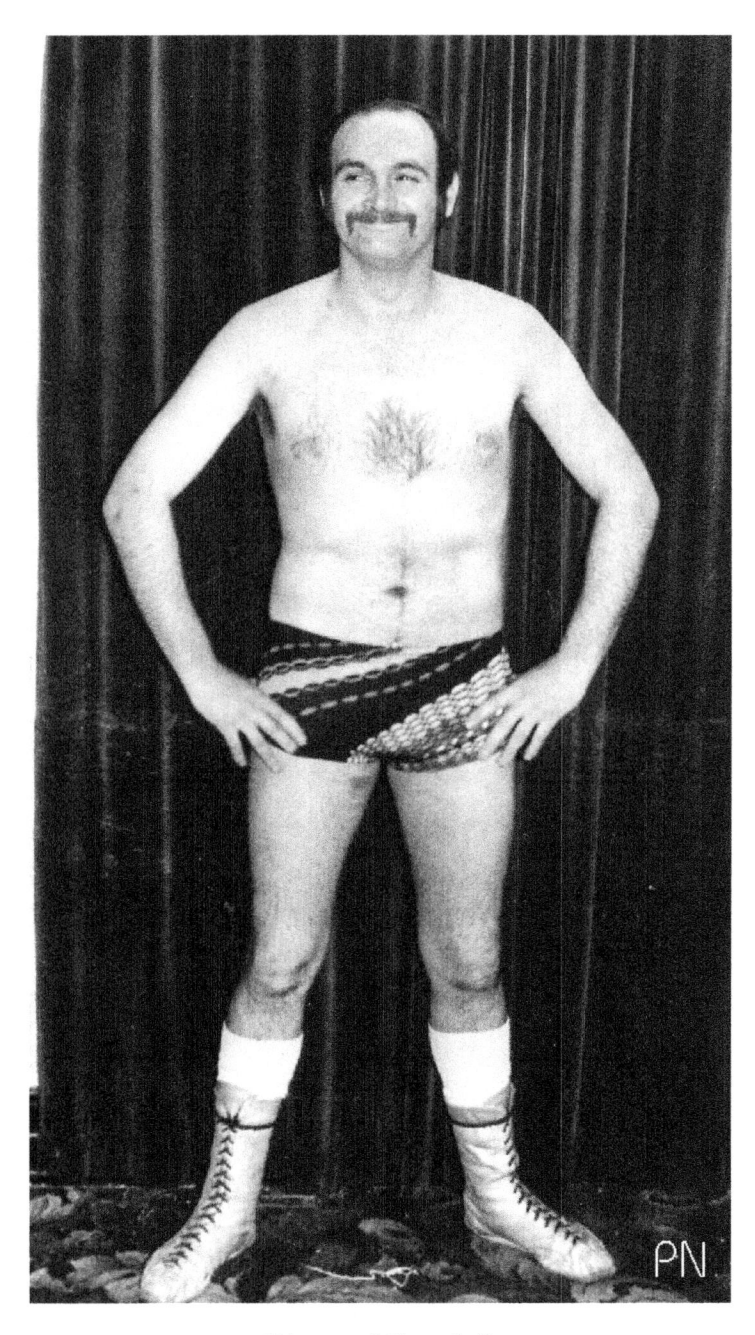

Diamond Shondell
wrestling funnyman
Picture credit to Peter Nulty

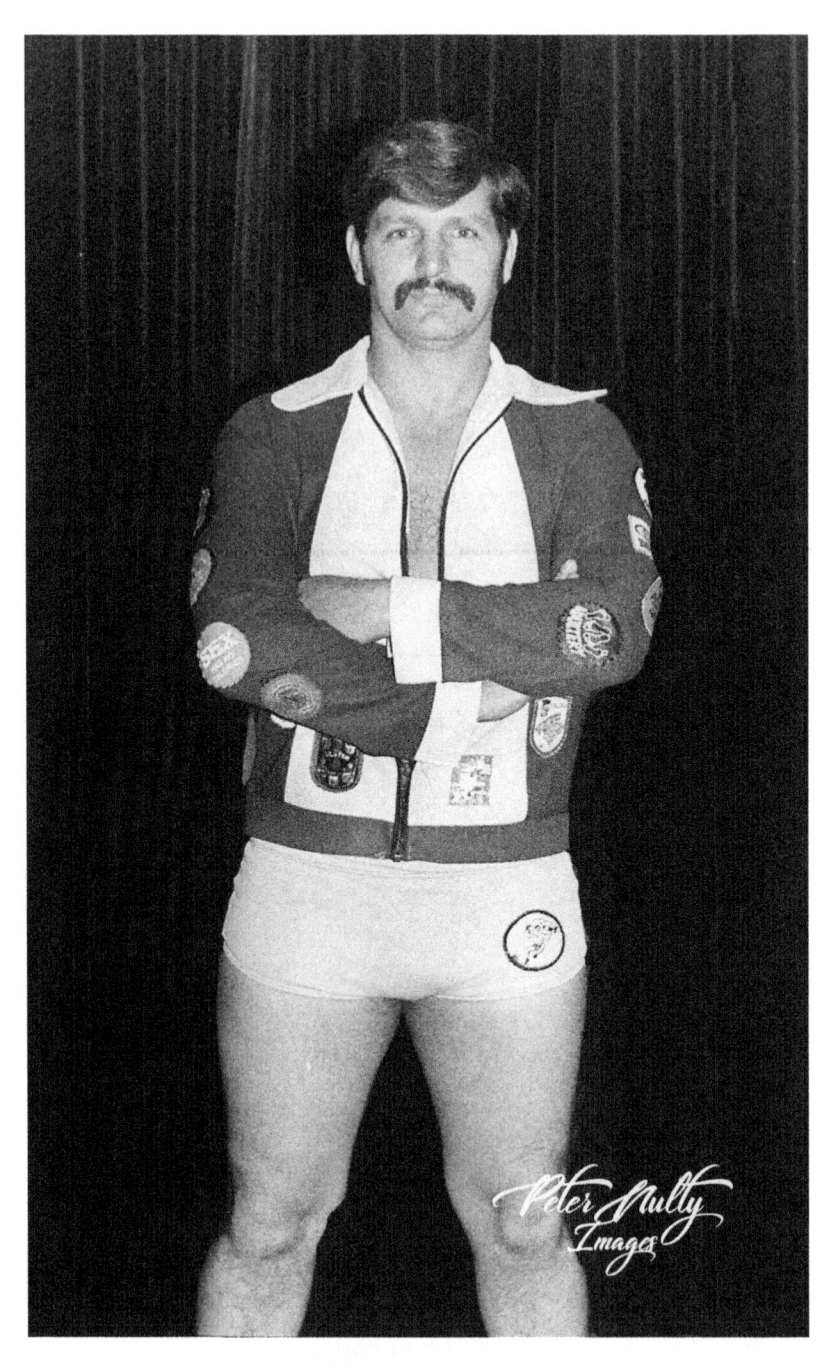

Rocky Hunter
Tag team specialist

Rocky Hunter and Diamond Shondell

Rocky Hunter: "Best one for me was the Diamond, we became great friends. I had a bout against him and during it I lifted him up and threw him out of the ring into the crowd. And you know, Dennis is a bit deaf, so he started shouting at me, 'come on out and finish it!', and I shouted back, 'come you in here and finish it!', and as all this goes on the referee is counting away, and counted him out."

Finding himself in the role of a funnyman Shondell was soon a regular in the ring billed as *"A Most Unusual Man"*.

Diamond Shondell: "Billy Joe was good, and Rocky was a good opponent too. He was hard to keep down though, like it was a workout just trying to keep him down. You'd knock him off his feet and he'd be back up before you'd blink. Would tag quite a lot with Rocky as well like."

Rocky Hunter: "Tagging with Dennis he'd do things like I'd throw the opponent in the corner, and he'd tie the tag rope round the neck, choking him. And I'd have the referee distracted, and Dennis would then jump down and tie the laces of the guy together too. So the referee would come over, and he'd take the rope off the neck of your boy, and go to help him out of the corner and inadvertently send the poor guy tumbling over, not realising the boots were tied together. Stuff like that Dennis was great at. The crowds loved Dennis. I always liked the tag team wrestling too, just enjoyed it more than the standard two in the ring."

Through the wrestling the real-life Dennis Millar and Ralph Hunter became best of friends. They also made for a terrific tag team, with the match itself being something of a specialty for Rocky in particular.
   34 year old Rocky Hunter was by then well established and very experienced on the Irish circuit. He'd wrestle frequently on Dave Finlay's features, as well as with Johnny "Rasputin the Mad Monk" Howard's club in Carrickmacross, and with his laid-back attitude Rocky was one of the easiest to get along among the grapplers in and out of the ring.

Rocky Hunter: "We had a great group lads for the most part, only the odd one out. I always got on with people, and I had no problem winning or losing. If a fella who might have only had a few fights wanted to make a name, I'd have no problem going down for him. You'd get a guy sometimes say, 'aw here Rocky I got the girlfriend and her parents watching me tonight, would you mind taking a dive?', no problem if it made him look good. And then maybe in the future, they'd return the favour, it be OK. Everyone worked well together for the most part."

Indeed while Diamond give the amateur grappling a go at Dave Finlay's club in Carrickfergus, Rocky was a regular at a new pro gym based in a youth club in Belfast.

- - - - -

Ricky Valentine: "I was a part-time youth leader down on Sandy Row, I'm from Sandy Row originally. The youth leader at the Charter Youth Club had asked me to come down as she had some unruly boys, and they couldn't keep a youth leader. And I went down and there was some lads there, didn't know who I was, didn't know I was from Sandy Row, and they weren't long finding out. So I turned it around and ended up with two good football teams, and a wrestling club. Had my own ring, it was an old boxing ring."

As early as 1975 Cecil "Ricky Valentine" Brown worked in the *Charter Youth Club* in Belfast and aiming to provide alternatives to the teenagers under his watch one of the outlets he eventually offered was the opportunity to learn pro wrestling from one the local league's best. Organising the first pro wrestling training sessions in a dedicated space since the demise of the Albion Street gym, Ricky Valentine, in his 30s, was a firm but fair coach whom, as was the tradition of the time, tested those interested first in shoot wrestling before allowing them insight into the more co-operative aspects of pro action.

As the sessions were at night and all ages were welcome, experienced wrestlers like Rocky Hunter and the Finlay father and son visited the *Charter Wrestling Club* to touch up on their techniques between bouts. The retired Whipper Billy Watson was even said to have stopped by the odd time too, with Ricky Valentine also learning sign language (like Noel Ewart and Dave Mack) in order to communicate with the Whipper.

Ricky Valentine
top technical wrestler and head coach of the Charter Wrestling Club

Ricky Valentine: "I taught this kid to wrestle, he was about 16 or 17 and overweight, and he was getting bullied, and I taught him how to wrestle. And the confidence that came out of him. His father, who's dead and gone now, came once to me and shook my hand and said, 'you have no idea the transformation you've made in my son. He was getting bullied, not anymore'. He did actually have a few bouts, but only a few and that was it."

While the vast majority of prospective pros weren't sticking to the wrestling since the turmoil of the Troubles began, two who were strong-willed enough to survive the weeding out process were 25 year old TV engineer Ian Shirlow (the nephew of Henry) and 24 year old lorry driver Bill Townsley (an in-law of Ricky's).

Ian Shirlow: "I came from a boxing background. My grandfather boxed in the army, my father, both my uncles and myself, we all boxed. That's how Henry got a forearm smash that was second to none. He was the only one I thought who could do a forearm correctly. He had the technique of it down to a tee. He would have pulled you in with two hands over the back of the head, then dropped his right shoulder and right arm, and brought the forearm up from underneath. No-one could fault him on his forearms."

Bill 'Judo Bill Weaver' Townsley: "I used to enjoy watching the Saturday afternoon wrestling, and I always thought to myself, at 14-15 years old, that's something I'd really like to do. Then later on in life my wife at the time, her cousin was Cecil Brown, Ricky Valentine. So he introduced me to it, I came with him to a few shows, then he took me to the Charter Youth Club in Belfast and it kicked off from there. We were in the club maybe three nights a week, and it was very intense. There was plenty of people who tried but never got anywhere with it, they couldn't handle the pain. There was nights I came home and probably didn't want to go back, but I did. I think it was because of pride."

Ian Shirlow: "Henry wasn't interested in me at all, he didn't want me to wrestle, he wanted to be the Shirlow who wrestled. So I got in *touch with Cecil Brown, who wrestled as Ricky Valentine, and who didn't live that far from me, he lived in Lisburn at the time. I got in touch, and asked about the club he had, and he says I could come down. So I went down to the Charter Youth Club, and was introduced by near getting my neck broke and shoulders pulled out. They'd have put you in holds, and then shown you how to get out of them. Same as any of the martial arts you see nowadays, a lot of it was just ground work. It was all taught in slow motion, 'this is how you do it', and you keep at it until it becomes almost second nature. Rocky Hunter would have been training there too, Dave Finlay Senior and his son, they'd have come by the Charter as well. You learned how to get in and out of moves. No-one knocked the living daylights out of each other, they learned how to use moves. I didn't even let on to Henry I was doing it."*

Born in Lisburn on May 29th 1952, like all the male members of his family, Ian Shirlow first and foremost was taught how to be a boxer. However, ever since he was 12 years old he had known his uncle Henry as Jack Flash Shirlow the pro wrestler, and Ian was intent on following in his footsteps.

While born in Belfast on September 21st 1953, Bill Townsley was an experienced judo player who after travelling to towns as a second for Ricky, decided to switch sports.

Tall and tough Ian Shirlow, with black hair and moustache, and fit and fast Bill Townsley, with a brilliant afro and goatee, rarely missed the chance to get down to the Charter club and be taught the techniques and tricks by Valentine – who'd since become the newest perfectionist of the dropkick in Irish wrestling.

Ricky Valentine: "I wrestled in bouts with Giant Haystacks, and he was a monster. I remember wrestling him up in Portrush, and I remember drop-kicking him in the chin, and I didn't think I was going to hit the canvas again I was up that high. I think I was near one of the only ones to dropkick him on the chin, cause he was near 7 feet tall. And I mind his feet were size 16, and I mind that from his foot being on my neck."

- - - - -

After the positive previous year Shirlow & Monroe started promoting their shows in the South too. Dublin and Castlebellingham, at a venue called *Bellingham Castle*, hosted top TV talent including new long-time World Lightweight Champion Johnny Saint as well as Ironman Steve Logan. Often opposing the Englishmen were Diamond Shondell and Rocky Hunter who were called to compete on cards across Ireland that year. It was a true testament to the toughness of the local lads that they were all part-timers / hobbyists and so balanced life between their regular jobs and wrestling, while those from the UK worked full-time as wrestlers, and weren't always without egos.

Rocky Hunter: "A good opponent was a guy you could work. Some guys thought they were superstars. They'd want to do six rounds of just throwing you about, so they could get all the attention. Over here there was very few like that, but when the English lads came over they could be like that, want to be the top dogs. You were OK as long as you could handle yourself."

Diamond Shondell: "You'd come out the shipyard, jump in a car and be on the road to a show. The bit that I would hate was when you went to Dublin, and you finished and then you seen the sign for Belfast; 100 miles. Back in them days that was like a four hour journey. So it was late night or early morning by the time you got home, and then you had to go to work the next morning. I mind my Dad some mornings having to put my feet on the ground to get me up. I was lucky in those days though, like I did get pulled a few times on my time-keeping but I never got the sack."

Rocky Hunter: "I remember there was a time I was on in Derry, and I was wrestling this guy with big long hair. He was a flying machine, but every time he got me in a hold, he seemed to be trying to drop me on my neck. So it came to the third round and I went over to Billy Finlay the referee and says, 'this guy doesn't want to wrestle me, he just wants to hurt me'. And Billy says, 'Rocky how long are you at this game?', and I says, 'a few years now', and he says, 'OK', and walked away. So I took that to mean, 'you need to look after yourself'. So when we got back at it, I got this guy and tied his hair round and round the rope, and you want to hear the screams of him when I started pulling."

Diamond Shondell: "I wrestled Johnny Saint, and he was World Lightweight Champion at the time, and he was like lightning. He'd get you in a hold, but he wouldn't hurt you, he'd just quickly change it to something else. And before you had time to think, 'how do I get out of this?' He'd have you in something else. You'd be like, 'slow down I'm still trying to think how to get outta that last hold!' He was so many steps a head of you."

Rocky Hunter: "The best compliment I ever got was when I wrestled Steve Logan. He just wrestled in the black pants you know. And after the bout in the changing room he said, 'Rock, you look around at all these guys and they have their fancy gear on to look good, but you, you're like me, we just go out to enjoy it. It was a pleasure out there tonight' and he shook my hand. That was nice to hear."

Then when the homegrown heroes weren't wrestling the best of the British scene they'd be squaring off against one another.

Lone Wolf: "Regular lads round here would be Ricky Valentine, Rocky Hunter, Pat Red Kelly. Diamond Shondell. Shondell I wrestled him a lot of times. I remember wrestling him one night in the Leighinmohr Hotel, and he made a mistake, he went to put my head under his knee and stamp down, but he mistimed it and cut my eye. And whenever we went into a hold, I said to him, 'work on it, work on it'. So he worked on it, and the next thing the blood was right down my face, my body, everywhere. And the Diamond was a dirty fighter and I was a clean guy, and the crowd was squealing and yelling at him. He was throwing me about, and rubbing his elbow into my eye, and oh they were fixing to kill him. Then at the end – and at that time some women wore these cork-heel shoes – a friend of my wife she took one of hers off and cracked him in the back of the head on his way back to the changing room."

Lee Hippie and The Lone Wolf
After dropping the hippie colours, Dennis McMillan kept the name but at times wrestled in a karate gi

Ricky Valentine: "I used to have some good bouts with Lee Hippie. I remember one time I was wrestling him in Ballynahinch I think. And I dropkicked him and he went out of the ring, and he landed on the lap of this big farmer. And this farmer punched Dennis in the back of the head as hard as he could. Could have killed him like. So I jumped out of the ring, like right over the ropes and landed on top of your man with both feet, and we both took into hammering him."

Pat Red Kelly: "Some of the boys liked to get blood drawn purposely. The likes of Johnny Howard, he had a soft left eye. Any time I'd wrestle him he'd say, 'don't forget the knuckles Paddy', next thing the blood would be flowing like a fountain."

Pat Red Kelly
one of the class of '64
and a talented wrestler and musician

On June 20th 1977 Shirlow & Monroe returned to the Ulster Hall with Rasputin the Mad Monk appearing in action, and with a big local bout on the bill in Pat Red Kelly vs. Roy Lynn.

Roy Lynn was the former Roy Digger Lynch (the fake Aussie). The heavyweight from Carrickfergus at this time was running his own health studio in his hometown. Lynn had been wrestling largely for Dave Finlay on his festival shows in previous years, but slotted in on the Shirlow & Monroe shows starting this year, Lynn would clash in bouts with other big men like Pat Red and Rasputin.

Wrestling at the Ulster Hall in the late 1970s

Pat Red Kelly: "Ulster Hall was packed. It was advertised on the radio and all. It was myself and Roy Lynn. He owned a gym down in Carrickfergus, and we chummed about a bit. So we went to his gym and practiced moves and didn't tell anybody. It was a fast match, all action, but Roy had two missing teeth so he wore fake ones, was a bit conscious about it. Well of course they got knocked out, and we then had to look around for them as the match was going on, scrambling about the mat looking for these teeth while also looking like we're still in a fight. Only for Billy Finlay, who was refereeing, to come over and be like, 'here lads I got them'. Still we had a fantastic match, and on the radio afterwards they had a person on to review it and they loved it too."

Meanwhile on the same show were three first class cross-channel clashes in Jack Flash Shirlow vs. Steve Logan, Whirlwind Monroe vs. Johnny Saint, and Darkie Arnott vs. Jackie Turpin. Jackie Turpin was the nephew of Randolph Turpin, who Darkie had toured Ireland with in the '60s. The match vs. Turpin was 48 year old Darkie's first in the Ulster Hall in over 25 years and a very memorable one for the respected veteran wrestler – who'd long since left the welding trade to go work in the civil service, inspecting sports clubs and their equipment.

Darkie Arnott: "The bout that stands out in my memory would have been in the Ulster Hall, I wrestled Jackie Turpin. He was one of the nicest people I've ever met in my life. No big head. His father had been a featherweight champion in boxing, and of course his uncle was Randolph Turpin. His father probably wanted him to be a boxer, but Jackie said his heart was never in it. He had a few professional fights then he was like, 'nah no more', and went into wrestling. So we had a really good bout, it went the distance and ended in a 1-1 draw. I think that was my last great bout, I did more after that here and there, but I think it was my last major bout. It went the full distance, and I was happy and the crowd was happy, so I was quite pleased with that."

That year Darkie became the last active wrestler left standing from the roster of Worldwide Promotions (nearly 20 years on from when it folded) after Strangler Stan Cooke retired from the ring.
     The one-time 3rd strongest man in Ireland may have been English by birth but lived out his life in Belfast, and spent close to twenty years on the Irish wrestling scene. The Strangler played an important part in the '60s as a founder of N.I. Wrestling Association and coach at the Milo club. Stan Cooke's finality is unfortunately unknown.

- - - - -

That same summer of 1977 Les Kellett was brought on board for one of Dave Finlay's most unique fixtures; an annual festival held in Tyrone at the *Benburb Priory.* Originally a Catholic monastery before being used as an army hospital during World War II, nowadays the Priory is a retreat welcoming all denominations in need of spiritual healing. Kellett was the wrestling's main attraction and, having recently quit Joint Promotions, the 60+ year old made the transition from TV star to one of the independent circuit's biggest draws. This event as well as some matches the next year being Kellett's final Irish appearances after 30+ years.

Dave Finlay himself was in a transitional period at the time, preferring growing the amateur sport than promoting pro shows.

Dave Finlay: "It was becoming more and more difficult to balance the two. Sometimes I was having to leave my wife Evelyn to run a show. So I thought, one of these has to go or they'll both suffer. I still wrestled professionally, did the tags with Fit. But the heart was in the amateur wrestling, the Olympic wrestling. We were trying to really get the scene going over here and it took a lot of work. The amateur people didn't really want any association with the professional game to tell you the truth."

So while Finlay kept his sold shows at festivals, he was no longer ringing around for them. If they didn't phone his Greenisland home to book a date, it wasn't a concern. Training local lads so they could successfully compete in national and international amateur competitions became Dave Finlay's main priority.

In turning his attention to amateur wrestling Finlay also passed his promotional partnership duties with Orig Williams over to one of their most loyal talents, 29 year old Dave Stalford. Stalford became the Welshman's co-collaborator on tours of Northern Ireland. Stalford was then trusted to drive the van carrying the ring around Europe and Africa, and still spent his summers wrestling full-time before returning to his car mechanic job at home during the autumn to spring months.

Notably, as reported on by the BBC, earlier that year in March 1977 Dave Stalford vs. English lady Viv Martell at a theatre in Belfast is the first found intergender wrestling match in Ulster's history – though not a regular occurrence, and likely just the result of Martell's original female opponent being injured or unavailable.

1978

Eddie Hamill: "It wasn't a big wage for TV. I think the top wage you got was £60. If you topped the bill at the Royal Albert Hall – I topped it a few times with Mick – it was £100. But you earned a living at it, and you got your expenses. I did like working for Joint."

Kung Fu's star was shining on World of Sport and the programme was experiencing its biggest boom in popularity since the mid '60s. This was owed in part to Big Daddy splitting away from Giant Haystacks to become a fan favourite (and an unlikely symbol of British national pride). That year Kung Fu tagged with the blonde-hair, big-bellied and beloved Daddy on television and seemed set to become even more prominently positioned on World Of Sport himself. Then suddenly Eddie Hamill quit Joint Promotions to rejoin the independent scene.

Eddie Hamill: "I left Joint as I was offered more money by Orig. I wasn't in it for the glory, I was in it to keep a family, I had a mortgage to pay. And after I had worked for Joint and been on TV, whenever I came back to work for Orig his houses were better because he now had a TV star. So I kept my word to him."

After four years of television exposure in front of millions of viewers, over the next few years Kung Fu wrestled extensively for Orig Williams as well as Brian Dixon's All-Star Wrestling – both of whom by then were behind only Max Crabtree in being the most successful promoters of pro wrestling in the UK.

- - - - -

Starring Kung Fu on their shows for the final time, Shirlow & Monroe were into their third successive and successful year as associates of Joint. Among the World of Sport sensations brought to bills around Ireland in 1978 were African action-man Honeyboy Zimba – who headlined the pairs' final Ulster Hall production that summer – and one of British wrestling's most beloved comedy characters, Catweazle.

AMAZING KUNG FU

Kung Fu unmasked

After his identity was revealed, on TV commentary and in newspaper interviews Kung Fu would always be acknowledged as Eddie Hamill. In a way his wrestling name was then "Kung Fu" Eddie Hamill

A Shirlow & Monroe show in Craigavon from May 13th 1978
These posters were designed and printed in England

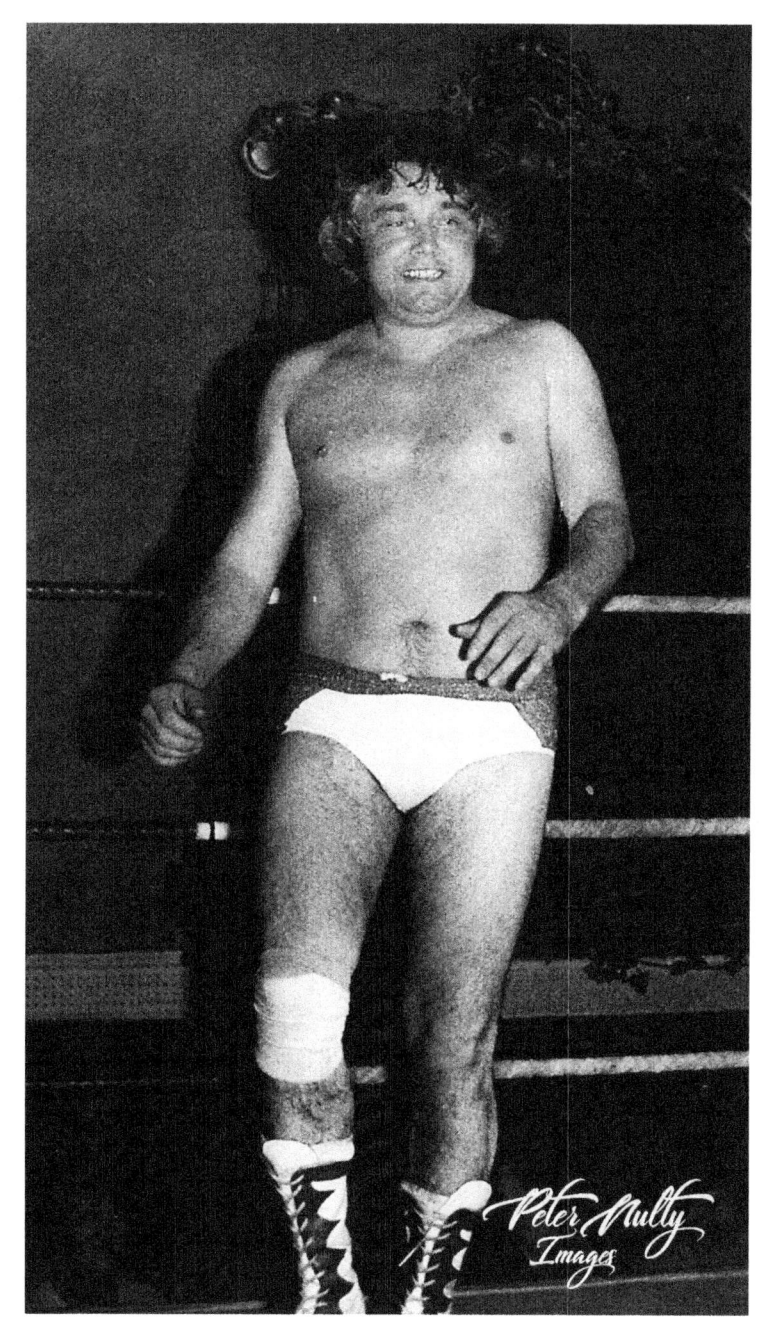

Whirlwind Monroe in the 1970s
Co-promoter of the Irish tours of World of Sport wrestling stars

277

Rocky Hunter vs. Brian "Goldbelt" Maxine in the 1970s
Billy Finlay is the referee

278

Johnny Saint vs. Ricky Valentine in the 1970s

Johnny Czeslaw vs. Billy Joe Beck in the 1970s
Picture credit to Peter Nulty

Rasputin the Mad Monk with Rocky Hunter in a headlock

The May, the Shirlow & Monroe shows also acted as the final found for bus driver Syd Waddell who after 15 years on-and-off as a referee just wasn't interested any longer and quit answering calls to oversee cards. Though finished with wrestling, Syd still shared old stories with long-time friend Darkie Arnott, with the two remaining comrades right up to Syd's passing in June 1997.

Darkie Arnott: "Syd was good fun, we were always pals. Funny story with Syd was; I was always a great motorbike man, always had a bike, and Syd and I were out on one up the country one evening on these rural roads. And I thought I heard him saying, 'Cops! Cops!'. So I says, 'never mind the cops, they'll have to catch us', and I opened up and sped off. But it wasn't about the cops he was shouting, it was about his cap which had come off his head. So we had to go back about 15 miles and somehow the cap was just lying there in the middle of the road."

Meanwhile at the Charter Wrestling Club both Ian Shirlow and Bill Townsley had persevered to become proficient in the pro style. Though it wasn't until the night that Henry Shirlow paid a random visit to Ricky Valentine at the Sandy Row youth club, that Ian and Bill would finally get their chance to wrestle on a live event.

Ian Shirlow: "Henry didn't even know I was training at the time, so when we walked into the Charter Youth Club it came as quite a shock to him. However he could see that I had stepped up and impressed, so he accepted it."

Fellow standout student Bill Townsley also impressed the undefeated Irish Light-heavyweight Champion, and was offered the opportunity to appear in action on his shows. Due to his background in mixed marital arts and ability to *weave* in and out of holds Townsley was given the gimmick name of "Judo Bill Weaver". Judo Bill wrestled barefooted and in a judo suit.

Judo Bill Weaver: "Henry Shirlow and Hugh Beattie were two absolute gentlemen. Two really fantastic guys. All the guys on the circuit were good guys. Though once you stepped through the ropes friendship was forgotten about. The English wrestlers whenever they came over, they always said there was a far tougher class of wrestlers over here than there was over there. The first bout ever I had was in the Lakeland Forum in Enniskillen, and it was something I'll never forget as they weren't expecting as many people as they got. It was nerve-wrecking, but I came out of it with a win and that was me on the way."

On November 13th 1978 it was Judo Bill Weaver vs. Rasputin in the *Lakeland Forum* in Enniskillen. The lorry driver making his debut on one of the biggest shows ever promoted by Shirlow & Monroe with a reported 2,000 jam-packed in the hall that evening. Wrestling wasn't just the attraction in itself, it was the appearance of the humongous Giant Haystacks in the west of Ulster. Fans scrambled from across Fermanagh as well as its neighbouring counties of Cavan and Monaghan to gawk at the sheer size of 'Stacks. Cameras from Irish television network *Raidió Teilifís Éireann (RTE)* were on hand to capture footage of the main event between Haystacks vs. Jack Flash Shirlow – with Billy Joe Beck filling in as the temporary referee.
	The bill also featured Butcher Donald vs. English wrestling Reverend Michael Brooks, and Hungarian army-man-turned-wrestler Tibor Szakcas vs. Whirlwind Monroe. Win or lose in his match, that night the real-life Hugh Beattie paid a very real price for being Haystacks' driver for this Irish tour...

Ian Shirlow: "Hugh Beattie was taking Haystacks back from that show, and they were in the biggest Ford Cortina on the road at the time. 'Stacks was in the passenger seat, and they came to an army checkpoint, and they couldn't get him out of the car. The army wanted him out just to get photographs with him, but he couldn't or wouldn't get out of the car. I think it was one of those things were if you got him out, you couldn't get him back in again. And when they got back to Belfast and got him out of the car, Hugh had to go the next day and get a new seat. It was totally flattened."

The huge success of the show solidified Enniskillen as another top spot for the wrestling. Haystacks' return the following year pulling in the punters yet again.

Diamond Shondell: "Biggest crowd I was ever in front of might have been a show in Enniskillen, it was packed. Giants Haystacks was on and it was in the papers the next day that it took two and a half hours to clear the car park. He'd pull some crowd. Like you wouldn't pay to see him wrestle, you'd pay to see the size of the man."

Lone Wolf: "Giant Haystacks was the biggest man I ever seen in my life. I seen him I said, 'Jesus Christ, look at the size of that man'. I couldn't believe there was a man that size."

Giant Haystacks vs. Jack Flash Shirlow
Enniskillen, November 13th 1978
Billy Joe Beck is the referee

- - - - -

The previous year in 1977 – following another period of dormancy – Mick Shannon had helped bring about another revival of pro wrestling in Derry by organising live events at *Templemore Sports Complex* and *St. Columb's Activity Centre* in the city.

The well-respected Mick called in all his contacts; Dave Mack (formerly of N.I.W.A) was matchmaker, Rasputin (formerly of the then defunct Carrickmacross Wrestling Club) was consistently on the cards, and at different times both Shirlow & Monroe and Orig Williams provided their rings and roster for a great night's entertaining to those from either side of the Foyle. However, it was Mick's good friend Dave Finlay Snr who aided him the most. Into this year Finlay and his faithful stable of wrestlers like Bruce McDonald and Noel Ewart featured on fixtures for Shannon. The Derry events also acted as the final found Irish appearances for legend-status wrestlers Les Kellett and Adrian Street.

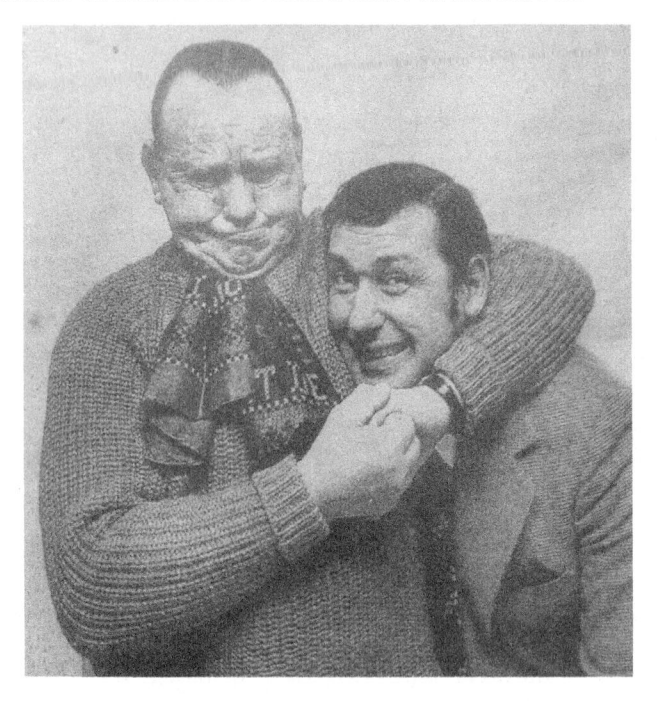

Les Kellett headlocks Mick Shannon

Dave Finlay: "I'd help Mickey out with the wrestlers, bring a car full of lads to Derry for him. Just said, you know, 'you got to pay them', and he always did. Sometimes if I brought over Kellett or Street, I'd share them over the shows. They might do somewhere for me, maybe Doagh, then go over to wrestle for Mickey in Derry."

Unfortunately age and injury played their usual part and so Mick Shannon decided to wrap up his days as a wrestler, and leave the promoting of shows in Derry to Shirlow & Monroe. The main event tag team match of Mick Shannon & Diamond Shondell vs. Dave Finlay & Young Apollo at Templemore Sports Complex on November 23rd 1978 is the final found match as an active pro wrestler for the real-life 41 year old Mickey Gallagher.

Mind you Michael Gallagher wasn't fully finished with wrestling. The following year in 1979 he established amateur wrestling as a sport in Derry by founding *The Buccaneers Wrestling Club*. Their base being the Marian Hall, Gallagher would train interested youngsters in the city in the Olympic sport and even arrange friendly competitions against Dave Finlay and his Carrickfergus club, as well as with clubs from the South of Ireland.

Mickey Gallagher demonstrating a move to the Buccaneers

Gallagher's Buccaneers and Finlay's Carrickfergus club were Ulster's only two amateur teams for years, until interest eventually waned in the Walled City and the Buccaneers ceased to exist circa 1984.

Mickey Gallagher was the heart of wrestling in his city for some 15 years and Derry's last local level pro wrestler until the new millennium. In January 2020 Michael Gallagher would pass away just a few weeks after his 83rd birthday. It is this authors greatest regret, regarding the book, that we never got to meet.

1979

Ian Shirlow: "My name was Chris Sommers because my first bout was going to be in winter time, but the posters were being made up over in England in the summer time before it. So winter, Christmas, Chris. Summer, Sommers. Chris Sommers. My wife at the time actually came up with it. I was a heavyweight, 16-17 stone. My first bout was in Castlebellingham against Judo Bill Weaver, I trained with him, and we knocked ten bells out of each other."

After impressing his uncle Henry at the Charter Wrestling Club, Ian Shirlow joined his crew on the strict condition that there remained only one "Shirlow" in wrestling. So on January 25th 1979 at Bellingham Castle, Ian debuted as "Chris Sommers" vs. Judo Bill Weaver – who'd since started tagging with Dennis "Lee Hippie" McMillan.

Judo Bill Weaver: "I was from Belfast but I moved to Lisburn and Dennis lived three doors below me in Lisburn at the time. Dennis and I we tagged together, cause he was into the karate and judo as well, so we done tag team a lot and had a few bouts against each other as well, and knocked ten bells out of one other. Dennis was a really good guy".

Ian Shirlow: "You were always travelling during the day. Some nights you'd be booked into a Bed & Breakfast, some nights if it was close enough to home you'd have just drove back. But if you went away for the week, that was you away for the week, you'd didn't return home until it was done. It was like the circus. I'd have had done quite a few matches with Rasputin, Rocky Hunter. A lot of English guys I faced, Cyanide Sid Cooper, Jimmy Breaks, you learned a lot wrestling those guys. We were only part-time and they were full-time."

Unknown at the time, Chris Sommers was to be the final notable homegrown name to debut as a pro wrestler in Northern Ireland of this era. Judo Bill Weaver and Ian Shirlow were graduates of the last class of the 20th century.

The speedy and skillful Judo Bill Weaver
Picture credit to Peter Nulty

Heavyweight wrestler Ian Shirlow aka Chris Sommers
Picture credit to Peter Nulty

- - - - -

That year, independent icon once Kung Fu was thrilling in tag team matches with Ricky Valentine or "Docker Dave Larson" – Dave Stalford renamed – on Irish bills for Orig Williams. They were supported on this tour by a women's match between the Cherokee Princess vs. Rusty Blair. Ireland didn't produce any women wrestlers in the 20th century so the English Princess and Scottish Blair were the next best thing.

Gloria 'Cherokee Princess' Pyne: "I was doing cabaret and I was asked if I would go on a tour overseas and train as a wrestler. They wanted wrestlers for a six month tour all over Asia. So I was to just learn a wrestling bout and I agreed, and then I was actually sent to Northern Ireland and did a week's training there with Carole Taylor who then became Rusty Blair. We both had a crash course in wrestling, and it was Orig Williams, he was doing the shows. So during the day we'd be trained in the ring by the guys and we just learned enough to do a bout on the tour. However then when we came back that's when we started training in earnest with Orig."

Born in England in 1956, Gloria Young was a hair-dresser turned cabaret / circus performer who aged 20 side-stepped into professional wrestling. After successfully surviving a week of learning the ropes, and literally how to run them, Gloria decided to purse wrestling as a full-time career and moved to Rhyl where she worked near exclusively with Orig Williams.

Owing to her exotic look Gloria was soon styled as a Native-American and rechristened "The Cherokee Princess", wrestling around the UK, Europe, Africa and Asia in the mid-to-late 1970s. From as early as 1977 the Cherokee Princess and Rusty Blair were frequently featured in action in Ireland. Troubles-torn Belfast was an experience for her unlike any other.

Cherokee Princess: "I think the first time I came over it was a little unnerving. You'd get off the boat and there were soldiers everywhere. And I remember we worked in a club that was either near the Falls Road or the Shankill and it was a little bit of a dodgy place to work. That was the most scary place. We were warned that if anything kicks off, just get out, just run basically. Belfast especially was a bit different to other places, getting stopped and getting searched, but you got used to it strangely. We'd go to Ireland once or twice a year, and maybe stay for a week or two at a time, and it was often in Northern Ireland and we'd stay in a place called Lisburn in a guest house there. I don't think there's a town we didn't work in. Everywhere that started with Bally we went to. We did a little bit in the South of Ireland but I think the wrestling was mostly up in Northern Ireland, it seemed to be where the majority of it took place. I loved coming over, we used to have a fantastic time. The audiences were fabulous, very responsive, we used to fill the halls, we always got such a wonderful welcome."

While Orig Williams was the top promoter of women's wrestling in Europe, Shirlow & Monroe's relationship with Joint Promotions (who were the traditional sort) meant they never booked women's matches. However, new local promoters did. New promoters inspired by the success of the Jack Flash & Whirlwind shows and the second big boom of wrestling on television fronted by Big Daddy.

- - - - -

Lone Wolf: "Roy Jordan had his own ring. He would have bought shows from Shirlow, but the risk then was that say it cost him £500 for the show, well if you don't make over £500 you've lost money. I remember the first night he run a show was in the Arcadia in Portrush. And Roy walked into the changing room and upped all our money from £8 to £16. He was a fan of wrestling. Him and the girlfriend would have come to shows and sat at ringside, this is before he got into it."

Roy Jordan was a scrapyard owner from Lisburn who initially bought shows to host as a hobby, even showing his appreciation for the wrestlers with a bump in pay (£16 being the equivalent of £50 today).

Starting in 1977, Jordan's shows were standalone all-Irish affairs in towns like Ballymena and Banbridge, and the Lone Wolf helped him in areas of promoting like putting up posters, etc. Though by 1979 Roy Jordan had respectfully cut out the middle men and began organising events with 34 year old Billy Joe Beck, who acted as the matchmaker.

Billy Joe Beck: "Roy Jordan wanted me to help him. So we did a few shows here, there and everywhere. Don't forget, you could pick a town to run a show and it would be no use, it wasn't a wrestling town. And you could pick another town and it would be bunged out. And you'd know to go back there because people like their wrestling."

Part-time local level performers were afforded even more action on the Jordan/Beck shows, which didn't bring in many notable male names from the British scene but did bring to bouts women wrestlers like the Latin-looking but English-born Paula Valdez – one of toughest and roughest in the ring, regardless of gender.
     Billy Joe remained a regular on the Shirlow & Monroe shows, so these Roy Jordan cards were carefully scheduled to not run in conflict to the Joint associates. However this wasn't upheld by everyone.

- - - - -

Dave Finlay: "Roy Lynn put together a few shows himself. There was a show of his down South somewhere, so I went down to wrestle but I get there and he says to me, 'I'd like you to do referee'. I says, 'what??'. He says, 'As a favour, please'. And he had these guys on from over the border and they were rotten in the ring, I had to talk them through it nearly the whole time. After it I says, 'never again'. Only he was a friend of mine. He had a lot of ambitions Roy."

Someone who did run shows in opposition to Shirlow & Monroe was 38 year old Roy Lynn who purchased a ring from Dave Finlay, and started running his own tours in many of the same venues as Shirlow & Monroe, like the Lakeland Forum in Enniskillen, Templemore Sports Complex in Derry and Bellingham Castle in Castlebellingham.
     As a wrestler Roy Lynn gimmicked himself as "Kojak Lynn" - playing to the popularity of TV detective show *Kojak* which

featured a bald-headed, tough-as-nails cop who chewed on lollipops played by Telly Savalas.

Roy "Kojak" Lynn

Bruce McDonald: "I liked Roy. I did a few shows for him. He was always square with me, always paid you."

While Lynn didn't have the connection to Joint Promotions, he was able to bring over recognisable wrestlers who'd previously appeared on TV but where currently independent. Irish fans got to see stars who'd previously been advertised on Shirlow & Monroe promotions like Honeyboy Zimba, as well fresh faces like "Iron Fist" Clive Myers – a wrestler who was so inspired by his match on television years before vs. Kung Fu, that he took up a martial arts gimmick of his own.

The heavyweight wrestler from Carrickfergus also used women wrestlers, being the first promoter to bring to Irish fixtures English wrestler Klondyke Kate whose superior size and strength saw her dominate the women's wrestling scene in the UK for years.

"Iron Fist" Clive Myers and Dave Mack in 1979

When the third man involved in the Shirlow & Monroe shows, Brian Page started MCing on their promotions for convenience sake, the dapper Dave Mack became the voice of Roy Lynn's promotions, working with Roy Jordan/Billy Joe Beck on their shows as well.

Two others of the old school, Darkie and Butcher, made changes in their part-time wrestling careers around this same time too.

Dave Finlay: "Darkie and Bruce were the sensible ones, they'd head home while the rest of us drank away our wages."

Bruce McDonald: "What we used to do was I would have picked Darkie up from his house, his wife Mary would have a flask and sandwiches ready for us, we would have went to the show, got ready, we'd be first bout, wrestle, finish up, take the funny clothes off, put the street clothes on, got paid and be back down the road as the third bout was going on.

As staples of the Finlay stable, Bruce McDonald and Darkie Arnott were the perfect car journey companions. They travelled to wrestling shows together for years, that is until Darkie was rushed to hospital one day after suffering a heart attack at home. Thankfully it wasn't fatal but it was enough of a scare to keep Darkie away from wrestling altogether for months.

Darkie Arnott: "I had a heart attack towards the end of my wrestling days. It must have been the late '70s. I had to have a bypass, but the surgery was successful."

At the time Billy Finlay was in high demand as the only dedicated referee left in Ireland, so the position was crying out for another level-headed character. After taking the time away to recover, and still too much in love with it to leave it Darkie returned to the scene as the regular referee for the Shirlow & Monroe shows, being found in this role as early as that summer of 1979.

Darkie Arnott "I liked refereeing. You'd get guys like Shondell there, he'd go down, then get up at the count of 6, then go down again. So I'd wait til he went down again to start going '2-4-6'. Got him up. I brought the cards into it too. White, yellow and red, and I used to bring extra. So when I first showed a card, up under a guy's nose, he'd take it and tear it up. Then I'd pull out another the same colour but with cellotape on it so they couldn't rip it."

Humorously, the former "Referee's Nightmare" became the nightmare referee for the villain wrestlers.

Jim Breaks vs. Diamond Shondell in 1979
with Darkie Arnott as the referee
Picture credit to Peter Nulty

- - - - -

While he enjoyed refereeing, Darkie did miss competing in matches. Eventually confident he was fit enough Darkie returned as a wrestler on shows for Roy Jordan and Roy Lynn in late 1979 / early 1980. Trusted to take care of the ring legend was of course Bruce McDonald who was happy to have his preferred passenger back, albeit with some initial reservations.

Bruce McDonald: "After Darkie had a heart attack, I was a little apprehensive, well more than a little, even though he had recovered well. But after the first one went OK, from there we settled. We had a good alliance, and we did a lot of first bouts. We trusted each other, so we could do good work together. Darkie was a villain originally but when he came back he just wanted to do the clever and fun stuff, which suited my style perfectly."

As Darkie winded down his wrestling days, his former tag team partner, the 48 year old Butcher Donald wrapped his up. Butcher's final found match is that summer in the South for Irish heavyweight "Big" Benny Sands who promoted his own shows for a couple of years, largely at Castle Bellingham (a popular spot).

Billy Joe Beck: "Butcher was a taxi driver and an ice-cream man. He was a lovely, easy-going guy. Everyone used to think he was an old man, but he wasn't that old, just looked it. He was so easy to wrestle, he was a treat to wrestle. He was generous in the ring, he didn't take take take."

Ian Shirlow: "I wrestled Butcher Donald one night, and it must have been very early on for me and very late on for him, and you couldn't catch him. He was quick even though he was older than me. He would have tied you in knots. He was always smiling too."

It was the end of a 17 year experience as a pro wrestler for Butcher Donald. Butcher had matched with virtually every notable name on the Irish circuit in his time, and though he finally submitted due to age and injury, his reputation for being reliable remained in the mind of Henry Shirlow in particular…

Butcher Donald in the late 1970s

That same eventful summer the Shirlow & Monroe shows hit another huge peak as thousands lined the stands around the outdoor *Recreational Grounds* in Portrush on July 13th 1979. Refereed by Darkie Arnott, the line-up was Jack Flash Shirlow vs. Big Benny, Whirlwind Monroe vs. Steve Logan, Ricky Valentine vs. The Lone Wolf, and Diamond Shondell vs. Judo Bill Weaver.

With 5 to 6 active promoters on the island, the Irish wrestling scene was red hot! Unfortunately the cool down wasn't far away…

Jack Flash Shirlow, July 13th 1979 in Portrush

Judo Bill Weaver vs. Diamond Shondell
Portrush Recreational Grounds
July 13th 1979

Brian Page
MC and one of the co-promoters of the TV talent tours

- - - - -

Away from the busy Irish wrestling scene, elsewhere in the world on August 8th 1977 in Kansas City, Missouri, USA it was "Black Angus" vs. *"Superstar"* Billy Graham for the *WWWF Heavyweight Championship.* 43 year old Angus would actually win the match by disqualification but not the title, as in America (unlike in the UK under the Mountevans Rules) wrestling belts didn't change hands on disqualification finishes. Though unsuccessful, the Irish highlander was the first Ulsterman to compete for a WWWF Title.

Wild Angus' career in America ended a year after, with the UK again becoming his home-base, and tours of Japan (with shoot wrestling legend Billy Robinson his tag partner) and tournaments in Germany/Austria again being common.

In 1979 Vincent J. McMahon rebranded the WWWF as the *World Wrestling Federation (WWF)*. At the time the WWF was working with Antonio Inoki's NJPW, and so that summer rugged 43 year old Sean Regan was wrestling in Toyko for NJPW when he unsuccessfully competed vs. Japanese wrestling legend Tatsumi Fujinami for the *WWF Junior Heavyweight Championship.*

- - - - -

By the age of 19, Dave Finlay Junior had five years experience as a part-time pro. However – like Eddie Hamill before him – Young Apollo knew that he needed to get off the island of Ireland if he was going to make it as a full-timer.

Fit Finlay: "I think it was September of '79 when I went to England. I had been wrestling, met all these wrestlers my Dad had brought over like Adrian Street and Les Kellett, and I just made the decision. I told my Mom and Dad, 'I'm going to England'. It was just like, 'hey I'm going' and sorta left the next day to go to Manchester."

Dave Finlay: "I said, 'I understand'. His mother really missed him, but all turned out all right."

Fit Finlay: "I wrestled for Orig, I wrestled for All-Star for Brian Dixon. My favourite place was the Liverpool Stadium, it was a boxing stadium, and it was wild. The crowds there were crazy. I was 19 years old having to fight my way to the ring. I never wanted to be liked or be a babyface, I always had this aggressive streak in me, maybe coming from growing up in The Troubles."

Though he'd won several competitions as an amateur with his father's club, Young Dave's passion was always the pro style. After starting a relationship with woman wrestler Paula Valdez (through her tours in Northern Ireland) the Greenisland grappler made the move to Manchester to live with Paula and wrestle full-time.
    Thankfully lost in the transition was his Roman soldier gimmick. Dave Finlay Jnr initially wrestled by his given name before being billed as the villainous "Belfast Bruiser". There was one notable name that he did bring with him from home though.

Fit Finlay: "In 1979 or 1980, I ended up wrestling with The Mummy gear on. One night in Liverpool Stadium I wrestled twice as someone didn't show up and I had the gear, so I pulled double duty and wrestled as myself and The Mummy on the same night. I had took the whole suit to England with me, thinking, hey never know when I might need this."

In the UK the Belfast Bruiser shot to the top as he also brought with him the many lessons in life instilled in him by his father. Among the most important advice Dave Jnr followed was going out and getting what you want rather than wasting time waiting for it to be handed to you.

Fit Finlay: "I didn't put people's standing in the business before mine, I respected others, yes, but I knew at an early age that no-one is going to give me this, I have to take it. I wasn't the biggest, I was 5 foot 11, not very heavy, 13-14 stone, so I had to work harder. I powered my way into positions, I outworked people. People hated me naturally, I think they thought all Irish people were terrorists, so I made the most of it. I was reliable, I was believable, I had a natural reaction from the crowd. I had this natural built-in arrogance. And again, the accent wasn't welcome."

Paula Valdez and Dave Finlay Jnr

Playing to the anti-Irish sentiment of some (as England was experiencing terrorist attacks related to the Troubles) soon the Belfast Bruiser was one of the most hated heels on the British scene and battling audience approved wrestlers like Kung Fu.

Eddie Hamill: "The Finlays, old Dave and young Dave were among my favourites in the ring. Young Dave was a great worker, he was a natural. Both the Finlay's were rough, tough, solid."

Fit Finlay: "The first time I wrestled Eddie it like it was meant to be. It was like two parts of jig-saw coming together, we just clicked. He was phenomenal."

Chapter 12

Fit & The TV Times

1980

Homegrown wrestlers / personalities active:
22

Billy Finlay, Billy Joe Beck, Bruce McDonald, Chris Sommers, Darkie Arnott, Dave Finlay Jnr, Dave Finlay Snr, Dave Mack, Diamond Shondell, Docker Dave Larson, Jack Flash Shirlow, Judo Bill Weaver, Kung Fu, Lee Hippie, Lone Wolf, Noel Ewart, Pat Red Kelly, Rasputin the Mad Monk, Ricky Valentine, Rocky Hunter, Roy Kojak Lynn and Whirlwind Monroe

- - - - -

For local level wrestling 1980 stands out as the last truly busy year, and it started off very memorably. On the January 30th edition of UTV's *Good Morning Ulster* programme an infamous incident in television history occurred when Giant Haystacks bodyslammed tiny TV presenter Jackie Fullerton.

Ian Shirlow: "Haystacks took it that they were trying to make fun of him, so he just lifted Jackie Fullerton up and piled him into the ground. I'm sure wherever we went that night it was packed."

Having just arrived into the Belfast studio, accompanied by Hugh "Whirlwind Monroe" Beattie, 'Stacks was only supposed to lift the little host up but, already grumpy and groggy from travelling, when snide remarks were made about pro wrestling by the television crew it was a step too far for the massive man who then bounced the Ballymena-born Fullerton off the floor, in a clip that has been used on blooper reels around the world ever since.

Despite breaking a few ribs Jackie Fullerton acknowledged that for as painful as it was, for better or worse it's probably what he's best remembered for. A decade later in 1990 on UTV talk show *Kelly*, Giant Haystacks and Jackie Fullerton were the special guests, appearing together for the first time since the slam heard round the studio to publicly make peace. When asked to explain, 'Stacks said it happened because Jackie had spoken to him like a "disbeliever", to which Fullerton quickly quipped he now believed.

Perhaps owing to karma for the bodyslam – or the new seat needed in Hugh Beattie's car from a few years earlier – Giant Haystacks would break his foot in a bout a few days later vs. Jack Flash Shirlow in Lisburn, and miss the rest of the scheduled shows for that week.

- - - - -

Lone Wolf is posted by Diamond Shondell
Billy Finlay is the referee

Lone Wolf: "It's actually how I met my wife was the wrestling. There was a night I was wrestling at the Arcadia in Portrush and I was thrown out of the ring and landed in the first row and I landed on this girl's lap, knocked her chair over. And afterwards we where at the bar and she was there, and I went over and said, 'I hope I didn't hurt you and I wonder could a buy you a drink?'. So I bought her a drink, and it was the most expensive drink I ever bought because 40 years later she's still here and I'm still paying for it!"

That year the Lone Wolf howled in a headlock for the last time, when 33 year old George Crothers moved away not just from wrestling but Lisburn, after falling in love with a girl local to Ballymena. George had been invaluable to the Shirlow & Monroe shows, and losing him was a big blow to their organisation. Losing a loyal wrestler was one thing but losing someone who was able to load the ring in a van, drive the van to a venue, unload the ring, set it up, set up the hall, sometimes wrestle, sometimes second, then take down the ring, load it back into the van, drive it back to where it was stored, and unload it again and do all that for a week left a huge hole in the production end of presenting events.

In later life George found great success as an electrical contractor, *Crothers Electrical* becoming a family business that his sons have since taken over. Their specialty being working on all the electrics on the ferries around Ireland. Now in his mid 70s George Crothers still lives in Ballymena with his wife and enjoys quality time with his grandchildren. A great storyteller The Lone Wolf was always one for socialising after the shows, and his close ties to Shirlow & Monroe meant he was sometimes the one who'd look after the TV talent too.

Lone Wolf: "We'd have the craic with the English ones. Cyanide Sid Cooper and I, one morning we were walking down this wee village down South in the middle of nowhere, and there was these three girls coming up and he wanted to know how to be sociable. So I says, 'see to these girls say 'pogue mahone', and just nod your head'. 'What's that mean?', I says, 'it means 'good morning''. Holy frig, walked up, 'pogue mahone' he says, and these three girls were about to friggin' kill him. He says to me 'what's going on??', I says, 'you just told those girls to 'kiss your arse!'."

- - - - -

Rasputin the Mad Monk hurls The Amazing Kung Fu across the ring

A full week's line-up for a series of Roy Jordan & Billy Joe Beck shows this year; with the Amazing Kung Fu as the main attraction, Lee Hippie in action, Billy Finlay as the referee, and the Cherokee Princess vs. Klondyke Kate supporting:

Monday February 11th at the *Valley Hotel* in Fivemiletown
Tuesday February 12th at the *Park House Inn* in Ballynahinch
Wednesday February 13th at *Three Oaks* in Aghadowey
Thursday February 14th at the *Royal Arms Hotel* in Omagh
Friday February 15th at the Orange Hall in Lisburn
Saturday February 16th at the Queen's Hall in Newtownards

After some final found matches in Ireland that summer, Gloria "Cherokee Princess" Young moved out of Wales and returned to living in England, going from a full-time to part-time wrestler. Gloria fully retired in 1984 age 28, feeling her best years were behind her, relinquishing the Native-American princess gimmick…

- - - - -

Chris Sommers: "My youngest son was born a night I was wrestling in March 1980. I was in La Mon House when I got the call. I can't remember who I was in the ring with, but when I came out of the ring, Henry told me the news, and also told me I was rubbish in the match! My head wasn't in it that night for obvious reasons."

- - - - -

A week's worth of Roy Lynn Promotions from that year; with former TV talent including Honeyboy Zimba, as well as Irish heavyweights Rasputin and Pat Red Kelly.

Monday April 21st at the *Millbrook Lodge Hotel* in Ballynahinch
Tuesday April 22nd at the *Imperial Hotel* in Dundalk
Wednesday April 23rd at Templemore Sports Complex in Derry
Thursday April 24th at *Leighinmohr House Hotel* in Ballymena
Friday April 25th at *Carrickfergus Leisure Centre*
Saturday April 26th at *Maysfield Leisure Centre*

Billy Finlay referees a women's tag team match on a Roy Lynn Promotion in the Republic of Ireland in May 1980
(L to R) the wrestlers are Lolita Loren, Nancy Barton, Paula Valdez and Nicky Monroe

Elmer Bendix: "They were stuck for a wrestler. They didn't have the right numbers, so they asked if I'd do it and I said I will surely. There was a wrestler, Honeyboy Zimba they called him. Big fella, looked like a Mr. Universe. Anyway, we were wrestling and I decided I'd headbutt him. Well that wasn't a good idea. I headbutted him, and I may as well have hit a wall. It was me that went bouncing, not him".

As well as bringing back 37 year old Portadown wrestler Elmer Bendix that April, Roy Lynn also staged Ireland's first women's tag team matches that May.

- - - - -

Unfortunately at the same time so many shows were happening the wrestling club at the Charter Youth Club faltered, Cecil "Ricky Valentine" Brown left his post as a youth leader and eventually the premises too were demolished as part of redevelopment plans.

Ian Shirlow: "There wasn't that many places you could train. We would have went to the army barracks the odd time. Billy Joe used to be a PI instructor in the Army, so Henry, Billy Joe and I would have trained there. Finlay had a spot we'd go to every Sunday at the Valley Leisure Centre. It just got that a few would get together and wherever you got to train, you trained. Your biggest worry was just keeping yourself fit."

Judo Bill Weaver: "When the Charter closed down we went to the Harland & Wolff club, down at the shipyard, and done training there. Albeit there was no wrestling ring, we just used mats. It was Rocky Hunter who introduced us as he worked at the shipyard at the time, and it was usually just myself, Rocky, Shondell and maybe the odd time Cecil. It wasn't just about the wrestling at the shipyard, it was just keeping fit in general, using the gym and the weights and all."

Sadly the grappling didn't keep at any new gym, no new local names emerged, and many more memorable ones departed. If 1940 was the beginning of local level wrestling in Northern Ireland, 1980 was the beginning of the end of it.

Missing their injured money-maker Giant Haystacks, Shirlow & Monroe would bring in "Mighty" John Quinn, a 6'5 Canadian heavyweight villain – who in a bit of dissonance would make his entrance to the cheerful tune of the *"Mighty Quinn"* by Manfred Mann. Quinn and Haystacks as enemies to the heroic Big Daddy actually helped British wrestling reach its highest peaks in '79 and '81, respectively. The two took part in much hyped matches vs. the Union Jack singlet-wearing Big Daddy at *Wembley Arena* with crowds of 10,000 and 7,000, respectively, reported.

Quinn was another big hit on Irish bills. However, this was his only tour with Shirlow & Monroe as he would depart Joint Promotions that summer – opening the door for something of an exodus as many more notable names would follow, inadvertently effecting the quality of stars available to Henry and Hugh.

Jack Flash Shirlow vs. The Mighty Quinn
Backstage before a match at Glenmore Activity Centre in Lisburn
May 2nd 1980

Darkie regrets giving the Mighty Quinn a yellow card

As Dave Finlay's festival circuit was nearly fully finished, his crew had start appearing on cards for Shirlow & Monroe. That late-April / early-May 1980 tour of The Mighty Quinn featured the final found appearance for The Mummy after 15 years on the Irish circuit – with some suggestion of Dave Finlay Snr himself being the final man to wear the crepe bandage costume.

Also found is 40 year old Noel Ewart's final found match, which was billed vs. Rocky Hunter. Ewart's step away from wrestling owing to age and injury. His match was the final too for anyone in wrestling who came through Larry Casey's gym. The Adonis of the Irish scene the last of the bodybuilders from the '60s.

In May 2011, age 71, Noel Ewart would pass away. A well-liked man in his local community Noel was fondly recalled by those in the wrestling fraternity as well.

Dave Finlay: "Noel Ewart was a good lad. He'd have done a good bit with me. I wrestled him the odd time but he was a lighter weight than me. He had a good build to him, being into his weight-lifting, very nice man."

- - - - -

(R to L) Billy Joe Beck, Ricky Valentine, Rocky Hunter, Cherokee Princess, Dave Mack, Diamond Shondell and Klondyke Kate before a Roy Jordan show in the summer of 1980

Darkie Arnott: "I made a bit of a comeback. Though I felt I was always trying to make sure I didn't do more damage, so after a while I decided to just referee."

After working some bouts with Bruce McDonald for Roy Lynn, a match that June of 1980 at the *Bay Hotel* in Cushendun – promoted by Roy Jordan / Billy Joe Beck – is the final found for Darkie Arnott after 30 years as a pro wrestler. Dave Mack the MC and Billy Finlay the referee, besides Cherokee Princess vs. Klondyke Kate, the all-Irish affair also featured Ricky Valentine vs. "The Exorcist" (likely Rocky Hunter in a mask) and Billy Joe Beck vs. Pat Red Kelly, with Darkie's bout being vs. Diamond Shondell.

Darkie Arnott: "Wrestling was really the thing in life I was most interested in, hobby-wise. I always respected it, and was grateful I got to do it for so long. My family always accepted it. Never a word about it, except if you came back saying 'oh my shoulders sore', 'oh my neck's sore'. 'Is it any bloody wonder?' they'd say. I made an awful lot of friends and it opened doors for me. I think I had probably some 300 bouts, maybe more, maybe less. When I think about it, I got through all those bouts without a serious injury, which is lucky."

After being Shirlow & Monroe's main referee for over a year, Darkie's final found appearance in the bow-tie is that September of 1980 on a show at the *Golden Grill Nightclub* in Letterkenny – with Billy Finlay taking over as the top referee of the TV talent tours thereafter.

Darkie Arnott: "I certainly enjoyed it. I never got a great deal of money out of it but that wasn't the point. We weren't big time. We were big time in Northern Ireland, but not on a wider degree, but I was happy with what I got. I think the thing I was always very proud of was that my picture got appearing in The Ring magazine. It was a boxing and wrestling magazine from America. I don't know if anyone else from here ever got that."

From a rookie at the Short & Harland gymnasium to a regular for Worldwide Promotions to relaunching homegrown pro wrestling in 1962, Darkie Arnott was truly the architect for the success of those who came after him; one of his trainees was a World of Sport star who travelled the world wrestling; another was first Ireland's #1 pro promoter and then the driving force behind the revival of the amateur sport in Ulster; and two more started their own shows and in spite of the Troubles brought some of the biggest names in British wrestling to Irish shores.

Everything from a local level in the prior two decades led back to Darkie Arnott, the grandfather of Northern Irish wrestling.

By then the 51 year old Noel Arnott was an actual grandfather too, and quietly faded way from wrestling to instead started spending more time with his family and friends away from the ring. Enjoying his career in the civil service helped with the transition away too, as Darkie didn't feel he needed to escape the lower points of life as he was very content with his lot in it.

Darkie Arnott: "I was recreation officer for all the training centres in Northern Ireland. You could pick where you wanted to go everyday. I did it for 24 years. Even when I had the heart attack and was off for six months they still paid me. Best job I ever had in my life. Though at my 90th birthday, we had a big party and my wife Mary joked that I was the most uncivil civil servant there ever was!"

Around the same time too Darkie was picking up another talent; playing the banjo. Moving off the mat and into music Darkie joined the *Belfast Banjo Club* and within a few years wasn't just a skilled banjo player but was also apt at building the instrument itself.

Today as Ireland's oldest living wrestler at 92 years old and counting, Noel Arnott is a great grandfather and still married to Mary, his wife of 60+ years. Still smoking a pipe he credits his long life with keeping fit while eating whatever he wants.

The referee's nightmare in the ring but an absolute gentleman outside it, there is no greater ambassador for the glory days of pro wrestling at a local level in Northern Ireland than Darkie Arnott.

1981

After a steady stream of shows, with tours of either fresh-off TV talent or all-Irish cards supplemented with women wrestlers, it may have been too much to manage as Roy Lynn staged less and less live events towards the end of 1980. There are no "Kojak" promotions found in 1981.

This year the Carrickfergus gym owner would quit the wrestling business and return to Australia. The former Digger Lynch was involved in the pro scene for at least 14 years and while his stint as a promoter was relatively short he still provided local wrestlers with many more matches and memories. As of 2022, in his late 70s Roy Lynn still lives in Australia.

- - - - -

Billy Joe Beck: "See with promoting, it's not easy, it's a lot of work. You have to get posters designed, and printed, and then put out. You have to keep publicity going so people don't forget it's on. And the only way you would really make money is if you could sell a show to somebody. You can charge them then, but if you have to do everything yourself it's a tough task. Sometimes a really good show would cover a bad show, money-wise, but it wasn't worth it usually. Unless you were a big promoter with years and years behind you like Joint Promotions, like Orig Williams, like Brian Dixon, you're making no big money from it."

That summer some sold shows to festivals in Lisnaskea and Newcastle are the final found promoted by Billy Joe Beck and Roy Jordan – the scrapyard dealer's fandom had subsided and he looked at wrestling events as too much of a financial gamble to justify any longer.

On these shows is yet another final finding in one of Irish wrestling's most popular performers 39 year old Pat Red Kelly in a tag team match as one of The Undertakers, reportedly partnering in this version with Rocky Hunter.

Pat Red Kelly: "I got fat! Too many pints! Nah I drifted away from it, I had work and whatever else. There was too much going on and going against it. Eddie went over to England and give it a go and ended up wrestling six nights a week and got on TV. He made it, not a lot do, only a small handful from thousands. I was offered to work with Orig after Eddie went and I went over and did a few shows with him, and there was talk that if I did this and did, that I might – might – get on the television. But I said 'no chance', they said 'why?', I said, 'well I don't think the legs of it would support the weight of me'! I have no regrets though, regrets slow you down and kill you."

After 17 years of action, the real-life Paddy Donaghue wouldn't be wrestling in his all-red or all-black gear any more. The cheerful character instead kept alive his other passions namely motorcycles and music, and in the latter Pat was joined by fellow guitar player Judo Bill Weaver.

Judo Bill Weaver: "Pat is a fantastic singer and sometimes after the shows we'd have brought our guitars and had a session together. It was really good, people really liked it. You could have been at a hotel and people would come down from their rooms to the bar to listen. We even had a band for a bit called Black Velvet, so the Black Velvet band. Might have been Pat's idea that, his sort of humour, he was good craic."

In later life Pat moved from the noisy city of Belfast to the quiet Donegal countryside, where he settled into life on the west coast by the sea. For a time too he taught traditional Irish music to interested youngsters. As someone who loved seeing the sights on his trips to wrestle around Ireland, even today being aged into his late 70s hasn't stopped jovial gent Paddy from adventuring far and wide in his trusty caravan.

Pat Red Kelly: "I go down into Europe in the winter months in a caravan, cross country in a caravan. The cost of living there is very very cheap. I've went down into Spain, North Africa. Used to be I'd have to bring all these different currencies, but when the Euro came in, it was brilliant. The wife used to travel with me, but she got tired of it, she'd rather fly. So now she just flies in to see me. I love getting away."

Pat was also very kind to gift this author with one of his ring jackets (a red one) during the writing of this book which, at 40-45 years old at time of writing, when worn on the modern day Irish wrestling scene the jacket will be tying two different generations of homegrown wrestlers together by literal threads!

- - - - -

Roy Lynn and Roy Jordan both out of the business, this year too Shirlow & Monroe pulled back significantly on promoting. Fewer of their shows are found than in previous years with this attributed to a decline in supply and demand. As a result, Irish wrestlers looked abroad for matches.

A frequent feature on all promotions during the boom period, 38 year old Johnny "Rasputin" Howard worked in the UK for Orig Williams, as well as in Europe on the German/Austrian tournaments dating back to at least 1979, where he is listed in matches against iconic French wrestler Andre the Giant.

Noteworthy, is that as Frank "Wild Angus" Hoy was still active and wrestled as Rasputin in Germany/Austria, whenever Johnny Howard appeared in action there he was sometimes billed as "Rasputin II". This could very confusing for anyone looking back on results for the tournaments.

Billy Joe Beck: "I used to work for the fire brigade, and I used to get leave, holidays, for twelve days in the spring time. For the summer, you got three weeks. And then in the autumn time you got another twelve days. So I was able to go for a week in the spring time, three weeks in the summer and then another week in autumn, overseas to England, to Scotland, to wrestle for Brian Dixon. And If you got it, you took it if you were free and wanted to. And I loved it, so I took it.

Bruce McDonald: "I would go over for Orig and work a week or a fortnight for him. It was usually during summer season, around Scotland, England, Wales and the Isle of Man. I would take leave, and my leave was extremely flexible because I worked out-of-hours an awful lot. I even did a bit for Orig in Kenya. It was very hot but very nice. Huge crowds. I worked with Brian Dixon too and a bit with Joint. Worked Adrian Street, Johnny Saint. The laziest worker in the world was Jackie Pallo. I worked with him and all he wanted to do was shout at the audience, give them stick. 'I have a castle in Spain Missus, do you want to come and hunt it?' all that."

Bruce McDonald (bottom left) and Dave Stalford with English wrestler Carla Sanchez and a flight attendant, at the airport in Kenya in 1981

Billy Joe Beck: "When I was in Scotland, I got to see Andy Robin and his bear. Andy Robin was a wrestler and he used to own and wrestle this bear as a bit of an attraction. So we had drove up to where he lived and were waiting for him, no sign. Next thing we look over into this field and there was the bear chasing after a horse. But they were playing, like the bear would chase the horse, then the horse would chase the bear and they were friendly with one another. It was unbelievable, my greatest regret is not having a camera to take a picture."

Someone who both Bruce McDonald and Billy Joe Beck crossed paths with on the British circuit was Scottish wrestling icon Chic Cullen.

Frank 'Chic' Cullen: "The first year I came to Ireland was with Orig Williams, it was always with Orig, and it was in 1977. I was 17 years old, I was a rookie, I did more putting the ring up and down than anything but that was my way of getting training from these guys – the quicker I got the ring up, the quicker the experienced guys got in the ring with me and coached me. Bruce McDonald taught me an awful lot about wrestling. I used to work with him a lot and he was so unselfish in the ring. He always tried to make you look the best he could and I've never forgot him for that. He seemed like the Jim Breaks of Ireland in that they'd put him in with young guys to get them along. He'd be on the tours in Scotland, he was a great guy. And Dave Stalford was one of my dearest friends in the business. He looked after me when I first started. Whenever I was in Northern Ireland I'd stay with Dave and his wife at their house."

Born in Scotland in 1960, as a wrestling-crazed teenager Frank "Chic" Cullen moved to Rhyl to join Orig Williams' motley crew. Through touring Ireland he learned from Bruce McDonald and Dave Stalford. Later Cullen would leave Rhyl and take up residence in Birkenhead, which was the base of Brian Dixon's All-Star Wrestling. It was working there that the speedy, rough scrapper would meet Billy Joe Beck, who himself was accompanied by another speedy, rough scrapper in 29 year old Dennis "Lee Hippie" McMillan. McMillan had joined Billy Joe on a trip to England when he was down on his luck after losing his job as a mechanic.

Billy Joe Beck: "I phoned Brian Dixon and says, I got another wrestler here and he'd maybe make a good villain, he looks the part, and he can move, he can work, do what he's told. And he says, 'ok I'll give him a chance, but he'll have to pay his own fare over, and if it works out, I'll pay his fare back'."

Chic Cullen: "I had met Dennis in Ireland when he was Lee Hippie and got on with him, then I met him again when he was in Birkenhead with Brian Dixon as Rocky Moran. He came there for six months and just never went home."

Thankfully on the British scene Dennis McMillan dropped the dreadful Lee Hippie gimmick and – in part tribute to his father, the international boxing referee "Rocky" McMillan – was repackaged as "Rocky Moran". In action for All-Star Wrestling, Moran impressed as a nasty Irish villain with a mighty moustache and even mightier mullet.

Enjoying the experience, and seeing no future for him nor his family in Northern Ireland, McMillan asked All-Star big boss Brian Dixon if he could stay on as one of his regulars in the UK, which Dixon agreed to. Proving his worth with consistent top class clashes, Rocky Moran became a full-time pro wrestler and one of the British scene's best all-rounders, able to adapt to any opponent, able to work slow or fast, and able to get a reaction from a crowd – especially as a villain.

Someone the ex-boxing prodigy gelled really well with was Chic Cullen. In fact, while McMillan worked out the logistics of bringing his two young daughters over to live with him, in the meantime he shared a flat with Cullen and women wrestler Klondyke Kate in Birkenhead.

Chic Cullen: "Dennis became one of my best friends, and we lived together, travelled together, wrestled against each other for years. We used to take everybody for their money at pool, here was the Irish guy and the Scottish guy coming together to beat all comers. Dennis was a very popular guy in the dressing room too and in the ring."

- - - - -

While All-Star Wrestling took on another dastardly Irishman in Rocky Moran, it lost its previous Paddy public enemy #1 to Joint Promotions.

Fit Finlay: "So I was working for Brian Dixon and what happened was Mighty John Quinn and Tony St. Clair left Joint Promotions and came to All-Star, and I was its top heel at the time. But when they came they were an established, made-up main event. You had a good-looking babyface in Tony St. Clair against the powerhouse in John Quinn, so I got moved down the ladder. So I talked to Tony, and he talked to Max Crabtree, and said 'hey I'm sending this Dave Finlay over to you', and within two weeks I was working for Max and quickly went to the top."

Though the public idolised Big Daddy, his fame frustrated many of his fellow wrestlers. Some felt that World of Sport had become a one-man showcase for the promoter's brother, and so slowly but surely many of those disgruntled exited Joint. On the independent scene, Dave Finlay Jnr rightfully guessed he could be washed away by the flood of big name TV wrestling stars coming in and so decided it was time to take the high ground and build his brand in front of millions on ITV.

Fit Finlay: "Before that I was wrestling as the Belfast Bruiser, I was given that name by Brian Dixon. But then Max Crabtree said to me 'you look quite fit so I think we'll call you... Fit Finlay'. I went 'OK', but I thought, that's so dumb. But even today everyone calls me Fit, I don't think they know my name's Dave at all!"

On the October 17th 1981 broadcast of World of Sport it was 21 year old Fit Finlay vs. Chris Adams; a world-travelled wrestler who rarely stayed in one place for too long. It was fitting really that Fit's first televised match was against a globe-trotting grappler.

- - - - -

Meanwhile at home the local wrestling scene was withering away.

Trying to keep the fire burning Judo Bill Weaver and his old coach from the Charter club and cousin-in-law Ricky Valentine had pooled together to promote their own shows in and around Belfast, Lisburn and the surrounding areas.

One of their venues included *Thiepval Barracks* as live events for the British army stationed in Northern Ireland dated back to the 1970s with Dave Finlay running them. The army camps were certainly an interesting invention in order to capture an in-house crowd as the soldiers really didn't have much in the way of entertainment elsewhere in Northern Ireland.

Ricky Valentine: "Did a lot of the British Army camps. The boys there they loved it, especially when the girls were on."

Unfortunately selling shows wasn't as easy as it once was nor were many festivals taking wrestling on as an attraction anymore, and so the Valentine / Judo Bill shows were very sporadic.

Judo Bill Weaver: "Ricky and I done a couple, the odd one here and there, to keep the thing going, keep a bit of interest in the circuit. But to put a show on you got to pay a lot of money out of your own pocket, which is tight going. We'd have guys like Rocky Hunter, Bruce, he was a very quiet, down-to-earth guy, Shondell, Rasputin. The referee was usually Billy Finlay, and MC usually Dave Mack, he was a gentleman."

Ricky Valentine: "Dave Mack was a character. Always wore a suit, always suave. He was brilliant as an MC."

Diamond Shondell: "I got to know Dave Mack well when he was doing the MC. He looked the part and was a really lovely guy. He didn't drink, so after the show I'd have a pint of Guinness and he'd have a cup of tea, and we'd have a few yarns."

On one of these Valentine / Judo Bill shows at the *North Belfast Working Men's Club* is the final finding of the slick-haired 68 year old Dave Mack as an MC at a live wrestling event. Dave Mack's then 12 year old daughter Tricia assisted that evening as the bell-ringer. Humorously, her father's suggestion at the family dinner table that she too could someday be involved in wrestling was instantly shot down by his disapproving wife – who especially wasn't happy when she heard her daughter nearly got flattened by Dave Finlay Snr flying out of the ring on that same show!

Dave Mack in the 1980s

A life-long cigarette-smoker who didn't touch alcohol, the real-life Dave McQuitty would pass away age 83 in December 1996. As a wrestler, referee, MC, coach, promoter, matchmaker, and gym owner Dave Mack experienced every era of pro wrestling at a local level in Northern Ireland in the 20th century, from its beginnings in the '40s to the heydays of the '50s, '60s and '70s, and was even there at its end in the '80s…

Costing much in effort and expenditure Ricky Valentine and Judo Bill Weaver would eventually cease running cards too.

Judo Bill Weaver: "The promotion end of it died off. We were hoping something would take off, nothing ever did, and everybody just sort of backed off and left it."

1982

While Shirlow & Monroe remained players, it was Orig Williams who became Ireland's top dog for pro wrestling promotion. Adding to his colourful character the 50 year old Welshman was by then wrestling as "El Bandito" were styled as a Mexican outlaw he wore a poncho, a sombrero and a handlebar moustache, and only give the gimmick away with his thick Welsh accent.

In time El Bandito and his gang took over all the top towns on the Irish scene including Enniskillen, Derry, Ballymena, Dublin and Castlebellingham. On the British circuit, he was still behind Max Crabtree's Joint Promotions and tied with the ambitious Brian Dixon and his All-Star Wrestling, but on the island of Ireland Orig was #1.

By now one of the Welshman's biggest billed attractions Kung Fu was working in Canada for Stampede Wrestling.

Eddie Hamill: "I went to Canada to work for Stu Hart. I think it was Chic Cullen that had mentioned me to the Hart's, and they had said 'I heard you used to wear a mask?'. They wanted me to wear it again, so I did, no problem, I started all over again in Canada."

The Hart family were to Canada what the Finlay family were to Ireland, with patriarch Stu Hart putting his full faith in his family to help him succeed in his wrestling shows. All five of Stu's sons were wrestlers, and in the late '70s they'd taken to touring the UK. Continuing the decades long connection between the British and Canadian wrestling scenes, the Hart brothers also convinced their father to bring some of the UK's best acts to Stampede Wrestling including Frank Cullen who put the good word in for Eddie, whom he'd met through working on shows for Orig and Dixon.

In October 1981 the Amazing Kung Fu – wearing a mask again – debuted with Stampede and became a fan favourite on another continent, even teaming in tag matches with a young Davey Boy Smith (the future British Bulldog).

In North America the rules of wrestling differed. There was no rounds system nor public warnings, and while the British independents had always allowed more leeway with the rules than Joint Promotions presented on ITV, in North America wrestling was still like the wild wild west / all-in wrestling where attacking your opponents after a match or interfering in a rival's bout or using weapons such as steel chairs, chains etc were all par the course for an organisation like Stampede.

Eddie Hamill: "Their style of wrestling was completely different from our style. I was used to British wrestling. I was used to rounds, they didn't work rounds, they just wrestled straight through, and actually in the end I thought that was better. I got used to how they worked over there, it's why they asked me to come back after the first time. I went there three months, came back, then they asked me to come back again. I said I couldn't again because I had a family, and Stu said to bring the family. So we moved all to Canada."

- - - - -

As his VISA only allowed 38 year old Eddie Hamill to stay for three months at time, between trips Kung Fu rejoined Joint Promotions in early 1982 and reignited his feud with Rollerball Rocco.

- - - - -

That February Eddie returned to Canada to wrestle full-time for Stampede, and this time with his family joining him for the three month stay. Though culture shocks when living in a new country are to be expected, unfortunately it was some shocking organisation in the wrestling that really blew Eddie's mind during his second stint as Kung Fu for the Hart family.

Eddie Hamill: "I mind I arrived at a hall once and there was no ring there. The punters showed up before a ring did. And then they had to put it up in front of all the people just sat there. One time too I got into the ring, and then this other fella came out, but he wasn't who I supposed to be on with. So he had to then go back, and the fella who I was supposed to be on with come out. I thought, what kind of place is this? You wouldn't have got away with it at home. It was so disorganised."

On a positive note, Kung Fu was billed in a six man tag with wrestling legend Bret Hart, who was considered the best of the Hart brothers and was soon snapped up by the WWF in America. This year 1982, Vincent J. McMahon signed over the WWF to his son Vincent K. McMahon, who would soon reshape pro wrestling or, as he termed it, "sports entertainment", across the world.
	Wrestling was about to take the great leap forward, but Eddie Hamill was happy to take one small step back when he returned to Wales with his family for good that spring.

Eddie Hamill: "After the next three months passed we moved back home again and I just thought, I'm not going out there again. I did like living in Canada but the travelling back and forth wasn't worth it. Especially with a family and having the kids in and out of school and all that, it wasn't practical. At that point I went back to working with Orig again. There was still plenty of work going."

As Kung Fu had only worn it again on request, on his final Stampede appearance, influential English wrestler The Dynamite Kid (another future WWF star) tore Kung Fu's mask off and ripped it to shreds. It was Eddie's last mask, so there were to be no more revivals of the Amazing one as a mystery man.

- - - - -

That same spring is the final finding for a Shirlow & Monroe show. Taking place on April 9th 1982 at the *Glenmore Activity Centre* in Lisburn with a crowd of 400 reported, after seven years of touring top World of Sport talent around Ireland the trio of Henry Shirlow, Hugh Beattie and Brian Page stopped promoting pro wrestling together.

Brian Page: "We stopped it because wrestling just sort of went out of fashion. Overall I would say it was quite successful, I wouldn't have done it for so long if it wasn't. I didn't have anything to do with wrestling afterwards, that was an end of an era for me really."

Shirlow & Monroe show from April 9th 1982 in Lisburn
Diamond Shondell replaced Chris Sommers on the night

The event also acts as the final found match for Whirlwind Monroe following an 18 year wrestling journey entertaining fans and endearing himself to everyone he came in contact across Ireland, the UK and Europe. Half of the notable names of the class of '64 were then finished with pro wrestling.

The real-life Hugh Beattie had other priorities; when he wasn't running his carpentry and property development businesses, Hugh was a dedicated family man with three daughters and two sons. Whenever he was able to get away from the city life and city sounds he'd take his family out on his self-built boat on sunny days, sometimes on the scenic Lough Erne in Fermanagh.

Meanwhile Henry Shirlow had started running Northern Ireland's first roller rink in Lisburn. *"Jack's"* (after his wrestling name) was a popular spot and all the rage of its time as the best pop and new wave beats blurred on speakers to thousands a week, who came along in clothes and hairstyles that were acceptable only in the '80s.

Brian Page however was fully finished with wrestling. Sadly in May 2021, just a month after the publication of this book, following an illness Brian Page would pass way age 86.

- - - - -

That year (or early the next depending on when the episode aired) Kung Fu was back on the small screen, but it wasn't on World of the Sport it was on a Welsh wrestling programme called *Reslo*.

Eddie Hamill: "Orig had his own TV show in Wales, Reslo. It was very popular there, and I worked on a lot of those shows."

That year the Welsh-language channel *C4S* was launched and on November 10th 1982 it started its own wrestling series called Reslo. Reslo is Welsh for quite simply "Wrestling". Orig Williams was the mastermind behind the series, though, unlike World of Sport on ITV, Reslo wasn't on C4S every week, it was like any other television show in that it would appear annually for a set number of weeks (the number of weeks was never consistent) and was broadcast for 30 minutes on a Tuesday night.

The commentary was in the Welsh language, however C4S could be picked up in parts of Ireland and England too. Reslo featured the likes of the Mighty Quinn, Tony St. Clair, the newest names to split from Joint in Rollerball Rocco and Johnny Saint, and was also the first British television show on which women wrestlers appeared.

Kung Fu and Rasputin were among the Irish names, as well as Dave "Docker Dave Larson" Stalford who even wrestled in a red, white & blue singlet with an emblem of the Northern Ireland flag on the front. Bruce McDonald also came close to being in an episode but his filmed bout wasn't broadcast in the end.

Billy Finlay: "With the refereeing you need to do know what you're doing and have confidence in it. Some ones tried it and just didn't look comfortable. They'd get in the road you know. A lot of times they'd have old wrestlers be referee and they didn't have a notion what they were doing".

Keeping order as an official on the very brightly coloured programme was 49 year old Billy Finlay. After years of part-time refereeing for all the promoters in Ireland, Billy decided to quit his day job selling engine parts and move to Rhyl to work full-time for Orig Williams, and anyone else in the UK with work going.

Billy Finlay: "The wrestling was stopped really at home, I think the Troubles stopped it. So I moved to Rhyl and refereed over here for years, six nights a week. Did the shows with Orig and Brian Dixon, few for Joint as well. Did the tournaments in Germany for weeks, and went to places like Sudan with it. I think biggest one I done was in front of 7,500 people at a big marquee in Germany. It was unreal. I did it all over, and you met people from all around the world".

The universally well-respected Billy Finlay would referee on Reslo as well as throughout Europe, and Africa as one of El Bandito's gang. Billy largely worked on the independent wrestling scene but still crossed paths on occasion with his nephew Fit Finlay, who was shining on World of Sport.

Billy Finlay in the 1980s

Billy Finlay: "I don't think anyone ever put two and two together that Fit was my brother's kid. He was a top wrestler, and could put on a great show too. One of the best I reffed for. Along with Tony St. Clair and John Quinn and Rollerball Rocco and Johnny Saint and Eddie Hamill. They were all tops."

- - - - -

That year Fit was the first Ulsterman to win a wrestling championship on ITV when he and his English tag partner Skull Murphy as *The Riot Squad* won a tag team tournament. The titles were rarely defended but were represented by physical title belts.

- - - - -

Fit Finlay: "I think I first went to Japan in '82. In those days they'd write you letters, you'd send letters, so a guy called Karl Gotch sent a letter inviting me to Japan, and I went with Pete Roberts, a great British wrestler. They wanted me to stay, but I had a lot of other commitments, and I didn't want to be locked down anywhere. So from '82 on I went to Japan maybe twice a year. I'd do the Super Juniors, then in the winter they had a tag team tournament. Through it I met a lot of guys from the States, Dick Murdoch, and Bam Bam Bigelow. Terry Funk became a good friend. It opened doors, and spread word of mouth, so I never had to send tapes or photographs to anyone, it was they always came to me."

That year Fit Finlay became the latest Irishman (and notably lightest as opposed to heavyweights Wild Angus and Sean Regan) to wrestle in Japan when he began competing for NJPW.
    As Japan was a hotbed for American wrestlers Finlay's reputation started to grow even greater as his path crossed with giants of the grappling game from across the Atlantic, who the grizzled young veteran quickly impressed with in-ring ability and all-round toughness and tenacity.

1983

This year is the swansong for Fermanagh's greatest gift to the world of pro wrestling; Wild Angus.

Wild Angus in the 1980s

In the UK, the great "Scot" worked wherever he wanted, with spells with Joint as a friend to Giant Haystacks and foe to Big Daddy on World of Sport in 1981 (with a final appearance on the programme in early 1982). Angus also appeared in action for Orig Williams, Brian Dixon and on the German/Austria tournaments. Soon after some finally found shows in Scotland and England in February 1983, the real-life Frank Hoy took off the kilt, put on a pair of trousers, and retired from the ring, age 49. To that point he was undeniably the most successful pro wrestler to come out of Ulster, having been paid good money to grapple in front of tens of thousands around the world in America, Canada, Germany, Japan, Australia and the UK for at least 20+ years.

Frank Hoy's legacy continued for a time after his retirement through his English-born son "Steve Casey", who at 6'2 and 16st (225lbs) debuted in 1979 tag teaming with dad on Irish tours for Orig Williams. Steve then followed in his father's global footprints and made his own mark in America, Canada, Germany, Japan and the UK up until his own retirement in 1996.

Taking his gimmick to heart, Frank Hoy – who loved to fish – lived out his life in Scotland, remaining there until his passing age 70 in April 2005.

- - - - -

After two years on the independent circuit, Dennis "Rocky Moran" McMillan was snapped up by Joint Promotions who were looking to sharpen up their shows, having also brought on board Moran's ring rival Chic Cullen.

On the July 30th 1983 broadcast of World Sport McMillan became the first of the Lisburn lads to compete on television when he challenged vs. deaf wrestler Alan Kilby unsuccessfully for the *British Heavy-middleweight Championship*.

Able to adapt to anyone Rocky Moran could wrestle straight as well as be the straight man to any comedy, and one of his trademark "bumps" (wrestling slang for when a wrestler takes a move) was an impressive tumble over the top rope after being whipped into a corner. Going forward the ex-boxer was showcased throughout British wrestling by Joint, including further TV appearances, vs. Vic Faulkner and vs. Chic Cullen.

Noteworthy too was that this year the "vintage" look of Fit Finlay began to take shape. Whereas previously Fit usually wrestled clean-shaven with short hair and red trunks or tights, to stand out on shows the former Young Apollo started to grow out his hair, and wear green and white tights with shamrocks for ring gear.

Another new addition to Fit's act was his then wife Paula Valdez, who both in real-life and at ringside became her young husband's manager. That November Paula became the first woman to appear prominently on World of Sport when she debuted as "Princess Paula", gimmicked as Native-American royalty and wearing a huge multi-coloured headdress.

Chic Cullen: "Dave's presentation with Princess Paula was good. They had a huge impact and I think that was the making of Fit Finlay. Wrestling is audio and visual, and they were a great visual act to all the seats in the house, from the front to the back. Their timing was great too, she'd give him a slap the odd time, or they'd kiss if he was doing good. Made them popular and made them a lot of money."

The odd couple visual of Irish-themed Fit Finlay and Native-American-themed Princess Paula worked wonderfully well together, and the two became British wrestling's first and only ever power couple on ITV.

The same November 17th 1983 episode as Paula's debut, Fit Finlay defeated English innovator Marty Jones to win a Lord Mountevans championship, the *World Mid-heavyweight Championship*.

- - - - -

While things were looking up for Irish wrestlers abroad, tragedy struck at home. In September of 1983, Hugh "Whirlwind Monroe" Beattie suffered a fatal heart attack age only 45, he left behind a young family and many grieving friends.

Henry Shirlow and Dave Finlay expressed their deepest condolences for their fallen comrade in the Belfast Telegraph – just under twenty years to the time that the paper's advertisement brought the three promoting pioneers together in the class of '64 at the Milo Wrestling Club.

A portrait of Hugh "Whirlwind Monroe" Beattie
kept by his youngest daughter Leanne

Unfortunately one of Hugh Beattie's best friends Eddie Hamill was left out of the loop on the death of his dear friend, as he was travelling at the time. It was a sad situation, though even decades later Eddie still treasures the times he shared with his pal.

> *"I only found out about Hughie's death two weeks after he was buried, it was the saddest day of my life, not only did I miss my old mate, but I was not there to pay my last respects, but we will meet again one day, so get them wrestling boots polished Hughie"*
> *- Eddie Hamill on the Belfast Forum website, in April 2013, 30 years after Hugh Beattie's passing*

Hugh Beattie was a well-liked and respected man. His funeral procession was huge, with many within the Irish wrestling scene paying their respects to one of its most charming and charismatic characters.

The eternal optimist, Hugh thrived on new experiences and opportunities, and though he was taken too soon the Whirlwind lived his short life to the fullest. Greatly missed by his family, another man who considered Hugh a best friend, Frank "The Blonde Duke" Hughes too still mourns the passing of his fellow thrill-seeking pal who way back in the 1960s he'd used to dynamite old shipwrecks with during the day and then tag team with in wrestling matches at night.

The Blonde Duke: "I still miss Hughie to this day. I feel even after all these years later I'm still grieving the loss of my friend. I'm just thankful that I'd got to spend time with him before it happened. A short while before he passed, I'd come back from working all around the world and met up with Hugh and it was like we didn't miss a beat. He and I would have had a couple of beers at my house every Friday night and just chatted, and those smaller moments really have a bigger meaning to you as time goes on."

1984

In England, Princess Paula wasn't the only woman in Fit Finlay's life involved in wrestling and neither was his uncle Billy the only active referee in the family anymore.

Born in Greenisland on February 25th 1963, Wendy Finlay, like her brother, idolised her dad and loved getting to help him with his pro shows. Whenever her father started investing serious time in developing the sport of Olympic wrestling in Northern Ireland, Wendy got coached up to referee amateur competitions and by the age of 19 was Ireland's first ever female referee in amateur wrestling.

It was after losing her job in Carrickfergus, 21 year old Wendy Finlay moved to Manchester to experience life over there, staying with Fit and Paula. It was during this time Wendy would be presented with the opportunity to follow in the trial blazed by her inspirational aunt Kim Starr, and referee pro matches.

Wendy Finlay: "I was over in England with Dave and travelling with him, and one day he said, 'Max Crabtree wants you to do a bit of refereeing'. I was shocked but very honoured, so I give it a go. It was nerve-wrecking, it was so different from amateurs, but once I got going it was OK and I enjoyed it. The first bout I actually reffed was with Johnny Howard, Rasputin and he was great, he really looked after me."

Rasputin was by then signed on as a star for Joint Promotions. Though his Mad Monk image was toned down considerably due to Max Crabtree not wanting to rile up any religious sorts with a huge villainous holy Irishman.

Since Kim Starr, women wrestlers had been utilised in the role of referee for ladies matches on rare occasion on shows in the UK, however women didn't referee the men's matches. So it was a shock when Joint Promotions – who never had womens wrestlers and only made the exception for Princess Paula so she could strictly be the manager of Fit Finlay – invited Wendy Finlay to make her own history as the first encompassing female referee in British wrestling history and, like a Finlay, she excelled in her role, albeit for a short stint.

Wendy Finlay: "It was only a few months. I didn't like the travelling, and the lady reffing didn't really take off. I think some of the men wrestlers were against it. After about a year in Manchester, I came home, I missed home too much and refereed amateur again. In the amateurs the boys accepted it."

On the amateur ranks that year, Wendy's dad Dave furthered embedded the Finlay family name in female sports history when his Carrickfergus club trained up two local teenage girls to become the first females to compete in amateur wrestling competitions on the Irish and British isles.

- - - - -

Friend to the Finlay family Orig Williams and his operation only got stronger that year when Giant Haystacks joined El Bandito's posse for his first tour of Ireland with them.
    The biggest man on British television decided he'd start taking independents bookings. Simply put, 'Stacks had become too big a money-maker for any promoter to control, and as Max Crabtree couldn't afford to lose the monster of a man, the Giant still appeared on ITV for Joint but was able to make extra money working the independents when he wanted to, and within reason – and Ireland wasn't on Crabtree's radar anyway.
    Proud of his Irish heritage, 'Stacks rarely missed the chance to compete on the Emerald isle going forward and, while the women wrestlers were one thing, when Haystacks came to town every hall was jam-packed wall-to-wall.
    Orig took Haystacks all over the island and to counties that hadn't got to witness the 45st megastar in person before. Such was the support that in February 1984 pro wrestling returned to the Ulster Hall after a 6 year hiatus. The Giant was the headliner, with Rasputin and Bruce McDonald on the undercard. In the return Ulster Hall fixture in April, Haystacks was absent so instead Rollerball Rocco and Johnny Saint entertained immensely with their specialised skills in manic matches and mat-wrestling masterclasses, respectively. On this one Kung Fu, Docker Dave Larson and Diamond Shondell were the local lads.
    Johnny Saint was by then wrestling in his third decade in Ireland, and while the English gentleman was never concerned

about wrestling in war-zone Belfast others tribulations brought on by the Troubles did bother him.

Johnny Saint: "I remember getting stopped at the borders, that was the worst part, just getting across it. We'd all be in a van and be stopped and the police would have you tip your bags out. Once you got in everyone was friendly, but getting in was the hardest part. Though I didn't mind going, I think the audience was starved for entertainment so the crowds were brilliant, it was just getting over the bloody border."

Orig Williams preferred to work with wrestlers who he could have the craic with in the pub after a show. Dave Stalford was one of his best friends because he could match the Welshman pint-for-pint, El Bandito had gained Haystacks as company at the bar too, at the expense of many a bar stool, and Johnny Saint was a lightweight only on the scales, and so fully enjoyed his experiences with Orig and his oddities on a night's drinking with traditional Irish music the soundtrack. However, even in social settings there was another humourous drawback for the World title-holder.

Johnny Saint: "Going out at night too if they heard your English accent you had to be very careful. Looking back it was funny, but back then it was a bit dangerous. I remember we were in a bar and I got chatting to this attractive young lady and I said 'oh will I run you home?', and she said 'oh no, once they hear your accent you'll be done for'. So that was that for the night, and I remember I was actually quite peeved about it; she was quite an attractive lady."

The Ulster Hall event being one of his final found appearances on the Irish isle, Johnny Saint would retire from full-time pro wrestling age 55 after a match in Japan in 1996. He would work as a truck driver, and then in 2007, age 66, Saint returned to the ring part-time and wrestled sporadically up until 2015 when, age 74, "The Man of a Thousand Holds" retired for good as an active wrestler. Today Johnny Saint is considered the living legend of the classic British style of wrestling.

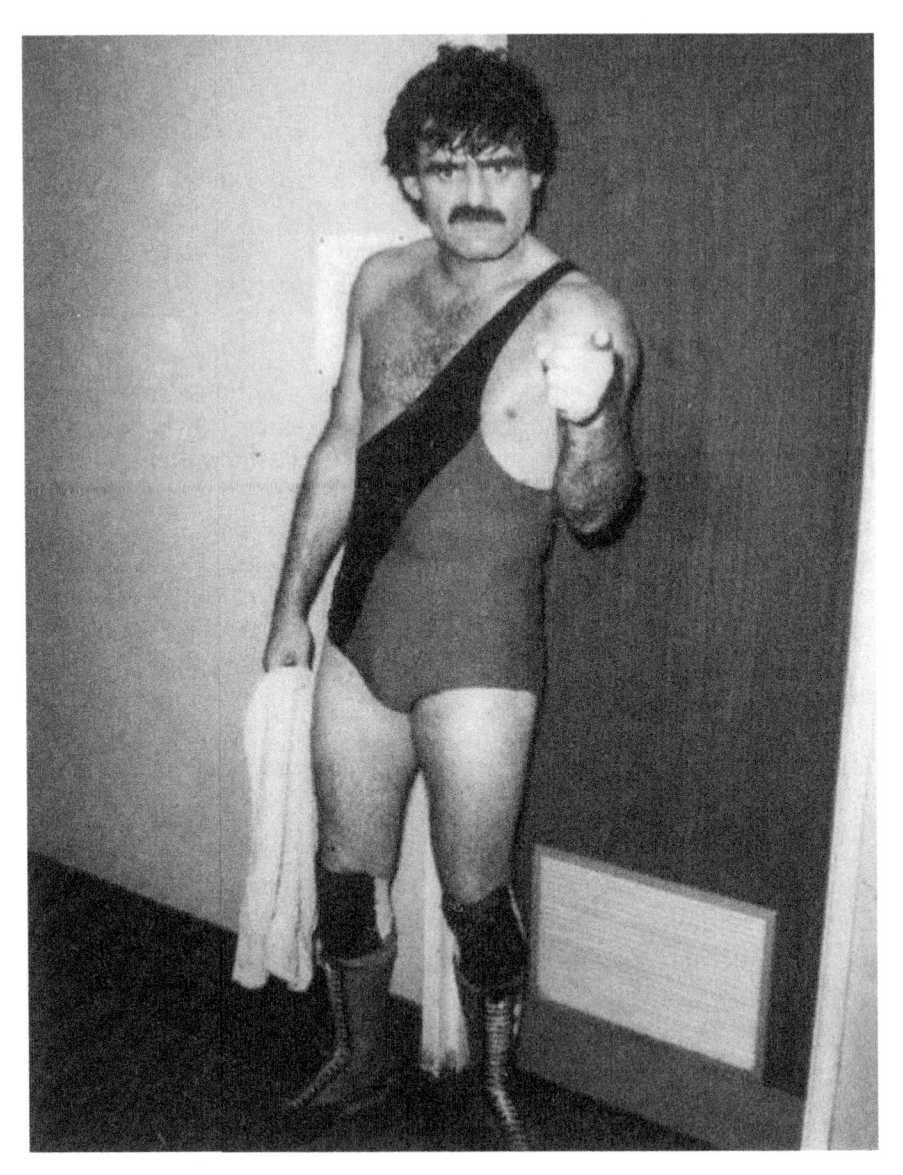

Dennis McMillan as Rocky Moran in the 1980s

On World of Sport that March – in one of his most memorable matches or rather pair of them – Rocky Moran teamed with Fit Finlay to represent Northern Ireland in a four team tournament.

Beating a Canada team that featured a young Owen Hart in the semi-finals, Finlay & Moran were bested by the English team, featuring Marty Jones, in the finals on that same show.

A month later on the very special April 28th 1984 edition of World of Sport there was an "Ireland vs. Scotland" themed show that included Rocky Moran vs. Chic Cullen as one of the matches were a decisive victory equalled one point for your nation. Also in action in his first ITV appearance was Rasputin who was bewilderingly presented as "Sean Doyle"; a fairly bland name for an otherwise highly entertaining character who never got to show his true style of wrestling on ITV due to the station having strict guidelines about what was and wasn't allowed to be shown. Completing the Irish team was 42 year old Jack Flash Shirlow, wearing his classic white trunks with a green shamrock emblem. Shirlow did battle and busted out his fierce forearm vs. brutish heavyweight Drew McDonald. Henry's time as a loyal associate for Joint Promotions finally rewarded with a TV appearance.

Moran, "Doyle" and Shirlow would all win their matches as Team Ireland sweeped Team Scotland to a 3-0 victory; a surprising result though perhaps explained by being a tournament of coincidence in that it seems Joint happened to book a trio of Irish vs. Scots matches on a taped show, and then just formatted it in post production to appear like it was meant to be this way by design.

The show proved to be Henry Shirlow's sole one, and it was also the only appearance of "Sean Doyle" though in a positive way as giant grappler Johnny Howard would make more appearances on ITV under his regular ring name of Rasputin.

Over the next few years, Rasputin would bounce between working with Joint and working on the independent circuit, becoming a very popular character in front of any crowd and with any crew of wrestlers he shared a car ride or locker room with.

The Irish invasion of Joint continued when Dennis McMillan was finally able to repay Billy Joe Beck a favour by getting him signed to be an exclusive part-time wrestler for Max Crabtree.

Billy Joe Beck: "Dennis had got with Joint Promotions. And then I was over, I had a free weekend, and Dennis was doing a show with Max Crabtree and he invited me to go along, and then introduced us.

And Max says, 'right kid, leave your name and address and phone number and I'll sort you out'. So next thing, I get a letter. And it says, 'come on over, and bring all your guns blazing and the wearing of the green'. That was in my contract! Guns blazing, and cowboy gear, and wearing of the green."

As his dad was Canadian, Billy Joe was given the gimmick of an Irish-Canadian cowboy and going forward he'd compete on Joint cards during his holiday breaks from fire-fighting.

On the December 22nd 1984 broadcast, Billy Joe Beck became the last of the Lisburn lads to appear on World of Sport in a match vs. English roughhouse Ringo Rigby.

- - - - -

By then Rocky Moran had departed Joint on his own terms owing to their taxing travel schedule.

Moran went back to work for All-Star Wrestling, whose base in Birkenhead meant he could spend more time with his two young daughters who'd since come over to live with him in England. At home Dennis was a loving father with a great sense of humour, the polar opposite of his villain persona in the ring.

- - - - -

That summer Henry Shirlow promoted his final events as an associate of Joint Promotions under the brand of *Dale Martin Promotions* (another one of Joint's banners, like Relwyskow & Green or Wryton).

On July 13th and 14th 1984 the roller rink kingpin was the public promoter for Joint in the seaside resort towns of Portrush and Newcastle, respectively, with Fit Finlay and Princess Paula along with smiley veteran Vic Faulkner, fresh faced teenage wrestler Danny Boy Collins, and Jack Flash Shirlow's television rival Drew McDonald all in action. As well as his heavyweight nephew Chris Sommers, Henry phoned up 53 year old Butcher Donald and the little taxi man from Rathcoole was delighted to come back to referee the bouts.

Though Shirlow openly expressed hope for a revival of the TV talent tours it wasn't to be. After 32 years these were the final shows organised in Ireland with any direct involvement or influence from Joint Promotions.

- - - - -

Sometime in the early 1980s Gerry Murphy the school teacher / Sean Regan the wrestler relocated with his family to South Africa, where as the country suffered from the segregation of Apartheid, Derry's good guy grappler Murphy worked with the black community to improve the education system in their schools.

No longer known as "Sean Regan" but rather wrestling under a mask as "Irish Mask", a villain, Murphy continued to compete in the German / Austria tournaments up until 1984 where-in his final found matches are recorded.

As of 2022 Gerry Murphy in his mid 80s still lives in South Africa. Among the many hats he's worn over the years is author, as he's written a series of autobiographies uniquely in the third person with the main character called "Sean Riley"; a school teacher by day, pro wrestler by night.

- - - - -

On July 27th 1984 Dave Finlay Snr promoted a special homecoming show for his son in Carrickfergus Leisure Centre. Fit Finlay returning as the World Mid-Heavyweight Champion, with some in the crowd being those who as kids used to watch him learn wrestling from his dad in the ring in their backyard. On the show, Billy Finlay and Wendy Finlay shared refereeing duties while Bruce McDonald and Diamond Shondell wrestled, and in the main event match it was Fit Finlay vs. arch-nemesis Marty Jones, with whom he traded the World title with several times.

The showdown between the high-intensity Irishman and the energetic Englishman was so successful that in December *Ballymena Leisure Centre* was booked for Finlay vs. Jones II, and then a few days later on December 27th 1984, Carrickfergus Leisure Centre was revisited as Fit Finlay vs. Marty Jones III in Ireland became the headline bout for the final found standalone pro wrestling promotion for Dave Finlay Snr.

By then the Finlay family business was amateur wrestling. Though these events achieved their simple aim; to celebrate the professional accomplishments of its famous son.

1985

In America, on March 31st 1985 the WWF hosted its inaugural *Wrestlemania* event, featuring a slew of celebrity appearances including boxer Muhammad Ali, *"Girls Just Wanna Have Fun"* singer Cyndi Lauper and *The A-Team* actor Mr. T. The biggest wrestling star on the bill was Hulk Hogan, who at 6'7 and over 300lbs (21st) with blonde hair and a handle-bar moustache would storm to the ring with endless energy in vibrant red and yellow colours before ripping off his shirt and posing with massive muscles. Nearly 20,000 wrestling maniacs packed into *Madison Square Garden* in New York to experience Wrestlemania that encapsulated everything anyone needed to know about American wrestling; it was bigger wrestlers, better production and excitingly over-the-top sports entertainment.

Meanwhile in the UK, that same night Big Daddy was wrestling in the much more minimalistic setting of a town hall or leisure centre in front of a couple hundred to a few thousand grapple fans. The presentation of pro wrestling on the British and Irish isles hadn't changed much in four decades, however it was about too. The Americans were coming…

As both were part-time performers for Joint Promotions, Billy Joe Beck and Henry Shirlow started travelling over to England together. Billy Joe's Irish-Canadian cowboy character proved especially popular with younger fans.

Billy Joe Beck: "I never wrestled Big Daddy but I worked on the same shows, and he was always the main event and the kids loved him and they'd all follow him to the ring. Well I remember once Max Crabtree had said, 'listen kid, you do the same, you keep going round and round the ring and the kids will love it, they'll want to follow the cowboy, they'll want to get the photographs and all that'. So I did what he said, and the kids followed me and got pictures and all. But afterwards I go back, and there's Max and he realised he made a mistake and says, 'listen kid, no more of that, because Big Daddy's the star of the show, he can't wrestle for crap but he's the star of the show, and all the kids are following you and if they're following you, they won't follow him'. I guess it was a compliment in a way."

Henry Shirlow lifts Billy Joe Beck up for a bodyslam, a demonstration for a newspaper in the 1980s

Joint Promotions poster for an event in England in 1985
Thank you to Tony Earnshaw for the poster

Big Daddy and Jack Flash Shirlow, backstage

Billy Joe Beck and Jack Flash Shirlow worked as good guys in matches in England, rare for any Irish wrestlers (besides Kung Fu) who were nearly always cast as villains. In fact not only were they embraced, there was even some sympathy at times for the Ulsterman and the situation they were coming from.

Billy Joe Beck: "I remember one time going over to England, Shirlow and I for Joint. And we went to the airport to get a flight. And the next thing we were pulled off the flight as there was a bomb scare. Well eventually it's sorted all out, and we fly over. And I didn't realise at the time, but because there'd been the bomb scare and we'd been held back they did an announcement at the show that the Irish wrestlers were held up because of a bomb warning. So you see whenever we went into the ring, what a roar! And these people thought this was great that we'd travel even though there was a bomb scare. We never thought anything of it because we were so used to it over here."

On September 28th 1985 Billy Joe Beck had the incidental honour of wrestling on the final ever episode of World of Sport, as the programme was cancelled after 20 years. Beck's match vs. Englishman Alan Kilby pitted him in the peculiar position of being against another deaf and mute wrestler (like his very first opponent Whipper Watson) in what was also Billy Joe's second and final television outing. Despite the cancellation of World of the Sport, wrestling still continued being broadcast on ITV on a Saturday afternoon, just once again as its own standalone show and called *Wrestling*.

Late in this year the Lisburn men Billy Joe Beck and Henry Shirlow finished up with Joint fixtures, and winded down travelling as much to wrestle.

- - - - -

While Reslo still offered Kung Fu, Docker Dave Larson and Rocky Moran wrestling on television on occasion, that year British wrestling gained its third series. Not on terrestrial TV but via a satellite station. *Satellite TV* was Europe's first cable channel system – the predecessor to *Sky TV* – and in 1983 the UK started receiving Satellite TV with *Screensport* being its sports channel.

In October 1985 Brian Dixon's All-Star Wrestling gained its own slot on Screensport. Similar to Reslo, *Satellite Wrestling* was an annual series shown on a Friday night for a set number of weeks. Also similar to its Welsh counterpart, it featured matches that were much more action-packed and violent than was permitted on ITV at the time, and shared stars with Reslo like Quinn, St. Clair, Rocco, Saint and a freed-up Chic Cullen.

There were then three wrestling programmes; Wrestling on ITV on terrestrial telly; Reslo on S4C in Wales; and Satellite

Wrestling on Screensport on cable, with Kung Fu and Rocky Moran being the only Northern Irish wrestlers to complete the hat-trick by competing on all three series, and Billy Finlay too by reffing on all three channels.

- - - - -

Rocky Hunter: "I had a fall at the shipyard and hurt my back and the doctor said to me, 'that's it, you can never wrestle again and you shouldn't be lifting anything too heavy'. So within four months I was back wrestling again, it was like a drug! I was always active, always very fit. I didn't enjoy it because you were performing, I just liked being fit. The wife wasn't happy of course but eventually I did pack it in. I loved it though. Like the pay was buttons, but then again the money was never there. But you met some really nice people, that was the loveliest part about it. I loved it, and I think most of the lads probably feel the same way. I have no regrets."

While Irish representation on televised wrestling was at its highest, that July is the final found match for Northern Ireland's original "Rocky". 42 year old Rocky Hunter on a show in the South as part of the *Tallaght Festival* in Dublin on July 19th 1985. A constant villain character, Rocky was actually one of most well-liked wrestlers in the locker-room, and his skills as a shooter and reliable hand in the ring leant to quality work for close to 15 years on the Irish wrestling scene.

Today in his late 70s the real-life Ralph Hunter balances between living in Bangor and Newtownabbey and shares similar traits with Pat Red Kelly in being a top storyteller with a great sense of humour and a love of travelling.

Rocky Hunter: "I would never have seen most of Ireland without the wrestling. I loved getting out and seeing places. Nowadays I'm always trying to get away somewhere. Donegal is one of my favourites, and then down round Mayo and Clare and that area. What I've been doing these last few summers is going away for 2-3 days at a time with my partner. Her and I will go on the bus, pensioners pass like, or a friend will drive us. It's great to get away. There's some really beautiful places about Ireland."

The Tallaght Festival bill is also the final found all-action appearance for Rocky Hunter's opponent that evening, 31 year old Judo Bill Weaver. Bill was still fit enough to continue in wrestling but, following the failed attempt to get pro wrestling promotion going again in the North, Judo Bill's heart just wasn't in it any longer.

Judo Bill Weaver: "I think after I stopped there was still a few guys on the circuit doing bits and pieces, but I had sorta lost interest for it, and wasn't in the shape for it after a while because I wasn't doing it. So I got a few phonecalls asking me about coming back but I didn't take it up again. I will say, it was one of those things you enjoy or you don't enjoy it, and for a time there really wasn't much else I was interested in. It was an experience and I thoroughly enjoyed it. I liked the travel and the wee bit of limelight. It was painful at times, there was brutal bouts, but you did it for the sport, the craic."

After wrestling the real-life Bill Townsley worked as a taxi driver in Belfast, and today in his late 60s is still working away. As Judo Bill Weaver he was one of the last to be trained in the classic style of wrestling in Ireland.

By 1985 shows in the South of Ireland outnumbered those in the North. Many were organised by Peter Nulty, a photographer from Dublin turned wrestler and referee who organised his own pro shows as well as being Orig Williams promotional partner in the South (Peter was the equivalent of Dave Stalford in the North).
    Two of Nulty's most trusted talents were Diamond Shondell and Bruce McDonald who were constant on cards, and who that summer travelled to a show way down South in the tiny village of Ballydehob in Cork to celebrate the 50th anniversary of the World Wrestling title win of its most famous resident, Danno O'Mahoney.

Bruce McDonald: "Dennis and I drove to Dublin, met Tony St. Clair and Jock Cameron at Dublin airport, with Peter Nulty there too of course. Then we flew from Dublin to Cork, and there was a parade, and Danno's daughter was there, and we did a show before flying back. I'm sure it was the only wrestling show that little village has seen before or since".

Diamond Shondell, Tony St. Clair (England), Jock Cameron (Scotland) and Peter Nulty pictured here outside the pub in Ballydehob named in Danno O'Mahoney's honour.

- - - - -

That October the comic wrestler from Carrickfergus and "Most Unusual Man" Diamond Shondell was warranted his chance to wrestle for Joint Promotions through the vouching of someone who'd always been entertained by the in-ring antics of the best dressed man on the local scene (since Dave Mack stopped styling and profiling anyway).

Fit Finlay: "Diamond Shondell was a character. He was so fun to watch."

Diamond Shondell: "With the help of Fit Finlay I got over to England. He had mentioned my name to Max Crabtree, and I actually got a letter from Max. To be honest, at that time I wasn't working. And he paid my fare over and I did four bouts for him; Kilby was two of them, Marty Jones was another one, and I really can't mind who else."

On October 30th 1985 it was the hard-at-hearing Diamond Shondell vs. the deaf Alan Kilby on Joint Promotion's final ever fixture in one of British wrestling's most prestigious venues, the Royal Albert Hall in London. Big Daddy was the figurative main event that evening, but the Shondell vs. Kilby match was actually chosen to close out the card with some light-hearted comedy – and despite being the villain Diamond's act was appreciated by many in attendance.

Diamond Shondell: "In the Royal Albert Hall, they had it that they'd book the hall for four hours, and the wrestling would be three of those hours. So after your match you were meant to go back, get dressed and go. Well they had us on last, so after the bout all these ones, the ones who'd been watching, they liked the bout and start coming up to the ring and asking for me to sign stuff and just wanting to chat. So I was staying out there, and eventually they had to send someone from the back to get me cause it was going to start costing them money!"

The very next day at television tapings, 35 year old Diamond Shondell was again vs. Kilby in a match that ended up being broadcast on the December 14th 1985 edition of Wrestling on ITV. The match – which has since been added to a DVD collection of Kilby's best bouts – showcased the comedic stylings of Shondell who managed to elicit a genuine laugh from commentator Kent Walton. Walton by that stage should have seen it all as he'd been the voice of wrestling on ITV since it started in 1955, so this was no mean feat.

Diamond Shondell: "When I was on with Alan Kilby for TV, it was before the bout and we were getting changed and Max Crabtree came in and he says, 'there's only one thing I don't want you to do; no biting'. Which I was very fond of doing at times, so just avoided that. Then at the end of that bout, yer man Kent Walton came back to the changing room and shook my hand and had a word for me. And I says, 'Kent you'll have to wait a minute for me to go get my hearing aid'. But he mustn't have heard me, because when I came back he was away! Nice of him anyway. I couldn't believe it when it was on TV. I got a lot of nice phonecalls saying it was brilliant. People stopped me in the street."

It was a life-long dream come true for the real-life Dennis Millar who grew up watching wrestling on television, and then as an adult as Diamond Shondell was the one being watched by millions on ITV, many of whom he brought to laughter like Kent Walton.

Diamond Shondell: "So Crabtree give me the four bouts, and I was about to leave to go home but I was told to wait, that he wanted to speak to me. And he wanted me to stay. He says, 'I got two years work for you if you can stay'. I says, 'I've already booked to go home, you never told me anything before'. Though he says when I come back, there'll be work, but unfortunately soon after ITV they split up the wrestling on TV I think. I often wonder what would have happened if I stayed in England. I would love to have gone back there again"

Unfortunately a return never materialised, and Diamond Shondell was to be the last of the Milo Wrestling Club to debut on TV.

Diamond Shondell: "There wasn't much wrestling about when I came back. To me it just seemed to die away. It just all stopped."

- - - - -

Riding high and on his way to becoming the Irishman with the most wrestling appearances on ITV at 50+ matches was Fit Finlay, who was the latest to work his way onto the German/Austrian tournaments.

Fit Finlay: "How I got into Germany was I was wrestling on TV, and wrestling in tags maybe twice a week against Big Daddy, then all the rest of the week against Marty Jones. And a referee called Jeff Kaye, old wrestler, asked me, 'hey do you fancy going to Germany?' – 'Heck yeah'. So Otto Wanz came to the Royal Albert Hall to watch me wrestle, and I actually signed a contract to come to their tournaments. I first went to Dortmund, then Bremen, and the next year, I think it was Linz in Austria, and these tournaments would go anywhere between three and eight weeks at a time, every single night, in the same arena, with the same wrestlers, some days not a lot of crowd, some days full."

Otto Wanz was an Austrian wrestler who operated the *Catch Wrestling Association (CWA)* in Austria and Germany – the countries being among the few who still used the "catch" branding. Fit Finlay was a huge hit at the tournaments and knowing his worth would approach any wrestling opportunity with a business mind to making money, and as much of it as possible.

Fit Finlay: "So two days before a tournament in Linz, Otto came to me and he was like, 'hey I think you're on too much money.' I was earning more money than some guys who'd been there for 15 years. So they said, 'I think we need to cut your money', and I said, 'nah I don't think so', so I left. I said 'when you can afford me, call me'. So I went back, wrestled in England some more, and then they called me. And not only did I get the money I was asking for, I bumped it up a little too."

Despite the minor money dispute, Fit loved working in Germany and Austria. Joining him on some trips too was Rasputin, someone Fit of course shared a mentor in Dave Finlay Snr.
	Between the tournaments and wrestling in Japan and the UK, there was rarely an off-day for the Greenisland grappler Fit Finlay who was then sporting a majestic mullet and moustache combo like a real man of the 1980s. Over a decade from his debut in a little fishing village on the Antrim coast, at 25 years old Fit was already regarded one of the best pro wrestlers this side of the Atlantic as well as one of the highest paid.

Fit Finlay: "I was wrestling every day. Sometimes I'd do the double, be the first match on one place, drive 100 miles and be on last in another. I was in it full-time. The travelling was part of it. The only time I took off was Christmas.

354

Princess Paula and Fit Finlay
one of ITV wrestling's greatest villain acts

- - - - -

Ian Shirlow: "There was always a venue round Boxing Day. It was a big day for the local lads to wrestle."

On Boxing Day 1985 Fit Finlay vs. Ricky Valentine was the big bout advertised for a show promoted by Henry Shirlow at the *Coach Club* in Hillsborough near Lisburn – making good use of ITV wrestling's then #1 villain being home for the holidays.

Ricky Valentine: "There was a lot of injuries. A lot of guys left it because of the injuries. I thought I had strong bones, but I was in a very bad car accident one time and I hadn't a bone in my body broken. And I said to the doctor in hospital, 'I must have really hard bones'. He says, 'on the contrary, you have soft bones'. And I remember one time seeing my arm bending in the ring, so after that I believed him on the soft bones. Never broken one."

The match vs. Fit Finlay is the final found for Ricky, whose decision to let go off the hold he had on wrestling age 40 was due to work. The shipyard labourer had moved up the corporate ladder to a prominent position involving the world's most famous fizzy drink.

Ricky Valentine: "I was a crane driver when I got into wrestling, then I took redundancy and by luck got in a post with Coke Cola as a relief driver. Then I got in full-time, then I applied for a manager job and got it. I was a manager for Coke Cola. Then an American company picked me up to sell equipment to Coke Cola, and I had to live in the Far East, Middle East and Africa for many years. I might have only been back home a few times a year. You got to see a lot of the world with that job. You were wining and dining clients to secure sales, living fast, it was really something."

Today in his mid 70s and happily retired, the real-life Cecil Brown lives the quiet life in Tyrone. As swimming was his other past-time passion, Cecil still swims miles a day and has passed his good genes in fitness down to his children and grandchildren.

Ricky Valentine: "I was always into swimming as well. I'm an Ulster Masters Champion. My daughter, she got dizzy eyes, she was an Ulster, Irish and British Champion in the 200 metres breast-stroke, so she took after me, nearly went to the Commonwealth Games. And my two grandsons, they're getting into the big time with rugby. So it's a good legacy to have led really."

The event in Hillsborough is also the last promoted by Henry Shirlow, and the final found local level live wrestling event of the 20th century, ending the era restarted by Darkie Arnott 23 years earlier. In the ring built by George "The Lone Wolf" Crothers, one of the referees was Wendy Finlay and the line-up was as follows: Bruce McDonald vs. Dave Finlay Snr, Chris Sommers vs. Docker Dave Larson, Ricky Valentine vs. Fit Finlay (with Princess Paula) and Jack Flash Shirlow vs. Rasputin.

The match vs. Bruce McDonald is also the final found for 49 year old Dave Finlay Snr as a pro wrestler. Dave was content to watch his son conquer the wrestling world in the professional style while he himself continued to evolve the amateur sport in Ulster.
      Supporting his friend all the way was Darkie Arnott, who even wrote into newspapers to publicly call to attention the dedication of Dave Finlay to developing amateur wrestling as well as providing youngsters with positive opportunities to travel and thrive in tournaments in the UK. Amazingly, considering the carnage of the Troubles, Dave Finlay was even able to convince clubs from as far as America to come to Carrickfergus for his own competitions around this time.
      While he was nearly fully finished with pro wrestling, in ten years Dave Finlay had achieved yet another accomplishment (under the umbrella of wrestling) by firmly establishing the sport of amateur wrestling in Northern Ireland.

Sadly at the same time – just under 40 years from when Jack McClelland hosted his first local level show in a Belfast gym – Ulster was no longer home to a homegrown pro wrestling circuit.

Chapter 13

Ring the Bell

1986

Homegrown wrestlers / personalities active:
11

Billy Finlay, Billy Joe Beck, Bruce McDonald, Chris Sommers, Diamond Shondell, Docker Dave Larson, Fit Finlay, Jack Flash Shirlow, Kung Fu, Rasputin and Rocky Moran

- - - - -

Orig Williams became the monopoly man of pro wrestling in Ireland. Due to the Troubles no-one else in the UK wanted anything to do with the North, and the South was always seen as too remote to take the risk on, and so the Welshman was the only active promoter left.

El Bandito and his outlaw gang of Giant Haystacks, women wrestlers and the best of the independents ruled the largely rural land unopposed. They were sometimes joined in their travels too by a wrestling-mad Reverend who was also a descendent of the classic music composer Johann Sebastian Bach.

Reverend John Bach: "Well if a show was rather weak, Orig relied on a good MC. If you have a great show, you don't necessarily need a great MC. However if the show is mediocre, you need someone with the gift of the gab who can play up to the crowd and get the excitement going. I suppose that's how I slotted into proceedings. I think I knew how to excite the crowd, how to build people up."

Orig Williams aka El Bandito

Born in London in 1940, John Bach's first foray into wrestling was working as an MC at big fun fairs in England in the mid 1960s. There would be both wrestling and boxing attractions at the fairs and Bach's job was to entice people with his brilliant booming voice into the marquees to see the matches. Ordained as a Reverend, Bach also taught math at one of the UK's most expensive "prep" schools for boys, and during his time there the school's boxing coach was a Jack Gutteridge, the real name of "Mr. TV" Jackie Pallo.

    In the early 1970s Reverend John Bach moved to Northern Ireland to professor at the then recently-opened *Coleraine University*. His reputation for being a tremendous public speaker preceded him, leading to a memorable introduction to Orig Williams in the mid 1980s.

Reverend John Bach: "Orig put on a show in Coleraine and I had went down to see it with my wife. Orig himself was wrestling as El Bandito and he was in the ring with a hold on his opponent when he recognised me in the crowd. And he actually came out of the ring and shook my hand, then went back in the ring and reapplied the hold he previously had on! I thought that rather nice of him. So then I done quite a bit of MCing for Orig. We got on quite well together. The thing about him was he was a great bluffer, and I pride myself on being a great bluffer too, so that's why we hit it off. He was always good for a pint or four as well."

The Welshman was actually the second promoter on the Irish isle to bring Bach on board as an MC. In the mid-to-late '70s the Reverend worked his magic on the mic to build up matches on some shows for Henry Shirlow after the two crossed paths while waiting for a train in Lisburn. Billed as the "Heavyweight Champion of Ireland" Jack Flash Shirlow was by 1986 also working for Orig Williams, and joined by Billy Joe Beck and Ian "Chris Sommers" Shirlow in wrestling for El Bandito whenever his shows came to Lisburn or the surrounding areas.

Reverend John Bach: "Derry always got a good crowd. It's always much easier for an MC to work a bigger crowd up. I suppose in places with a history like Derry it's quite easy to stir the people there up. There was Enniskillen and Portrush and Dublin too. I believe I MC'd at the Ulster Hall as well. Of course Coleraine and Ballymena were much closer to home for myself. I didn't travel too far too often, I didn't want a fortune spent paying my fuel costs."

Balancing between his religious duties, his University work and wrestling announcing, eventually Reverend John cut back on being a compère in the mid-to-late 1980s. Today in his 80s John Bach is retired from all and still lives with his wife (also a Reverend) in Northern Ireland.

Reverend John Bach: "I think wrestling was an important part of my life. It was good fun and it made people happy. I spent a part of my life teaching psychology at University and I believe watching *wrestling was actually very good for people. It got rid of aggression. You could shout and scream at a wrestling match, save you from doing it at home. Everyone is to a certain degree aggressive. And the great question is what do you do with that aggression? How do you express that aggression without hurting anyone else or yourself for that matter? And the usual answer is sport, and wrestling works in a similar way. I reckon we had a therapeutic function really, you could express that aggression without anyone being harmed. Though I suppose there were the grannies with their loaded handbags and sharpened umbrellas. A critic of course could say it encourages violence too, so you had to be responsible. You weren't there to promote a riot. You were there to promote a good evening."*

- - - - -

In January 1986 Rocky Moran defeated Chic Cullen to become the *British Heavy-Middleweight Champion* and successfully defended the belt for two months before trading it back to his former flatmate that March.

- - - - -

That spring the Scot then helped line-up his Irish friend with a trip to Canada for Stampede Wrestling. In the spring/summer months of 1986 Dennis McMillan took on his third name change, albeit temporarily, as "Chic Scott". In Stampede, heel Chic Scott shared the squared structure once again with a young Owen Hart, as well as a young Chris Benoit. Both the high-flying Owen and technical-talented Benoit eventually ending up in the WWF where they are considered among the greats in the history of the company.

- - - - -

After his short stint with Stampede, and back to his best billing, Rocky Moran would rejoin All Star Wrestling's broadcasts of Satellite Wrestling on Screensport in the summer/autumn of 1986. Moran would soon be back on ITV too when Joint Promotions finally lost its stranglehold on wrestling on the station.

1987

When Max Crabtree's contract with ITV was on the verge of expiring, Brian Dixon jumped in to negotiate an agreement with the big bosses of the UK's second channel. A deal was then reached to share the television slot between Joint Promotions and All-Star Wrestling (ending the latter's stay on Screensport). This shift in power was significant in a positive way for wrestlers as Joint losing control of TV meant it lost control of calling the shots on whose shows its top talent could and couldn't appear on, and so wrestlers could finally work wherever they wanted and with whomever they wanted.

The sharing didn't end there either. There was a third promotion that Joint and All-Star would have to further split their ITV screen time with… the WWF, whose first broadcast on British terrestrial television was January 17th 1987. WWF owner Vince McMahon was eyeing worldwide expansion, and though they were only given limited slots, viewers around Ireland and the UK then got to see a very different type of pro wrestling – one that was more aesthetically attractive; being set in huge stadiums with larger-than-life muscle men like Hulk Hogan and the colourful and charismatic "Macho Man" Randy Savage.

Furthering his retrospective reputation of being trusted to test future famous international wrestlers, Rocky Moran would complete another trifecta that January, the week after the arrival of the Americans. The previous year the scowling Lisburn slugger had jousted with a genuine Japanese high-flyer on Satellite Wrestling AND on Reslo, and that year on ITV for the third time and on a third channel, it was Rocky Moran vs. Fuji Yamada. Yamada would go on to be repackaged with a full bodysuit and mask as "Jushin Thunder Liger" – who today is considered one of the most iconic Japanese wrestlers of all time.

Meanwhile after working a few more TV matches in 1986 for Joint (his third stint with them), revered veteran Kung Fu remained on ITV employed by All-Star.

On Reslo, Eddie Hamill sometimes appeared in action as El Bandito's tag team partner. Kung Fu sightings on the innovative Welsh series also seen him in matches vs. top talent like Johnny Saint, and vs. long-time rival Rollerball Rocco.

"Kung Fu" Eddie Hamill whips Docker Dave Larson in the 1980s

Self-admittedly, Eddie had cut back on bouts the previous year after he started working as a life guard in Rhyl. After nearly fifteen years as a full-time wrestler Eddie was content to balance between working a real-life job as a supervisor for the *Royal National Lifeboat Institute (RNLI)* and competing part-time as a wrestler.

Eddie Hamill: "I'd still wrestle in Ireland at least once a year. Orig used to do tours, two weeks at a time, and it might be a few shows in Northern Ireland and a few shows in Southern Ireland."

- - - - --

Free to wrestle wherever he wanted Fit Finlay was instantly booked by Orig Williams on the very next Irish tour, which included a heavily-hyped main event match vs. Giant Haystacks in the Ulster Hall that February of 1987.

The Finlay families friendship with El Bandito still strong after almost twenty years, Fit and Haystacks were the first names fixed to be featured on cards whenever the Welshman spotted the Emerald isle coming up on his calendar going forward.

- - - - -

Dave Finlay Snr's festival circuit was by then non-existent. Though there was one unique presentation involving pro wrestling that he'd held onto; wrestling at the Medieval nights events at Carrickfergus Castle in the summer months. That June of 1987 is the final finding of these throwbacks to the days of King Arthur and his Knights of the Round Table, with Diamond Shondell and Bruce McDonald being all that remained of the Finlay stable.

Diamond Shondell: "In Carrick Castle they used to have these Medieval nights. Everyone dressed up like Robin Hood and Maid Marion and all that, eating chicken off the dish with your hands and drinking wine out of the big tumblers. And I'd go up to the King and say, 'you got anyone round here who wants to challenge me?'. Though I don't mind anyone ever having a dig. And there would always be a sword laying across the table and I'd lift it, and if it was a wooden one I'd bust it, and if it was a steel one I'd bend it. Anyway, after about the third time doing that Dave Finlay said not to touch the sword because it cost too much money to get another one."

Bruce McDonald: "It was usually just Shondell and I, with Davey as the referee. There was no ring involved, you were just scuffling on the floor, maybe tossing over tables. It was fun. Any money for it went towards Dave's amateur club. It was maybe only ten minutes a night, so nothing too strenuous, and it helped Davey."

Diamond Shondell: "I remember once after we'd finish, they had a magician on, and he had all his stuff set on a table and I don't know why I did it but I stood on the table and the legs buckled and everything shot everywhere, pigeons flying about the place. Then there'd be times at the end of it I'd say, 'right where's my reward?' and I'd go and grab a woman from the audience and carry her out. But believe me you had to have a look first, because you didn't want to pick a heavy one you can't lift. So you'd pick them up, carry them out, set them down, and they'd go back in again, all show. A few of the women would have even thrown their underwear at you when you were wrestling, I'm not even kidding you! It was a laugh like."

Bruce McDonald vs. Diamond Shondell
Pictures courtesy of Carrickfergus Museum

Bruce McDonald vs. Diamond Shondell
with Dave Finlay Snr as referee
Pictures courtesy of Carrickfergus Museum

As this is the final found year for this festival in Carrickfergus, it also acts as the final found involvement for 51 year old Dave Finlay Snr in organising pro wrestling of any kind. During his 23 years of activity in pro wrestling Dave Finlay was for a time one of its top wrestlers and then its top promoter and throughout of it all he built the legacy of one of the world's most famous wrestling families, the Finlay's.

Dave's amateur club continued to thrive, competing in amateur tournaments around the world and winning multiple gold medals. The grey-haired ex-grappler continued to spearhead the sport in Northern Ireland into the early 2000s. Today in his mid 80s Dave Finlay Snr has remained active in coaching the craft of amateur wrestling around the Antrim area, offering half a century of experience, knowledge and advice to young hopefuls.

- - - - -

Later in the year Ireland's other wrestling family, the Shirlow's, would be broken up when 35 year old Chris Sommers was booked for a bout on October 21st 1987 at the Lakeland Forum in Enniskillen that unfortunately proved, painfully, to be his final.

Ian Shirlow: "I got my left shoulder broke. It was the night that Omagh was flooded and the road to Enniskillen was washed out, so I was late getting there. Orig Williams was the promoter, and he had me off the card because he didn't think I was coming. So the only way he could put me on was in the tag match, me & Fit Finlay tagging against Bearcat Brodie & 'Stacks. So I started getting changed, trunks on, socks, and I was putting my boots on when he says I was to go out as the last bout was over. So no warm-up or anything, in there with 'Stacks and he fired me into the ropes, and I came off and into a dropkick, but as soon as I hit the deck, he hit the deck after me on top of me, and broke my shoulder. Popped it out. And I was counted out, it was counted as a fall. Finlay says, 'what the hell happened?', and I says, 'my shoulder's broke', and he didn't believe it until he seen the bone sticking out. I ended up of course in hospital and I was told not to wrestle again, and that was it finished. Though after I had my shoulder broken and got out of the ring, I actually did better training that I did when I was wrestling. I became a weight-training instructor, did a lot of stuff in the health club, tug-a-war coach, boxing coach."

Ian's injury would thankfully heal and in fact his recovery went so well that he was spurred on to open his own health studio in Lisburn (his uncle Henry's by then defunct). Ian Shirlow was one of the last of a dying breed; a wrestler trained in Northern Ireland in the 20th century. The retirement of Chris Sommers ending the legacy of the Charter Wrestling Club too. Today in his late 60s Ian is still working away.

Ian Shirlow: "I enjoyed every moment of wrestling, well some nights maybe not as much as others. But everyone was friendly. If you got hurt, they tried to help you. It felt like a big family."

On that same tour for El Bandito, the live event at the *Lisburn Leisure Centre* originally advertised the family feud of Jack Flash Shirlow vs. Chris Sommers for the Heavyweight Championship of Ireland. The match was cancelled following Ian's injury, so instead that evening English wrestler Barry Douglas (the nephew of George de Relwyskow) was the hand-packed replacement vs. Jack Flash Shirlow. Shirlow retaining his title to thunderous applause from his hometown crowd.

On the undercard for that same show it was: El Bandito vs. Jack Flash Davey (Peter Nulty), Princess Paula vs. Tracey Kemp, Billy Joe Beck vs. Docker Dave Larson, and Kung Fu & Fit Finlay vs. the humongous Giant Haystacks & big Bearcat Brodie in a tag team match – which ended with the dream team of Eddie and Fit picking up the victory.

The split between homegrown wrestlers and the best of British wrestling being nearly 50/50, this show on October 29th 1987 in Lisburn served as the last time for significant homegrown representation on a live wrestling event in Northern Ireland until the new millennium.

- - - - -

That December, on the final ITV broadcast of wrestling for 1987, all of Ulster's finest television star wrestlers featured in the one match. The dream team disbanded, it was Fit Finlay & Rocky Moran vs. Kung Fu & the inspired Clive Myers in an excellent match to end the year. This is also the final found match for Dennis McMillan.

Similar to old boxing buddy Ian Shirlow, Dennis McMillan cut his wrestling career short at 35 years old due to injuries. The Lisburn man's 17 year stint in pro wrestling was a successful one. As Rocky Moran he was one of the best and most believable all-round action-men in the UK. Dennis' dad being especially proud of his son, and the McMillan family being sure to video tape the wrestling anytime Moran was on.

In later years Dennis would run a pub in Birkenhead and work his wonders as a car mechanic again too. Living out his life in England, sadly Dennis McMillan would pass away age only 53 in July 2005. He remains much missed by his family, friends and fellow wrestlers.

1988

Bruce McDonald: "It was becoming a monster mash, they had started paying wrestlers by the pound and I'm not that big. Orig had monsters he was bringing in from Germany, big heavy guys, so smaller guys didn't stand a chance. That's when they wanted cowboys and indians and indians and cowboys, and I just decided it was time. My last ten matches were probably for Orig."

Since the beginning of the decade, Bruce McDonald had been one of the more constant local lads on Orig Williams cards in Ireland, often vs. Dave "Docker Dave Larson" Stalford or Peter "Jack Flash Davey" Nulty. It was after a match vs. Peter Nulty on February 27th 1988 at *Downpatrick Leisure Centre*, 38 year old Bruce McDonald accepted his final payslip from El Bandito. The American influence of bigger wrestlers being better was creeping into the matchmaking of British promoters, and the lighter-weight Bruce decided his days were numbered.

Unilaterally well-liked by all his contemporaries and considered a quality wrestler too, in over 21 years of opportunities on the Irish and British isles and going as far as Africa, Bruce McDonald was Irish wrestling's cool-hand. Bruce was trusted to debut young grapplers like Dave Finlay Jnr and respectfully retire legends like Tiger Joe Moore, Darkie Arnott and Dave Finlay Snr.

Today the real-life Bruce Stevenson, in his early 70s, is happily retired from the health service and spends time between his native Newtownards and a holiday home in France.

On March 1st 1988 Lisburn loudly cheered on 46 year old Jack Flash Shirlow one last time as he successfully defended his Heavyweight Championship of Ireland in a rematch vs. Barry Douglas in a bloody bout. After the match Henry Shirlow, the grey-haired renaissance man and one of Irish wrestling's biggest personalities for 24 years, retired from the ring surprisingly quietly.

In the mid 1990s Henry helped raise £4000 for charity by walking 300 miles around Northern Ireland. In later life he co-founded *Hillsdown Water Services* that is still in operation as of 2022 and supplies hotels, restaurants, universities and many other businesses with water filtration systems.

Jack Flash Shirlow vs. Barry Douglas
Lisburn, March 1st 1988

Ian Shirlow: "Henry never really talked about wrestling afterwards. It was just another era he had went through. Same as cricket, once he was finished, he just moved on. He made a name for himself in a way with it though. He was well-liked round the wrestling circles in Europe. The guys in England would all have had a good word about him. He treated everyone well, and did run a professional show and a professional outfit. Henry had a massive personality, a hell of a voice too, would been one of those to get up and sing at a chance. He was a likeable rogue. Successful in business as well, even towards the end of his life he was still working and running his business. Right up until he got sick and when he got sick I looked after him."

In December 2012, age 71, Henry Shirlow would pass away after a battle with illness. He was one of the most memorable mat-men of his era, and as a co-promoter with Hugh Beattie and Brian Page provided many of the local lads the chance to compete against some of the best British wrestlers of the time.

When the bell sounded to end the main event of that March 1st 1988 show in Lisburn, it also signalled the end for Butcher Donald involvement in live wrestling events too.

The 56 year old taxi driver had been personally recommended to Orig Williams by Henry Shirlow. Reportedly Shirlow wanted a referee he could trust to avoid any shenanigans, and Butcher's family remembered that he was thrilled the day that Shirlow showed up at their house to request the Butcher don the dickie-bow for the first time in four years.

Butcher Donald referees Mighty Quinn vs. Giant Haystacks
Lisburn, March 1st 1988

It was a final farewell for Butcher after 25 years. He'd been a wrestler, a coach, a promoter, a referee and surely done many more odd-jobs not usually listed on a poster or in a programme.

Cliff Donaldson's passion for wrestling continued for the rest of his life, as he still enjoyed watching it when it was on TV. In fact, so important was wrestling to Cliff that upon his passing in September 2006, age 75, his family all included in the newspaper memorials to their beloved father, *"In Memory of Cliff Donaldson (Butcher)"*.

- - - - -

That May it was announced that 1988 was to be the last year that wrestling would be broadcast on ITV. A new boss for the channel called Greg Dyke made the decision to cancel the Saturday afternoon slot in an aim to modernise the station, viewing wrestling as working-class and unappealing to advertisers.

In its final year Fit Finlay accompanied by Princess Paula made two appearances, vs. familiar face Johnny Saint, and then vs. young gun Danny Boy Collins. The influence of the American product was further highlighted as Wrestling on ITV had started having its wrestlers cut promos (hype up a match through talking) to cameras backstage before a bout was aired.

Having appeared on ITV for All-Star Promotions as recently as that summer, this year is also the final found for Billy Finlay as a referee.

Billy Finlay: "The travelling was getting me down. You'd be in Scotland one day, then expected to drive the whole way down to the bottom of England the next. It was a lot of hours in a car and it's not what you want to be doing as you get older, for me anyway. So I stopped it. I had really enjoyed it though."

56 year old Billy had travelled the world and been the third man in the ring for many great matches. After getting off the road Billy Finlay remained in Rhyl, working as a green-keeper and still attending wrestling shows at the local town hall but strictly as a spectator. Sadly in September 2021 Billy passed away aged 88. He was very fondly remembered by his surviving peers, with many considering Billy Finlay one of, if not thee greatest pro wrestling referee in Europe of his era.

The last Irishman to appear on the Wrestling on ITV was Rasputin, who wrestled in a series of notable scraps including a heavyweight six-man tag match, a heavyweight battle royal, tags vs. Big Daddy, and even a singles bout vs. Giant Haystacks. Notably, despite being a regular opponent of Big Daddy, Rasputin achieved something of an anomaly in reportedly never being pinned by Britain's favourite wrestler.

Giant Haystacks and Rasputin in the 1980s

On December 17th 1988 ITV aired *"The Final Bell"* a compilation episode of some of the most memorable matches and moments from wrestling over its 33 year run on the channel. After the credits rolled, British and Irish wrestling would never be the same again.

Johnny Saint: "It effected the whole business after a while. The promoters stopped running a lot of the halls as after it came off television it didn't take long for a lot of the people to forget you. When a programme comes off television you soon forget about it. So the business went into a bit of a decline really."

1989

That year the cable channels were showing wrestling from the WWF as well as its chief competitor *World Championship Wrestling (WCW)* who too aimed for global domination by conquering international markets. It was the WWF though who struck first with a live wrestling show in the UK.

Fit Finlay: "I guess at the time they had to use local wrestlers for the VISA or something. I was actually in Hanover, Germany when Orig Williams called me and said, 'hey this might be a great opportunity for you, the WWF are coming to the UK and they need some wrestlers and I thought about you'. And I said, 'I really don't want to do that Orig'. But I felt obligated to Orig because how good he had been to me in years gone by."

On October 10th 1989 the WWF aired live on *Sky One* from the *London Arena*. Top of that evening's programme was Hulk Hogan defending his *WWF World Heavyweight Title* vs. Macho Man Randy Savage. At the bottom of the bill was a six man tag team match pitting low level American wrestlers Al Perez, Tim Horner & Dale Wolfe vs. three of the best British wrestling had to offer in Fit Finlay, his Riot Squad tag partner Skull Murphy and Rollerball Rocco. Despite his team getting the win, Fit felt the experience overall was a loss.

Fit Finlay: "It was not a good experience. They treated us like dirt. So when Pat Patterson came to me and said, 'we're really interested in working with you in the future', I said, 'you know what you can do with your job...' But I did the show, and left, and when Orig asked me how it went, I said, 'don't ever ask me to do that again, I will never talk to those guys in my life again'."

Chapter 14

The Real Americans & Albion Street Alumni

1990

Homegrown wrestlers / personalities active:
4

Docker Dave Larson, Fit Finlay, Kung Fu and Rasputin

- - - - -

Eddie Hamill: "Towards the end the joints started going, and the injuries were taking longer to recover from. And the council offered me a job as a beach lifeguard, and in keeping with the wives long-time wishes to get a proper job, I took it. I still wrestled in Rhyl or when it was nearby, and some of the holiday camps, but it became I had the real job, and wrestling became the hobby, and eventually it just fizzled out and I finished. I'm not sure when my final match was or who it was against."

Following a final tour of Ireland the year before, 46 year old "Kung Fu" Eddie Hamill would wrestle some of his final found matches in England for Orig Williams in January 1990. Eddie had been an active pro wrestler for 26 years of his life, in a remarkable career were he wrestled around the world.

Eddie Hamill: "I wrestled in Turkey, Sudan, Zimbabwe, Germany, France, Sicily in Italy. Actually the story about Sicily, I was wrestling there, and every show I was on there was all these old farmers stood at the back of the hall. So I asked the promoter, 'these old farmers *what are they here for?' He says, 'they're the local Mafia, and you can't put a show on unless you give them a cut'. So they just came to see how many people were there and to get their money. So I always tell people, 'I once worked for the Mafia!' You see the Mafia on TV, they're big guys in suits, and these were just little farmers in caps and wellies."*

Kung Fu Eddie Hamill in the 1990s

From his humble beginnings at the grim gym above a garage on Albion Street, Eddie Hamill went from the highest regarded local level regular to one of the most successful Irish wrestlers of his time. In his retirement from the ring, Eddie was also the last of the class of '64 to wrestle a match.

Today in his late 70s Eddie is retired from his work as a lifesaver with the RNLI and still lives in Rhyl, only visiting Northern Ireland on occasion to see his daughter. Among his peers in the Irish and British wrestling communities, Eddie Hamill is well-remembered for not only being one of the top talents of his time but being a genuine gentleman and one of the real-life good guys.

Eddie Hamill: "I still go down to the hall here in Rhyl when there's wrestling on. Me and some of the old wrestlers like Johnny Saint meet up, catch up. There's some good workers even today. It's very nice when sometimes you go and some of them ask me advice or show me one of my moves they wanted to try out. They'd ask me how to do it, and I'd say, you have to do it this way instead of that. It's good to see it's still going. I have no regrets from it, even with the injuries, I'd do it all over again tomorrow."

- - - - -

That year wrestling cards in Northern Ireland started being advertised as *"American Wrestling"*. Orig Williams embraced the popularity of the phenomenon from across the Atlantic, with the Welshman even billing many of his wrestlers without name value as "Yanks" to try and trick the crowd into believing they were seeing actual American wrestlers.

Main event matches in 1990 included Giant Haystacks in cage matches with the tiny town of Irvinestown in Fermanagh among the first to host this type of match in Ireland. Another new match type were chain matches, were wrestlers could use a steel chain tied to their wrists as a weapon to choke, whip or wrap up in a fist and punch their opponent with. Then if 'Stacks wasn't being stuffed into a cage or on the chain gang he would wrestle two wrestlers at once in "handicap" matches. English up-and-comer Steve Regal was one of the men to try and team up against the mighty man in Ireland. Indeed on Reslo, Regal even partnered unsuccessfully with Docker Dave Larson in these matches vs. the mammoth Manchester man.

The Mountevans Rules went the way of the dodo as Americanising pro wrestling made the classic British style, as a collective identity, virtually extinct.

- - - - -

Rasputin with George "Jamaica Kid" Burgess on the ropes
Peter Nulty is the referee

Within the year Rasputin would also wrestle his final found matches in England. For the same reasons and at the same age as Eddie Hamill – the man he'd made his unforgettable ring invasion "debut" against – the real-life Johnny Howard would finish up shortly after a few final bookings on bills for Max Crabtree (who after losing TV made money by touring Big Daddy around every worthwhile town in the UK).

Johnny Howard came a long way from learning wrestling in the Finlay's living room to being regarded as arguably one of Europe's best big men and was indisputably one of Irish and British wrestling's most entertaining and endearing characters.

"Ras" as he was known to many, lived out his life near Banbridge, Co. Down repairing and selling cars and motorcycles. In August 2013 Johnny Howard would pass away age 70. Tributes would pour in from his many friends in the wrestling business, including his coach Dave Finlay Snr whom he'd remained close to.

Dave Finlay: "If Johnny had of went to America he would have done well, because he had this great look. He was a wild man in the ring, but he was a gentle giant in real-life."

1991

On April 26th 1991 real American wrestling came to Ireland for the first time when the WWF stopped in Belfast during its UK tour, returning wrestling to the King's Hall for the first time in 23 years. The sold-out show included Jake "The Snake" Roberts, "Rowdy" Roddy Piper and the legendary Andre the Giant – who would appear in action in Japan and Mexico afterwards, but this bout in Belfast was actually one of the famous Frenchman's final WWF matches before his death in 1993.

- - - - -

Meanwhile the British wrestling scene was on the sharp decline with less and less regular shows. As being a full-time wrestler based in the UK was becoming more difficult 31 year old Fit Finlay continued his career by taking up permanent residence in Germany. Separated and later divorced from Paula, Fit's full focus was then on rising to the top in mainland Europe.

Fit Finlay: "Same as England, I quickly rose to the top through sheer determination. I give them ideas on how to bring people in, and as years went by we started doing cage matches and chain matches and street fights. Ended up I bought a caravan and just started travelling round Europe in that. Most of the tournaments were in large tents, could hold a couple thousand people. In Vienna, it was an open-air ice rink. Germany was unbelievable, it was like you were on holiday the whole time. And you could spend the whole year just travelling around Germany and Austria wrestling."

Ruthless in the ring and in business, in the coming years it could be argued that Fit Finlay was Europe's #1 professional wrestler. The angry Irishman was nearly untouchable in terms of match quality and money-making. In his autobiography *A Lion's Tale*, wrestling icon Chris Jericho cited Fit Finlay as one of the best wrestlers at the German/Austrian tournaments, which became the new epicentre for pro wrestling in Europe in the early-to-mid 1990s.

1992

The Americanisation of British wrestling went further when the Welsh wizard of promoting went into his old playbook and started advertising wrestlers with similar names to those appearing on WWF television (just as he'd done in the 1960s with the stars of World of Sport).

"The Renegade Warrior" instead of the extremely popular Ultimate Warrior was one of the first of many many more rip-offs "Superstars". That year – among names like "American Demolition" and "The Wild Samoan" - are the final found matches for Giant Haystacks (in Ireland) and for Fit Finlay, on tour for Orig.

Fit Finlay: "I thought it was the wrong thing to do, and a little bit insulting. I told Orig that. I thought we were good enough to be our own personalities, so I didn't do many of those shows because I didn't agree with it. I thought it was disrespectful. Then again those guys kinda had to do it to get work."

Surprisingly, whenever the Welshman's Irish tour stopped in Lisburn that February it featured comedic villain Diamond Shondell vs. hometown hero Billy Joe Beck.

Irish Middleweight Champion Billy Joe Beck in Lisburn, 1992

On that same show Billy Joe and Diamond took part in an over-the-top-rope battle royal, that also featured Fit and Docker Dave Larson – so all four remaining Northern Irish wrestlers in one match.

All four wrestled in a ring with aprons owned by WCW. As rivals to the WWF, the previous year WCW brought their brand of wrestling action across the Atlantic and stopped in Dublin for their first ever Irish show. The story goes that Orig Williams loaned WCW one of his rings for their show and either the Americans forgot to take the aprons back home with them OR someone on the Welshman's ring crew accidentally on purpose forgot to return them.

Billy Joe Beck vs. Diamond Shondell
in Lisburn in 1992

- - - - -

Darkie Arnott and Dave Finlay pictured with Dave's Coach of the Year award presented to him by the *Northern Ireland Institute of Coaching* for his success in amateur wrestling

1993

In August 1992 the British Bulldog defeated Bret Hart to win the *WWF Intercontinental Championship* in front of the biggest wrestling crowd ever assembled in Europe; a reported 80,000 at *Wembley Stadium* in London for the WWF's annual *Summerslam* event. So as a result of the British Bulldog becoming the UK's new national hero, his cousin who was also a wrestler started performing for Orig Williams as… "British Bulldog II".

This trend of tribute acts – similar to the world of music with Elvis Presley impersonators and U2 cover bands, etc – became the chief promoting tactic in the UK, with one of the most infamous being "The Legend of Doom" which was a rip-off of colourful American tag team Legion of Doom. Drew McDonald (who wrestled Jack Flash Shirlow on TV) was even rechristened "The Ultimate Chippendale" as any sort of sensational American pop culture (in this case, male stripper act the Chippendales) would seemingly do on a wrestling show. Wrestling in the UK and Ireland by proxy was becoming more and more Americanised, however its final form was still a little while away…

Amidst all this, on the same show as The Legend of Doom, The Ultimate Chippendale and British Bulldog II is the final ever match-up between two Albion Street alumni.

42 year old Diamond Shondell vs. 47 year old Billy Joe Beck on February 16th 1993 at the Lisburn Leisure Centre was the end of era. Fifty five and a half years after Bob/Bert Cowan wrestled a school teacher for Bill Bankier in the King's Hall in 1937, Beck vs. Shondell was the final ever pro match on home turf between local wrestlers of the 20th century.

Billy Joe Beck: "The two of us had a cracking match. Dennis was a treat to work with and he made you look great. Though I had to have a speech in the ring after my match with Diamond to say I was finished for good so Orig would stop putting my name on the posters! The manager of the Lisburn Leisure Centre used to say to me, 'Billy Joe you've had more comebacks than Frank Sinatra'. Every time Orig would go there, he'd have me on the poster."

One last one-off, this match was the final found for both men who still treasure their time as pro wrestlers.

Diamond Shondell: "*I remember wrestling in Fivemiletown, hotel down there. I was wrestling once and this wee boy came up to the ring and put a tape recorder at the side of the ring and turned it on. And then I found out later on that he was blind, and did it so he could listen to the recording of me wrestling. That was lovely like. I actually made a point of going out after the show, and meeting him along with his mother and father. He'd come all the time. Things like that you always remember.*"

Billy Joe Beck: "*You get asked sometimes, was there good pay for it? There wasn't but it didn't matter. You did it because you loved it. It had to be in your blood. You had to enjoy it. If you didn't enjoy it, you wouldn't have stuck it. It was great for keeping you fit. It was great for making you fit. I'd love it.*"

Diamond Shondell: "*Once the wrestling stopped, I just lost touch with everybody. The only one I kept in contact with was Rocky. Rocky and I worked in the shipyard together, and I used to have a car then so I'd take him home. Whenever we went to the shows, even if we weren't wrestling each other, we'd have a yarn after. Even today we'd call each other from time to time to catch up.*"

Today the real-life Dennis Millar lives in Carrickfergus and in his early '70s is an active member of the town's *Royal Antediluvian Order of Buffaloes,* "the Buffs", who are a friendly society that helps raise money for charity. Dennis and Ralph 'Rocky' Hunter have been close friends for the best part of fifty years.

Today in his mid 70s Billy Joe Beck is involved in a tremendous charity cause too, having started working for *Race Against Multiple Sclerosis (RAMS)* in Lisburn shortly after his last match. Along with his colleague Vivienne McAloney, over the last 25 years Billy Joe has done amazing work helping treat those suffering a multitude of illness through maintaining one of Ireland's only oxygen chambers. To raise money to support the *RAMS Therapy Centre*, Billy Joe – a talented MC as well – also hosted many different fundraisers, with one in particular in 2005 being a pro wrestling show with help from Orig Williams. Indeed, taking this into account the Irish-Canadian cowboy was involved in pro wrestling from start to finish for around 37 years (the 3rd longest of anyone in Irish wrestling besides Dave Mack and Fit Finlay).

- - - - -

On March 16th 1993 WCW brought its muscle-bound brawlers to the King's Hall. The main event that evening featured face-painted *WCW World Heavyweight Champion* Sting, who had been interviewed in the lead-up to the event by local public relations guru John Noble.

John Noble: "I remember I got an interview with Sting who was coming over with WCW at the time to Belfast. There was a guy called Michael Keating who was the son of Gloria Hunniford, and he worked for a PR company in London, and I had some dealings with him before in various things, and then out of the blue he phoned me one day and said, 'We've got WCW coming to Belfast and we'd like to get them some extra publicity'. So doing that sort of sparked my interest, and it grew from there. Michael Keating actually give me some tickets to go up to the King's Hall to watch the show, but unfortunately there wasn't a great crowd. It might have only been half-filled."

It was to be WCW's only ever event in Northern Ireland. However, in a positive piece of history the following evening on St. Patrick's Day in Dublin, Sting would actually lose his WCW Heavyweight title to the vicious Vader – which remains the only time a major American championship has ever changed hands in Ireland.

- - - - -

This year British idol Big Daddy retired from the ring, and his brother Max Crabtree rebranded as *Ring Wrestling Stars (RWS)*. However, it was fresh paint on an old fence and so after a short time spinning his wheels in a post-Daddy world, Crabtree called it a day in 1994. The legacy of Joint Promotions would actually continue into 1995 when Anne de Relwyskow then finished promoting; the Relwyskow & Green brand seeing out the heritage of Joint after 43 years.

- - - - -

After an interview with the Belfast Telegraph earlier in the year reminiscing about his days as a pro wrestler, and stating the fact that his son's success started in the amateur sport, Dave Finlay Snr left his number for any of his old ring rivals to get in contact. Spurred on by this idea and seeking to raise funds for a national amateur wrestling squad he was preparing for the *Commonwealth Games*, Dave then organised the *Northern Ireland Wrestlers Association Reunion* for that December.

      Hosted at the *R.A.F. Social Club* in Belfast, the venue was sorted by Noel Ewart who invited Whipper Watson, who still sported a tremendous head of hair. Darkie Arnott of course showed his support along with his mates Syd Waddell and Ricky Doak, and also caught up with his old car journey companion Bruce McDonald – in a rare pub appearance for both, though standard fare for Dave Stalford. Butcher Donald reminisced about old times breaking in beginners at the Albion Street, while two of his proteges Rocky Hunter and Diamond Shondell shared a drink at the bar as they had many times before and since. Henry Shirlow, Ian Shirlow and Billy Joe Beck travelled together from Lisburn, Mick Shannon from Derry, and Tug Wilson all the way from England to attend. Though home for the holidays Fit Finlay covered the most miles. And that night Northern Ireland's greatest wrestling export spent time for the final time with an elderly Dave Mack who, only sporting a few grey hairs, sat content with a cup of tea and still looked as suave as ever in his finest suit.

      It was the last time many of these men would ever see each other.

Dave Finlay: "So we all met up after all the years and do what old wrestlers do, lie to each other!"

The event successfully helped raise money for Dave Finlay's Northern Ireland amateur wrestling team who travelled to compete in their first ever Commonwealth Games in Australia in the summer of 1994.

Henry Shirlow, Dave Stalford, Dave Finlay Snr, Noel Ewart and Eric Wilson

Bruce McDonald and Billy Joe Beck

Fit Finlay, Mick Shannon and Dave Finlay Snr

Henry Shirlow and Syd Waddell

Darkie Arnott, Tommy "Ricky" Doak (friend of Darkie and wrestler in the early-to-mid 1960s), Butcher Donald and Billy Joe Beck

Diamond Shondell and Rocky Hunter

Noel Ewart and Whipper Watson

Chapter 15

Ulster Turns Tribute

1994

Homegrown wrestlers / personalities active:
2

Docker Dave Larson and Fit Finlay

- - - - -

In previous years the WWF sent over to Belfast some of its most famous superstars like The Undertaker and Bret Hart. That March of 1994 the biggest name on the bill at the King's Hall was the Macho Man Randy Savage. The event itself however was poorly-received with tickets and merchandise considered overpriced. The WWF was by then touring throughout Europe up to twice a year, but they ran just one more show in Dublin the next year before dropping Ireland completely from the calendar.

    The WWF were the last to host a wrestling event at the King's Hall in the 20th century. The building remained operational for different functions until closing for good as an entertainment complex in 2012. Currently it is being developed into a "Health and Well-being Park".

1995

John Noble: "I reviewed a couple of Orig's shows for the newspapers. I remember there was one up in Portrush I think, and I did an article for the Coleraine Chronicle. And I was able to meet Orig."

Born in Downpatrick, Co. Down on February 11th 1969, John Noble had grown up watching wrestling on ITV with some of his favourites being Chic Cullen and Danny Boy Collins – who both featured on an Orig Williams event at the Ulster Hall that John attended in the late '80s during his fandom.
  By 1995, 26 year old John's career was in PR, working largely with the music industry, with record labels in London employing John as their Northern Ireland representative. A successful freelancer John also wrote for several magazines and newspapers, and so with experience and contacts – and most importantly, interest in getting involved in the wrestling business – John's meeting with Orig went so well that he began helping the Welshman promote events in NI.

John Noble: "I did a few jointly with Orig around '95, '96, and maybe one in '99 too. I would have helped him with shows around Downpatrick, Newcastle, Ballynahinch, those areas. Orig was really the only one coming here at that time."

Despite ruling wrestling in his home away from home, there wasn't much for Orig to celebrate in July 1995 when Reslo would air its final episodes (with Fit Finlay among those featured in the last season) as after a 13 year run the old Bandit lost his TV deal with S4C. Any future effort by a British group to get wrestling back on television in any meaningful way failed, as Americanised wrestling events took over.

Fit Finlay in the 1990s

1996

In mainland Europe and Japan, Fit Finlay was kept busy battling with some of the best wrestlers in the world including Chris Benoit, Jushin Thunder Liger, beloved Latino wrestler Eddie Guerrero (styled as "Black Tiger" in NJPW), first-class Canadian wrestler Lance Storm, and Japanese star Masa Chono. At times too the former Roman soldier teamed with heavyweight American brawler John Hawk (later to be better known as John Bradshaw Layfield aka JBL).

Against all Finlay held his own, heralded much praise and solidified his status as Europe's top action-man.

- - - - -

Fit Finlay: "I got call, I think I was in Vienna, at the CWA office, and it was WCW. William Regal had given them where to get hold of me. They wanted me to come over but I really wasn't interested. They kept calling me, so I said I'll come over for a few months, see what I like, see what I don't like. I think I went from January 1996 to May, because I promised Otto Wanz I'd be coming back. It was a culture shock to me WCW."

After Hulk Hogan jumped from the WWF to the WCW in 1994, it helped the latter gain a lot more exposure and for a period become the #1 pro wrestling promotion in the world.

Backed by media mogul Ted Turner's billions, WCW had a bottomless budget and splashed out on signing international wrestling stars from across the globe. Steve Regal had went to WCW in early '93 and worked his way into a good position as cocky English noble "Lord Steven Regal" (later "William Regal"), and having established himself as an entertaining mid-card act, Regal vouched for Fit Finlay who subsequently signed a short-term contract to join the already overcrowded WCW roster.

On the January 27th 1996 broadcast of *WCW Saturday Night* 35 year old Fit Finlay made his debut and an immediate impact by attacking Regal. Wearing a jacket reading "Northern Ireland" Finlay then cut a politically-charged promo claiming his attack on the Englishman was retribution for the British occupation of Ireland…

Ignoring the controversial content (which harkened back to "The Irish Rebels" tag team days) Fit Finlay was finally on a worldwide platform, and soon the fighting Irishman was wrestling on the company's premiere programme *WCW Monday Nitro* which was watched by millions on Ted Turner's own *TNT* channel.

In his first spell with WCW Fit showed off his skills against superstars such as Randy Savage (who too had made the move to Ted Turner's company) and Diamond Dallas Page (who helped popularise the RKO move; known in his incarnation as the "Diamond Cutter").

As well, before returning to Germany, Finlay met Steve Regal in an "Ireland vs. England" match on the pay-per-view (PPV) event *WCW Uncensored* in March 1996 in a hard-hitting fight to a stalemate finish that is considered something of a cult classic with wrestling fanatics.

From the outside looking in wrestling for a company like WCW was the dream job, however for the former Belfast Bruiser it was a nightmare as he found himself lost in the shuffle of the American powerhouse promotion.

Fit Finlay: "I didn't like it at all. It wasn't a good place to be, it wasn't run right, and I was used to being involved in everything, and now I was usually sitting doing nothing. They didn't know who to put with me."

1997

WCW however were so impressed by what they saw in Fit Finlay that they were desperate to bring him back to the States. So when they made him an offer he couldn't refuse, Fit reluctantly relocated his family to Georgia, near WCW's base of operations.

Fit Finlay: "They offered me ridiculous money. I think I came over in September '97 and I stayed. I didn't like it, I hated WCW. I was maybe in the ring five times a month which was driving me mad. It was a low in my career."

Despite his frustrations, Fit's decision to re-sign with WCW was a smart business move. Within the next few years the wrestling business collapsed in Germany and Austria, leaving America as one of the only real options, along with Japan and Mexico, left for those who wanted to work full-time in wrestling.
    Over the next three and a half years in WCW Finlay squared off with popular wrestlers like the unstoppable Goldberg, high-flying innovator Rey Mysterio, the latest to switch leagues in wrestling legend Bret Hart, and even old rivals like Eddie Guerrero. As WCW maintained a relationship with NJPW Finlay was also allowed to travel to Japan to wrestle on occasion, which was some relief at least.

1998

On April 10th 1998 the *Good Friday Agreement* was signed in Northern Ireland and viewed as a historical end to the Troubles.
    Then on May 4th a new-look Fit Finlay with short blonde hair defeated American wrestler Booker T on that night's episode of Nitro to win the *WCW Television Title*; one of two major championships he would win in the States.
    Fit Finlay was on television during a time in American wrestling known as the *"Monday Night Wars"* when the WWF and WCW battled for brand supremacy. Times had also changed, edginess and counter-culture were "in", and America blazed the way as its movies, music and media in general heavily influenced the youth of Ireland and the UK.

1999

The year the *"WWF Tribute"* shows began in earnest, and when British wrestling was viewed as reaching its lowest point. The Tribute shows of the late '90s to early '00s made the Americanised events of the early-to-mid '90s look tame by comparison as British wrestlers began not just portraying tweaked versions of popular WWF Superstars but actively began "playing" them as characters. So on posters it would be advertised for example as *"Rick Masters is The Undertaker"* or *"Gary B. Ware as Kane"* (Kane being The Undertaker's brother in the WWF). Indeed, going forward the only pro wrestling Orig Williams presented in Ireland was WWF Tribute shows.

Much chagrin has been aimed at these cards, however making money in professional wrestling in the UK was by then incredibly difficult, and one of the only ways to get paid was putting on or performing on these Tribute shows.

2000

On November 23rd 2000 this author, aged 9, attended their first ever live pro wrestling event, with his dad and brother at *Omagh Leisure Centre.* It was a poorly attended WWF Tribute show featuring, among others, a fake Rock, a fake Undertaker, a fake Kane, a fake Mankind, a fake X-Pac and a fake Hardy Boy. The most memorable moment was coming across several of the wrestlers, still in costume, smoking together at a fire exit during the interval.

- - - - -

That same November, Fit Finlay wrestled his final match for WCW and it was actually in Germany and on a Germany-exclusive PPV called *Millennium Final.*

2001

That April the WWF bought WCW and became the unequivocal #1 pro wrestling company in the world, and the most successful in history. Many of WCW's performers weren't picked up by the WWF after the deal was done, but Fit Finlay was. Praised by past associates like JBL and Eddie Guerrero (then active wrestlers for Vince McMahon) and owing to his 27 years of experience, Fit Finlay took on the behind the scenes role of a trainer for the WWF, and quietly retired as a wrestler.

- - - - -

By 2001 PR guru and freelance writer John Noble from Downpatrick was interested in promoting his own wrestling tour and embarked on an ambitious tour, hoping to capitalise at wrestling's huge peak in popularity at the time – the WWF's Wrestlemania 17 event that April was the biggest box office success in their history to that point.

John Noble: "I did a big ten day tour. I did the Maysfield Leisure Centre in Belfast, the leisure centre in Downpatrick. I did Lisburn, Bangor, Newry, other places up the country, Derry. And I think on average I was getting a thousand people to those shows. It was hard work but once I got it all in place the ten day tour went extremely well. I was very lucky in my PR background. Obviously newspaper coverage was a much bigger deal back then than it is now, and I got massive coverage in the Irish News, the Belfast News-Letter, the Telegraph. I actually got page 3 of the Belfast Telegraph. I got BBC News, UTV – Live at 6 I think it was called, and all the radio stations as well, and that all really helped sell it. I never did any of the Tribute stuff. I brought in some Americans, Christopher Daniels and Mike Modest, and I blended them in with UK guys, and they all worked really well to put on a great tour. I'm a great believer in supporting local talent, but there really wasn't anyone local doing it at the time, that I knew of anyway. I used Scott Conway's ring and some of his wrestlers. Drew McDonald was one, and he was very keen, obviously because it was ten days work. By doing a ten day tour it cut the costs, for example if you were booking a flight that cost was then divided by ten. Everything was worked out on that basis, and it was beneficial to bring in the Americans because you were spreading your costs over ten days."

Working closely with English promoter Scott Conway – who would send one of his rings over in a ferry – the tour John organised in May 2001 was such a huge success he would continue to promote shows going forward.

John Noble: "Any time I did shows I turned a profit. The ten day tour was a massive profit. Each show turned a profit. I was lucky at the time because I got massive publicity. Even if they hadn't made a profit I think I would have enjoyed the experience."

John Noble was the first successful homegrown pro wrestling promoter of the new millennium, predating a new era for Irish wrestling that was to start the following year.

- - - - -

Though in recent years he'd appeared less and less as an actual wrestler, Dave Stalford was reportedly still competing on cards for his pal Orig Williams during the '90s into the '00s. In fact during the tribute times Stalford too took on an American gimmick, becoming one-half of "The Bushwhackers", based on a New Zealand tag team of the same name prominent on WWF programming in the late '80s to mid '90s.

Chic Cullen: "Towards the end Dave Stalford did wrestle as the Bushwacker but he wrestled as Docker Dave Larson too. Though he didn't do much in the ring by then, he filled out the bill. He was down the middle of shows with Orig so it saved paying someone else."

In September 2001 the real-life Dave Stalford passed away from an illness, age 53. He was active as a co-promoter with El Bandito on the WWF Tribute shows in Northern Ireland right up to when he became sick, and was the last full member of the Milo Wrestling Club to wrestle a professional match.

After Dave Stalford's passing, Peter Nulty (retired from wrestling since 1990 to focus on promoting and refereeing) became the Welshman's organiser for all of Ireland.

Meanwhile Scottish sensation, and friend to many an Irishman, Frank "Chic" Cullen wrestled regularly up to 2004, and then sporadically until 2017, age 57. Back living in Scotland after many years residing in Canada, Frank is still a friend of the Hart family, and has kept himself involved in wrestling by recently helping found the first wrestling school in Dubai.

- - - - -

On November 27th 2001 a recently-formed touring Australian outfit called *World Wrestling All-Stars (WWA)* hosted the first live pro wrestling event at Belfast's newest sports and entertainment venue, the *Odyssey Arena*. The Odyssey opened a year earlier as the successor of sorts to the King's Hall.

The WWA was headed by Andrew McManus, a successful concert promoter in the land down under. McManus' business model was built on touring venues around Europe as well as his native Australia and nearby New Zealand, filming the events and then trying to sell them on PPV in America. The WWA roster was composed of faces fresh from worldwide TV exposure with WCW as well as former WWF superstars. At the time McManus shows were actually second in star-power only to Vince McMahon.

The reported attendance for the WWA event that year at the Odyssey was 5,000 with the main event featuring guitar-breaking American grappler Jeff Jarrett vs. his real-life cousin and former rapping WWF star Road Dogg.

2002

The WWA returned to the Odyssey in 2002 with big names Belfast hadn't seen in years like Sting and Lex Luger. However, this outing would be one of the last for Andrew McManus' operation. WWA ceased the following year after failing to find firm footing in business matters, ending the Australian's excursion into the world of pro wrestling. Andrew McManus would later bring such music legends as Whitney Houston to Australia.

- - - - -

On the losing end of a lawsuit with the other WWF – the animal rights group *World Wildlife Fund* – that year the wrestling WWF changed its name to *World Wrestling Entertainment (WWE)*.
      The WWE then turned its attention to other challenges. That year cease and desist letters were sent out to British promoters, including Orig Williams, to say that if they didn't stop promoting Tribute shows that legal action would be forthcoming. Under the might of Vince McMahon, the Brit's backed down and the much-maligned tribute era of British wrestling ended.

On October 25th 2002 the WWE returned to Belfast for the first time in eight years. Its new base being the Odyssey Arena, home of the hockey team the *Belfast Giants* – so just like the hey-day for wrestling in the King's Hall, modern day shows take place on top of an ice rink. This return show featured future idols of sports entertainment in John Cena and Brock Lesnar, and on the undercard Fit Finlay accompanied fan favourite Rikishi to the ring for his match. It was the 42 year old Finlay's first public appearance in a wrestling capacity in Northern Ireland in 10 years.

The WWE have continued to regularly include Northern Ireland as a stop during its European tours once or twice a year ever since. The Odyssey Arena is currently known as the *SSE Arena*.

- - - - -

On his own Irish tours going forward Orig Williams tried to bring in former WWE or WCW wrestlers with name recognition to draw up interest. Business was never the same as it was in the '60s, '70s and '80s but the Welshman just kept working away on live wrestling events.

In November 2009, age 78, Orig Williams would pass away in his homeland. His shows planned for early 2010 in Ireland were cancelled by his grieving friend and business partner Peter Nulty, as the legacy of the wonderful Welshman's promotions ended with him. Orig's funeral was an event in itself however.

Reverend John Bach: "The last time I was in Rhyl, quite sadly was for Orig's funeral. It was an enormous funeral, many many people came to pay their respects. In a way, a celebratory way of course, a good time was had, which is really how Orig should and how I imagine he would have wanted to be remembered."

Orig Williams was involved in professional wrestling for at least 46 years, with 45 of those spent travelling all over the Irish isle. A year after his death Orig's autobiography *El Bandito* would be released. It recanted just some of the stories from the career of one of Europe's most prolific promoters in history of pro wrestling, and expressed strongly how close in connection the Welshman felt to Ireland and its people.

- - - - -

In the WWE Fit Finlay's job as a trainer had settled into a speciality area; coaching its women's wrestlers. While some in the wrestling world viewed it as strange that the hard-boiled brawler from the mean streets of Northern Ireland would be put in a position to be responsible for training women, considering his family history it shouldn't have come as surprise. His father Dave Finlay Snr had actively got women involved in pro and amateur wrestling for decades, and his aunt Rosemary and sister Wendy both broke down barriers in "he-man" sport/entertainment. At a much larger level Fit Finlay continued his families unique legacy as trail-blazers for women in wrestling. Even though the WWE had a habit of signing female fitness models with no prior experience, Fit mentored many women like this from scratch. Both 7x time WWF/WWE *Women's Champion* Trish Stratus (herself a former fitness model) and lucha libre-inspired Lita both credit Finlay with developing them as wrestlers.

Fit Finlay finally found happiness in his work in America. In WWE he was treated well and to this day is respected and revered by many of its superstars past and present.

Fit Finlay: "My family has basically been fed off wrestling my whole life. It's in a great place now. Some people might not agree with a lot of it, but that's the way it is. Movies change too, I don't think my kids have ever watched a John Wayne movie. They make movies with car crashes and explosions, same as wrestling, it moves and changes. In the early 1900s it was way different than it was in the '60s and '70s. It's hugely different nowadays, things change. You have to move with the times to survive."

- - - - -

Though local level pro wrestling sat dormant since the mid '80s, this year two companies were founded in the South of Ireland.

In January 2002 *Irish Whip Wrestling (IWW)*, owned by promoter Simon Rochford from Dublin, announced its intention to start running regular shows. Shortly thereafter *NWA: Ireland* in County Wicklow announced it was offering pro training to anyone interested, with English trained wrestlers Fergal Devitt and Paul Tracey at the helm.

From here the Irish wrestling scene restarted at a local level, again first in the South and followed soon after in the North.

Epilogue

On the January 20th 2006 edition of *WWE Friday Night Smackdown*, 45 year old Fit Finlay would come out of retirement as a wrestler and debut on WWE TV. His viciousness seeing him vilified as a heel, Finlay played up to the part by using a shillelagh to attack his opponents before, during and after matches. Something more Irish than a Native-American princess was added to Fit's act too when the man who "loves to fight" was given a leprechaun character called Hornswoggle to aid him in his matches (just like Shillelagh O'Sullivan!).

Over the next four years Finlay would wrestle full-time for the WWE and feature on its premiere Wrestlemania event on four occasions. His most memorable match being branded a *Belfast Brawl* at the 2008 edition vs. JBL – his former tag team partner in Germany. On television and on PPV Finlay shared scraps with some of sports entertainments most famous faces; The Undertaker, Kane and future Hollywood film stars John Cena and Dave Batista.

In 2010 Finlay again quietly retired from in-ring action as behind the scenes he became one of the WWE's most trusted producers; helping other wrestlers put their matches together.

That same year a documentary by director Ronan McCloskey called *The Fit Finlays* aired on RTE and is now available to view for free on *YouTube.* The film details the career of Fit and includes interviews with his father Dave Snr, mother Evelyn and sister Wendy, as well as "Kung Fu" Eddie Hamill and the late Johnny "Rasputin the Mad Monk" Howard.

During a brief spell away from the WWE in 2011-2012, Finlay returned to wrestling cards on the independent scene, and bruised up a new generation in bouts around the world. This involved special appearances with American organisations *Ring of Honor* and *Pro Wrestling Guerilla* as well as returning to wrestle in Germany for their *Westside Xtreme Wrestling* promotion and even a one night only return to All-Star Wrestling in England.

As of 2022 All-Star Wrestling are still active, with Brian Dixon the longest-tenured pro wrestling promoter in the world at 52 years and counting.

Fit Finlay wrestling on the American independent circuit in 2012
Picture credit to Dr. Mike Lano
wrealano@aol.com

Re-signing with the WWE in the summer of 2012 and regaining his producer role, Finlay would still see out his commitments on the independent scene. On December 22nd 2012 in Germany in what is so far his final match, 52 year old Fit Finlay teamed with his 19 year old son Dave Finlay III in a successful tag match vs. British wrestling veterans Danny Boy Collins & Robbie Brookside. It was his son's first ever pro match and the beginning of the next chapter in the Finlay family wrestling legacy.

- - - - -

The Irish wrestling scene relaunched in 2002 continues to this day. In 2003, John Noble began working in partnership with Irish Whip Wrestling. John would promote shows until 2010.

Northern Ireland's most notable recent success story is Damian Mackle aka "Big Damo" who is from Belfast. Damo was trained in Scotland and by coincidence actually looks a little like Wild Angus. From 2016 to 2021, Damo wrestled in WWE as "Killain Dain". He is currently back on the independent circuit.

- - - - -

Fit Finlay: "Now it's given, you don't really earn it, you pay however much money to do it. In the Albion Street in Belfast they would grapple around, they were submission wrestlers, they were tough guys, but you had to be, because if you weren't you were out the door. Therefore you've gone through this initiation of sorts, you've gone through these hard times, so you're not going to let anyone speak badly about the profession you've chosen to to do. Even though back then it was largely part-time wrestlers, fortunately I'm blessed to have journeyed a little bit longer than most, I'm 46 years into it and still going. But all those guys at the Albion Street gym were all a part of what I became."

Dave Finlay: "Orig Williams paid a great tribute to us, he said the Finlays are the royal family of wrestling."

Fit Finlay: "I've got a ring in my house, I train my kids. My son Brogan he's turning 18, I'm training him, he's going to the gym everyday. My eldest son he works in New Japan Pro Wrestling. My daughter she's going to get into it too. The tradition is going on."

Sadly in 2019 the matriarch of the family, Evelyn Finlay, passed away. She is sadly missed but is forever remembered as a loving sister, a supportive wife, a proud mother and a doting grandmother.

    Today Dave Finlay Snr is 86 and Darkie Arnott is 92. They are living legends of local wrestling and still friends after first meeting at an N.I. Wrestling Association event at the King George VI hall in Belfast 58 years ago.

    In the legacy of homegrown pro wrestling the line of succession in continued coaching ended up as Harry Joyce > Harry Browne > Darkie Arnott > Dave Finlay Snr > Fit Finlay.

Homegrown wrestlers / personalities active:
1

Fit Finlay

Dave Finlay III, Dave Finlay Snr, Darkie Arnott and Fit Finlay in 2019

Acknowledgements

In alphabetical order, I would like to thank the following pro wrestling personalities:

Bill Townsley, Billy Finlay, Billy Joe Beck, Brian Page, Bruce Stevenson, Cecil Brown, Dave Finlay Jnr, Dave Finlay Snr, Dennis Millar, Eddie Hamill, Elmer Benson, Eric Wilson, Frank Cullen, Frank Hughes, George Crothers, Gloria Pyne, Ian Burns, Ian Shirlow, Jayne Porter, John Lowing, John Miller, John Noble, Rev. John S. Bach, Noel Arnott, Paddy Donaghue, Peter Nulty, Ralph Hunter, Rosemary Gault, Sean Montgomery, Steven Hoy and Wendy Finlay.

As well my thanks for the contributions of the families of those who are no longer with us:

Andy McClea's family, Billy Beattie's family, Billy Watson's family, Cliff Donaldson's family, David McQuitty's family, Dennis McMillan's family, Frank O'Donnell's family, Gerry McSorley's family, Joe Moore's family, Harry Browne's family, Harry Corr's family, Hugh Beattie's family, Johnny Howard's family, Liam White's family, Michael Gallagher's family, Noel Ewart's family, Peter McElhatton's family, Syd Waddell's family and William Willis' family.

Thank you all so much for your time, effort, patience and invaluable help with this book. It was always my absolute pleasure to converse with you all, and when possible be in your company.

A special thank you to Billy Joe Beck, Dave Finlay Snr, Dennis Millar, Eddie Hamill, Eric Wilson, Ian Shirlow, Peter Nulty, Rocky Hunter and Hugh Beattie's daughter Shirley who all provided me with contact information for others.

Sincere thanks too to Billy Joe, Darkie Arnott, Dave, Dennis, George Crothers, Ian, Pat Donaghue, Rocky, Wendy Finlay, all the families and particularly to Peter for the fantastic photographs. Additionally the scrapbooks kept by Darkie, Dave, Rocky and the families of Butcher Donald and Harry Browne were vital in research. Their scrapbooks were my treasure.

Further thanks to the following for their help:

BBC Radio Ulster, Belfast Telegraph, Carrickfergus Museum, Craigavon Museum Services, Glen Folk Village, and RAMS Therapy Centre.

My great appreciation to the following websites without which this book would be very thin indeed:

Ancestry.com, *"British Wrestling Posters"* on Facebook, BritishNewspaperArchive.co.uk, BritishWrestlersReunion.com, Cagematch.net, *"Henry Shirlow 1941-2012"* on Facebook, IrishNewsArchive.com, ITVwrestling.co.uk, MapleLeafWrestling.com, and WrestlingHeritage.co.uk

Also to the following books for inspiration and additional information:

"Have A Good Week... Til Next Week" by John Lister, *"Imagine What I Could Do To You"* by Adrian Street, and *"The Wrestling"* by Simon Garfield.

And to British wrestling historian Darren "Tarzan Boy" Ward, American wrestling historian Dr. Mike Lano, Stampede Wrestling historian Heath McCoy and Irish boxing historian Barry Flynn for their help in providing information and materials.

Finally my greatest thanks to:

My (now) fiancée Hayley for her endless support throughout the time it took to complete this project. Love you.

Steven "Cambo Cray" Campbell for his terrific work designing the cover of this book, as well as thinking up the title for it. Nice one.

My dad Peter, my brother Matthew and my friend Ryan Mulgrew for all their support. Cheers lads.

...and of course my mother Louise for proof-reading and advice. Any creative writing ability I have is because of her good genes. Thank you Mum.

Northern Ireland Wrestler's Reunion 2021

On Sunday October 10th 2021 the first Wrestler's Reunion held in Northern Ireland since 1993 was organised by this author and hosted at the *Lansdowne Hotel* in Belfast.

In attendance were the Lone Wolf George Crothers, Dave Finlay Snr, Wendy Finlay, Rocky Hunter, Pat Red Kelly, Bruce McDonald, Ian Shirlow, Diamond Shondell, Ricky Valentine and Judo Bill Weaver, as well Peter Nulty and family members for Noel Ewart, Dave Mack, Whirlwind Monroe and Syd Waddell.

It was a great day, well worth writing this book for alone. It ended with all expressing the same sentiment "we have to do this again". Here's hoping we can make it an annual tradition.

(from L to R) Pat Red Kelly, Peter Nulty, the author Nick Campbell, Bruce McDonald, Lone Wolf, Rocky Hunter, Diamond Shondell, Ricky Valentine, Dave Finlay Snr, Judo Bill Weaver and Ian Shirlow

Going forward: 2022 update

My intention is to write a sequel of sorts to this book. Originally I suggested I would cover the history of pro wrestling in Northern Ireland from 2002 to 2032 so both books together would chronicle 100 years combined, however I've since come to the realisation that I'm really not as interested in the more modern history. Of course a lot can change in a decade, indeed a lot has changed in the one year since this book was originally published, so who knows. I believe the sequel may be more semi-autobiographical, recounting my own experiences on the Irish wrestling scene with modern history mixed in. What a sell for the sequel: uncertainty!

As far as further updates I intend this to be the last… until the online archives for the Derry Journal or Londonderry Sentinel from 1955 onwards are published!! Every so often additional years are added to the Irish and British newspaper archives and these provide me with all-important new info. The Derry newspapers I hope will reveal even more details on wrestling in the city / county so I'll save my next big update for then.

    Until then I will include any further interesting trivia, tidbits or photos I come across on the Facebook group Whose Clothesline is it Anyway? (feel encouraged to join). Please feel welcome to email me on any book-related matters at wciiawrestling@hotmail.com as well.

Finally, since the original publication of this book two of those interviewed have sadly passed away, Brian Page and Billy Finlay. Brian I interviewed very near to the original publication date and by his own admission he wasn't in the best of health, passing away just a month later. Billy did me the kindness of phoning me upon receiving a copy of the book to thank me for it and praise its production. The last time we spoke he politely declined an invitation to the Irish wrestling reunion I was organising, and this was just a few weeks before his passing. I wish I had met both Brian and Billy, they were both gentlemen in conversation.
    I dedicate this second edition to them.

About the Author

Darkie Arnott and Nick Campbell in October 2021

I was born in Omagh, Co. Tyrone in 1991, years after many of my new-found favourite wrestlers had already retired from the ring.

In 2014 I started on the Irish wrestling circuit as an MC. In 2015 I bought a wrestling ring and started organising my own local level shows. During this time is when I became fascinated with the history of pro wrestling in Northern Ireland.

Falls, Brawls and Town Halls was two years work and one of my proudest achievements in life.

Thank you for reading it - - Nick

Printed in Great Britain
by Amazon